T4-AQL-658

Linda S. Schearing is Associate
Professor of Hebrew Scriptures,
Religious Studies Department,
Gonzaga University, Washington.
Steven L. McKenzie is Associate
Professor of Old Testament at
Rhodes College, Memphis,
Tennessee.

JOURNAL FOR THE STUDY OF THE OLD TESTAMENT
SUPPLEMENT SERIES
268

Sheffield Academic Press

Those Elusive Deuteronomists

The Phenomenon of Pan-Deuteronomism

edited by
**Linda S. Schearing &
Steven L. McKenzie**

Journal for the Study of the Old Testament
Supplement Series 268

Copyright © 1999 Sheffield Academic Press

Published by
Sheffield Academic Press Ltd
Mansion House
19 Kingfield Road
Sheffield S11 9AS
England

Typeset by Sheffield Academic Press
and
Printed on acid-free paper in Great Britain
by Bookcraft Ltd
Midsomer Norton, Bath

British Library Cataloguing in Publication Data

A catalogue record for this book is available
from the British Library

ISBN 1-84127-010-5

CONTENTS

ABBREVIATIONS

AB	Anchor Bible
ABD	David Noel Freedman (ed.), *The Anchor Bible Dictionary* (New York: Doubleday, 1992)
ABRL	Anchor Bible Reference Library
AnBib	Analecta biblica
ANET	James B. Pritchard (ed.), *Ancient Near Eastern Texts Relating to the Old Testament* (Princeton, NJ: Princeton University Press, 3rd edn, 1969)
ATANT	Abhandlungen zur Theologie des Alten und Neuen Testaments
ATD	Das Alte Testament Deutsch
BEATAJ	Beiträge zur Erforschung des Alten Testaments und des antiken Judentums
BBB	Bonner biblische Beiträge
BBET	Beiträge zur biblischen Exegese und Theologie
BDB	Francis Brown, S.R. Driver and Charles A. Briggs, *A Hebrew and English Lexicon of the Old Testament* (Oxford: Clarendon Press, 1907)
BETL	Bibliotheca ephemeridum theologicarum lovaniensium
BEvT	Beiträge zur evangelischen Theologie
BHS	*Biblia hebraica stuttgartensia*
BHT	Beiträge zur historischen Theologie
Bib	*Biblica*
BJS	Brown Judaica Studies
BKAT	Biblischer Kommentar: Altes Testament
BN	*Biblische Notizen*
BWANT	Beiträge zur Wissenschaft vom Alten und Neuen Testament
BZ	*Biblische Zeitschrift*
BZAW	Beihefte zur *ZAW*
CBC	Cambridge Bible Commentary
CBQ	*Catholic Biblical Quarterly*
CBQMS	*Catholic Biblical Quarterly*, Monograph Series
CE	Cahiers Evangile
ConBOT	Coniectanea Biblica, Old Testament
CR:BS	*Currents in Research: Biblical Studies*
DBAT	*Dielheimer Blätter zum Alten Testament*

DBSup	*Dictionnaire de la Bible, Supplément*
DJD	Discoveries in the Judaean Desert
DSD	*Dead Sea Discoveries*
EBib	Etudes bibliques
EF	Erträge der Forschung
ErIsr	*Eretz Israel*
ETL	*Ephemerides theologicae lovanienses*
EvT	*Evangelische Theologie*
FOTL	The Forms of the Old Testament Literature
FzB	Forschung zur Bibel
FRLANT	Forschungen zur Religion und Literatur des Alten und Neuen Testaments
HAT	Handbuch zum Alten Testament
HALOT	*Hebrew and Aramaic Lexicon of the Old Testament*
HSM	Harvard Semitic Monographs
HTR	*Harvard Theological Review*
IB	Interpreter's Bible
IBS	*Irish Biblical Studies*
ICC	International Critical Commentary
IDB	George Arthur Buttrick (ed.), *The Interpreter's Dictionary of the Bible* (4 vols.; Nashville: Abingdon Press, 1962)
IDBSup	*IDB*, Supplementary Volume
IEJ	*Israel Exploration Journal*
ITC	International Theological Commentary
JBL	*Journal of Biblical Literature*
JSOT	*Journal for the Study of the Old Testament*
JSOTSup	*Journal for the Study of the Old Testament*, Supplement Series
KHAT	Kurzer Hand-Kommentar zum Alten Testament
LD	Lectio divina
MB	Le Monde de la Bible
NCB	New Century Bible
NEB	Neue Echter Bibel
NedTTs	*Nederlands theologisch tijdschrift*
NICOT	New International Commentary on the Old Testament
OBO	Orbis biblicus et orientalis
ÖBS	*Österreichische biblische Studien*
OBT	Overtures to Biblical Theology
OTG	Old Testament Guides
OTL	Old Testament Library
OTS	*Oudtestamentische Studiën*
RB	*Revue biblique*
RSR	*Recherches de science religieuse*
SBA	Stuttgarter biblische Aufsatzbände
SBB	Stuttgarter biblische Beiträge
SBLEJL	SBL Early Judaism and its Literature

SBLDS	SBL Dissertation Series
SBLMS	SBL Monograph Series
SBT	Studies in Biblical Theology
SJOT	*Scandinavian Journal of the Old Testament*
SKGG	Studien der Königsberger Gelehrte Gesellschaft, Geisteswissenschaftliche Klasse
SPAW	Sitzungsberichte der preussischen Akademie der Wissenschaften
SPT	Studien zur praktischen Theologie
ST	*Studia theologica*
TBü	Theologische Bücherei
TDOT	G.J. Botterweck and H. Ringgren (eds.), *Theological Dictionary of the Old Testament*
TLZ	*Theologische Literaturzeitung*
Trans	*Transeuphratène*
TRE	*Theologische Realenzyklopädie*
TZ	*Theologische Zeitschrift*
VT	*Vetus Testamentum*
VTSup	*Vetus Testamentum*, Supplements
WBC	Word Bible Commentary
WMANT	Wissenschaftliche Monographien zum Alten und Neuen Testament
ZAW	*Zeitschrift für die alttestamentliche Wissenschaft*
ZBK	Zürcher Bibel Kommentare
ZDMG	*Zeitschrift der deutschen morgenländischen Gesellschaft*

LIST OF CONTRIBUTORS AND EDITORS

A. Graeme Auld, University of Edinburgh, Scotland

Joseph Blenkinsopp, University of Notre Dame, South Bend, IN

Marc Zvi Brettler, Brandeis University, Waltham, MA

Richard Coggins, formerly of King's College, London

Stephen L. Cook, Protestant Episcopal Theological Seminary in Virginia

James L. Crenshaw, Duke University, Durham, NC

Robert A. Kugler, Gonzaga University, Spokane, WA

Steven L. McKenzie, Rhodes College, Memphis, TN

Norbert F. Lohfink, Sankt Georgen School of Theology, Frankfurt am Main, Germany

Corrine L. Patton, University of St Thomas, St Paul, MN

Thomas C. Römer, University of Lausanne, Switzerland

John Van Seters, University of North Carolina, Chapel Hill

Linda S. Schearing, Gonzaga University, Spokane, WA

Robert R. Wilson, Yale University, New Haven, CT

Ehud Ben Zvi, University of Alberta, Edmonton, AB, Canada

INTRODUCTION

Linda S. Schearing

> ...the Deuteronomists have sometimes been praised or blamed for virtu-
> ally every significant development within ancient Israel's religious prac-
> tice...[1]

It is now over 50 years since Martin Noth wrote his ground-breaking
work on the Deuteronomistic History (DH). Little did he know then
how the next five decades of scholarship would expand upon his observations! Increasingly viewed as the *Ur*-document of the Hebrew Scriptures, the DH is credited with influencing (formally or informally)
almost every level of the Hebrew Bible's composition. Before the fever
of this pan-Deuteronomism reaches epidemic proportions, it is perhaps
wise to step back and ask some hard questions: What do the terms
deuteronomic, *deuteronomistic* and *deuteronomism* mean? What makes
a text *deuteronomistic*? Can one talk about *deuteronomistic influence*?
If so, to what does this refer? Was there a 'school' with which such
texts were formally connected? Or does it merely mean that writers of
such texts are responding (either in support or in challenge of) deuteronomistic themes? Or can it simply describe a similarity of rhetorical
style or vocabulary between these texts and Deuteronomy? Little did
Noth envision that, by the end of the twentieth century, his lone
deuteronomistic writer sitting in exilic Palestine would blossom into a
'school' spanning half a millennium and impacting all divisions of the
Hebrew canon.

The writers in this book address the growing epidemic of pan-
Deuteronomism that has infected scholarship on the DH. Two articles
reprinted in this volume (Coggins' and Lohfink's) are essays published
in 1995 that significantly addressed the rise of pan-Deuteronomism and

---

1. R.J. Coggins, 'Prophecy—True and False', in H.A. McKay and D.J.A.
Clines (eds.), *Of Prophets' Visions and the Wisdom of Sages: Festschrift for R.N.
Whybray* (JSOTSup, 162; Sheffield: JSOT Press, 1993), pp. 80-94 (85).

warned scholars of its shaky foundations. Nine of the remaining eleven essays in this book are papers delivered in the Deuteronomistic History Section at the Society of Biblical Literature's 1996 meeting in San Francisco, a section that addressed pan-Deuteronomism in both of its sessions. The two remaining essays (Wilson's and Ben Zvi's) were recruited for this volume because of their appropriateness for our topic. Finally, the epilogue, written by Steven McKenzie—my co-editor and a notable DH scholar in his own right—concludes this study of pan-Deuteronomism with McKenzie's own reflections on both the subject and the authors' positions.

I

The first essay is a reprint (with minor authorial changes) of the 1995 article written by Richard Coggins. In 1993 Coggins alerted readers to the dangers of pan-Deuteronomism. In 1995 he returned to his earlier warning in an article entitled 'What Does "Deuteronomistic" Mean?' The article presents readers with a succinct survey of the extreme diversity underlying contemporary scholarly usage of 'deuteronomistic' and other related terms. Indeed, almost all of the writers in this volume cite Coggins' work in their discussion of pan-Deuteronomism.

In 1995 while Coggins was asking his English-speaking readers to ponder the meaning of the term *deuteronomistic*, Norbert Lohfink was asking German readers to reflect upon an adjacent question: 'Gab es eine deuteronomistische Bewegung?' ('Was There a Deuteronomistic Movement?'). The second essay in this volume is a translation of a shorter version of Lohfink's German article. Like Coggins, Lohfink was concerned with clarifying the terminology surrounding the issue of deuteronomistic influence. Lohfink's essay raises five questions for consideration: (1) When would it be better not to use the word 'Deuteronomistic'? (2) What criteria allow for the designation of a text as deuteronomistic? (3) When may we speak historically of a movement? (4) What in reality were 'books' in biblical times? And (5) Was there a deuteronomistic movement? To this last question Lohfink gives a somewhat mixed answer. While he recognizes various 'movements' in ancient Israel—a 'national and religious restoration movement' during Josiah's time, an 'exilic conversion movement' (which later became the 'Babylonian return movement') and a Maccabean movement—Lohfink argues that none *necessarily* carried the label 'deuteronomistic'.

Concluding the introductory section is a previously unpublished essay by Robert Wilson entitled 'Who Was the Deuteronomist? (Who Was Not the Deuteronomist?): Reflections on Pan-Deuteronomism'. Wilson expands upon Coggins' earlier survey of scholarship addressing deuteronomistic influence in the Pentateuch, the Prophets and the Writings. At the conclusion of his survey, Wilson makes two important observations: (1) although many scholars agree that much of the Hebrew Bible is deuteronomistic, they do not agree on what makes it so; and (2) no one has provided a coherent explanation as to why the deuteronomists engaged in such a 'massive and thoroughgoing literary enterprise'. Wilson's last thought—'if everybody is the Deuteronomist, then there may be no Deuteronomist at all'—highlights the nebulous nature of the term *deuteronomistic influence* and underscores the concrete implications such ambiguity holds for scholarship.

II

While Part 1 of the book explores the history of scholarship and problems inherent in the terminology surrounding pan-Deuteronomism, Part 2 addresses pan-Deuteronomism in the Pentateuch, the Former Prophets, the Latter Prophets and the Writings.

The first essay in this section is Joseph Blenkinsopp's treatment of the Pentateuch. Writing in the period after the demise of J and E as continuous sources, Blenkinsopp addresses the suggestion that non-P material in Genesis, Exodus and Numbers belongs instead to the deuteronomic writer. Limiting himself to the core of the Sinai-Horeb pericope (Exod. 19–34), Blenkinsopp finds evidence of materials reflecting 'pure deuteronomic doctrine' as well as other indications that the pericope 'owes a debt' to Deuteronomy. Blenkinsopp concludes that instead of using the term 'Yahwist' for this material, one might just as well talk about 'a deuteronomic account of national origins'. Where and by whom such an account would have been written, however, are questions he declines to answer in this article.

Although Coggins described belief in the Deuteronomistic History as the 'received wisdom of Hebrew Biblical scholarship' (see pp. 22-35 below), A. Graeme Auld questions such an assumption in his essay 'The Deuteronomists and the Former Prophets, or What Makes the Former Prophets Deuteronomistic?' Auld surveys scholars who struggle with whether or not a DH ever existed and, if it did, what it entailed—

crucial questions at a time when others are seeing the influence of such
a history throughout the Hebrew Bible. Positing a late date for Deuteronomy, Auld prefers to think of the flow between Deuteronomy and
Kings as *moving from* Kings *to* Deuteronomy (rather than the more
popular image of *from* Deuteronomy *to* Kings) and suggests that the
Former Prophets contains a pre- or proto-Deuteronomism. According to
Auld, scholars need to 'go with the flow' and concentrate on the
sources and levels of redaction prior to dtr1 or on extant texts with
which our final text can be compared (such as LXX or Qumran documents).

Robert Kugler's treatment of pan-Deuteronomism and the Latter
Prophets has as its goal the selective assessing of 'evidence cited in
favor of the notion of a deuteronomistic redaction' of the prophets.
According to Kugler, such a redaction would go a long way toward
'confirming the existence of a social movement that actively promoted
that theological outlook'. In order to determine the presence of this
redactional activity, Kugler suggests four rough categories of influence:
category 1 evidence consists of passages that contain notions and literary traits typical of the deuteronomic tradition; category 2 evidence
consists of passages that lack obviously deuteronomic concepts or ideas
but do exhibit the distinctive literary traits of the deuteronomic tradition; category 3 evidence consists of passages that do address a theme
or concept known only from the deuteronomic canon but that do not
exhibit its peculiar diction or language; and category 4 evidence consists of passages improperly associated in past scholarship with
deuteronomic themes, content or style. Of the 15 books in the Latter
Prophets, Kugler concludes that five show no dtr imprint (Joel, Obadiah, Jonah, Nahum and Habakkuk) while others contain complementary category 1, 2 and 3 evidence—but none of dtr redaction (Second
Isaiah, Third Isaiah, Haggai, Zechariah and Malachi). Of the rest—First
Isaiah, Amos, Hosea, Micah, Zephaniah, Jeremiah and Ezekiel—Kugler
finds strong hints of redaction only in Amos and Jeremiah.

Concluding Part 2 is James Crenshaw's essay on pan-Deuteronomism and the Writings. After lamenting the similarities between the
pan-Sapientialism of the 1960s and the pan-Deuteronomism of the
1990s (both of which he condemns for their lack of methodological
integrity), Crenshaw surveys contemporary trends towards linking
Deuteronomy with Proverbs, Ecclesiastes and late liturgical prayers.
When he finds no persuasive evidence to suggest any formal connection,

he concludes his essay with methodological observations that critique the cogency of various 'proofs' of deuteronomistic influence. Crenshaw also complains that the issues of literacy and the accessibility of books in the ancient world are often ignored by scholars in their quest for finding evidence of pan-Deuteronomism.

III

The last section contains six essays focusing on specific passages and books thought to contain deuteronomistic influence or, as in the case of Marc Brettler's article, on passages which may have influenced Deuteronomy. Since the Latter Prophets have drawn the lion's share of scholarly attention concerning pan-Deuteronomism, it should come as no surprise that the last four essays (two-thirds of Part 3) are devoted to case studies involving prophetic books.

John Van Seters's essay asks the question 'Is There Evidence of a Dtr Redaction in the Sinai Pericope (Exodus 19–24, 32–34)?' Unlike Blenkinsopp, who finds enough evidence to warrant talking about a 'deuteronomic account of national origins', Van Seters concludes that Exodus 19–24 and 32–34 are post-deuteronomistic. While the Sinai Pericope transforms rather than repeats dtr concepts and perspectives, there is, Van Seters insists, 'no dtr redaction in the Tetrateuch'.

Unlike the rest of the essays in this part, Marc Brettler's article does not confront pan-Deuteronomism in the Hebrew Scriptures directly, but instead discusses 'Predestination in Deuteronomy 30.1-10' and in allied prophetic texts. He concludes, for example, that Deut. 30.1-10 draws its inspiration from Jeremiah 31, not vice versa, and thus reverses the direction of influence normally assumed between Deuteronomy and Jeremiah.

Thomas Römer's article titled 'How Did Jeremiah Become a Convert to Deuteronomistic Ideology?' poses two questions for consideration: (1) How should we describe the dtr redaction of Jeremiah (if there was one)? And (2) what is the relationship between the dtr redactors of Jeremiah and those of the historical books? Römer concludes that there are two dtr redactions of Jeremiah. The first dealt with chs. 7–35 and took place at the same time as the dtr redactions of Amos and Hosea and, with them, resulted in the kernel of a 'dtr' prophetic canon. The second dtr redaction was framed by chs. 1 and 45 and took place some time before the end of the exile.

While Römer addresses Jeremiah, Corinne Patton tackles the issue of pan-Deuteronomism and Ezekiel. According to Patton, Ezekiel—unlike Jeremiah—shows little evidence of wholesale dtr redaction. Patton turns instead to specific passages thought to contain isolated examples of dtr presence. Patton concludes that while some of these texts simply reflect Ezekiel's ability to manipulate deuteronomistic ideas in light of his own ideology, others suggest that Jeremiah and Deuteronomy may have found inspiration from Ezekiel and not the other way around.

The book concludes with two essays on the Book of the Twelve that provide readers with quite different assessments. At one end of the spectrum is Stephen Cook who, in his essay 'Micah's Deuteronomistic Redaction and the Deuteronomists' Identity', not only argues for a direct deuteronomistic redaction of Micah, but suggests that it coheres with earlier Mican prophecy and concludes that the circles that produced Micah (Northern Levites, according to Cook) were also responsible for dtr reforms and the composition of the DH. At the other end of the spectrum is Ehud Ben Zvi's article, 'A Deuteronomisitic Redaction in/among "The Twelve"? A Contribution from the Standpoint of the Books of Micah, Zephaniah and Obadiah'. Ben Zvi argues that similarities between Micah, Zephaniah and Obadiah and the DH can be explained by their association with the same general period and social group rather than the presence of deuteronomistic redaction.

In an epilogue, co-editor Steven McKenzie furnishes some concluding remarks on the future of pan-Deuteronomism. After a quick survey of the history of Deuteronomy's relationship to other parts of the canon, McKenzie reaffirms his belief in dtr—that is, in Noth's single exilic historian who was responsible for the DH. He rejects the notion of systematic editing produced by subsequent 'dtrs' in a school or as part of a movement. This does not stop McKenzie, however, from insisting that Deuteronomy as elaborated by the deuteronomistic historian exercised a considerable influence on the formation of Hebrew Scripture. For McKenzie, *deuteronomistic influence does not mean deuteronomistic editing.* Thus, in the final analysis, scholars would do well to content themselves with the 'enormous influence' the DH had on both the composition of the Hebrew Bible and upon nascent Judaism, without constructing fictitious deuteronomistic schools that bear the weight of the entire Hebrew Scriptures on their shoulders.

Concerning the collection of the above articles into this volume, several points need to be made. First, no attempt was made to make sure terminology was used consistently between articles. Indeed, as one reads through these pieces it becomes obvious that the lack of consistency in usage between terms like *deuteronomic, deuteronomistic* and *deuteronomism* is a very real part of the problem—one that many of our writers struggle to resolve both in this book as well as in the discipline of DH studies.

Secondly, some of the essays use Hebrew, while others use transliteration or a combination of the two. We allowed this mixture to stand as it is, although in some ways we were prone to make transliterated Hebrew the norm. We chose not to do so because some of the essays—noticeably Marc Brettler's—would have suffered in the transition.

Finally, we would like to thank all those without whose help this volume would have been impossible to assemble. Special thanks go to the writers for presenting papers, allowing us to reprint past essays or for writing specifically for this publication. Of particular importance to the project were: Ehud Ben Zvi (the then co-chair of the Deuteronomistic History Section) for taking on the planning and implementation of the 1997 and 1998 sessions while I edited this volume; the Deuteronomistic History Section Committee of the National Society of Biblical Literature (Richard Nelson, Pauline Viviano, Ehud Ben Zvi [as well as Steven McKenzie and myself]—and our two more recent members, Thomas Römer and Marc Brettler) for their suggestions and hard work in making our section an unusually productive one; Philip Davies from Sheffield Academic Press for his belief in our project; Ed Crowley for his translation of Lohfink's article from the French, and Philip Davies and his wife, Birgit, for their help in checking it against the original German; and my colleague Robert Kugler, whose chance remark concerning his syllabus gave me the seed that blossomed into this project. Of course, standing behind all these friends and supporters are our families—without whose understanding it would have been impossible to devote the time needed to such a project. So—to Angel, Brittany, Sean, Ariel, Vilma, Christina and Bonnie—a heartfelt thanks for your patience, love and support!

Part I
PAN-DEUTERONOMISM: THE PROBLEM

What Does 'Deuteronomistic' Mean?*

Richard Coggins

Half a century ago 'Deuteronomy' and 'Deuteronomic' were words applied in biblical studies either specifically to the book of Deuteronomy, or to the proposed Pentateuchal source D. In practice the difference between the two usages was not great, for in most versions of Pentateuchal criticism D was largely confined to the book of Deuteronomy. Even as recently as 1951 the well-known survey of current developments in Old Testament scholarship, *The Old Testament and Modern Study*, contained just one index reference to the Deuteronomic history work.[1]

Today all is changed. The additional adjective 'Deuteronomistic' has been coined, and its influence is all-pervasive. Graeme Auld refers to Deuteronomism (*sic*) as 'an internationally traded currency'.[2] I myself wrote recently that 'the Deuteronomists have sometimes been praised or blamed for virtually every significant development within ancient Israel's religious practice', and tried to warn against the danger of 'pan-Deuteronomism'.[3] The problem has been steadily increasing. Not just the book of Deuteronomy and the Pentateuchal source D (if a four-document hypothesis relating to the Pentateuch is still accepted), but also

---

* Except for minor authorial changes, this article is the same one that originally appeared in Jon Davies, Graham Harvey and Wilfred G.E. Watson (eds.), *Words Remembered, Texts Renewed: Essays in Honour of John F.A. Sawyer* (JSOTSup, 195; Sheffield: Sheffield Academic Press, 1995), pp. 135-48.

1. H.H. Rowley (ed.), *The Old Testament and Modern Study* (Oxford: Clarendon Press, 1951), p. 374.

2. A. Graeme Auld, 'Reading Joshua after Kings', in Davies, Harvey and Watson (eds.), *Words Remembered, Texts Renewed*, pp. 167-81 (170).

3. R.J. Coggins, 'Prophecy—True and False', in H.A. McKay and D.J.A. Clines (eds.), *Of Prophets' Visions and the Wisdom of Sages: Festschrift for R.N. Whybray* (JSOTSup, 162; Sheffield: JSOT Press, 1993), pp. 80-94 (85).

the Former Prophets, Joshua–2 Kings, the editing of Jeremiah, the editing of other pre-exilic prophetic collections (?Amos ?Hosea ?parts of Isaiah ?a major part of the Book of the Twelve) can all be attributed to the work of Deuteronomists. In addition Deuteronomistic influence is claimed for or detected in practically every part of the Hebrew Bible, so that one may note with an element of surprise that the books of Job or Ecclesiastes are said to be free from, or perhaps are only rebelling against, Deuteronomistic influence or tendencies. When a word or a concept has taken over so much of our thought it seems only right to pause and explore its appropriate meaning; is it as pervasive as at first appears? Is the orthodoxy of ancient Israelite religion really laid down along Deuteronomistic lines, as has recently been claimed?[4] What in practice do we mean when we use the term Deuteronomistic? In what follows a number of references will be made to recent authors and con-temporary usage; it should be understood that these are intended only as illustrative, rather than as offering negative judgments upon the books and articles referred to.

I

Deuteronomic and Deuteronomistic. One bone of contention can prob-ably be removed quite quickly. There has been dispute as to whether we need two adjectives at all, and some scholars have suggested that 'Deuteronomistic' is an unnecessary coinage. But the sheer prevalence of the usage would suggest that two words are necessary, one to describe that which pertains specifically to the book of Deuteronomy, the other more general, to denote the influence or thought-forms asso-ciated with the work of the Deuteronomists and expressed more widely and diffusely in the literature. The usage followed in this essay will largely be dependent on that of the particular authors being referred to; no element of consistency can as yet be detected.

II

An issue that is often discussed, but from which no satisfactory con-clusions are reached, is that of dating. Once again the conventional

---

4. M. Barker, *The Older Testament* (London: SPCK, 1987), pp. 142-60; *idem*, *The Great Angel* (London: SPCK, 1992), pp. 12-18.

wisdom used to be relatively straightforward.[5] Northern origins could be traced in Deuteronomy through its sceptical view of kingship, its understanding of the prophets as 'covenant mediators', its links with Hosea and its use of 'love' terminology rather than the terminology associated with the Jerusalem tradition. It was thought likely, therefore, that following the fall of the Northern Kingdom in 722/721 religious leaders had fled to the South, and had encapsulated their ideas in what would later become the book of Deuteronomy, but had been forced to hide the results because of the persecution under Manasseh. Only in the new atmosphere brought about by Josiah's reform was it safe for them to bring those ideas out into the open. On such an understanding as this, Deuteronomy—or at least its nucleus—was clearly pre-exilic: certainly no later than the seventh century, when the law-book was discovered, and perhaps significantly earlier, if the northern connection were taken seriously.

But then problems arose. The theory of a Deuteronomistic History, as the appropriate description for the books Joshua–2 Kings, first propounded by M. Noth in 1943 (ET 1991) has won all but universal acceptance, and this brings the dating down to the middle of the sixth century, since the last event referred to is Jehoiachin's restoration to at least partial favour at the Babylonian court (2 Kgs 25.27-30). Now we have to assume that the Deuteronomists survived for some 60 years at least after the discovery of the law-book under Josiah. For Noth the concept was still manageable, since he was convinced that one editor was responsible for the whole of the Deuteronomistic History, and he suggested that the final verses of 2 Kgs 25.27-30 were added by the Deuteronomist 'from his own knowledge'.[6] But for the most part this view of unitary authorship is the one aspect of Noth's thesis which has not been accepted. Instead there have arisen various theories of levels of Deuteronomistic redaction which can be traced in the Deuteronomistic History, and that has led to proposed dates even further into the sixth century as the most likely background.

Two main types of proposals have been put forward. On the one hand, and largely in the USA, F.M. Cross and his pupils have suggested

5.   E.W. Nicholson, *Deuteronomy and Tradition* (Oxford: Basil Blackwell, 1967), pp. 58-82.

6.   M. Noth, *Überlieferungsgeschichtliche Studien* (Schriften der Königsberger Gelehrten Gesellschaft, 18.2; Halle: Niemeyer, 1943), pp. 1-110; *The Deuteronomistic History* (ET; JSOTSup, 15; Sheffield: JSOT Press, 1991), p. 117.

that the basic form of Joshua–2 Kings is pre-exilic, but that it underwent a further redaction during the period of the exile. Alternatively, and this time mainly in Europe, those who have followed R. Smend have taken the view that the whole work is essentially exilic, and that particular prophetic and 'nomistic' redactions (DtrP and DtrN) took place at a later stage. Thus, to give but one example of many that could be put forward, J. Vermeylen has claimed to detect three redactional levels which he identifies as 'Dtr 575', 'Dtr 560' and 'Dtr 525', the numbers referring to the dates of supposed activity.[7] A very useful sum–mary of the main views of the development of the Deuteronomistic History is provided by Provan.[8]

Difficulties have also arisen in assessing our knowledge of the earlier stages of this movement. In many reconstructions of the history of Israel, Josiah's reform and the discovery of the law-book have been taken as fixed points which could be relied upon where much else was controverted. But is this as firmly based as is sometimes assumed? We need not doubt that Josiah, rejoicing in new-found opportunities of showing his independence of Assyrian control, engaged in a religious reform which cleared his cultic places of what were deemed to be alien practices. But the story of the finding of the law-book, as has often been noted, fits somewhat awkwardly into the overall account. Could it be that this is an editorial construct, aimed in part at least at providing an acceptable contrast in behaviour over against the wicked Jehoiakim, who when he was confronted with a scroll rent the scroll (Jer. 36)? Josiah by contrast rent his garments and showed himself a model of deuteronomistic piety. Parallels also exist between the account of Josiah's reaction to the words of the Torah and the picture offered in Nehemiah 8 of Ezra reading from the Torah to the assembled congregation. How much in all of this is ideology and how much history must remain open to further scrutiny. The survey by Ahlström seems not to be wholly self-consistent, as the existence of a scroll at the time of Josiah appears to be sometimes affirmed, sometimes denied, but his work still offers a valuable introduction to the problems posed by the account in 2 Kings 22–23.[9]

7. J. Vermeylen, *Le Dieu de la promesse et le Dieu de l'alliance* (LD, 126; Paris: Cerf, 1986), pp. 123-27.

8. I.W. Provan, *Hezekiah and the books of Kings* (BZAW, 172; Berlin: W. de Gruyter, 1988), pp. 2-31.

9. G.W. Ahlström, *The History of Ancient Palestine from the Palestinian*

Whatever conclusion we reach in these matters, the fact remains that the exilic and even postexilic periods are now regarded as the age at which Deuteronomistic influence was at its height. Thus R.F. Person, writing on Zechariah 9–14, is concerned to show that 'the Deuteronomistic school', defined as 'a scribal guild active in the exilic and post-exilic periods' was responsible for the final redaction of those chapters, commonly regarded as among the latest additions to the prophetic corpus. He devotes the first part of his study, entitled 'Deuteronomic Redaction in the Post-Exilic Period', to establishing that traces of Deuteronomic redactional activity can be found in the post-exilic period, and affects books generally regarded as postexilic in origin. His argument is based both on specific textual usage and on themes regarded as characteristically Deuteronomic.[10] This concentration on the 'postexilic' period has been a feature of much Hebrew Bible study in recent years. Thus, for example, P.R. Davies's search for 'Ancient Israel' has led him to conclude that much of the material once regarded as embodying ancient traditions was the product of 'scribal schools' and may be as late as the third century. As he rightly sees, it then becomes almost meaningless to talk of a 'Deuteronomistic history', a usage which he suggests should be abandoned.[11]

We thus find ourselves confronted with dates ranging from the eighth to the third centuries as the suggested period in which Deuteronomistic influence was at its height. (All this, of course, is purely within the range of critical scholarship; if we include within our consideration conservatives who claim to detect signs of traditions going back to Moses himself that will of course extend the range of possible dates still more widely.) Yet of so wide-ranging and influential a movement there is no external evidence of any kind; the whole history of tradition has to be worked out by inference. Deuteronomistic influence may be traced, but there is still no agreement as to who the Deuteronomists were.

Period to Alexander's Conquest (JSOTSup, 146; Sheffield: Sheffield Academic Press, 1993), pp. 772-77.

10. R.F. Person, Jr, *Second Zechariah and the Deuteronomic School* (JSOTSup, 167; Sheffield: JSOT Press, 1993), pp. 40-78.

11. P.R. Davies, *In Search of 'Ancient Israel'* (JSOTSup, 148; Sheffield: JSOT Press, 1992), p. 131.

III

It is scarcely possible, in an essay of this kind, to enter in detail into the discussions as to the identity of the Deuteronomists. As is well known, three views have been particularly influential: that the Deuteronomists were Levites;[12] that they were part of, or heirs to, the prophetic tradition;[13] or that they were to be associated with wisdom schools.[14] It is noteworthy that all these theories were proposed in work from at least 20 years ago; more recently the tendency has been simply to take the Deuteronomists on their own terms, as it were, and to decline to identify them with some other group known to us in ancient Israel. Thus R.E. Clements[15] suggests that the most precise designation possible is to call them 'a "Reforming Party" with members drawn from more than one group'. The view of R.E. Friedman, that the Deuteronomist was an individual, either the Baruch of the book of Jeremiah, or 'a collaboration, with Jeremiah, the poet and prophet, as the inspiration, and Baruch the scribe',[16] has not been taken up to the best of my knowledge, and is rebutted by Clements.[17]

Reference to 'schools' has proved another potent source of confusion. Sometimes the 'Deuteronomistic School' is used in terms which imply something analogous to an institution, as in Weinfeld's reference to 'wisdom schools'. (Here again we have the problem of the complete lack of any direct reference to such 'schools'.) But often 'school' seems to mean little more than what we might term a 'school of thought'—a particular mode of expression, a particular theological stance, which is widely found and then described as 'Deuteronomistic'.

IV

Reference has just been made to the supposedly massive programme of redaction in which the Deuteronomists are alleged to have engaged. In

12. G. von Rad, *Studies in Deuteronomy* (SBT, 9; London: SCM Press, 1953), pp. 60-69.

13. Nicholson, *Deuteronomy*, pp. 58-82.

14. M. Weinfeld, *Deuteronomy and the Deuteronomic School* (Oxford: Clarendon Press, 1972), pp. 260-74.

15. R.E. Clements, *Deuteronomy* (OTG; Sheffield: JSOT Press, 1989), p. 79.

16. R.E. Friedman, *Who Wrote the Bible?* (London: Cape, 1988), p. 147.

17. Clements, *Deuteronomy*, p. 77.

what follows no attempt is made to be exhaustive; the quotations are given in an illustrative way, to show something of the range of alleged Deuteronomistic literary influence on the Hebrew Bible as it has come down to us.

One can begin at the beginning, with the Pentateuch. In the older days of the four-document hypothesis the amount of D redaction in the first four books was always regarded as minimal; S.R. Driver, for example, analysed the material in Genesis–Numbers, attributing sections to J, E and P, but without leaving any room for a significant input from D.[18] More recently, however, theories of a much more elaborate Deuteronomistic contribution have been put forward. Thus R. Rendtorff identifies a 'whole series of texts dealing with the events of the exodus from Egypt, Sinai, and the beginning of the occupation of the land which refer back to the patriarchal story, and especially to the promise of the land to the patriarchs'. All of these, in his view, are 'stamped with deuteronomic language'.[19] This understanding has been developed further by Rendtorff's sometime pupil, E. Blum, who claims that beneath the present form of the Pentateuch one can detect a Deuteronomistic level of redaction (K^D in his terminology, standing for D-Komposition). In this the different older traditions were shaped into a history stretching forward from Abraham. In Blum's view this was a product of the early postexilic period.[20]

Working in greater detail on a smaller block of material, W. Johnstone has isolated Deuteronomistic cycles of 'signs' and 'wonders' in Exodus 1–13.[21] This takes further an approach he had already adumbrated in outline in his earlier work, where a D version of Exodus was proposed and its characteristic theological concerns set out.[22] Similarly L. Perlitt, in his investigation of the origins of the notion of covenant,

18. S.R. Driver, *An Introduction to the Literature of the Old Testament* (Edinburgh: T. & T. Clark, 9th edn, 1913).

19. R. Rendtorff, *The Problem of the Process of Transmission in the Pentateuch* (JSOTSup, 89; Sheffield: JSOT Press, 1990 [German original, BZAW, 147; Berlin: W. de Gruyter, 1977]), pp. 194-95.

20. E. Blum, *Studien zur Komposition des Pentateuch* (BZAW, 189; Berlin: W. de Gruyter, 1990), pp. 7-218.

21. W. Johnstone, 'The Deuteronomistic Cycle of "Signs" and "Wonders" in Exodus 1–13', in A.G. Auld (ed.), *Understanding Poets and Prophets: Essays in Honour of George Wishart Anderson* (JSOTSup, 152; Sheffield: JSOT Press, 1993), pp. 166-85.

22. W. Johnstone, *Exodus* (OTG; Sheffield: JSOT Press, 1990), pp. 105-10.

had already identified a later part of Exodus, chs. 32–34, as essentially a Deuteronomistic composition.[23] The whole theme has indeed been taken further by S. Boorer, who explains in her introduction to the discussion of the theme of the promise of the land in the Pentateuch that she uses the symbol 'Dtr' to 'refer broadly and loosely to any text in Deuteronomic/Deuteronomistic style'.[24] She also draws attention to the practice of Rendtorff, who, as we have seen, speaks of Dtr texts in Genesis–Numbers without specifying their relation to Deuteronomy itself. Instead he spoke in more general terms of a 'Deuteronomistic school' or 'Deuteronomic-Deuteronomistic circles'.[25]

That the books Joshua–2 Kings owe their existing shape to Deuteronomistic editing, so that it is proper to describe them as forming a Deuteronomistic History, has now become part of the received wisdom of Hebrew Bible scholarship, and detailed support for this understanding need not be offered, though Davies's reservations, already mentioned, should be borne in mind. Similarly, among the prophets the presence of a substantial amount of Deuteronomistic editing in the present form of the book of Jeremiah is now widely accepted, and scarcely needs documentation. With the other prophetic collections this Deuteronomistic influence is less widely recognized, yet, as already noted in the introduction, has come to be quite widely proposed. Thus, for Isaiah, Vermeylen's detailed study of the growth of the whole Isaiah tradition, from the figure of the prophet himself down to the apocalyptic imagery of the later parts of the work, led him to find a significant place for Deuteronomistic editing. Many passages which had traditionally been considered as emanating from the prophet himself were regarded as later. Thus, the analysis of the 'Song of the Vineyard' in Isa. 5.1-7 is held to show features which are best explained as arising from a Deuteronomistic milieu at the time of the exile.[26]

Ezekiel, too, has entered into this discussion. Whereas much older scholarship was sceptical as to any connections between Ezekiel and the broad stream of Deuteronomistic tradition, there have been recent

23. L. Perlitt, *Bundestheologie im Alten Testament* (WMANT, 36; Neukirchen–Vluyn: Neukirchener Verlag, 1969), pp. 203-32.

24. S. Boorer, *The Promise of the Land as Oath: A Key to the Formation of the Pentateuch* (BZAW, 205; Berlin: W. de Gruyter, 1992), p. 3.

25. Boorer, *Promise*, p. 31.

26. J. Vermeylen, *Du prophète Isaïe à l'apocalyptique* (2 vols.; Paris: J. Gabalda, 1977–78), I, p. 168.

writers who see closer links. Thus R.R. Wilson maintains that, while 'it is not possible to isolate a specifically Deuteronomic editorial layer', the theology of the book as a whole has 'Deuteronomic features'.[27]

When we turn to the Minor Prophets the issue of Deuteronomistic redaction is very much a matter of current debate. It has long been noted that the books of Hosea, Amos, Micah and Zephaniah all have similar introductory verses, in which the activity of the prophet is associated with the reign of a particular king or kings. Since we know of those kings mainly through the books of Kings, and since the books of Kings are part of the Deuteronomistic History, it is natural to regard these four books as having undergone Deuteronomistic redaction, offering them as an alternative and expanded version of the story being unfolded in the books of Kings, even though the lack of reference to them in 2 Kings remains an unexplained puzzle. This has been worked out in considerable detail by J. Nogalski, as part of his reconstruction of the editorial process underlying the complete 'Book of the Twelve'. While acknowledging the 'tentative' nature of this proposal of a Deuteronomistic corpus consisting of Hosea, Amos, Micah and Zephaniah, he nevertheless concludes that 'the language and perspective of this corpus bears signs of Deuteronomistic theology and the use of both Northern and Southern traditions in creating a historical compendium of prophecy'.[28] This point is taken a stage further by T. Collins, in his redaction-critical study of the prophetic corpus. For him, it is not only that 'the theology of those responsible for producing [the final text of the twelve] was broadly in line with that of the Deuteronomist writers', but also some of its later parts 'were written with an eye to the Deuteronomist theology in general, like Malachi, or to the Deuteronomist view of prophecy in particular'.[29]

This perception of Deuteronomistic influence is not, however, confined to the introductory verses of these collections. In Hosea and Amos in particular, more detailed traces of deuteronomistic influence are often claimed. Thus, for Hosea, N.P. Lemche argues that 'the religious message of the book is not far removed from Deuteronomistic theology',

27. R.R. Wilson, *Prophecy and Society in Ancient Israel* (Philadelphia: Fortress Press, 1980), p. 284.

28. J. Nogalski, *Literary Precursors to the Book of the Twelve* (BZAW, 217; Berlin: W. de Gruyter, 1993), p. 278.

29. T. Collins, *The Mantle of Elijah: The Redaction Criticism of the Prophetical Books* (The Biblical Seminar, 20; Sheffield: Sheffield Academic Press, 1993), p. 62.

and goes on to 'counter the accusation of "pan-Deuteronomism" by showing how the Deuteronomists themselves tried to monopolize the religious expression of early Judaism'.[30] The conclusion reached by G.A. Yee, in a detailed study of the way in which the book of Hosea reached its final form, is that the final redaction took place in Deuteronomistic circles. She traces two levels of redaction, the first 'very steeped in deuteronomistic ideology', the second also betraying a 'deuteronomistic orientation', but dating from a later period, when the exile had become a reality.[31] The notion of being 'steeped in deuteronomistic ideology' is a point to which we shall need to return.

With Amos the emphasis has been on particular expressions as characteristically Deuteronomistic rather than larger claims for the whole thrust of the theology of the book. Thus, to give but two examples, the condemnation of Judah with its reference to the *torah* of Yahweh and his 'statutes' (*ḥuqqāyw*) (Amos 2.4), and that to 'his servants the prophets' (3.7) are commonly held to be characteristic Deuteronomistic vocabulary.

V

Reference to 'his servants the prophets' invites consideration of yet another area in which the influence of the Deuteronomists in shaping our perceptions has been claimed. R.P. Carroll maintains that our understanding of prophets as those who speak the divine word, who must be listened to and obeyed, is essentially a Deuteronomistic one.[32] At this point it becomes difficult to be certain whether we are meant to think of a particular group of people, identifiable in principle as 'Deuteronomists', who successfully impose this radical shift of perception, or whether the reference is rather in more general terms to the spiritual and intellectual climate of the period of early Judaism, when the search for identity and for the causes of the transformation which

30. N.P. Lemche, 'The God of Hosea', in E. Ulrich *et al.* (eds.), *Priests, Prophets and Scribes: Essays on the Formation and Heritage of Second Temple Judaism in Honour of Joseph Blenkinsopp* (JSOTSup, 149; Sheffield: JSOT Press, 1992), pp. 241-57 (255).

31. G.A. Yee, *Composition and Tradition in the Book of Hosea* (Atlanta: Scholars Press, 1987), pp. 308-309.

32. R.P. Carroll, 'Coopting the Prophets: Nehemiah and Noadiah', in Ulrich *et al.* (eds.), *Priests, Prophets and Scribes*, pp. 87-99 (90).

had affected the community could broadly be described as 'Deuteronomistic'. This is the same issue as that raised by the terms in which Yee
describes the reaction of Hosea: her expression, it will be recalled, was
that the process was 'steeped in deuteronomistic ideology', and this
more naturally refers to a climate of thought than to a precise literary
process of redaction. Similar questions arise with the well-known
ascription by Perlitt of the importance of $b^e r \hat{\imath} t$ (covenant) to Deuteronomistic influence; at times it is clear that he is engaged in precise analysis of distinctive vocabulary usage;[33] elsewhere a much less specific
ideological approach is more characteristic.[34]

This uncertainty is what seems to me to underlie David Clines's
judgment, in a private communication, where he expresses doubts
whether he believes in Deuteronomists at all. 'Maybe all the "Deuteronomic" language doesn't imply the existence of people called
"Deuteronomists", but is just a kind of language', the kind that was
thought especially appropriate for writing pompous religious prose.
Parts of this are interestingly reminiscent of the argument used by
J. Bright in his attempt to challenge the assumption of Deuteronomistic
editorial activity in the shaping of the book of Jeremiah. Discussing the
prose material in Jeremiah, he wrote that

> the style of these discourses, though indeed closely akin to that of the
> Deuteronomistic literature, is a style in its own right...it is by no means
> glibly to be classified as 'Deuteronomistic'. It is, moreover, not a late
> style, but a characteristic rhetorical prose of the seventh/sixth centuries.[35]

The last point to raise relates to those parts of the Hebrew Bible
where there are signs of revolt against the accepted norms of religious
belief and practice; most obviously the books of Job and Ecclesiastes.
Sometimes these works are seen as rebelling against the norms of the
wisdom movement, as exemplified by the book of Proverbs. (And, of
course, if the views of Weinfeld and others, that close links should be
seen between Deuteronomy and Proverbs, are to be accepted, then what
is implied is a rebellion against Deuteronomic 'orthodoxy'.) But it has
also not been uncommon to see Job's attitude to the question of suffer-
ing, in particular, as a rejection of 'the Deuteronomic doctrine of the

33. Perlitt, *Bundestheologie*, pp. 8-30.
34. Perlitt, *Bundestheologie*, pp. 54-128.
35. J. Bright, *Jeremiah* (AB, 21; Garden City, NY: Doubleday, 1965), p. lxxi.

rigid correlation of desert and fortune'.[36] Rowley saw this as an application at the individual level of what the Deuteronomists applied only to the nation, but it may be questioned whether a strictly individual reading of the book of Job is appropriate. Here once again we find belief in a generalized Deuteronomistic ideology shaping the character of Judaism's self-awareness. More generally, however, writers on Job and Ecclesiastes are cautious about defining what precisely is being rejected; instead, they concentrate rather on the viewpoint being expressed by their books, and only speak in more general terms about the Deuteronomistic character of Israel's understanding of its position before God.

VI

Perhaps enough has been said to illustrate the extreme diversity underlying contemporary scholarly usage of 'Deuteronomistic' and related terms. Reference was made at the beginning of the essay to *The Old Testament and Modern Study*. A contrast can be drawn between the views expressed there and those to be found in the successor volume, *Tradition and Interpretation*, in which the editor notes in his introductory essay that 'the range of its [Deuteronomy's] creative influence is seen as so extensive that it is not entirely out of place to speak of a pan-Deuteronomic phase in Old Testament study'.[37] In the same volume W. Zimmerli noted the urgency of the challenge 'to develop criteria more keenly differentiated for the phenomenon of "Deuteronomism", which certainly did not fall suddenly complete from heaven'.[38] J.R. Porter has raised important questions concerning the existence of a 'Deuteronomic school', as a notion which becomes 'more tenuous and vague' as its implications are examined in greater detail, and he goes on to identify as a danger 'the tendency to attribute almost all Israelite literary activity, from the period of Josiah to some time after the exile, to the Deuteronomic school, and thus to ignore the richness and variety of the religious expression in Judah during these years'.[39]

36. H.H. Rowley, *Job* (NCB; London: Thomas Nelson, 1970), p. 22.
37. G.W. Anderson (ed.), *Tradition and Interpretation* (Oxford: Clarendon Press, 1979), p. xix.
38. W. Zimmerli, 'The History of Israelite Religion', in Anderson (ed.), *Tradition and Interpretation*, pp. 351-84 (380).
39. J.R. Porter, 'The Supposed Deuteronomic Redaction of the Prophets: Some

The questions that Porter raises with regard to the specific question of the redaction of the prophetic collections can, it seems, be extended a good deal further. We need to balance his perfectly legitimate reference to 'richness and variety' with the recognition that there were ideological pressures at work to impose a particular view of Israel's past, of its relation with its God, of the meaning of the various events that had befallen it, culminating in the destruction of Jerusalem and the deportation of its leading citizens. It is obviously convenient to have some overall name by which to describe and refer to this ideological movement. Whether it is also convenient to describe it as 'Deuteronomistic' must be more open to question, for as we have seen there is then real danger of confusion. In short, it seems as if the use of the terms 'Deuteronomic' and 'Deuteronomistic' may have any one of at least three different implications. First, there is the long-established and traditional usage of that which relates to the book of Deuteronomy itself. Whether the theory of a Deuteronomistic History will continue to attract such widespread support, so that it can in effect be bracketed with this first usage, must be open to question: the points raised by Davies, suggesting a much later date of composition than has been customary, will need to be given fuller consideration than has so far been the case. Secondly, there is the much more disputed issue of Deuteronomistic redaction of other parts of the Hebrew Bible: possibly the remainder of the Pentateuch; more frequently substantial elements of the prophetic literature. Here Deuteronomistic influence is characteristically recognized because of distinctive vocabulary features, but as we have seen there is also a tendency to set down alongside this various ideological features which are regarded as distinctively Deuteronomistic. These should really be regarded as a third usage of the term.

That there is some linkage between these various usages is obvious enough; scholars have not simply applied the term 'Deuteronomistic' to them all in a wilful fashion without some justification. Nevertheless the question must be asked whether confusion is not being increased by applying the same description to what are essentially different phenomena. We need, it seems, to be clearer than we have often been in distinguishing between what can properly be said about a particular book and its immediately related congeners; what can be said by way of describing a literary process through which other pieces of literature reached

Considerations', in R. Albertz *et al.* (eds.), *Schöpfung und Befreiung: Für Claus Westermann zum 80. Geburtstag* (Stuttgart: Calwer Verlag, 1989), pp. 69-78 (71).

their final form; and what can be said about an ideological movement which played a major part in shaping the self-understanding of Judaism. To use the same name for them all is to invite a breakdown in under-standing.

WAS THERE A DEUTERONOMISTIC MOVEMENT?*

Norbert F. Lohfink

G. von Rad considered Deuteronomy to be a later, written record of homilies 'of a Levitical reform movement which preceded the cultic transformations carried out under Josiah', at the time of the 622 reform. Thus the prophetic reform party, presumed since Wellhausen to be behind Deuteronomy, was replaced by a 'Deuteronomistic movement' attributable to militant rural Levites. This shift of perspective took place almost unnoticed.

The expression 'Deuteronomistic movement' is accompanied by 'Deuteronomistic school'. Thus H.W. Wolff, in his commentary on the twelve minor prophets,[1] spoke of 'this great Deuteronomistic school' in which 'was born that vast historical work and which is concerned with the preservation and the understanding of the prophetic books from before the exile'. Wolff was definitely thinking of an identifiable group. In English, as in German, the word 'school' can designate a few, more or less connected, authors or compilers of texts, who are associated with the language and content of Deuteronomy, just as one can speak of a 'school' of a painter. For many, 'Deuteronomistic school' doubtless means nothing more than that.

*   This translation was prepared from an abbreviated version, in French, of Professor Lohfink's original article, 'Gab es eine deuteronomistische Bewegung?', in W. Gross (ed.), *Jeremia und die 'deuteronomistische Bewegung'* (BBB, 98; Weinheim: Beltz Athenäum, 1995), pp. 313-82. We are grateful to Dr Ed Crowley for his help in translating the French version: 'Y a-t-il eu un mouvement deutér-onomiste', in N. Lohfink, *Les traditions du Pentateuque autour de l'exil* (CE, 97; Paris: Cerf, n.d.), pp. 41-63. We are also grateful to Professor Lohfink for his suggestions on the English translation and to Dr Philip Davies and Birgit Mänz-Davies for their reading of this English translation in light of the German.

1.   H.W. Wolff, *Dodekapropheton* (BKAT, 14; Neukirchen–Vluyn: Neukirchener Verlag, 1965), p. 20.

According to O.H. Steck,[2] the Deuteronomistic movement, supported by Levites from the Judaean countryside, existed over an astonishing period of half a millennium! For him, the movement persisted and produced literature until around 200 BCE, when it broke up into the vast Hasidic movement. Such a prolonged duration of the 'Deuteronomic' or 'Deuteronomistic' movement seems also to have been accepted without reservation by Old Testament scholarship.

In the meantime, of course, the members of this movement are hardly thought to be passing through the villages as Levite preachers; the teachers of the Deuteronomistic school never do this. However, the Deuteronomic movement and the Deuteronomistic school, as categories in Old Testament exegesis, are constantly appealed to, particularly in Germany, and recently in the form of an even more imprecise term, 'Deuteronomism'. The number of authors belonging to this 'movement' constantly increases—especially in the exilic, Persian and Greek periods—and the number of biblical texts composed, edited or at least added to by them also expands. Some years ago, in order to be considered good, an Old Testament specialist had to reconstruct a primitive decalogue or a new festival; today, a self-respecting doctoral student has to find the hand of a Deuteronomist somewhere in the Bible. This is the only way into the guild.

This situation calls for re-evaluation. To be sure, I can offer only a few loosely related remarks. The phenomenon conveyed by the suggestive name 'pan-Deuteronomism' covers almost all the problems of the Old Testament.

When Would It Be Better Not to Use the Word 'Deuteronomistic'?

I begin with some thoughts about the label 'Deuteronomistic', now being affixed to more and more texts. Wellhausen reflected on the terminology that would establish itself later on, when he described the beginning of the book of Joshua in his *Composition of the Hexateuch.*[3] His definition can serve as a starting point:

> Josh 1 is purely Deuteronomistic, that is to say, composed by the writer who inserted the Deuteronomic law into the history and who rewrote the

2. O.H. Steck, *Israel und das gewaltsame Geschick der Propheten* (WMANT, 23; Neukirchen–Vluyn: Neukirchener Verlag, 1967).

3. J. Wellhausen, *Die Composition des Hexateuchs und der historischen Bücher des Alten Testaments* (Berlin: W. de Gruyter, 1963), p. 117.

history according to the Deuteronomic Law. That writer could be designated the Deuteronomist, to distinguish him from the author of the actual
Deuteronomy.

A distinction is therefore made here between 'Deuterono*mic*' (pertaining to Deuteronomy) and 'Deuterono*mistic*' (pertaining to material
influenced by Deuteronomy). Later in his treatment, Wellhausen accepted a direction of dependence from 'Deuteronomic' to 'Deuteronomistic': he assumed the Deuteronomic Law (Deut. 12–26) to be earlier.
Texts can therefore be considered 'Deuteronomistic' if from the point
of view of language or content they have contacts with Deuteronomy,
or even with only the Law of Deuteronomy 12–26, and are derived
from it.

This idea lies at the root of the current usage. Connections of a text
with Deuteronomy, generally on the level of vocabulary, are established, and as a result the text is labelled as Deuteronomistic. But over
time two approaches have been developed, which, to simplify matters, I
will call 'Approach 1' and 'Approach 2'.

In Approach 1, one no longer proceeds simply from the Deuteronomic Law or the book of Deuteronomy but assumes an extended
canon of Deuteronomistic texts. To the book of Deuteronomy has been
added the history that runs from Joshua to 2 Kings, as well as the
'Deuteronomistic' parts of the book of Jeremiah. On this very broad
basis some texts can be shown to be 'Deuteronomistic' that would not
have been labelled as such if the comparison were limited to Deuteronomy 12–26. For example, in the entire book of Deuteronomy there is
not even one example of the 'Deuteronomistic portrait of history' that
makes it possible for Steck to detect the Deuteronomistic movement as
late as the third century. Likewise in the whole Deuteronomistic History, such a portrait is only found in one place: 2 Kgs 17.7-20. On the
other hand, there are some references to it in the book of Jeremiah. The
occurrence in 2 Kings 17, however, is still not typical. Steck's designation of this historical portrait as 'Deuteronomistic' is based solely on
the occurrences in Jeremiah. While it seems to me justifiable to declare
this historical portrait 'Deuteronomistic', it may not be justifiable to
stick this label on every bit of later writing in which this historical portrait occurs and then almost automatically to attribute such writings to
authors from an alleged 'Deuteronomistic movement'.

In Approach 2 even texts that contain nothing typically Deuteronomistic are identified as Deuteronomistic. All that is necessary is that

they have some relationship with the texts that belong to the basic Deuteronomistic canon or have been classified as Deuteronomistic with the help of Approach 1. For example, for some time there has been a growing consensus that the Book of the Twelve taken as a whole is a Deuteronomistic creation because the titles of the books are attributed to the hand of Deuteronomistic redactors. Now it is clear that even if the dating formulas of the Twelve are borrowed from the books of Kings, we cannot find in these titles any combinations of specifically Deuteronomistic terms or typically Deuteronomistic ideas. Yet, according to the mysterious rule of Approach 2, we must still speak of 'Deuteronomistic' titles. In such a case, I see no difficulty in speaking of a 'relationship' with the Deuteronomistic literature or of 'features' or even 'elements' that *also* appear in Deuteronomistic writings. However, it seems to me exaggerated to describe such literature as Deuteronomistic even more readily than when isolated and perhaps authentic Deuteronomistic features appear. Where this happens, something more than a mere description of textual phenomena is lurking under the surface: the Deuteronomistic movement has made an appearance!

When all is said and done, I would like to argue in favour of reserving the use of the word 'Deuteronomistic' for describing textual affiliation, thereby avoiding pan-Deuteronomistic chain reactions. If I am not mistaken, whole books can still be designated Deuteronomistic, but only within the basic Deuteronomistic canon already known. Beyond that we could use the word, exclusively as an adjective, for some concrete phenomena in such expressions as 'Deuteronomistic formulation' or 'Deuteronomistic *theologoumenon*' or 'Deuteronomistic narrative pattern'. This convention would make it obligatory to add supplementary arguments if one wished to look for authors or groups of protagonists in order to explain these literary or thematic features.

The fact that today less effort is expended in looking for the connection of texts with the Deuteronomic Law than with the whole basic Deuteronomistic canon necessitates a brief additional remark. To be sure, the reason for this is the ever-expanding notion of 'Deuteronomism'. But at the same time specific information comes to light at the very heart of the Deuteronomistic literature. On this subject, just one remark. R. Smend[4] was able to write about the 'so-called Deuteronomist': 'This accepted designation rests on the fact that the way of

---

4. R. Smend, *Die Entstehung des Alten Testaments* (Stuttgart: W. Kohlhammer, 2nd edn, 1981), p. 83.

thinking and of expression itself is met in a particularly concentrated way in Deuteronomy. But [the term] is not very appropriate, since it suggests that this style is derived from Deuteronomy, which is far from being proved.' This claim clearly contradicts the citation of Wellhausen that I quoted at the beginning of this article. In recent publications, the original Deuteronomy of Josiah actually seems to be more and more distant.

We must nevertheless not throw out the baby with the bath water and, as in a recent doctoral dissertation, identify the Covenant Code of Exodus 20–23 with the lawbook of Josiah.[5] Moreover, we can assume that large parts of the text of our Deuteronomy, not yet in the book found in 622, are nevertheless from the time of Josiah. But these are at least related to the book of Joshua, and therefore, according to the usual language, 'Deuteronomistic'. The idea that the Deuteronomistic phenomenon is out of the question before the exile, the point of view attributable to M. Noth,[6] is in complete opposition to the position of Old Testament exegetes of the last century, even if it is commonly held in Germany today.

It is quite possible that there was not very much in the covenant law of Josiah aside from the basic texts of the Deuteronomic legislation on cult and the social laws. But only what was then found in this lawbook would be 'Deuteronomic', according to Wellhausen. The remainder would be 'Deuteronomistic'. In this case, the linguistic, theological and literary characteristics that we call 'Deuteronomistic' would be derived only slightly from the 'Deuteronomic', but would instead be something original. It is therefore quite appropriate to start from a large basic canon of Deuteronomistic writings. But if we still wish to identify other texts as 'Deuteronomistic', research on the strata within the basic Deuteronomistic canon becomes all the more imperative.

What Criteria Allow for the Designation of a Text as Deuteronomistic?

What I have discussed to this point is essentially the question of curbing the inflationary usage of the label 'Deuteronomistic'. While remaining

5.   E. Reuter, *Kultzentralisation: Entstehung und Theologie von Dtn 12* (BBB, 87; Frankfurt: Hain, 1993).

6.   M. Noth, *Überlieferungsgeschichtliche Studien* (Tübingen: Max Niemeyer, 2nd edn, 1957); *The Deuteronomistic History* (ET; JSOTSup, 15; Sheffield: JSOT Press, 1991).

with the surface of the text, and without trying for now to define the authors and the groups of protagonists, I come to the next question: What criteria can be used to identify real Deuteronomistic material?

Criteria for identifying Deuteronomistic material are often based on linguistic features. Ordinarily, scholars identify words and expressions that have parallels in the basic Deuteronomistic canon. But the method is not limited to that; obviously we refer as well to common contents and interests, such as the themes of centralization of cult, of the veneration of YHWH alone, of observance of the Torah, of the land promised and endangered. We can discover common narrative patterns, such as the laws on the unfolding of history which lead to blessing or curse. But in my opinion we do not take style sufficiently into account. For example, in the rhetorical sequences of Deuteronomistic texts, series using infinitives are favoured, whereas in Priestly texts parallel sentences with finite verbs are constructed instead. Compositional devices at different levels are added to these (such as the framing of texts with exhortatory formulas or the linking of long historical narratives through the insertion of interpretative discourses). Finally, we think that we can point to individual cases of dependence on specific Deuteronomistic texts. In theory we can agree with such a list of criteria. But what does it amount to in practice?

An initial question is: what significance does counting occurrences of individual words have and what do the corresponding lists of parallel words prove? Given the limited extent of our textual corpus and still more the isolated occurrences of the fragments which are supposed to be Deuteronomistic, it would be very dangerous to work in a purely statistical way on the level of vocabulary. With our small numbers, the statistics on words can be completely distorted by a few citations and commentaries that go against the general sense, while they would disappear in the mass of large textual complexes. In the case of our texts, it is probably never permissible to start from isolated words and their distribution. These texts can only be evaluated from groups of words and combinations of words. And it is necessary then to move beyond the statistics and examine and judge each particular case. M. Weinfeld,[7] in his appendix on terminology, has sensed this necessity quite well and, unlike the older lists, isolated terms are rare in his lists. However his way of doing things does not seem to have gained widespread

8.   M. Weinfeld, *Deuteronomy and the Deuteronomic School* (Oxford: Clarendon Press, 1972), pp. 320-65.

acceptance as yet among the Deuteronomistic treasure hunters.

Furthermore, the use of verbal statistics requires a countercheck from a control corpus; in the contributions referred to, this feature is missing most of the time. In many cases, if it is a matter of particular terms, a simple glance at the tables in Part 3 of Anderson's and Forbes's *Vocabulary of the Old Testament* [8] could reveal, all things considered, whether there is something specifically Deuteronomistic about a word or it is frequently used in other biblical settings as well.

Searching for groups or collections of words, with characteristic turns of phrase, has become easier in recent years. In the past concordances were primarily useful for searching for isolated words, while for more complicated searches it was necessary to engage in difficult and time-consuming research. But now we have computerized aids for research which would be inexcusable not to use. What is more, I think there is a certain moral obligation to resume, to complete, or even, if necessary, to correct the arguments of our predecessors, since they often relied on chance finds or on deliberately simplified questioning.

Three Examples from the Book of Amos

In the examples that follow I will choose arguments that rely not on isolated words but on characteristic expressions. To avoid diffusing the argument, I will limit myself to the presentation of W.H. Schmidt[9] on 'the Deuteronomistic redaction of the book of Amos'. This example is interesting for the history of research, since it forms the basis for many later works.

Amos 2.10. I would like first of all to focus on the exodus formula 'I brought you up [$\sqrt{\,}$ *'lh*] out of the land of Egypt; and led you 40 years in the wilderness, to possess the land of the Amorite'. To prove its Deuteronomistic character, Schmidt presents just three parallels: Judg. 2.1; 6.8-9; 1 Sam. 10.18. But other examples of the phrase, in divine discourse, exist as well outside the Deuteronomistic canon (Exod. 3.8, 17; Lev. 11.45; Mic. 6.4; Ps. 81.11).

Now, in the Deuteronomistic canon, there are more than 48 instances of the exodus formula with the verb *yṣ'*, 'go out', instead of *'lh*, 'go up'.

8.   F. Anderson and A.D. Forbes, *The Vocabulary of the Old Testament* (Rome: Pontifical Biblical Institute, 1989).

9.   W.H. Schmidt, 'Die deuteronomistische Redaktion des Amosbuches', *ZAW* 77 (1965), pp. 168-93.

In Deuteronomy it is the verb *yṣ'* that is used (there is only one *'lh*). Given the fact that outside the basic Deuteronomistic canon there are as many instances of the exodus formula with *'lh* as with *yṣ'*, the countercheck shows that this discussion is purely academic. W. Gross, just to quote another opinion, puts Amos 2.10 outside of Deuteronomistic literature, because it is connected with the 'prophetic indictment' or lawsuit (*rîb*).

Amos 3.1. The title of the book and the transition formula in 3.1 ('Listen to this word that Yahweh pronounces [speaks] against you, people of Israel, against the whole family that I brought up out of the land of Egypt') form the starting point of all of Schmidt's research. This procedure is easily understandable since redaction naturally tends to add a text in the transitions from one literary unit to another. Schmidt's argument for the Deuteronomistic character of Amos 3.1 is summed up in the following statement: 'The expression in Amos 3.1, slightly modified by a word displacement "word of Yahweh which he *spoke*", is a Deuteronomistic turn of phrase that comes up again and again in the Deuteronomistic parts of the books of Kings (1 Kgs 14.18; 15.29; 16.12, 34; 22.38; 2 Kgs 1.17; 10.17; 24.2)'. Has Schmidt found only the texts that he cites or has he really reduced the list? What emerges from an examination of the list?

I have limited my research to passages in which the verb 'to speak' (*dbr*) is used in relative clauses, although I have included those cases in which 'Yahweh' occurs as the subject of the noun 'word' (*dbr*) or of the relative clause. Instead of the eight occurrences retained by Schmidt, the result is 48, of which 12 are outside Deuteronomy–2 Kings and Jeremiah (including Exod. 4.30; 24.3; Num. 22.35; Isa. 16.23 [37.22; 38.7]; Ezek. 12.8). In the books of Kings there are 16 references to fulfilment statements in the narratives of the prophets. Are these instances (cf. also Josh. 14.6) Deuteronomistic or do they come from earlier sources? The example of 1 Sam. 20.23, where David and Jonathan speak together ('As for the *word* which we have *spoken* [√*dbr*], you and I...'), shows, contrary to all statistics, that these words are an everyday expression and not specifically Deuteronomistic.

Amos 2.4-5. Schmidt's third example is Amos 2.4-5: 'Thus says Yahweh: ...because they rejected the law of Yahweh and have not kept his statutes, but their lies have led them astray, after which their fathers

walked. So I will send a fire upon Judah and it shall devour the strong-
holds of Jerusalem.'

This is the cornerstone of the edifice of proofs for the Deuteronomistic redaction of Amos. The title of the book and the transition
formula of 3.1 cannot, by themselves, sustain the thesis of a Deuteronomistic redaction of Amos. Deuteronomistic additions and expansions
must still be found elsewhere. However, except for two specific verses
(3.7 and 5.26) Schmidt only finds such additions in chs. 1 and 2 (1.9-10,
11-12; 2.4-5, 10-12). Only if there is this proof of Deuteronomistic
insertions in chs. 1 and 2 can we then think of an overall Deuteronomistic redaction of the book. But even here the identification of the
oracle against Judah as Deuteronomistic must bear almost alone all the
weight of this argument. Schmidt identifies five elements of 2.5 as
Deuteronomistic 'literary formulas'. But a close examination shows
that not one of these elements constitutes solid proof of the Deuteronomic character of Amos 2.4-5. Consider the following:

1. *'To reject the teaching* [torah] *of Yahweh'*: This is a prophetic
    expression (Isa. 5.24; Jer. 6.19; 8.8-9 and Hos. 4.6) and not
    Deuteronomistic. The verb 'reject' (*m's*) is found also in Eze-
    kiel and in the Holiness Code. Moreover, Deuteronomy does
    not speak of the Torah of Yahweh, but of the Torah of Moses.

2. *'Keep the statutes of Yahweh'*: 'statute' is used with 'keep'
    alone in Exod. 12.24 (?); Deut. 16.12; Pss. 105.45; 119.5, 8
    (with *ḥq*) and Lev. 19.19; 20.8; Ezek. 18.19, 21; 37.24 (with
    ḥqh). These passages indicate that this expression is at home in
    later periods or in the priestly tradition, but not in the Deuter-
    onomistic tradition—provided the statistics are valid with such
    small numbers.

3. The parallel *'teaching / decree'*: Schmidt puts forward as
    examples Deut. 17.19 and 2 Kgs 17.37. But there are 19 non-
    occurrences where these two words are found in the same
    verse. These two words certainly do not represent a stereo-
    typed Deuteronomistic series or parallelism in the strict sense.

4. *'Follow other gods'*: This is a specific Deuteronomistic
    expression, but 'follow' on its own is definitely not. 'Their
    lies' can refer to strange gods, but also to kings or false pro-
    phets. In any case there is not a single Deuteronomistic pas-
    sage where false gods would be the subjects of an active verb.

5.   The double accusation of 'having rejected the laws of God and
     followed idols' comes up often in the Deuteronomistic corpus,
     but it is not exclusive to that corpus. The entire Holiness Code
     is also influenced by this juxtaposition (see, e.g., Lev. 26.1, 3).

Moreover, this conclusion could be reinforced with other literary
arguments. It makes perfect sense to want to verify the old assertions on
Deuteronomistic terminology with the help of a computer. Doing so
reveals that there is only one chapter of the basic Deuteronomistic
canon that has several passages parallel to Amos: 2 Kings 17. Therefore, we can ask whether, in this chapter which speaks of Israel's rejection of the Torah preached by the prophets, the Deuteronomistic authors
have not systematically made allusions to earlier prophetic writings,
including Amos 2.4. I say this hypothetically. But in any case whenever
the dependence of one text on another is considered, it must be kept in
mind that such dependence need not be uni-directional.

When May We Speak Historically of a 'Movement'?

The German word *Bewegung* (movement) is best understood in combination with other words: 'workers' movement', 'youth movement',
'liturgical movement', 'African liberation movement', 'peace movement', 'ecology movement'. As the six-volume Duden dictionary
defines it, the word *Bewegung* designates 'a large number of humans
come together to realize a common (political) project'.

It seems to me very important that, in all the examples cited, the idea
of a movement, even if it is embodied in institutions and groups of supporters, goes beyond the limits of an organization created *ad hoc*, of a
given political party or of individual groups. Numerous and differentiated groups and even isolated individuals can join a movement. A
'movement' does not exist without an *interior reaction* of the people it
touches, that is, without some form of emotion. It cannot flourish inde-
finitely. If it has no success, it peters out at the end of a certain time,
even if institutions that originated from it continue to exist. A movement *wants to set in motion*. It is aimed at social and often political
change. One of the oldest references in German literature to the concept
of 'movement' comes from the final lines of *Herrmann und Dorothea*
where Goethe,[10] in 1797, in reference to the French Revolution says 'It

10.   Johann Wolfgang von Goethe, *Herrmann und Dorothea*, vv. 305-306 and
309-10.

is not the task of the Germans to continue the horrifying movement', and calls for a fight against this movement on the banks of the Rhine 'for God and the Law, for parents, the women and the children'.

Can we transpose the conception of 'movement' that has been developed within the contemporary world into ancient Israel? The social level in which 'movements' would have arisen and developed, at least at the end of the monarchy, in the exile and in the following period, did not include the whole population, but only one social and political class. Below the royal household were the agents of the state administration, the priestly class, the commanders of the army and the landowning aristocracy, to which should be added, naturally, the craftsmen who are certainly subordinate but who have a professional status. On the fringe there is still the mercantile group. In this rather limited circle of persons, linked together in other respects by family ties, real 'movements' are conceivable. They can quite naturally become 'parties', especially in the royal palace. But they have no future if they cannot count on at least tacit support from the population of the towns and countryside. Still, the milieu in which movements are found is that of society's upper level.

Movements are defined more by their goals than by their literary style. If we want to construct a hypothesis of a 'Deuteronomistic movement', we must support the hypothesis with proofs drawn more from the objectives of the Deuteronomists than from the analysis of their style. Each movement develops its own rhetoric, perhaps even in writing. But when a movement encompasses several groups, the same goals may possibly be presented using different rhetorical styles. Although this is not the time to present a thesis, we could think, by way of example, that at the same time of the weakening of the Assyrian Empire, Deuteronomy, as well as the book of Nahum, a new edition of the book of Isaiah, the Deuteronomistic history and some chapters of Jeremiah addressed to the former Northern Kingdom could all support the following goals without the texts resembling one another from the literary point of view:

1. to obtain greater national freedom;
2. to regain all the territory of the twelve ancient tribes;
3. to make Zion the unique religious centre for the whole nation.

Movement does not, then, mean linguistic uniformity, even if the different groups within the movement mutually influence one another's language and develop some common slogans. From this understanding, the existence of a specifically Deuteronomic or Deuteronomistic movement does not suggest itself, though it is not to be excluded either. In any case, without a historical investigation, and depending only on style and the general orientation of a text, we cannot conclude that a 'movement' existed. The existence of a text merely means that someone wrote on a papyrus scroll.

What in Reality Were 'Books' in Biblical Times?

We speak of 'books' that stemmed from the Deuteronomistic movement. This shows how easily we project our modern concept of reading culture back into ancient Israel. While we can probably transpose the idea of 'movement' to antiquity without much difficulty, it is an entirely different matter when it comes to the written word that so overwhelmingly permeates our life. The artifact closest to 'book' in the ancient world is the scroll, first made of papyrus, then of leather. We must examine how scrolls were made, who owned them and how they utilized them. This investigation is not just a matter of scrolls being covered with writing as such, but raises a more crucial question. In our society, printed media both contributes to and presupposes the phenomenon of 'publication'. But to what extent can we speak of scrolls 'being published' in the ancient world?

The Circulation of Writings

After its invention, writing was first used in the ancient Near East for economic transactions, juridical documentation, the exchange of letters, and inscriptions glorifying kings. At a very early stage, texts were inscribed on the walls of temples and palaces and engraved on jewelry. They were used in magic and in the cult of the dead. In the archives of the palaces and temples and in the learning and teaching activities associated with them, other forms of literature were developed: annals, lexicographical lists, divinatory collections, compilations of laws, wisdom teachings, ritual prescriptions, epics and myths. Such texts were used in the functioning of the institutions associated with them and were not intended for circulation. Of course an Ashurbanipal, in the seventh century, could have had copies of them made for his library at Nineveh. But normally new copies of ancient writings were made only when it was necessary to replace an old tablet or an old scroll or when a separate institution needed a text and financed copying it. Our modern idea of 'publication' of a text does not fit in such a context.

It was certainly the same in Israel and Judah in the period of the monarchy. From the eighth century onward we can envisage a more developed administration, and in connection with it a development of literacy in the upper levels of society. A rudimentary ability to read must have been developing in broader circles. But only a small number of copies of the texts in which we are interested here could have been made and distributed. In any case we have no information, no iconographic evidence and no archaeological trace of any possession of books by private individuals or of any circulation of scrolls in a sort of circle of readers.

On the contrary, it is conceivable that the sources and early versions of many of our present biblical books existed for a long time in the form of a single copy. They must not have been altogether unknown or ignored in Jerusalem. It is easily conceivable that they would have sometimes been added to and revised, especially when they were used for teaching in the Temple school. From time to time new copies of these old texts were made in order to maintain their readability.

Deuteronomy. What is more, texts of an official character were not multiplied. 'Ur-Deuteronomy' evidently was not found in the Temple as a copy of juridical erudition but as a document in its original version; earlier copies did not exist. The assertion that *'the* book of the Law' (2 Kgs 22.8) had been found at the time of the work in the Temple and the fact of a public commitment to observe this book are best understood from this background. Modern exegesis is at fault in ignoring the information that it could find in any Hebrew dictionary and in speaking continually of a 'book of the Law'. We are dealing here with a charter, an official document. Deuteronomy, in its present form, takes into account the fact that the Torah recorded by Moses exists in one copy only, deposited 'before the Levites' (Deut. 17.18) and 'beside the ark of the covenant' (Deut. 31.26). The king was not to have *one* other copy, among many, but *'the* second copy' (Deut. 17.18: *'the* copy of *that* Law'), to read from each day. Even if historically this never actually happened, it nonetheless reflects the imagination of things in the period of the exile. According to Deuteronomy itself, the general knowledge of the text does not come about through the circulation and reading of scrolls. It takes place through a public reading of the text every seven years, through individual memorizing and meditated recitation of the text, and by the use of prescribed texts for wall inscriptions according to Deut. 6.9, which probably comes from the period of Josiah. Even if these prescriptions were never carried out, they reflect the environment of these texts. However, the theory of knowledge of the text from liturgical proclamation, apprenticeship, and recitation is only valid for the Deuteronomic Torah, which was intended to be a charter. It does not apply to all the texts existing on scrolls.

The Prophetic Texts. Our only information about what was written outside the official archives and schools comes from the opposition. Prophets driven 'underground', such as Isaiah (8.1-2) and Jeremiah (36), put their earlier messages into writing. From the simple existence of many other collections of prophetic writings, we can conclude that this often happened. In Ezekiel's surroundings, the writing of texts is already something so typically prophetic that the prophet sees the reception of the message as the eating of a scroll (Ezek. 3.1-3).

It seems, at least at the end of the monarchy, that there would have been a sort of propaganda using short narratives. Some of these accounts are preserved for us in the books of Kings and Jeremiah.

We do not know if the prophetic writings were reproduced and circulated. Probably for a long time many of them only existed in a single copy, which was looked after, read, commented upon, annotated and from time to time rewritten in a circle of pupils. Perhaps there were contacts between the families or the circles of prophets that kept alive the prophetic traditions. They may have exchanged written copies of these traditions as well. But that was all.

Even the short narratives to be used for propaganda or collections of prophetic speeches, like the scroll that Jeremiah dictated to Baruch to be read in the Temple (Jer. 36), were not freely reproduced. They served rather as communication for a specific purpose and for use in planned situations foreseen in advance instead of satisfying a cultural need for reading that only exists for us. Multiple copies of these writings probably did not exist.

Even at the end of the monarchy and during the exile, this is the way it must have been. Some families or small circles who possessed and carefully preserved a text—the speeches of a prophet, for example— would probably not have handled it differently from the scrolls in the archives or schools; at most their behaviour was a little less professional. What with the fragility of the materials and the need for individual reproduction each time, the condition of the text was constantly under threat.

The oldest writings of the prophets, at least those from the Northern Kingdom, could have found their way very early on to the Jerusalem Temple, the archives of the palace or the library of one of the notable families of Jerusalem. The divinatory lists from Mesopotamia attest interest in oracles and predictions of the future on the part of the educated.

During the time of the exile we should perhaps pay greater attention to the Babylonian Golah than to the land of Israel itself, since it was the community of exiles among whom was found the major part of the really dominant class, locally dispersed, with several centres (or central families) who possessed and took care of the scrolls. After the exile it is once again Jerusalem alone that is in question, at least in the case of the writings now found in the canon.

The Qumran Library

To look at things from the other end of the spectrum, we are now familiar with the astonishing and rich post-Maccabaean library at Qumran with about a thousand scrolls and documents at the time of the site's destruction in 68 CE. According to the illuminating analysis of H. Stegemann[11] it was comprised of four sections. There was first of all a collection of model manuscripts which were used in the making of other copies. Next there were the scrolls used by the occupants of Qumran, often available in several copies. In addition, there were works on specialized subjects and on current events, among them the scrolls in Greek or the Temple Scroll. The fourth group was made up of used and discarded manuscripts.

The existence of the first group shows that Qumran was a sort of centre of manuscript production. This is connected with the fact that the residents produced leather for the scrolls there using the chemicals from the banks of the Dead Sea. We can suppose there was a similar collection of models for making copies in the Temple at Jerusalem as well. Qumran was in a certain way the rival Essene enterprise. Without doubt they also produced manuscripts for non-Essenes.

---

11. H. Stegemann, *Die Essener, Qumran, Johannes der Täufer und Jesus* (Herder Spectrum, 4128; Freiburg: Herder, 1993); *The Library of Qumran: On the Essenes, Qumran, John the Baptist, and Jesus* (ET; Grand Rapids: Eerdmans, 1998).

The second group of manuscripts was first and foremost made up of biblical scrolls (33 copies of the Psalter, 27 of Deuteronomy, 20 of the book of Isaiah, and often several copies of other books), then the book of *Jubilees* (16 copies), other works common in Jewish tradition and specifically Essene writings. The existence of this library could have been duplicated in other Essene colonies as well as in non-Essene centres in the whole country. It is evident that there had developed in the meantime a sort of book culture. The canonization of biblical books and Greek cultural influence had such an effect that there was now a public for reading. Personal reading and public reading during worship services formed a part, at least for some forms of Judaism, of obligatory religious exercises.

The Canonization of Biblical Books
Although the understanding of the state of our sources is still debated to a great extent, at least one important link to connecting the situation at the beginning of the exile with that attested at Qumran was the canonization of the sacred Scriptures. That certain texts were considered holy and therefore used in worship services and in education connected with the synagogue presupposed the reproduction of these texts and the fixing of their content. They must have been copied from other texts, lists of which must have existed. A few anecdotes in the book of Maccabees, whose historicity admittedly remains a little uncertain, show that we cannot give the beginning of this new situation a very early date.

According to 1 Macc. 1.56-57, at the time of the religious persecution of 166 BCE 'the books of the Law' were burned. A royal decree prescribed the execution of those in whose home a 'book of the covenant' was found. These two designations must refer to the Torah, which was already canonized at this time. The least we can say is that at that time the Torah was already distributed in a certain number of copies and was found in the possession of individuals. In this episode there is no mention either of schools or of synagogues.

The Torah nevertheless may be an exceptional case. According to a passage in the second letter of Hanukkah, quoted at the beginning of 2 Maccabees, Judas Maccabaeus had again collected in Jerusalem the scrolls dispersed by the war (2 Macc. 2.14). By way of hinting at the tradition behind Judas' actions, the author alludes in 2.13 to the 'Memoirs of Nehemiah' (probably from the third century), a book which has not come down to us. In his time Nehemiah must have founded a library at Jerusalem containing, besides the archival documents coming from the royal grants, the books of (Samuel and) Kings, the scrolls of the prophets and the Davidic writings (the first Psalter?). The historical value of this account matters little; what interests us is that in the third century BCE the existence of these scrolls seems to be linked to that of a unique library in Jerusalem. The list is a point in favour of the beginning of a process of canonization of these scrolls, since other scrolls could have been named. There is no reason to think of a wide diffusion of these writings in numerous copies. The Torah is not mentioned in this context. Its existence in a large number of copies, especially in view of judicial administration, seems to have been obvious at that period.

Therefore, except for the book of Deuteronomy itself, we have no positive indication that the scrolls that would have come into existence in the Deuteronomistic movement circulated as official and public documents up to the third, or even the second century. Canonization made them official documents to hear and to read; this had to be done from Jerusalem, since it was there as well that the official models for scrolls were found. Their Greek translation could already have begun in Alexandria.

We can perhaps reconstruct an intermediate phase before the official canonization created a new intellectual market, and this is the historical nucleus of what we read about Nehemiah. At Jerusalem, the Temple and the school bought little by little, or at least copied, the writings that existed in various places—in families that took care of them or in small institutions—to bring them into their own collection. Perhaps authors of new works also deposited their own scrolls there. After all, this was the only place where they could hope to have them read and eventually even copied. In Greece, literature had a public character much earlier. But about 500 BCE Heraclitus still 'published' his work in this way by placing a scroll in the sanctuary of Artemis at Ephesus. There, those who were interested in it could read and copy it. The copies of scrolls that had been kept in Babylon must also have been archived together in Jerusalem, even if they came from different centres in Babylon. Thus the Jerusalem copies must have been the models for copyists at the time of the canonization. In concrete terms, this canonization at Jerusalem, alongside the establishment of a list, probably should be seen as the last alteration of the text and the establishment of model copies. After this, the production of copies was encouraged.

During the Persian and Greek periods, lengthy texts, uniquely destined again for internal use, could have been created: I would include among these the books of Chronicles and late non-canonical writings such as the Temple Scroll from Qumran. On the other hand, books like Esther or Judith or the legends of Daniel could have been texts intended to be reproduced and distributed immediately to well-read circles of the elite. The arrival of this minor literature, which had not existed previously in this form, was a sign of the cultural change introduced by Hellenism, which progressively led, even in Judah, to a public literature. If such writings partially penetrated even into the third part of the canon (the Writings), it is due to the late formation of this collection and its complicated prehistory, which cannot be discussed further here.

The 'Publication' of Biblical Books

This overview of the function of scrolls still needs some rounding off. I have stressed the importance of Jerusalem. However, we must not forget that even after the return from exile there remained a Golah, with owners of scrolls and school centres in the diaspora, including Mesopotamia and Egypt. Even in Samaria there was probably a library. There were exchanges between these centres up until the point that the scrolls sent by Jerusalem were translated into Greek at Alexandria. However, in the process of canonization, Jerusalem played a major role.

I have stated that the idea of the 'publication' of a text before the establishment of the canon is inaccurate. I must now complete that assertion. Although not published, many texts provided the basis for the educational curriculum. At least part of the elite must have received a formal education. Account should be taken of the fact that rich people had recourse to private tutors and that parents could teach their children to read and write. However, education normally took place in the institutions that possessed and preserved the scrolls. From the moment in the educational process when students read a text, which at that time meant memorizing it as well, it became naturally 'public' in one sense. A certain number of cultured people were acquainted with it and knew also that other people were acquainted with it; this is the definition of 'public character'. If, in this sense, a text was educationally foundational, it could then provide a model for thought and expression without the user necessarily participating in the particular group that had a monopoly on it.

With regard to Deuteronomy, a still more extensive knowledge than the one mentioned above must be taken into account. Deuteronomy came about not in the setting of a book-culture but in that of public worship and regular private meditation. It therefore becomes clear that the content and the language of the Deuteronomistic Law were not the private property of any closed circle. Those who knew the Deuteronomistic Torah could reflect it in their own literary creations.

Returning to the system of libraries and schools: even if it is logical that the text of a prophet was at first taken up by his own disciples, it did not stay that way. The texts of different prophets could be consulted and used as soon as they came into a library or a school. Thus, it was not necessary to be the member of a prophet's circle of disciples in order to know a particular prophetic text and exploit it from a literary point of view.

Finally there is no reason to doubt that within the same school, teachers would have different ideas and different linguistic and literary tendencies. This is even more probable if we consider what happens in our schools and universities. If, in a certain period, there was a religious, political or social movement, or even several concurrent movements, then the members of the institution that had charge of books and of teaching could have been affected very differently. Some could even have belonged to several movements.

All these considerations of the circumstances in which text scrolls appeared in Israel can be related to our exegetical analysis of the texts, at least in principle.

Is There a Relationship between the
Form of the Text and 'Movements'?

I want to begin with the most important point. In the old theories on the Pentateuch, there was a 'supplementary hypothesis' that was superseded by 'the documentary hypothesis'. In a modified form it has reemerged lately to serve as a model in the reconstruction of the prehistory of the books of the Old Testament: first of the prophetic books, but also of the historical books, the laws, the Pentateuch and even the Psalter. In all of these works, one posits supplements, amplifications, commentaries and glosses of older texts. Like a climbing literary plant, the 'rereadings' have overrun the literary walls, either in the form of patches or in a systematic way. They have grown intermittently in many phases. Very often, it is no longer possible to combine different 'rereadings' to one strata/layer of the development of the text, or to distinguish between activities of practical 'rereading' and of 'redactional work'. While I am rather dubious of this type of analysis, it does not mean that I am sceptical in every case. Hypotheses worked out as a result of 'redaction history' can often best clarify a very complicated literary situation.

The problem that interests those who study the relationships between literature and society is this: how can texts that are widely dispersed in a community be constantly reshaped? This problem is definitively resolved by the portrait of the circulation and conservation of text scrolls before the creation of the canon, as I developed it above. As long as a piece of writing only exists in a single copy or as long as there is only one copy of the written work that is considered authentic, and as long as it is at the same time scrutinized, discussed and confronted with new questions by a body of scholars and teachers, *the supplementary model fits the literary indications about the prehistory of the text.*

Conversely, it follows that if a text can only be analysed legitimately with the help of the supplementary model, it must have formerly existed in a copy *that was unique or considered authentic in a single copy.* It was not widely circulated and perhaps not even published. It would be a matter of just one text in a small library or in a small scholarly circle. But as long as that situation persists, the text scarcely comes into question as a 'manifesto' of a 'movement'.

Of course, some further explanations and details must still be provided. We should perhaps distinguish more clearly than is generally done the phenomenon of literary supplementation from the textual modifications and expansions that occur in the late stages of a text from the activity of copyists, and that here and there could have important consequences for the text's understanding. A small addition to the text made by a copyist can obviously also happen in a text that has been published and distributed in many copies, but it is easily recognizable.

In addition to the careful revision of a text by supplementation, there are other ways of creating and changing texts, as long as they exist only in single copies in a library or school. Even for internal use only, *new texts can be composed* from isolated written or oral texts (the old fragmentary hypothesis) or from two parallel texts (the documentary hypothesis). It is consequently unacceptable to conclude that a text was only then received in a single copy and in a single place if an analysis of it indicates that it has developed according to the supplementary model.

As far as 'movements' are concerned, we come to the following conclusion: the fact of revision of a text cannot lead directly to the conclusion that a corresponding movement existed. The phenomenon of rereading is sufficiently explicable as an outcome of the mechanisms of its connections with libraries and education.

Was There Therefore a 'Deuteronomistic Movement'?

I now present some historical theses. Did the 'Deuteronomistic movement', promoted so much recently, really exist? If so, to what extent and in what form?

The Northern Kingdom

Just before and during the exile, authors of Deuteronomistic texts could have done their work under the inspiration of Hosea. That could have happened intentionally. Hosea's texts were actually in their library. Or, the specific language of Hosea was handed down by Jeremiah, since it is clear that he personally knew the texts of Hosea. That is all it takes to explain why there are traces of certain Hosean ideas and language in Deuteronomistic writings. But this kind of late acquaintance and utilization should not lead to Hosea being considered a proto-Deuteronomist nor make us think that his book demonstrates the existence of proto-Deuteronomistic groups in the northern Kingdom before its fall.

Hezekiah

I take into account the arrangements made by Hezekiah in connection with the preparation of the revolt against Assyria that led to the terrible disaster of 701. Because of this revolt the kingdom of Judah was reduced to the city of Jerusalem and some surrounding villages (46 fortified towns of Judah were taken), and the population of Judah deported by Sennacherib was more significant than that deported later by Nebuchadnezzar (according to Assyrian sources it would have amounted to 200,150 persons). The revolt had been prepared for not only militarily, but also socially and psychologically. Quite obviously the measures included the suppression of the traditional ancestral cult in the country as well as, perhaps, other cults within Jerusalem or in the other large towns. The goal of these measures was to make it possible to concentrate the rural population in the fortified cities in case of war. This reduction of cults corresponds to the redaction of the document of the

Torah discovered later under Josiah in the Temple. This document deals especially with new regulations for worship. We have no information from the time of Hezekiah about any ritual covenant making based upon this text, as happened later under Josiah.[12]

It is possible that, at that time, an ancient version of the book of Kings, reaching its high point with Hezekiah, was composed. But it is difficult to consider it as already Deuteronomistic.

All these phenomena, even if we gather them together, do not justify speaking of a 'movement'. Rather, they have to do with royal enactments. We could discuss the motives for them. By royal command scribes or competent priests composed the accompanying texts. As if by chance, we read in Prov. 25.1 that 'the officials of Hezekiah king of Judah' gathered together, composed or compiled a collection of the Proverbs of Solomon. At the court, therefore, there were specialists and arrangements for this activity.

If we do not go too far in our claims, the document of the Torah produced at the time of Hezekiah would appear to be the first of a more elaborate Torah drawn from the text of the covenant of Exodus 34 and the Covenant Code. Perhaps it was not very long and only dealt with questions of cultic reform. It is usually referred to as 'Ur-Deuteronomy'. It was followed by a history of preceding centuries that showed Hezekiah and his centralization of worship in a flattering light. It was an initiative from above and not the product of a 'movement'. It is possible that these actions were supported by a 'movement', but we have no information on this subject. If such a movement actually did exist, it is not absolutely certain that it must be called 'Deuteronomistic'.

Josiah
The situation changes with Josiah. This time it seems that there was actually a 'movement'. At least this is the opinion of two recent works: *The History of Israelite Religion in the Old Testament Period* by R. Albertz[13] and *The Torah* by F. Crüsemann.[14] These are the first

12. Cf. the important contribution of B. Halpern, 'Jerusalem and the Lineages in the Seventh Century BCE: Kinship and the Rise of Individual Moral Liability', in B. Halpern and D.W. Hobson (eds.), *Law and Ideology in Monarchic Israel* (JSOTSup, 124; Sheffield: JSOT Press, 1991), pp. 11-117.

13. R. Albertz, *The History of Israelite Religion in the Old Testament Period* (trans. J. Bowden; Louisville, KY: Westminster/John Knox Press, 1994).

14. F. Crüsemann, *The Torah: Theology and Social History of Old Testament*

German works of this kind for a long time, marked by an expressed interest in sociology. Whereas H. Donner[15] in his *History of the People of Israel and their Neighbours* had clearly explained the events connected with Deuteronomy as essentially a reform of worship by King Josiah, we find in the two later works the designation 'Deuteronomistic movement'.

Crüsemann is perhaps a little too imaginative when he speaks of a 'peasant liberation movement' that allowed the 'people of the land' to take power after the murder of Amon (640) and to protect Josiah beyond childhood. He is certainly right in seeing in the forefront of the movement a series of aristocratic families of Jerusalem, whose names are known to us. They are indeed those headed by the priest Hilkiah and those controlled by Shaphan, the two most important royal officials. But he describes the movement in question with equal accuracy as a mixture of various traditions and groupings.

Albertz, whose discussions are broader and more detailed, notes from the outset that what is called the reform of Josiah was much more than a simple reform of worship. It was at the same time an extensive movement of national, social and religious renewal that made use of the historical opportunity offered by the decline of Assyrian power to reconstruct resolutely and thoroughly the State of Israel. According to Albertz this movement included the landed nobility of Judah, the 'people of the land' (*'am hā-'āreṣ*), a group of officials from the Jerusalem court, influential and educated in wisdom, and a large part of the clergy from the Temple of Jerusalem. Many of the prophets and their circles of disciples also belonged to this movement.

We can presume here that the movement not only had a textual basis in Deuteronomy, but that it produced at the same time all sorts of other texts. Albertz lists the book of Zephaniah, a re-edition of the book of Isaiah and some texts of the young prophet Jeremiah that later went into the book of Jeremiah. He even speaks of a 'circle of disciples of Hosea', a phenomenon which is undemonstrable in my view.

One observation of Albertz seems very important to me. According to him the movement 'was able to find broad support in Judean society.

Law (trans. A.W. Mahnke; Minneapolis: Fortress Press, 1996; trans. from *Die Tora: Theologie und Sozialgeschichte des alttestamentlichen Gesetzes* [Munich: Chr. Kaiser Verlag, 1992]).

15. Trans. of *Geschichte des Volkes Israel und seines Nachbarn in Grundzügen* (2 vols.; ATD, 4; Göttingen: Vandenhoeck & Ruprecht, 1984–86).

It was made up of a broad coalition among some of the Jerusalem officials, the priests of Jerusalem, the middle classes of Judea, some isolated prophets and the Davidic royal house.' In view of the very diverse special interests of the different groups in this coalition, it is easy to understand why the movement, which developed in the years 630–609 BCE, broke up relatively quickly after the catastrophic death of Josiah in 609. On all the points that concern this present essay, I readily agree with his reconstruction.

This reconstruction reveals all the characteristics of a 'movement'. I ask only one question: Is it relevant to refer to this movement as 'Deuteronomistic'? The Deuteronomy of that period must have been its most important text. I go even further than my two colleagues. I think that shortly after the solemn commitment of Judah and Jerusalem to the Law that they had just found, this text was reworked and noticeably revised. That work was already 'Deuteronomistic'. I think too that, even while Josiah was still living, the production of the Deuteronomistic History began. At first it only consisted perhaps of the presentation of isolated periods, but soon an edition of the episodes from Moses to Josiah was drawn up, giving the first elaboration of a part of the Deuteronomistic History. The reworked Law was inserted into the presentation of the journey in the desert and the conquest of the land. In a new style, it became a collection of discourses addressed by Moses, just before his death, to Israel. A literary production stemming from the strength of this movement, it served as a historical legitimation for the ambitious scope of their objectives. However the authors of this Deuteronomistic writing—educated members of the families who had power in Jerusalem or intellectuals in the service of these families— represent only one element of the movement. The movement also found literary expression in other language and from other traditions of Israel.

In my opinion it is necessary to avoid the expression 'Deuteronomistic reform movement' and to speak instead of a national and religious restoration movement of the period of Josiah. This movement sought to unite the nation again under just one king, to regain the whole country that belonged to the ancient twelve tribes, and to make Jerusalem the unique religious centre of the God of Israel, YHWH. It considered this agenda to constitute a restoration. Therefore a temptation to extend the life of this movement up to the period of the Maccabees disappears.

There was, then, a movement. Deuteronomy and the incipient

Deuteronomistic History played first violins. And yet this was not a 'Deuteronomistic movement'. Under Jehoiakim it immediately disintegrated. The death of Josiah destablilized everything; the power of Egypt did the rest. The king was quickly replaced. The landed nobility was rendered powerless by high taxes. The administration was changed, even if this happened slowly, as we see from the very different groups of people mentioned in the brief accounts of the book of Jeremiah for the period of Jehoiakim and Zedekiah. Even among the priests things changed. The groups that had collaborated in a happy period were soon back at their old rivalries. The single movement was dead; the many parties at court returned.

If Hardmeier's interpretation of the Hezekiah–Isaiah narrative is correct,[16] Jeremiah and the Shaphanites (pro-Babylonians, who clearly were at the head of the production of Deuteronomistic texts) found themselves, shortly after the fall of Jerusalem, in deadly conflict with the circles of political leadership. The latter, out of national arrogance and confidence in the divine election of Jerusalem, continued to think of themselves as heirs of Josiah's reform. Of course, we cannot immediately consider Jeremiah and the Shaphamites to have been 'Deuteronomists'.

The favour of exclusive worship of YHWH in Jerusalem, while in line with the restoration movement of Josiah, is not, in itself, specifically 'Deuteronomistic'. The theological key-word in the Hezekiah–Isaiah accounts, 'have confidence' (*bṭḥ*), is not at all Deuteronomistic. In contrast to the Psalter, it is absent from Deuteronomy and the Deuteronomistic historical texts.

Faced with this situation we no longer ask ourselves about the continuation of Josiah's restoration, but only about those who adopted the Deuteronomistic texts then available and made of them something new. Our information is not very extensive. We do not even know who saved these scrolls by taking them in their baggage as Jerusalem was being demolished.

The Deuteronomistic Literary Work during the Exile
We are so lacking in information that we can only try to draw some conclusions from the character of the texts on their fate and their line of transmission. We can combine two observations. On the one hand,

16. C. Hardmeier, *Prophetie im Streit vor dem Untergang Judas* (BZAW, 187; Berlin: W. de Gruyter, 1990).

blocks of text were introduced into Deuteronomy and the Deuterono-mistic History, though more often interpretative supplements were made here and there. On the other hand, it was only in the exile that the book of Jeremiah, closely related to Deuteronomy and the Deuterono-mistic historical books in language and content, was composed. It was not done all of a sudden, but intermittently, and, in part at least, as a rereading of a particular point or part of a text. In accordance with my previous remarks, everything leads us to believe that in the time of the exile these texts were not widely circulated in numerous copies. Each one existed perhaps in only one copy—guarded, studied, discussed and reworked in just one locality.

In Babylon. The Deuteronomistic History and the book of Jeremiah were cared for in the same place. Otherwise it would be difficult to explain their numerous connections (without, however, glossing over their differences). Perhaps this work was done by the same authors. I am thinking of a locality in Babylon rather than at Jerusalem or Miz-pah. The *Tendenz* of the narratives of Jeremiah, the important thematic points in these narratives and the prose discourses of Jeremiah argue in favour of Babylon. Perhaps we can connect the formation of all this lit-erature to the Shaphan family.

Preaching? In researching the place and persons connected with the Deuteronomistic literary output, we are under no obligation to postulate the existence of a Deuteronomistic 'movement'. There is no proof either that systematic homiletic activity was implanted in this Deuteronomism.

But even though we cannot discern a 'Deuteronomistic movement' during the exile, I believe that we must nevertheless take up the theme of 'movement' in this context. We should merely note that things are more difficult to grasp than in the case of the restoration movement of Josiah. The explanations that follow suppose that the Deuteronomistic work was composed in distant Babylon. It is conceivable, however, contrary to what I propose, to connect its composition with the Shaphan family, still living in Judah even after Gedaliah. Then we would have to consider the possibility that surprisingly good communication existed between Judah and Babylon. However, it is still better to suppose that the greatest part of the elite of Judah and Jerusalem, to the extent that they survived, were in Babylon.

Deuteronomy and the exilic writings. In exilic Babylon several different literary collections were being formed. This was done at different times in different places, mainly using the technique of progressive supple- mentation. Besides the Deuteronomistic writings, there was the Ezekiel collection, the Priestly History, and the book of Isaiah, which was enlarged by Second Isaiah. Perhaps other books were developed as well.

These literary works are clearly distinguished from each other by the themes they take up, the traditions they go back to, their theology and their way of expressing themselves. We observe, however, thematic and verbal intertextual correspondences between them that increase with time. All these works are clearly preoccupied with the past and try to make sense of it. Except for the Priestly Writing, for example, we rec- ognize a unique leitmotif that develops around the root 'to turn around, to convert' (*šûb*). In one way or another, all of these writings are con- nected to the prophetic phenomenon, even the Priestly Writing which contradicts Ezekiel's visions of the future, and which, partially at least, develops a contrary vision.

These different texts indicate the existence of a single movement, more religious and intellectual than concrete and political, that formed little by little and caught hold in the whole Babylonian Golah. It wanted to recover its own identity, through reflection and a turning inward. We should perhaps speak of an 'exilic conversion movement'. Out of it came this group of the Golah, which would later return to Jerusalem and would want to mark the new city with the imprint of its fairly rig- orous ideas. Even the Priestly Writing, from which the word *šûb* is cer- tainly not missing by accident, goes along in a dialectical way with this same unanimity of expression. It, too, thinks of the possibility of a return, but, in opposition to the prophets and the Deuteronomist, does not envisage it as the consequence of human penitence but solely of divine favour.

In the exile, then, there was apparently again a 'movement'. But, once again, this would not be a 'Deuteronomistic' one, even less so than that which existed in Josiah's time. We could perhaps say that there was *in the interior* of this movement a Deuteronomistic school as well as other schools. Still, the word 'school' in this case would have a very broad meaning. The members of similar schools were perhaps teachers or pupils in a sort of scholastic institution in the Golah. But in our context, this is not what the word 'school' means. Rather, the people in question would be considered members of a Deuteronomistic (or other) 'school' because they formed their thought and their way of speaking according to the Deuteronomistic texts that were found in their library and read as part of their instruction. They felt themselves to be the inheritors of those texts, and they continued to work on them.

I cannot go into details. It would be important, for example, to do precise analyses comparing the Deuteronomistic History, including Deuteronomy, and the Deuteronomistic work carried out on the book of Jeremiah, in order to see whether it is possible to determine if the composition of these works was spread out over time or different layers became intermingled because they were composed during more or less the same period.

Legislation for the exiles? I would like to touch lightly on another aspect: the Babylonian return movement must have been supported very strongly in its different centres by jurists. Far from the concrete realities of their own country, these people had to restore morale by developing juridical utopias. This is the only way to imagine the emergence of texts as varied as Leviticus 25 in the Holiness Code (sabbatical year and jubilee year), the prescriptions about officials in Deuteronomy 16–18, and different features of the assistance measures of the Deuteronomistic Code as well as the project of a political constitution in the book of Ezekiel.

I have inferred above that the primitive Deuteronomy which became public and legally enforceable through the affirmation of the covenant under Josiah, was a relatively short text but that the law, as extended by the Deuteronomists, first at the time of Josiah and then later during the exile, did not remain a legally enforceable text in the same way. This is important for the question of its publication and the eventual procedures for its promotion. It was a juridical text expanded in a literary way. It was set as the initial piece in the Deuteronomistic History. Consequently, the programme of preaching, instruction and meditation on the law found in the texts was not introduced or applied in Jerusalem before the exile. The exilic supplementation of these texts had neither the aim nor the possibility of modifying the law then in force. This does not rule out the possibility of serious and enterprising jurists having a hand in it, but they were not legislators; this made it easier to sketch utopian pictures.

The Persian Period

The redaction of groups of texts stemming from the exilic return movement was brought to a close, not in out-of-the-way places in Babylon, but in Jerusalem after the return of the intellectual elite. There, different groups, parties and perhaps even movements developed their own designs for the world and society. We have little information on this period. Did similar social formations have their own institutions for preserving scrolls, for discussing them and for the production of new texts? Does the literature that has come down to us reflect these social entities, as well as the institutions whose existence we assume? It seems to me very doubtful that outside of Jerusalem and Judaea there would have been libraries or schools. Yet something of this type is generally accepted without discussion. It seems to me, however, that there is a simpler hypothesis, namely that in connection with the Temple there was a single centre for archives, study and teaching, eventually with several sections.

I would not want to rule out the presence of smaller scrolls in rich families. But the work of updating old texts is more likely to have been carried out in the central institution where those well versed in different literary and theological styles, from different groups of families or parties, must have been at work. Only in such a place could individuals have felt entitled to modify the traditional texts. Redactional activity, even on texts like Deuteronomy, continued in spite of the fact that the 'canonical formula', 'You must not add anything...you must not take away anything...', occurs twice (Deut. 4.2; 13.1). When the phenomenon of canonization began to take place, it is possible that after deliberation by the different groups concerned (perhaps even the fraternity of priests and the council of elders), there would have been agreement on the redactional activity to be carried out on the texts. The final phases of the history of the redaction of the Pentateuch appear to me to be best explained in this way.

With regard to the supposed parties and interested groups in Persian and Hellenistic Jerusalem, I do not think that it would be appropriate to call them 'movements' and this is one more reason to reject a 'Deuteronomistic movement'. The Deuteronomistic aspect of many writings of this period can be explained in another way.

With the canonization of the Pentateuch, the Deuteronomic Law came into the public domain. It was already known since the elaboration of the Pentateuch, perhaps even earlier, at least to those who dealt with law. It was even proclaimed during worship services and used by the people for meditation. Thus, its content and rhetorical style were already very public.

As far as other Deuteronomistic writings are concerned, we must consider the fact that at Jerusalem, in the library and school of the Temple, all the texts of the basic Deuteronomistic canon were represented and served as educational materials. As such, they possessed a public character. The literate persons who composed new texts or who prepared a new redaction of the old ones knew the Deuteronomistic writings, or at least some of them, by heart and could read them any time they wanted. It is understandable, therefore, if Deuteronomistic content or language appear here and there in their own work or even permeate it entirely.

This explains the language of Chronicles as well as the Deuteronomistic texts later added to the Pentateuch. It is the same for many of the Qumran texts. Through allusions or citations, these authors or glossators could refer their readers directly to Deuteronomy or to the Deuteronomistic writings. These readers were as learned as the authors and expected such allusions. According to R. Hanhart,[17] Zech. 1.1-6 is an intentional citation of an earlier writing (the book of Jeremiah). But nowadays there is a tendency to speak of the Deuteronomistic framework of the book of Zechariah and therefore of a Deuteronomistic redaction. A particularly significant case of a simple appropriation of style or of conscious allusion are the plusses in the Masoretic text of the book of Jeremiah and the imitations of the Deuteronomistic prose of Jeremiah in Daniel 9 or the book of Baruch. The authors who were thus inspired by Deuteronomy or who referred to it were not necessarily 'Deuteronomists' or members of a 'Deuteronomistic' school. In all these instances, therefore, it is inadmissible to assume the involvement of a Deuteronomistic 'movement'.

The End of the Persian and Greek Periods

The arguments just presented all apply from the moment that the Pentateuch was published as law. From that point on it became the code of law in use and at the same time the first component of the canon on the way to formation. Each new writing or rewriting of a text was consecrated by the recognition of Deuteronomistic language within it because

---

17. R. Hanhart, *Sacharja* (BKAT, 14.7; Neukirchen–Vluyn: Neukirchener Verlag, 1990), p. 17.

that language penetrated the Torah. This language would have been recognized from the outset. From a certain date (impossible to specify) the Torah was used in liturgical reading. When the Chronicler relates that Jehoshaphat, in the ninth century, sent a group of dignitaries, Levites and priests into Judah with the book of the Torah of YHWH to instruct the people (2 Chron. 17.7-9), the Chronicler is not relating a fact of the ninth century but one of a period of the redaction of Chronicles. In that period the Levites travelled up and down the country. But this was something other than a 'movement'. Besides, they did not propagate Deuteronomy, but the Pentateuch.

Even more numerous are the conscious references to the canonical Pentateuch in the last redactional additions framing the Book of the Twelve or the whole canon of the prophets. For example, the typical Deuteronomistic formulae that are accumulated at the beginning of the book of Joshua or at the end of that of Malachi are nothing more than deliberate cross-references to the canonical Pentateuch. What sense does it make to speak here of 'Deuteronomistic' redactors or of a Deuteronomistic movement?

It would be even less appropriate here than elsewhere to see a Deuteronomistic movement or school at work. How and where to put the scrolls of the 'enlarged' Torah found at Qumran (and not yet published) still remains to be determined. These additions are witnesses to the last phases of the supplementation of the laws and above all of Deuteronomy itself, before the canonization of the Pentateuch. Textually, they went beyond the scrolls that had become authoritative. Even if they were written in a very 'Deuteronomistic' way, they have nothing to do with any kind of 'Deuteronomistic movement'.

The next real movement, and a powerful one too, that can be recognized in the history of Israel was that of the Maccabees. It was a bloody uprising. This event really shows how incongruous it is to posit on the basis of some short redactional phrases the existence of a Deuteronomistic movement that spanned centuries and from which, finally, almost the whole Old Testament originated.

WHO WAS THE DEUTERONOMIST? (WHO WAS NOT THE DEUTERONOMIST?): REFLECTIONS ON PAN-DEUTERONOMISM

Robert R. Wilson

Some readers will already be familiar with the literary allusion in the title of this paper. It recalls some lines in the Sumerian King List, a remarkable document that traces the history of kingship from the time it was 'lowered from heaven' to reside in the city of Eridu (or the city of Kish in some editions) to the time it finally came to rest in the city of Isin, the place where the scribe who created the list obviously thought kingship properly belonged. As the scribe lists the succession of cities through which kingship passed, he also lists the succession of rulers who exercised kingship within each of those cities. Thus the text is based on the notion that kingship could reside legitimately in only one city at a time, and within a given city kingship could legitimately be exercised by only one king at a time. This ideology of kingship is unswervingly displayed in the list until the kingship reaches the city of Agade, where the real world of political upheaval finally forces the author to depart from the formulaic presentation of the list. According to Thorkild Jacobsen's translation, after listing the early kings of the dynasty of Agade, the apparently exasperated scribe describes the political instability in the dynasty with the following words:

> Who was king? Who was not king? Was Igigi king? Was Nanum king?
> Was Imi king? Was Elulu king? Their tetrad was king and reigned 3
> years![1] (vii 1-7)

This description of a chaotic time when kingship seemed to be everywhere can also serve as an apt characterization of the situation that seems to be rapidly developing in the field of biblical studies with respect to the extent of Deuteronomistic influence in our present biblical

---

1. T. Jacobsen, *The Sumerian King List* (Chicago: University of Chicago Press, 1939), pp. 112-15.

text. Traditionally scholars have seen the hand of the Deuteronomists in an impressive amount of biblical literature, but their influence was still confined to a relatively small portion of the biblical corpus. They were responsible for Deuteronomy, of course, and for most of the so-called Deuteronomistic History—Joshua, Judges, Samuel and Kings. Outside of these obviously Deuteronomistic books, the Deuteronomists were usually thought to be responsible primarily for the non-narrative prose in Jeremiah, for Isaiah 36–39 (paralleled almost verbatim in 2 Kgs 18–20), and for small units in Amos and Hosea.

In recent years, however, this situation has begun to change radically. Modern Pentateuchal studies seem to find the Deuteronomists represented in most of the books of the Torah, and some scholars have even gone so far as to suggest that the Deuteronomists were in fact the compilers, if not the authors, of the Torah as we now have it. In the Deuteronomistic History itself the Deuteronomists are being given credit for creating most of their material out of whole cloth, and, in some extreme circles, they are being credited with shaping virtually all of the prophetic books, not to mention a number of the Psalms. Indeed, even a casual reading of recent scholarly literature suggests that we are rapidly entering an era of pan-Deuteronomism. Whenever the authorship of a particular piece of biblical literature is investigated, the identity of the author(s) always turns out to be the same: the Deuteronomists. Thus the title of this paper: Who was the Deuteronomist? Who was *not* the Deuteronomist?

Because the Deuteronomists are appearing with increasing frequency in discussions of all sorts of biblical literature, it may be useful to attempt to chart the overall extent of this trend and to assess its implications. In the discussion that follows I will at least begin this task, although a full treatment of the topic would obviously require considerably more space than is available in a brief paper. My interest in the following survey is not to provide a comprehensive account of the scholarly discussion; nor will I give a critique of the various positions being advanced. Rather by citing representative examples of recent scholarly trends I wish to trace the general outlines of the growth of pan-Deuteronomism and then to suggest some of the implications of the phenomenon.

I

The Deuteronomists in the Torah

Since Wellhausen's development of the classical form of the Documentary Hypothesis, the Deuteronomistic contribution to the Torah has usually been thought to be restricted to the book of Deuteronomy itself. Even around the turn of the century, when the excesses of source criticism were so clearly visible in the scholarly world, particularly in Germany, scholars only rarely identified the hand of the Deuteronomist in the first four books, although from time to time they did notice similarities between the Deuteronomist and the work of the Elohist. It is difficult to determine precisely when this situation began to change, but a convenient benchmark is the influential work of Lothar Perlitt. In 1969, at a time when George Mendenhall's work on covenant had convinced most scholars of the centrality and antiquity of this central concept, Perlitt published a thoroughgoing revisionist treatment of the issue.[2] He focused his inquiry on the theology of covenant, rejecting from the start the relevance of the alleged parallels between biblical covenants and ancient Near Eastern treaties. After a survey of the uses of the word $b^e r \hat{\imath} t$, Perlitt concludes that the term refers to the notion of obligation and locates the most complete development of the concept in the work of the Deuteronomists, which he dates to the eighth and seventh centuries. Perhaps, under the influence of prophets such as Hosea, the Deuteronomists developed the idea of covenant and then imposed it on other biblical literature, including the central part of the Torah, the Sinai section (Exod. 19–24, 32–34). With this theory Perlitt set in place two of the cornerstones of much of later pan-Deuteronomism: (1) Deuteronomistic editing is much more pervasive than scholars have previously thought, particularly in the Torah; and (2) Deuteronomistic editorial activity was relatively late, certainly no earlier than Josiah and possibly later, perhaps much later.

Although scholars were quick to point out a number of problems in Perlitt's analysis (and I will return to some of these later), his work had an enormous impact on critical thought, particularly in Germany. While Perlitt confined his work to the study of covenant, it did not take long for scholars to expand on his concept of Deuteronomistic editing in the

2. L. Perlitt, *Bundestheologie im Alten Testament* (WMANT, 36; Neukirchen–Vluyn: Neukirchener Verlag, 1969).

Torah. In 1976 H.H. Schmid published a major re-examination of Pentateuchal criticism that drew heavily on the work of Perlitt.[3] Focusing primarily on themes or motifs in the first four books (such as the promises of land, increase and blessing made to the ancestors), Schmid concludes that the traditional Yahwist source does not exist but that material usually attributed to J is in fact the work of much later editors writing at about the same time as the Deuteronomists and under their influence. Although few scholars have followed Schmid in the details of his argument, a number have accepted the suggestion that the Deuteronomists were responsible for shaping much of the Pentateuch and have then dated this editorial activity to the exile or even later.[4] Thus it is no longer unusual to see scholars identifying Deuteronomistic material in all of the first four books (including Gen. 1–11). The work of the Deuteronomists is even being detected in passages usually thought to contain archaic traditions and to be pre-Yahwistic. For example, a recent monograph by H. Hagelia[5] argues that Gen. 15.1-21 (the supposedly ancient 'covenant between the pieces') is linked through vocabulary, phraseology and theological content to crucial passages in the Deuteronomistic History, including 2 Samuel 7, 1 Kings 3, and 2 Kgs 17.1-23 (also Isa. 7.1-17). These connections, in the author's mind, demonstrate the Deuteronomistic origin of the Genesis passages (Gen. 15.1-6, 7-21) and point to thoroughgoing Deuteronomistic literary activity in the Torah outside of Deuteronomy during the exile or later. In a similar vein, Martin L. Brenner analyzes the Song of Moses in Exod. 15.1-21 and argues that it is by no means the ancient victory song that scholars have traditionally thought it to be.[6] Rather, the song is full of Deuteronomistic language and in addition shows influence

---

3. H.H. Schmid, *Der sogenannte Jahwist: Beobachtungen und Fragen zur Pentateuchforschung* (Zürich: Theologischer Verlag, 1976).

4. R. Rendtorff, *The Problem of the Process of Transmission in the Pentateuch* (JSOTSup, 89; Sheffield: JSOT Press, 1990); E. Blum, *Die Komposition der Vätergeschichte* (Neukirchen–Vluyn: Neukirchener Verlag, 1984); *idem, Studien zur Komposition des Pentateuch* (BZAW, 189; Berlin: W. de Gruyter, 1990); W. Johnstone, 'The Deuteronomistic Cycle of "Signs" and "Wonders" in Exodus 1–13', in A.G. Auld (ed.), *Understanding Poets and Prophets: Essays in Honour of George Wishart Anderson* (JSOTSup, 152; Sheffield: JSOT Press, 1993), pp. 166-85.

5. H. Hagelia, *Numbering the Stars: A Phraseological Analysis of Genesis 15* (Stockholm: Almqvist & Wiksell, 1994).

6. M.L. Brenner, *The Song of the Sea: Ex 15:1-21* (Berlin: W. de Gruyter, 1991).

from Second Isaiah, a fact that demonstrates that the song must be later than the exile. Brenner finally traces the authorship of the song to the Sons of Asaph, who composed it sometime after the rebuilding of Jerusalem's walls by Nehemiah.

Carrying the argument one step farther, some scholars are now seeing the Deuteronomists, writing presumably in the exile or later, as the final editors or shapers or even authors of the present form of the Torah. David Noel Freedman, among others, has long advocated such a position and has claimed that the Bible's 'Primary History' (Genesis through Kings) was put together by Deuteronomists working in the exile not long after the last events recorded in Kings.[7] Taking another tack, Suzanne Boorer has detected the hand of the Deuteronomists in five Torah texts (Exod. 13.3-16; 32.7-14; 33.1-3; Num. 14.11b-23a; 32.7-11) and then has argued that all but one of these texts predate their parallels in Deuteronomy.[8] This suggests Deuteronomistic editorial activity in an extensive body of biblical literature over a fairly long period of time.

Deuteronomists in the Deuteronomistic History
It will come as no surprise that contemporary scholars see the Deuteronomists as the primary shapers of the Deuteronomistic History. This notion has been assumed since the beginning of critical scholarship, and whether one accepts the theory of Martin Noth that the History was essentially the work of a single creative mind or prefers to see in it two or more layers of editorial activity, the fact remains that the History, along with the book of Deuteronomy, remains the Bible's chief repository of Deuteronomistic language and thought. However, in recent years even here scholars have begun to see the Deuteronomist's contributions as more extensive than previously thought.

In modern times, the notion that the History is the work of a single creative genius has usually been associated with the name of Martin Noth, who argued strongly against the idea that it grew more slowly

---

7. D.N. Freedman, 'The Earliest Bible', in M.P. O'Connor and D.N. Freedman (eds.), *Backgrounds for the Bible* (Winona Lake, IN: Eisenbrauns, 1987), pp. 29-37; cf. J. Van Seters, *In Search of History: Historiography in the Ancient World and the Origins of Biblical History* (New Haven: Yale University Press, 1983), pp. 322-53.

8. S. Boorer, *The Promise of the Land as Oath: A Key to the Formation of the Pentateuch* (BZAW, 205; Berlin: W. de Gruyter, 1992).

over time through the work of several editors.[9] However, even Noth conceded that the History's author made extensive use of earlier blocks of traditional materials, including written documents and archives. Some of these 'books' are mentioned explicitly in the text, where they seem to function as a sort of scholarly reference for the reader who desires additional information. In addition to these references, Noth accepted the common notion of traditional collections of stories, such as those of the judges, the throne succession narrative and the prophetic tales in Kings. Some of these materials contain relatively little in the way of Deuteronomistic language or theology and have simply been set by the Deuteronomists in a larger Deuteronomistic framework. Recently, however, even this rather traditional assumption has been challenged. John Van Seters, for example, in his study of historiography in Israel, concludes that the Deuteronomists were in fact the Bible's first historians and that they created much of the Deuteronomistic History out of whole cloth. They had in fact very few sources to work with, and Noth's pre-existing blocks of tradition on closer examination turn out to be either *post*-Deuteronomistic additions or free creations of the Deuteronomist. In keeping with the general trend of pan-Deuteronomism, Van Seters dates the Deuteronomist's work to the exile or later. He arrives at this conclusion by seeing in Deuteronomism heavy influence from the prophets and close parallels with the techniques of Greek historiography.[10]

The notion that the Deuteronomists were creative writers more than they were historians utilizing earlier sources has been generally adopted by scholars concerned to read the Bible as literature. A prime example is the work of Robert Polzin, who sees in the Deuteronomistic History the product of a literary genius responsible for virtually all of the text as we now have it.[11] Approaching the same idea from another direction, A. Graeme Auld has recently argued that the Chronicler did not base his work on the present text of the Deuteronomistic History but that both the Chronicler and the Deuteronomist creatively transformed an earlier history of Israel and Judah. Both works are therefore best seen as works of literature and theology offering competing visions of Israel's past,

9. M. Noth, *The Deuteronomistic History* (JSOTSup, 15; Sheffield: JSOT Press, 1991).

10. Van Seters, *In Search of History*.

11. R. Polzin, *Samuel and the Deuteronomist* (San Francisco: Harper & Row, 1989).

and the Deuteronomistic History is certainly not to be considered a reliable historical record.[12]

The Deuteronomist in the Prophetic Books
Scholars have long seen Deuteronomistic influence in the prophetic books. Standard commentaries have often identified Deuteronomistic editing in Amos, primarily on the basis of vocabulary. This suggestion is usually traced to the work of Werner H. Schmidt[13] and his suggestions have been accepted and extended by a number of other scholars, including Hans Walter Wolff in his commentary on Joel and Amos.[14] What is new in the present debate is the extent and relative lateness of the Deuteronomistic editing. Among the more recent commentators, J. Jeremias falls in line with current trends by seeing the book as the product of the exile, and this dating of the material would place the Deuteronomistic editing of the book correspondingly late.[15]

Among the other prophets Micah has often been thought to contain Deuteronomistic layers, with some scholars assigning chs. 6 and 7 solely to a Deuteronomist. Hosea, of course, often reflects Deuteronomistic language and thought, although in this case the prophetic book is usually considered an early source of what later becomes the Deuteronomistic movement. An exception to this point of view is expressed in a recent monograph by Else Kragelund Holt, who has the book originating in the late exilic period.[16]

Isaiah actually contains chapters paralleled in Kings and thought by some scholars to be late Deuteronomistic additions (although the contrary case has also been argued[17]), and Deuteronomistic writing has been detected in various postexilic prophetic books, particularly Malachi. However, scholars have traditionally found the greatest amount of Deuteronomistic influence in the book of Jeremiah. Beginning in 1901

---

12. A.G. Auld, *Kings without Privilege: David and Moses in the Story of the Bible's Kings* (Edinburgh: T. & T. Clark, 1994).

13. W.H. Schmidt, 'Die deuteronomistische Redaktion des Amosbuches', *ZAW* 77 (1965), pp. 168-93.

14. H.W. Wolff, *Joel, Amos* (Philadelphia: Fortress Press, 1977).

15. J. Jeremias, *Der Prophet Amos* (Göttingen: Vandenhoeck & Ruprecht, 1995); cf. D.U. Rottzoll, *Studien zur Redaktion und Komposition des Amosbuches* (BZAW, 243; Berlin: W. de Gruyter, 1996).

16. E.K. Holt, *Prophesying the Past: The Use of Israel's History in the Book of Hosea* (JSOTSup, 194; Sheffield: Sheffield Academic Press, 1995).

17. C.R. Seitz, *Zion's Final Destiny* (Minneapolis: Fortress Press, 1991).

with the commentary of Bernhard Duhm,[18] scholars have noted particularly close affinities between the Deuteronomistic History and the non-biographical prose passages in Jeremiah. These passages received their classic treatment in the work of Sigmund Mowinckel, who argued that a number of passages in the book contained Deuteronomistic vocabulary and concepts and were therefore added by the Deuteronomists, probably during the exile.[19] Mowinckel's analysis, involving the prose passages in 3.6-13; 7.1–8.3; 11.1-5, 9-14; 18.1-12; 21.1-10; 22.1-5; 25.1-11a; 27.1-22; 29.1-23; 32.1-2, 6-16, 24-44; 34.1-7, 8-22; 35.1-19; 39.15-18; 44.1-14; and 45.1-5, has been accepted by most scholars as proof of a Deuteronomistic layer in Jeremiah, although there remains a great deal of debate concerning the relation of this material to the book's biographical prose and to the prophet's poetic oracles.

With all of this traditional discussion of Deuteronomistic material in the prophetic books, it would seem unlikely that much more Deuteronomistic influence could be uncovered. Such, however, is not the case. A quick survey of recent research on prophecy reveals that pan-Deuteronomism has in fact run rampant in the prophetic corpus in the past few years. To take Jeremiah as an example, Ronald Clements has recently argued that in addition to contributing Mowinckel's prose material, the Deuteronomists were also responsible for giving the final canonical shape to Jeremiah 1–25. He presses this argument by showing that motifs and themes from 2 Kings 17, the retrospective on the history of the northern kingdom, have governed the arrangement of the Jeremiah material.[20] This argument would make the Deuteronomists in fact the final editors of the book and would place their activities sometime in the exilic or postexilic period.

Clements's theories on the Deuteronomistic editing of Jeremiah seem to be heavily influenced by the work of Robert Carroll, who in his commentary on the book suggests that much of the material in Jeremiah comes to us through a thoroughly Deuteronomistic filter.[21] Going even further in other scattered publications, he also argues that almost noth-

18. B. Duhm, *Das Buch Jeremia* (Tübingen: J.C.B. Mohr, 1901).

19. S. Mowinckel, *Zur Komposition des Buches Jeremia* (Kristiania: Jacob Dybwad, 1914).

20. R. Clements, 'Jeremiah 1–25 and the Deuteronomistic History', in Auld (ed.), *Understanding Poets and Prophets*, pp. 93-113.

21. R.P. Carroll, *Jeremiah* (OTL; Philadelphia: Westminster Press, 1986).

ing in the prophetic corpus actually reflects the realities of pre-exilic
Israel and that what we know as pre-exilic prophecy was actually created in the postexilic period by the Deuteronomists and then retrojected
into an earlier period, a view which is shared, at least in part, by Auld.[22]
This would seem to make the Deuteronomists responsible not only for
the shaping of prophetic books but also for the creation of Israelite
prophecy itself, a position that would seem to be the ultimate expression of pan-Deuteronomism.

The current trend toward Deuteronomizing Isaiah seems to have
begun with a monograph by Hermann Barth.[23] Barth argued that many
of the oracles attributed to the First Isaiah were in fact created or
shaped by editors working in the time of Josiah and within the circles
responsible for the Deuteronomistic movement. These editors were
responsible for reviving interest in the earlier prophet, whose words
were reformulated to fit the basically hopeful outlook of the Deuteronomists during Josiah's early reign. The argument for a basically
Deuteronomistic presentation of Isaiah is based on the observation that
many of Isaiah's oracles are 'congenial' to the characteristic Deuteronomic view of reality, although it must also be noted that traditional
Deuteronomistic language is largely lacking in Isaiah. As shaky as this
theory seems to be, it has had a major influence on commentaries on
Isaiah, and the theory of a major Deuteronomistic editing of the First
Isaiah is beginning to be presented in 'state-of-the-art' redaction
histories.[24]

22. A.G. Auld, 'Prophets through the Looking Glass: Between Writings and
Moses', *JSOT* 27 (1983), pp. 3-23; note also the immediate responses of R.P. Car-
roll, 'Poets not Prophets: A Response to "Prophets through the Looking Glass" ',
JSOT 27 (1983), pp. 25-31, and H.G.M. Williamson, 'A Response to A.G. Auld',
JSOT 27 (1983), pp. 33-39, and the later reactions of R.P. Carroll, 'Inventing the
Prophets', *IBS* 10 (1988), pp. 24-36; T.W. Overholt, 'Prophecy in History: The
Social Reality of Intermediation', *JSOT* 48 (1990), pp. 3-29, and 'It Is Difficult to
Read', *JSOT* 48 (1990), pp. 51-54; R.P. Carroll, 'Whose Prophet? Whose History?
Whose Social Reality? Troubling the Interpretative Community Again: Notes
towards a Response to T.W. Overholt's Critique', *JSOT* 48 (1990), pp. 33-49; A.G.
Auld, 'Prophecy in Books: A Rejoinder', *JSOT* 48 (1990), pp. 31-32; and H.M.
Barstad, 'No Prophets? Recent Developments in Biblical Prophetic Research and
Ancient Near Eastern Prophecy', *JSOT* 57 (1993), pp. 39-60.
23. H. Barth, *Die Jesaja-Worte in der Josiazeit* (Neukirchen–Vluyn: Neukirchener Verlag, 1977).
24. T. Collins, *The Mantle of Elijah: The Redaction Criticism of the Prophetical*

In the book of Ezekiel, Walther Zimmerli has noted the presence of Deuteronomistic themes, although characteristic Deuteronomistic language seems to be lacking.[25] These hints of Deuteronomistic activity have been analyzed in greater detail by Karl-Friedrich Pohlmann, who sees in them the hand of editors favoring the exilic community.[26]

Finally, studies of the Book of the Twelve have begun to see much more Deuteronomistic editing in these books. I have already indicated something of the current state of thinking about Deuteronomistic editing in Amos, Hosea and Micah, but I should also note here a thoroughgoing attempt by Raymond F. Person, Jr, to demonstrate that Second Zechariah (Zech. 9–14) is the product of Deuteronomists working in the postexilic period.[27] Person makes his case primarily by comparing Second Zechariah with Deuteronomistic portions of Jeremiah, and in this way he also demonstrates that Deuteronomistic editing of the prophetic literature continued over a fairly long period of time.

Beyond the detection of Deuteronomistic influence in individual prophetic books, scholars have suggested that the organization of books within the Book of the Twelve also shows Deuteronomistic influence. The most comprehensive case for such overall Deuteronomistic editing has been mounted by James Nogalski, who argues that Hosea, Amos, Micah and Zephaniah once circulated together before they became part of the present Book of the Twelve. These four books formed a Deuteronomistic corpus that was compiled sometime after 586 in order to explain the exile and destruction of Jerusalem.[28] Although Nogalski mounts the most recent case for overall Deuteronomistic editing of the Book of the Twelve, the idea itself has been around for some time and has been advocated in a less thoroughly developed form by Joseph Blenkinsopp and Norman Gottwald, among others.[29] On a broader

Books (The Biblical Seminar, 20; Sheffield: Sheffield Academic Press, 1993), pp. 37-58.

25. W. Zimmerli, *Ezekiel 1: A Commentary on the Book of the Prophet Ezekiel, Chapters 1–24* (Hermeneia; Philadelphia: Fortress Press, 1979), pp. 44-46.

26. K.-F. Pohlmann, *Ezechielstudien* (Berlin: W. de Gruyter, 1992).

27. R.F. Person, Jr, *Second Zechariah and the Deuteronomic School* (JSOTSup, 167; Sheffield: JSOT Press, 1993).

28. J. Nogalski, *Literary Precursors to the Book of the Twelve* (BZAW, 217; Berlin: W. de Gruyter, 1993); *idem*, *Redactional Processes in the Book of the Twelve* (Berlin: W. de Gruyter, 1993).

29. J. Blenkinsopp, *Prophecy and Canon* (Notre Dame: University of Notre Dame Press, 1977), pp. 96-123; N.K. Gottwald, *The Hebrew Bible: A Socio-Liter-*

scale, the most recent edition of Otto Kaiser's introductory textbook sees Deuteronomistic editing throughout the prophetic books wherever there are narratives describing prophetic activity.[30]

The Deuteronomists in the Writings
Although there have been relatively few attempts to detect Deuteronomistic influence in the Writings, there is one major exception: the book of Psalms. On the basis of linguistic and conceptual parallels between certain psalms and biblical literature usually thought to be of northern origin, a number of scholars have suggested that Psalms 9–10, 16, 29, 36, 45, 53, 58, 74, 116, 132, 133, 140, 141, the Korah Psalms and the Asaph Psalms also originated in the north. If one argues that Deuteronomistic literature is also of northern origin, then it might be possible to argue for the Deuteronomistic origin of these same Psalms. It is not surprising, therefore, that the notion of Deuteronomistic editing in the Psalter is becoming more common in current psalms research and has begun to influence commentaries on the book.[31] However, a number of methodological problems are raised by these arguments, not the least of which is the question of the link between Deuteronomism and northern biblical Hebrew. On this point there is still no scholarly agreement, and thorough arguments have been mounted on both sides of the issue. So, for example, Gary A. Rendsburg argues on linguistic grounds for the northern origin of some of the psalms but then denies the northern origin of the Deuteronomistic literature.[32] On the other hand, Harry P. Nasuti finds linguistic and thematic links between the Psalms of Asaph and the Deuteronomistic literature and so concludes that the two are ultimately related to each other.[33]

When all of the pieces of this survey are pulled together, it appears that we are left with a picture of pan-Deuteronomism of epidemic pro-

---

ary Introduction (Philadelphia: Fortress Press, 1985), pp. 464-68.

30. O. Kaiser, *Grundriss der Einleitung in die kanonischen and deuterokanonischen Schriften des Alten Testament. II. Die prophetischen Werke* (Gütersloh: Gerd Mohn, 1994).

31. F.-L. Hossfeld and E. Zenger, *Die Psalmen I* (Würzburg: Echter Verlag, 1993).

32. G.A. Rendsburg, *Linguistic Evidence for the Northern Origin of Selected Psalms* (Atlanta: Scholars Press, 1990).

33. H.P. Nasuti, *Tradition History and the Psalms of Asaph* (Atlanta: Scholars Press, 1988).

portions. These individual studies, when taken together, suggest a picture of a Deuteronomistic group, working sometime in the exile or early postexilic period, that is responsible for much of the biblical material as we now have it. They either edited, collected or shaped much of what we have in the Torah and the prophets, or in some cases were actually responsible for writing it. It would seem, then, that we have a basically Deuteronomistic Bible, and the answer to Richard Friedman's question 'Who wrote the Bible?'[34] is absolutely clear: the Deuteronomists wrote the Bible. Who was the Deuteronomist? Who was *not* the Deuteronomist?

II

Now what is to be made of this picture of pervasive Deuteronomistic influence? What are the implications of the arguments that have been made, and what conclusions might be drawn from this recent explosion of pan-Deuteronomism? The answer to this question must obviously be based on a careful assessment of each individual case and argument. However, even on the basis of this broad survey it seems possible to make two general observations concerning the new pan-Deuteronomism.

First, although a growing number of scholars agree that much of the Hebrew Bible is Deuteronomistic, they do not agree on what makes it Deuteronomistic. A variety of criteria have been employed to identify Deuteronomistic influence, but to date there is no consensus on what makes a particular passage Deuteronomistic. This lack of commonly accepted criteria gives the impression that a number of scholars are playing the same game, but without a commonly agreed upon set of rules. It should come as no surprise, then, that there are often disputes among the players.

In spite of the fact that scholars have not yet agreed on how to identify Deuteronomistic material, it does seem clear that some criteria are more persuasive than others. Although I have not made a thorough or comprehensive study of the subject, I would suggest that the most persuasive case for Deuteronomistic influence can be made on linguistic grounds. The book of Deuteronomy and the acknowledged Deuteronomistic material in Joshua through Kings do have a distinctive

---

34. R.E. Friedman, *Who Wrote the Bible?* (London: Cape, 1988).

vocabulary and prose style, which has often been studied.[35] It would seem fair to assume, then, that wherever characteristic Deuteronomistic language appears, Deuteronomistic influence is present. However, it must be remembered that this method of identification is not without its limitations. To begin with, the number of characteristic Deuteronomistic vocabulary items is relatively small when compared with the vocabulary of biblical Hebrew as a whole. Furthermore, many of these items are not really peculiar to Deuteronomy but can often be found, although more rarely, in non-Deuteronomistic sources. This picture might change even more dramatically if we knew more about Hebrew in the biblical period outside of the Bible. Some scholars have suggested that the distinctive prose of the Deuteronomist is in fact simply a common dialect of the period. This would throw into question the identification of Deuteronomistic influence on purely linguistic grounds, but at the moment we simply do not have enough data to resolve the issue. Until we do, I would suggest that the use of linguistic criteria remains the most reliable way of identifying the hand of the Deuteronomists.

Less reliable than linguistic criteria, although more often employed in scholarly analysis, is the identification of Deuteronomistic influence through the use of characteristic ideas, concepts or themes. Although it is relatively simple to identify such phenomena in the undisputed Deuteronomistic corpus, it is much more difficult to argue successfully that they are exclusively the property of the Deuteronomists. To take a few obvious examples, Perlitt is undoubtedly correct in identifying the notion of covenant as a central Deuteronomistic concern, but he clearly goes too far when he suggests that only the Deuteronomists employed the concept. Extrabiblical parallels, however distant, and undoubtedly non-Deuteronomistic biblical material suggest that other groups and authors used the concept as well, although they may well have understood it differently. Similarly, a strong concept of retributive justice is certainly a hallmark of Deuteronomism, which holds rather simplistically that good behavior brings reward while disobedience brings punishment. However, it is far from certain that only the Deuteronomists held this view. As Bertil Albrektson pointed out some time ago, similar ideas appear in Near Eastern literature generally, and it would not be

---

35. S.R. Driver, *An Introduction to the Literature of the Old Testament* (Edinburgh: T. & T. Clark, 9th edn, 1913), pp. 99-102; M. Weinfeld, *Deuteronomy and the Deuteronomic School* (Oxford: Clarendon Press, 1972), pp. 320-65.

surprising to find them in the Bible outside of the Deuteronomistic cor-pus.[36] Even more improbable is the suggestion of Carroll and others that interest in prophecy is peculiarly Deuteronomistic. To be sure, the Deuteronomists *are* interested in prophecy. They give a good bit of attention to it in their literature, and they have their own characteristic understanding of the phenomenon. But the Near Eastern evidence and the studies that have been made by anthropologists suggest that prophecy was much too common in the ancient world to permit the claim that it was invented by the Deuteronomists.[37]

Even less persuasive than the citation of alleged Deuteronomistic concepts, motifs and themes are arguments for Deuteronomistic influence based on the discovery of concepts, motifs and themes that might have been 'congenial' to the Deuteronomists. Much of Schmid's argument for a Deuteronomistic Torah works in this way. For example, the promise motifs in the ancestral stories are said to be Deuterono-mistic because they would have been congenial to Deuteronomists living in the time of Josiah or in the exile, or whenever. This may well be true, but one ought not to overlook the fact that undisputed Deuter-onomistic literature makes very little of the promise theme (with the exception of 2 Sam. 7), and in spite of the efforts of Frank Moore Cross, I can find very few notes of hope in the Deuteronomistic His-tory.[38] It is probably more plausible to believe that the promise motifs in the Torah, wherever they came from, survived because they had meaning to the later generations of Israelites who preserved, edited and copied these texts; it is unlikely that the promises found their way into the Torah because they were congenial to the Deuteronomists.

At the bottom of the list of plausible arguments for Deuteronomistic influence is the bizarre theory advanced by some Isaiah scholars that certain passages are Deuteronomistic because they can supposedly be dated to a time and place when Deuteronomists are *thought* to have been active.

In assessing the extent of pan-Deuteronomism, then, it is important to remember the lack of consistent criteria being employed in the discus-sion, and it is equally important to keep open the possibility that pan-Deuteronomism may be less pervasive than it first appears. However,

36. B. Albrektson, *History and the Gods* (Lund: C.W.K. Gleerup, 1967).
37. Barstad, 'No Prophets?', pp. 39-60.
38. F.M. Cross, *Canaanite Myth and Hebrew Epic: Essays in the History of the Religion of Israel* (Cambridge, MA: Harvard University Press, 1973), pp. 274-89.

even if the claims of the pan-Deuteronomists are somewhat exaggerated, enough remains to make the claim of extensive Deuteronomistic
literary activity worth taking seriously. It is therefore important to make
a second observation concerning pan-Deuteronomistic scholarship. All
of the work that I have surveyed, when taken together, provides no
coherent account of Deuteronomism as a social, political or religious
movement. On the basis of these scholarly hypotheses, it is difficult to
see the activities of a specific group working at a specific time and
place and having specific interests.

To be sure, individual scholars working on particular problems and
texts are quite capable of giving a plausible picture of the Deuteronomists, but when all of this research is taken together, the picture begins
to blur considerably. To begin with, there is no consensus on when this
explosion of Deuteronomistic literary activity took place. A popular
suggestion is that it began in the Josianic period, although recent
research on the Deuteronomistic History has suggested dates as early as
Hezekiah. Even more popular is the idea that Deuteronomists shaped
the bulk of our literature sometime in the exile or in the early postexilic
period. It seems impossible with our present knowledge to opt for one
or another of these dates. Furthermore, it is always necessary to keep
open the possibility that all of these suggestions may be correct and that
the Deuteronomists were active over a very long period of time, a
possibility that may find support in the textual history of books such as
Jeremiah, where Deuteronomistic editing seems to have continued in
the Hebrew text after it had stopped in the Greek.

Even more important, recent research on Deuteronomistic influence
can provide no coherent account to indicate *why* the Deuteronomists
engaged in this massive and thorough-going literary enterprise. In
almost each case where Deuteronomistic literary activity can be
detected, the authors seem to have been shaping earlier texts for different reasons. So, for example, the Deuteronomistic hand at work in the
non-biographical prose of Jeremiah may have been concerned to provide interpretive clues to earlier Jeremiah oracles that immediately preceded the Deuteronomistic additions. But this interest is not at all the
same as the interest of the alleged Deuteronomistic shaper of Jeremiah
1–25, who, according to Clements, was trying to illustrate the theology
of 2 Kings 17. Different still were the intentions of the alleged Deuteronomistic shaper of Isaiah, who wanted to provide prophetic support
for the Deuteronomic reforms during Josiah's reign. None of the above

seems to have had anything to do with the alleged Deuteronomists who shaped the Torah to provide comfort for the Babylonian exiles. In short, if the pan-Deuteronomists are correct in their arguments, then they are suggesting something much more pervasive and complex than the work of a single group, guided by a single rationale and working at a specific time and place.

These observations on pan-Deuteronomism, then, suggest one of two things. First, if Deuteronomistic literary activity was as extensive as the pan-Deuteronomists have suggested, then it may be necessary to alter our concept of Deuteronomism. Instead of thinking of the Deuteronomists as a small discrete group working at a particular time (whenever that may have been) and with particular interests in mind, it may be necessary to explore the possibility that Deuteronomism was a wide-ranging movement that was much more diverse than scholars commonly think and that was active over a very long period of time. There is, however, a second alternative. Recent research may in fact have demonstrated, unwittingly, that the concept of Deuteronomism has become so amorphous that it no longer has any analytical precision and so ought to be abandoned. At the moment I still lean toward the first alternative, but the second is becoming increasingly attractive. It is one that the ancient author of the Sumerian King List would have understood. If everybody is king, then in fact nobody is king. Current trends in Deuteronomistic research may thus force scholars to take seriously the possibility that if everybody is the Deuteronomist, then there may be no Deuteronomist at all.

Part II

PAN-DEUTERONOMISM AND HEBREW SCRIPTURE STUDIES

DEUTERONOMIC CONTRIBUTION TO THE NARRATIVE IN GENESIS–NUMBERS: A TEST CASE

Joseph Blenkinsopp

Until about a quarter of a century ago the distinctive character and literary history of Deuteronomy vis-à-vis the first four books of the Bible could be taken for granted. Most scholars accepted de Wette's placing of Deuteronomy in the seventh century preceded by other literary corpora—an annalistic and prophetic source—though surprisingly not much attention was paid to a possible relationship or overlap between these early sources and Deuteronomy. The distinctiveness of Deuteronomy came even more clearly into view with the widely accepted traditio-historical studies of Martin Noth in the 1940s, especially his thesis that, with the exception of some parts of chs. 31–34, Deuteronomy was written as an introduction to Joshua–2 Kings—the Deuteronomistic History (hereafter Dtr)—in the period of the Babylonian exile.[1] From time to time throughout the modern period commentators have drawn attention to passages in Genesis and Exodus stylistically or thematically reminiscent of Deuteronomy, and some were inclined to read the elusive Elohist as an example of what was loosely called proto-Deuteronomism. But as long as the Documentary Hypothesis remained basically unchallenged these observations never coalesced into a systematic study of Deuteronomism in Genesis–Numbers.[2]

---

1. M. Noth, *Überlieferungsgeschichtliche Studien* (Tübingen: Max Niemeyer, 3rd edn, 1967), pp. 1-110; *idem, The Deuteronomistic History* (ET; JSOTSup, 15; Sheffield: JSOT Press, 1991); *idem, Überlieferungsgeschichte des Pentateuch* (Stuttgart: W. Kohlhammer, 1948); *A History of Pentateuchal Traditions* (ET; Englewood Cliffs, NJ: Prentice–Hall, 1972).

2. Noth himself found Deuteronomistic ideas and expressions in Exod. 19.3-9, 23.20-33 and 32.9-14; see his *Exodus: A Commentary* (London: SCM Press, 1962 [1959]), pp. 157, 192; *idem, The Deuteronomistic History*, p. 104 n. 2. Among later

Now that the existence of early, continuous sources (J and E)—an essential feature of the Documentary Hypothesis—has turned out to be problematic to say the least, new options are being explored, among them the possibility of a significant role for the Deuteronomic[3] school in the production of the larger narrative complexes in Genesis, Exodus and Numbers. At one end of the spectrum much of the material formerly classified as J and E is simply reassigned to a Deuteronomic writer, or the Yahwist (J) is more or less completely assimilated to the Deuteronomic *oeuvre* and reclassified as Deuteronomic.[4] Others argue that the first consecutive account of national origins, though not in direct historiographical form, is to be found in Deuteronomy and dated no earlier than the seventh century BCE. The non-P narrative in Genesis, Exodus and Numbers is then taken to represent a filling out of this Deuteronomic outline. Taking this a step further, others read the same narrative complex, with the exception of the so-called primeval

essays see C.H.W. Brekelmans, 'Eléments deutéronomiques dans le Pentateuque', *Recherches Bibliques* 8 (1967), pp. 77-91; W. Fus, *Die deuteronomistische Pentateuchredaktion in Exodus 3–17* (Berlin: W. de Gruyter, 1972); and M. Vervenne, 'The Question of "Deuteronomic" Elements in Genesis to Numbers', in F. García Martínez *et al.* (eds.), *Studies in Deuteronomy in Honour of C.J. Labuschagne on the Occasion of his 65th Birthday* (VTSup, 53; Leiden: E.J. Brill, 1994), pp. 243-68, who gives some account of the prehistory of the question.

3.   To avoid confusion in the use of 'das schreckliche Wort' (L. Perlitt, *Bundestheologie im Alten Testament* [WMANT, 36; Neukirchen–Vluyn: Neukirchener Verlag, 1969], p. 2 n. 2), I use the terms 'Deuteronomism' and 'Deuteronomic' in a general sense with reference to the book of Deuteronomy in any of its putative editions together with other material assigned to the same school, reserving the word 'Deuteronomistic' for the history so designated (= Dtr). Further clarification will be attempted in the concluding section of the paper.

4.   The earliest elaborated proposal was that of H.H. Schmid, *Der sogenannte Jahwist: Beobachtungen und Fragen zur Pentateuchforschung* (Zürich: Theologischer Verlag, 1976), followed by M. Rose, *Deuteronomist und Jahwist: Untersuchungen zu den Berührungspunkten beider Literaturwerke* (Zürich: Theologischer Verlag, 1981). J. Van Seters uses some of the same arguments but opts for an exilic J writer later than and influenced by the Deuteronomists. See his 'Confessional Reformulation in the Exilic Period', *VT* 22 (1972), pp. 448-59; 'The So-Called Deuteronomistic Redaction of the Pentateuch', in J.A. Emerton (ed.), *Congress Volume: Leuven 1989* (VTSup, 43; Leiden: E.J. Brill, 1992), pp. 58-77; and most recently *The Life of Moses: The Yahwist as Historian in Exodus–Numbers* (Louisville, KY: Westminster/John Knox Press, 1994), especially pp. 247-360 on Exod. 19–34.

history,[5] as a long introduction to Dtr edited by members of the Deuter-onomic school or even as the first volume of a two-part Deuteronomic historiographical work. A more cautious approach contents itself with Deuteronomic editorial linkage between the major sections of the Tetrateuchal narrative. This is usually said to appear in the form of the promise of land and peoplehood to the ancestors (e.g. Gen. 50.24; Exod. 33.1-3), a major leitmotif in Deuteronomy.[6]

The only way of attaining a reasonable degree of probability in a matter of this kind is by careful and detailed scrutiny of specific nar-rative passages in Genesis, Exodus and Numbers to determine whether they exhibit terminology, rhetorical and stylistic features, and themes either peculiar to or highly characteristic of Deuteronomy and other Deuteronomic writings. To avoid being misled by what is after all an easily imitated if rhetorically distinctive type of discourse, conclusions must be based on an accumulation of several kinds of indicators. That is the easiest part, for we are then left with the task of *explaining* these stylistic and thematic similarities. Is the text in question contemporary with, earlier or later than related passages in explicitly Deuteronomic writings—Deuteronomy itself, Dtr, D-type editorial matter in prophetic books, especially Jeremiah? Does it represent an early type of Deuter-onomism (proto-Deuteronomism?) or is it the work of a later writer, committee or editor (e.g. the late J advocated by Van Seters or the D Composition of Blum) influenced by Deuteronomic ideology and style?

Since the task of surveying this relatively recent field of investigation in its entirety is potentially interminable and in any case out of the question in the present context, I propose to limit myself to the core of the Sinai-Horeb pericope (Exod. 19–34). The problems involved in the interpretation of this much-studied narrative have contributed in a major way to the radical questioning of the classical Documentary

---

5.   On the distinct character of Gen. 1–11 in the context of the formation of the Pentateuch see F. Crüsemann, 'Die Eigenständigkeit der Urgeschichte: Ein Beitrag zur Diskussion um den "Jahwisten" ', in L. Perlitt and J. Jeremias (eds.), *Die Bot-schaft und die Boten: Festschrift für Hans Walt Wolff zum 70. Geburtstag* (Neu-kirchen–Vluyn: Neukirchener Verlag, 1981), pp. 11-29; J. Blenkinsopp, 'P and J in Genesis 1:1–11:26: An Alternative Hypothesis', in A.B. Beck *et al.* (eds.), *For-tunate the Eyes that See: Essays in Honor of David Noel Freedman* (Grand Rapids: Eerdmans, 1995), pp. 1-15.

6.   R. Rendtorff, *The Problem of the Process of Transmission in the Pentateuch* (JSOTSup, 89; Sheffield: JSOT Press, 1990), pp. 60, 72, 78; *idem, The Old Testa-ment: An Introduction* (London: SCM Press, 1985 [1983]), pp. 160-63.

Hypothesis, and it has been at the center of the debate in the modern period, especially following on the important contributions of Lothar Perlitt and Ernst Kutsch in the late 1960s and early 1970s.[7] However one judges their proposals, they have at least shown that the pericope can no longer be adequately explained on the basis of the classical Documentary Hypothesis.

Introductory Address (Exodus 19.4-6a)

> You have seen what I did to the Egyptians, and how I carried you on eagles' wings and brought you to myself. And now, if you will diligently obey my voice and observe my covenant, you will be for me a special possession from among all the peoples, for all the earth is mine. You will be for me a kingdom of priests and a holy nation.

The address follows the familiar pattern of Deuteronomic parenesis: appeal to collective experience, immediate or vicarious, followed by the promise of a special relationship contingent on obedience and covenant-keeping. It is also Deuteronomic in the choice of language and images.

'attem r^e'îtem ('you have seen'): we find identical wording in appealing to experience in Deut. 29.1 and Josh. 23.3; with the verb *r'h* ('you have seen' or 'your eyes have seen') in the plural (e.g. Deut. 1.19; 4.3; 11.7) and often also in the singular.

'^a šer 'aśîtî l^emiṣrāyim ('What I did to the Egyptians'): the expression occurs with reference to hostile acts at Deut. 1.30; 6.22; 7.18; cf. Josh. 23.3. Perlitt, who reads 19.3-8 as an *Einschub* (insertion) from the Deuteronomic school active in the post-disaster period, suggests comparison with Israel's experience of what God has wrought in Babylon referred to in Isaiah 40–48 and other prophetic texts from that time.[8] I take this and other echoes of exilic and postexilic prophecy in the pericope as a whole to be important indicators of the spiritual climate in which it was composed. For the reader of that time Babylon is Egypt, Egypt is Babylon.

---

7. Perlitt, *Bundestheologie*; E. Kutsch, *Verheissung und Gesetz: Untersuchungen zum sogenannten 'Bund' im Alten Testament* (Berlin: W. de Gruyter, 1973). Some of the more significant recent commentary on the pericope will be noted in the course of this essay.

8. Perlitt, *Bundestheologie*, pp. 170, 176.

wā'eśśā' 'etkem 'al-kanpê nᵉšārîm ('and how I carried you on eagles' wings'): the same striking image occurs elsewhere only in the Song of Moses, Deut. 32.11, and the verb *nś'* describes metaphorically God's providence for Israel in the wilderness at Deut. 1.31; similarly, the verb *bw'*, as in *wā'ābi 'etkem 'ēlāy*, is standard in Deuteronomy for divine providential action in the same narrative context (4.38; 6.10, 23; 7.1; 8.7; 9.4, 28; 11.29; 26.9; 30.5; 31.20, 21, 23).

wᵉ'attâ 'im-šāmôa tišmᵉ'û bᵉqōlî ('and now, if you will diligently obey my voice'): Deut. 4.30; 5.23; 8.20; 9.23; 11.13; 13.5, 19; 15.5; 26.14, 17; 27.10; 28.1-2, 15; 30.2, 8, 10, 20 all refer to listening to and obeying God's communications as a condition for the promised special relationship. The attached phrase, *ûšᵉmartem 'et-bᵉrîtî* ('and obey my covenant'), is the necessary follow-up to the way of listening, *šmr* + *bᵉrît* being a typical Deuteronomic combination; see Deut. 7.9, 12; 29.8 and cf. 1 Kgs 8.23; 11.11; Jer. 11.2, 3, 6.

wihyîtem lî sᵉgullâ mikkol-hā'ammîm ('you will be for me a special possession from among all the peoples'): see Deut. 4.20 and 9.26 where the same idea occurs but with *naḥᵃlâ*; *sᵉgullâ* is one of the most characteristically Deuteronomic terms; see Deut. 7.6; 14.2 (with *mikkol hā'ammîm*); also Deut. 26.18; cf. Mal. 3.17; Ps. 135.4; in different contexts *mikkol hā'ammîm* expresses the unique status of Israel in contrast to other nations, as in Deut. 7.6 (2×), 7 (2×), 14; 14.2; 30.3.

kî lî kol-hā'āreṣ ('for all the earth is mine'): this phrase is not found elsewhere; *'ereṣ* in Deuteronomy usually refers to Israel but also occurs in familiar combination with *šāmayim* as in Deut. 3.24; 4.36, 39; 5.8; 11.21; and in such phrases as *mayim mittaḥat lā'āreṣ*: Deut. 4.18; 5.8; *miqṣēh hā'āreṣ*, Deut. 13.8; 28.49, 64; *kol mamlᵉkôt hā'āreṣ*, Deut. 28.25. The point is the same as is made throughout Isaiah 40–48 (e.g. Isa. 42.5-6): the God who created the universe is also the one who has chosen Israel.

wᵉ'attem tihyû-lî mamleket kōhᵃnîm wᵉgôy qādôš ('you will be for me a kingdom of priests and a holy nation'): This much discussed expression is not found in Deuteronomy, but its essential components occur in the book: Israel is designated as a *gôy* at Deut. 4.7-8, 34; 26.5; cf. 2 Sam. 7.23, in the Deuteronomic prayer of David; also in the promise that Israel will be a mighty nation (*gôy 'āṣûm*), Deut. 9.14 cf. Gen. 12.2; Exod. 32.10; Num. 14.12; etc. Here, too, Perlitt plausibly explains the use of this designation in terms of the exilic situation, in which the issue of Israel's relation to other ethnic groups became particularly acute.[9] The phrase *'am qādôš* as used of Israel occurs only in Deuteronomy (7.6; 14.2, 21; 26.19; 28.9). The essence of the idea is expressed in Deut. 7.6: 'For you are a people holy to YHWH your God. Your YHWH your God has chosen to be a people for his own possession (*'am s^egullâ*) from all the peoples that are on the face of the earth'. The expression *mamleket kōh^anîm* does not occur elsewhere; interpreting it in its present context, I see it connected with *gôy qādôš* as another way of expressing the apartness and unique status of Israel, since priesthood encapsulates the essence of holiness and being set apart. It is also reminiscent of prophetic texts in which Israel is assigned priestly status vis-à-vis other nations (e.g. Isa. 61.6). The expression provides no justification for assigning the passage to P.[10] That Israel is a holy or priestly people means, for the Deuteronomists, that Israel is chosen and set aside by God as his *s^egullâ* (7.6; 14.2; 26.19), a status that is given concrete expression by observing the law including the dietary rules (Deut. 14.21).

I conclude, then, that this short parenesis is thoroughly Deuteronomic in style and substance. It appeals to collective experience, with reference to events in Egypt and in the wilderness, as the basis for covenant observance; and observance of the laws is essential for maintaining Israel's special relationship (*b^erît*) and status (*s^egullâ*). This is pure Deuteronomic doctrine expressed in Deuteronomic language, and its purpose is to provide a theological summary of and introduction to the Horeb event.[11]

9. Perlitt, *Bundestheologie*, pp. 174-75. See also E. Blum, 'Israël à la montagne de Dieu', in A. de Pury (ed.), *Le Pentateuque en question* (Geneva: Labor et Fides, 1989), pp. 288-92.

10. E.g. H. Cazelles, 'Pentateuque IV: Textes sacerdotaux', *DBSup* 7 (1966), cols. 833-34. Actually, this short piece has been assigned to practically every known source at one time or another—J (Gressmann), E (Eissfeldt, Beyerlin), a D-type addition to J (Noth). K. Baltzer, *The Covenant Formulary in Old Testament, Jewish and Early Christian Writings* (Oxford: Basil Blackwell, 2nd edn, 1971 [1964]), pp. 28-29, gives a sample of opinion but perhaps wisely refrains from stating his own. For a brief summary on sources see my *The Pentateuch: An Introduction to the First Five Books of the Bible* (New York: Doubleday, 1992), pp. 187-88.

11. This doctrine is, as Perlitt picturesquely expresses it, 'Die Lesebrille die jene Erben des Dt dem Leser der Sinai-Erzählung auf die Nase setzen wollten' (*Bundestheologie*, p. 171). The further question as to the identity and location of these 'Erben' is difficult and with our available resources perhaps impossible to answer. I am in agreement with much of Van Seters's analysis of Exodus texts, including the

The Framework of the Address (Exodus 19.3b, 6b)

The passage discussed above is introduced with the words: 'Thus you shall say to the house of Jacob and announce to the Israelites' (19.3b). I note, first, that the incidence of the expression *bêt ya'ªqōb* is almost entirely restricted to texts from the exilic period or later.[12] The more solemn *higgîd* occurs often in Deuteronomy for the promulgation of the *bᵉrît* (4.13) as also for a *dᵉbar YHWH* (5.5) and *dᵉbar hammišpaṭ* (17.9). The parenesis concludes with 'These are the words which you shall speak to the Israelites'. *'ēlleh haddᵉbārîm* is a Deuteronomic formula of frequent occurrence (Deut. 1.1; 12.28; 28.69). Since *dābār* is also used of a legal ordinance (e.g. Deut. 4.2; 27.3, 8, 26; 31.12, 24), or covenant stipulation (28.69; 29.8, 18), it often occurs in contexts that are ambiguous, perhaps deliberately so.[13] The same ambiguity is in evidence here as we move from v. 6 to v. 7, since the latter can only refer to the law communicated to Moses to which the people give their assent. The word *dābār*, therefore, refers successively to discourse (v. 6), law (v. 7) and discourse (v. 8).

The Address in Context

After the P introduction, which moves the Israelites from Rephidim into the wilderness of Sinai (19.1-2),[14] Moses makes the first of several ascents of the mountain. Symbolically, the mountain occupies the space intermediate between the deity and the people. Moses is the intermediary, and as such he is told to speak. The sequel (vv. 7-9)

Sinai-Horeb pericope (in *The Life of Moses*) but see no reason to retain the siglum J for an exilic author, or narrative strand, distinct from but influenced by Deutero-nomic writings. Since it is established that these writings come from a multi-generational school, I find the data in Exodus more consistent with successive literary essays from the same school, especially the recasting of first-person historical reminiscence in the form of direct historical narrative. We will attempt to be somewhat more precise at the conclusion of our analysis.

12. Isa. 2.5; 10.20; 14.1; 29.22; 46.3; 48.1; 58.1; Jer. 2.4; Ezek. 20.5; Amos 9.8; Obad. 17-18; Ps. 114.1.

13. Deut. 1.1; cf. 1.3; 4.2, 10, 12, 36; 5.5, 22; 6.6; 9.10; 11.18.

14. The temporal indication is certainly P, but the repeated notice that they came to the Sinai wilderness and that they camped there created complications for the documentarians; e.g. Martin Noth assigned vv. 1 and 2a to P, 2b to J, and 3a to E. See the analytical outline provided by the translator in Noth's *A History of Pentateuchal Traditions*, p. 270. Van Seters (*The Life of Moses*) assigns v. 2 to his exilic J.

makes it clear that the speaking is now understood to consist of a promulgation of the laws. For Moses summons the elders and sets the words (i.e. the laws) before them for their approval. After the public reading of the laws the people give their assent, and Moses reports back to God (v. 8b). The repetition in practically identical terms of Moses' reporting back to the deity (*wayyaggēd mōšeh 'et-dibrê hā'ām 'el-YHWH*, v. 9b; cf. *wayyāšeb mōšeh 'et-dibrê hā'ām 'el-YHWH*, v. 8b) suggests that v. 9b is a resumptive phrase added after the addition of v. 9a, which emphasizes the legitimation of Moses' role ('See, I am about to come to you in a thick cloud so that the people may hear as I speak with you, and may also for ever believe you'; cf. Exod. 4.1, 5, 8, 9; 14.31). Needless to say, acknowledgment of the authority of Moses and therefore of the law is a point of decisive importance for Deuteronomy (Deut. 5.5, 23-27, 31; 9.9, etc). This is one more indication, therefore, of an intent to recast the Sinai theophany tradition, alluded to in v. 9a, in a form consistent with the overall Deuteronomic understanding of the event in terms of law and covenant.[15]

I conclude, then, that the parenesis of vv. 4-6a with its narrative setting was composed by a Deuteronomic author as a recapitulation or proleptic summary of the Sinai-Horeb event, one that encapsulated its theological significance as understood among Deuteronomic *litterati*. Further confirmation of this interpretation is the important role assigned by Deuteronomy to elders in connection with the law (e.g. Deut. 5.23; 27.1; 29.9; 31.9, 28). Also, the terms in which the people assent to the law (Exod. 19.8a) recur in the actual covenant-making later on (24.3, 7), as also in the retelling of the event in Deuteronomy (5.27), to which we shall return. This giving of assent (*na'ăšeh*), a performative utterance like the 'I do' of the marriage ceremony, is clearly a feature of decisive importance in the Deuteronomic understanding of covenant, not least because the honoring of commitments on the part of the deity is, for the Deuteronomists, contingent on this assent being uttered and implemented (see also Deut. 30.11-13).

15. A further possibility is that v. 9a represents the original continuation of v. 3a, and that therefore the Deuteronomist has replaced an address of the deity dealing with the imminent theophany with his own parenesis in which the giving and assent to a covenant is central.

What Are We to Make of This?

A *theoretical* possibility is that the kind of D-type language we find in this Exodus passage gave rise to the rhetoric and themes of the book of Deuteronomy, that it represents a sort of proto-Deuteronomism.[16] While it is difficult to exclude this option absolutely (or, for that matter, any of the other proposed solutions of this issue), it does not seem at all likely since no essential difference can be detected between this and similar passages in Exodus on the one hand and parallel texts in Deuteronomy on the other that would justify qualifying the former as proto-Deuteronomic. I have just noted, on the contrary, that Exod. 19.3-6 betrays rather clear affinity with biblical texts from the neo-Babylonian period, about the time of the composition or final draft of Dtr or later, and we shall see indications of dependence on both Deuteronomy and Dtr at later stages of the narrative, especially in Exodus 32–34.

Mention of Dtr leads me to the further suggestion that editorial procedures observable in this work may provide clues about the presence of Deuteronomic activity in Genesis–Numbers. The historian has certainly incorporated sources, some comparable in length to source material in the Tetrateuch (the Ark History, the Court History, cf. the Joseph story), some in parallel versions (e.g. the rejection of Saul, David sparing Saul's life), and some even with contrasting names for the deity (e.g. the famine and plague at the beginning of David's reign).[17] It was such features that at one time led some scholars to pursue J and E down into the history of the kingdoms. The hand of the editor(s) is also detectable in occasional interpretive observations, in the linkage between one incident and another, and even, as in our test case, in an initial paranetic address put in the mouth of the deity or the deity's representative (e.g. Josh. 1.1-9; Judg. 2.1-5). It therefore makes sense to seek an explanation of alleged D-type passages in the Tetrateuch along the same lines, that is, by analogy with Dtr.[18] In passing from

16. See A. Phillips, 'A Fresh Look at the Sinai Pericope', *VT* 34 (1984), pp. 39-52, 282-94.

17. The relevant texts are: 1 Sam. 3.1–7.1; 2 Sam. 11–20 and 1 Kgs 1–2; 1 Sam. 13.7b-15a, cf. 15.1-35; 1 Sam. 23.14–24.22, cf. 26.1-25; 2 Sam. 21.1-14, cf. 24.1-25.

18. Many parallels between narrative incidents in Genesis–Numbers and Deuteronomy-Dtr have been noted, e.g. the 'end of an era' schema in Judg. 2.8-10 (cf. Gen. 50.26; Exod. 1.6-8), the anti-Amalekite jihad in 1 Sam. 15.2-3 and Deut. 25.17-19 (cf. Exod. 17.8-16), and the *zēker* and *zikkārôn* of Exod. 17.14, cor-

Deuteronomy to the Tetrateuch we shift from first-person historical reminiscence of Moses to more or less direct history-like narration. The scope and limitations of Deuteronomic activity in both the Tetrateuch and Dtr would presumably be dictated in some way by the historical horizon of the reminiscence of the Deuteronomic Moses. In Deuteronomy Moses looks forward prophetically to a history of infidelity leading to exile and, eventually, the possibility of a new beginning, and this outline is filled out in Dtr. The reminiscence or retrospect begins with Horeb (1.6), and Horeb remains its primary focus (4.10-14; 5.2-33; 9.8-21; 9.25–10.5; 10.10-11). The historical context of the Horeb event called for an account of the sojourn in Egypt and the wilderness experience only (10.22; 26.5). Hence the *relative* absence of D-type narrative or parenesis in Genesis, except where it is a question of the ancestral promise, corresponds to the almost total neglect in the reminiscence in Deuteronomy of allusion to events or situations prior to Egypt, except where the ancestral promise enters into play.[19]

After this initial address and the repetition of Moses' reporting back to YHWH the assent of the people (19.9b), Moses is instructed to prepare the people ritually for the giving of the law, and he does so (19.10-15). There follows a theophany, which appears to combine elements of a storm on the mountain with volcanic phenomena, and the description

responding to the injunction *zākôr...lō' tiškaḥ* of Deut. 25.17-19.

19. The only exceptions are the allusion to the fate of the cities of the plain (29.22) and the *"rammî 'ōbēd* (26.5), presumably Jacob. Without attempting to address the issue in detail, I simply observe that passages in Genesis in which the ancestral promise is linked to the observance of law and covenant (especially 18.17-19; 22.16-18; 26.4-5) give every appearance of being Deuteronomic. The 'covenant of the pieces' in Gen. 15 is a special case in which several recent commentators have found significant evidence of Deuteronomic activity. For example, see J. Van Seters, *Abraham in History and Tradition* (New Haven: Yale University Press, 1975), pp. 249-78, whose late J here and elsewhere is influenced by Deuteronomic themes; Schmid, *Der sogennante Jahwist*, pp. 35-36; R. Rendtorff, 'Gen 15 im Rahmen der theologischen Bearbeitung der Vätergeschichten', in R. Albertz *et al.* (eds.), *Werden und Wirken des Alten Testaments: Festschrift für Claus Westermann zum 70. Geburtstag* (Göttingen: Vandenhoeck & Ruprecht, 1980), pp. 74-81; *idem*, 'Covenant as a Structuring Concept in Genesis and Exodus', *JBL* 108 (1989), pp. 385-93 (391-92) (also found in *Canon and Theology: Overtures to an Old Testament Theology* [Minneapolis: Fortress Press, 1993], pp. 125-34); M. Anbar, 'Genesis 15: A Conflation of Two Deuteronomic Narratives', *JBL* 101 (1982), pp. 39-55; J. Ha, *Genesis 15: A Theological Compendium of Pentateuchal History* (Berlin: W. de Gruyter, 1989), esp. pp. 94-95.

of which continues after the giving of the decalogue (19.6-19 and 20.8-21). While the sequence of events (promulgation of the decalogue, expostulation of the people, private communication of the lawbook to Moses) runs parallel with the Deuteronomic account (Deut. 5.2-33),[20] the actual description is not particularly close. Deuteronomy has no ritual preparation,[21] and its characteristic expressions ('the mountain burning with fire', 4.11; 5.23; 9.15; 'from the midst of the fire', 4.12; 5.4, 22, 24, 26; 9.10; 10.4; 'darkness, cloud and gloom', 4.11; cf. 5.22, 23) are missing from the Exodus version. These features would be consistent with the view that Deuteronomic editors have reworked an existing literary tradition of a Sinai theophany into a paradigm of covenant making in keeping with their own ideological agenda. It is at any rate worth noting that there is no mention of the giving of the law in the description of the theophany, the preparation for it and the sequel to it (19.10-25; 20.18-21).

The Literary Framework of the Lawbook (Exodus 20.22; 23.20-33)

The covenant lawbook is preceded by language similar to the recapitulatory passage we have been discussing, with the same appeal to experience (19.3-6): 'YHWH said to Moses, "thus you shall say to the Israelites: you [pl.] have seen that I have spoken to you from heaven" ' (20.22). That God speaks from heaven is a well-attested Deuteronomic way of expressing the ultimacy of authority inhering in divine communications in general and the law in particular. It is amply illustrated in Solomon's prayer at the dedication of the temple, acknowledged to be an exilic Deuteronomic composition.[22] We are here near the beginnings of the idea of a *unique* divine communication at

---

20. Exod. 20.18 follows on smoothly from 19.19, suggesting that, in addition to the decalogue, the curious sequence of events recorded in 19.20-25 has been inserted somewhat awkwardly into the storyline, perhaps to make room for the priests and Aaron in the ceremony. For Noth (*Exodus*, p. 160) it is 'secondary'. At any rate, there is nothing specifically Deuteronomic about it.

21. These preliminary ritual acts (Exod. 19.10-15) are fairly standard and well attested, perhaps the closest parallel being the ceremonial preparation for the Bethel cult carried out by Jacob and his household at Shechem. These include a purification ritual (*hiṭṭahᵃrû*, cf. Josh. 3.5 and 7.13) and a change of clothes (Gen. 35.1-4).

22. 1 Kgs 8.22, 23, 30, 32, 34, 36, 39, 43, 45, 49, 54; see also Deut. 4.36; 26.15 and several late texts, e.g. Isa. 63.15; Neh. 9.13, 27-28.

Sinai-Horeb. The epilogue to the lawbook (23.20-33), if that is what it is,[23] deals primarily with the theme of divine guidance after the Israelites have left Sinai behind and wandered off into the wilderness and into their history. It assumes the absolute necessity for a mediating agency by which the Sinai experience would be perpetuated and embodied in fully authorized institutional forms. The key to understanding this Deuteronomic theme as stated here is its parallelism with the Deuteronomic understanding of prophecy as the continuation of the role and mission of Moses. In 23.20-33 the *mal'āk* is sent by YHWH, communicates divine commands and must be heeded and obeyed since the angel-messenger speaks in YHWH's name (Exod. 23.20-22). This is exactly parallel to what Deuteronomy has to say about the *nābî'* (Deut. 18.15-20) and will help to explain why *mal'āk* eventually became a synonym for *nābî'*.[24]

The rest of this concluding discourse dealing with the situation obtaining after the occupation of the land (23.23-33) is strung together out of Deuteronomic *topoi* and turns of phrase: the injunction to take heed (*hiššāmer*), a standard feature of Deuteronomic rhetoric; the list of indigenous nations (cf. Exod. 3.8; 33.2; Deut. 7.1; Josh. 24.11); prohibition of alien cults and the command to destroy the *maṣṣēbôt* (cf. Deut. 7.1-2, 5; 12.1-3); blessings contingent on the worship of YHWH alone, some of them couched in practically identical language (cf. Deut. 7.12-16; 11.13-15, 23-25; 28.1-14); the divine terror (*'êmâ* cf. Deut. 32.25; Josh. 2.9); hornets drafted in the fight for possession of the land (cf. Deut. 7.20; Josh. 24.12); the conquest as a gradual process (Deut. 7.22; cf. Judg. 2.21-23); the boundaries of the Promised Land reaching, optimistically, as far as the Euphrates (cf. Deut. 1.7; 11.24; Josh. 1.4); the prohibition of making covenants with the native populations and

---

23. In fact, it at no point refers back to the preceding legal compilation. However, W. Johnstone, 'Reactivating the Chronicles Analogy in Pentateuchal Studies, with Special Reference to the Sinai Pericope in Exodus', *ZAW* 99 (1987), pp. 16-37 (25-27), finds analogies in Judg. 2.1-5 and Deut. 27–28 functioning as codas to the account of the settlement and the Deuteronomic law respectively. Judg. 2.1-5 is certainly very close linguistically to Exod. 23.20-33, but I find no indication that it functions as an *excipit* to the conquest and settlement, as Josh. 21.43-45 clearly does, and Deut. 27–28 is quite different from Exod. 23.20-33.

24. E.g. Hag. 1.13; Mal. 3.1, cf. 3.23. At Judg. 2.1-5 a *mal'āk YHWH* delivers a prophetic address in the Deuteronomic fashion. As generally understood, Hos. 12.13 refers to Moses as a prophetic guide for Israel in the exodus and wilderness; cf. Num. 20.16 in which a *mal'āk* brings Israel out of Egypt.

their deities (Deut. 7.2; cf. Exod. 34.12, 15); these same deities represented as a snare (*môqēš*, Deut. 7.16; Josh. 23.13; Judg. 2.3; cf. Exod.
34.12). In other words, the passage is as Deuteronomic as anything in
the book of Deuteronomy itself.[25]

So much is reasonably clear, but it is by no means equally clear that
these two passages represent a deliberate framing of the lawbook.
Neither of them alludes to it; 20.22 refers back to the promulgation of
the decalogue, perhaps with the purpose of linking the lawbook with the
decalogue, and 23.20-33 looks forward to the journey towards and
arrival in Canaan. Whatever the circumstances under which the lawbook was inserted into the Sinai-Horeb episode, it seems more likely
that 23.20-33 was intended not so much as an epilogue to it but as the
first of several thematic allusions to the journey that remained to be
undertaken (33.1-6, 12-16; 34.11-16), a point alluded to at the beginning of Deuteronomy (1.6-8). The topographical-symbolic link between
Horeb and Moab, that is, between the first and the second covenant (cf.
Deut. 28.69), was clearly of great importance for the Deuteronomists.

Many of the same motifs and much of the same language recur in the
first of these parallel passages dealing with guidance on the journey,
which is located in the interval between the punishment of the calf-
worshipers and the remaking of the law tablets (Exod. 33.1-6). The
summons of YHWH to Moses to move on (cf. Deut. 1.7) at the head of
'the people whom you have brought up [*he'elêtā*] out of the land of
Egypt' sounds Deuteronomic, but this is one of those small points that
warn us against one-dimensional solutions. For Deuteronomy uses the
verb 'bring out' (*hôṣî'*), never 'bring up' (*he'elôt*), in exodus contexts,
and the bringing out is attributed to YHWH not to Moses. In Dtr and
other Deuteronomically authored or edited texts, however, '*lh* (hi.)
predominates, though *yṣ'* (hi.) also occurs, and there are places where

25. In this essay I omit discussion of a possible D redaction of the decalogue
(Exod. 20.1-17) and the covenant lawbook (Exod. 20.23–23.19). In my *The Pentateuch*, pp. 207-208, I argued that both versions of the decalogue have been worked
over by a D editor, and I believe the arguments presented there could be amplified.
For the thesis of a D recension underlying P argued at much greater length see
W. Johnstone, 'The Decalogue and the Redaction of the Sinai Pericope in Exodus',
ZAW 100 (1988), pp. 361-85. The issue of D editing in the *Bundesbuch* is still in
need of study. It is not part of my present agenda, but see N. Lohfink, 'Gibt es eine
deuteronomistische Bearbeitung im Bundesbuch?', in C.H.W. Brekelmans and
J. Lust (eds.), *Pentateuchal and Deuteronomistic Studies* (BETL, 94; Leuven:
Leuven University Press, 1989), pp. 91-113.

both occur together.[26] This would be consistent with the view that Exod. 33.1-6 is related to but later than the first draft of the book of Deuteronomy. I note further that here and elsewhere in Exodus Moses is the agent (3.10-12; 14.11; 16.3, 32; 17.3; 32.1, 7, 23; 33.1), whereas the only instance in Deuteronomy in which Moses does the 'bringing out' occurs at the beginning of Deut. 9.12-21, a passage clearly synoptic with Exod. 32.7-20, as we shall see shortly. Taken by itself, this would favor the priority of the Exodus version (32.7-20) over the corresponding passage in Deuteronomy (9.12-21) and raise serious questions about the Deuteronomic character of Exod. 33.1. But other expressions occurring in 33.1-6 are more straightforwardly of Deuteronomic vintage, including 'the land [about] which I swore to Abraham, Isaac and Jacob', which is standard in Deuteronomy with or without the names of the ancestors;[27] 'a land running with milk and honey', of frequent occurrence in Deuteronomy and related writings;[28] 'a stiff-necked people', also favored by the Deuteronomists.[29] The angel-guide or messenger-guide (*mal'āk*) is not featured in Deuteronomy, but both here and at Exod. 23.20, 23 this theologoumenon seems to be a derivate of the Deuteronomic understanding of the prophetic office, as noted earlier. The list of six or seven autochthonous peoples is generally taken to be a Deuteronomic topos. It occurs twice in Deuteronomy (7.1; 20.17) and five times in Dtr (Josh. 3.10; 9.1; 11.3; 12.8; 24.11) but about an equal number of times in the Tetrateuch, and not much can be concluded from the order in which the peoples are listed. What is specifically Deuteronomic is the occurrence of the list in association with the promise of land, as here, elsewhere in Exodus (3.8, 17; 13.5) and in the 'covenant of the pieces' (Gen. 15.18-21).

26. '*lh* (hi.) Josh. 24.17; Judg. 2.1; 6.13; 1 Sam. 8.8; 10.18; 2 Sam. 7.6; 1 Kgs 12.28; 2 Kgs 17.7, 36; also Jer. 11.7; 16.14; 23.7. Both come together at Judg. 6.8 and in the valedictory discourse of Samuel, 1 Sam. 12.6, 8.

27. With the names: Deut. 1.8; 6.10; 9.5; 29.12; 30.20; 34.4; cf. Exod. 32.13; 33.1; without the names: 1.35; 4.31; 6.18, 23; 7.8, 12, 13; 8.1, 18; 10.11; 11.9, 21; 19.8; 26.3, 15; 28.11; 31.7, 20, 21, 23; cf. Exod. 13.5, 11.

28. Generally, as here, associated with the land promise: Deut. 6.3; 11.9; 26.9, 15; 27.3; 31.20; Josh. 5.6; Jer. 11.5; 32.22; cf. Exod. 3.8, 17; 13.5; 33.3.

29. Deut. 9.6, 13; see also related phrases in 10.16; 31.27; 2 Kgs 17.14; Jer. 7.26; 17.23; 19.15; cf. Exod. 32.9; 33.3, 5; 34.9.

Sealing the Covenant (Exodus 24.1-18)

Exodus 24, at the center of the Sinai-Horeb narrative, has proved to be mined terrain for proponents of the Documentary Hypothesis.[30] I propose to take as a starting point the broadly accepted opinion that this complex account of what happened subsequent to the promulgation of the decalogue and the communication of the lawbook to Moses is a conflation of several scenarios that differ as to location, participants and ceremonial:[31]

1. Verses 1-2, 9-11: location: on the mountain; participants: Moses, Aaron and his sons, Nadab and Abihu, with 70 elders; event: a vision of the enthroned deity and a meal.
2. Verses 3-8: location: at the foot of the mountain; participants: Moses, 'young men' (*nᵉ'ārîm*), the people; event: the law is written and read publicly with sacrifices and a blood ritual.
3. Verses 12-15a, 18b: location: on the mountain; participants: Moses and Joshua; event: Moses receives the stone tablets.
4. Verses 15b-18a: location: on the mountain; participant: Moses; event: a vision giving specifications about the cult.

The first and fourth scenarios need not concern us. Whatever the origin and affinities of (1),[32] it has no counterpart in Deuteronomy, which

---

30. A brief survey of opinion can be found in my *The Pentateuch*, pp. 189-92. A full and thoroughly documented treatment of Exod. 24 is that of E.W. Nicholson, *God and his People: Covenant and Theology in the Old Testament* (Oxford: Clarendon Press, 1986).

31. In identifying these strands, I do not overlook the possibility that their arrangement and reciprocal relationships are exegetically significant, but I would resist the suggestion that they can be somehow unified with reference either to a cultic act or to the treaty-covenant formulary. These and other exegetical issues including the amalgamation of the D material with P cannot, however, be pursued in this paper.

32. See Nicholson, *God and his People*, pp. 121-33, who argues that eating and drinking simply indicate that they survived the encounter with God. The closest parallel is the meal with sacrifice on another 'mountain of God' in which Jethro, Moses, Aaron and elders participate (Exod. 18.12), which may emit an echo of the Kadesh tradition. This strand has been variously attributed to L (Eissfeldt), N (Fohrer), J (Mowinckel, von Rad), and E (Noth, Beyerlin); on which see Perlitt, *Bundestheologie*, pp. 181-82. The description of the lapis-based throne (*kᵉma'ᵃśēh libnat hassappîr*) (cf. Ezek. 1.26; 10.1) also suggests Priestly (P) affinities.

betrays little interest in or sympathy for Aaron and does not even mention Nadab and Abihu. The fourth (4) represents the climax of the P account of the Sinai event and is continued in the detailed instructions for the establishment of the wilderness cult (25.1–31.17), the implementation of the same (35.1–40.38), and then on into Leviticus.

As I noted earlier, the prologue to (2) has been used in the D-type inaugural address of YHWH, as will be apparent from the following synopsis:

Exodus 24.3	*Exodus 19.7-8*
way^{e}sappēr lā'ām 'ēt kol-dibrê YHWH w^e'ēt kol-hammišpāṭîm.	*wayyābō' mōšeh wayyiqrā' l^{e}ziqnê hā'ām wayyāśem lipnêhem 'ēt kol-hadd^{e}bārîm hā'ēlleh '^{a}šer ṣiwwāhû YHWH.*
wayya'an kol-hā'ām qôl 'eḥād wayyō'm^{e}rû, kol-hadd^{e}bārîm '^{a}šer dibber YHWH na'^{a}śeh.	*wayya'^{a}nû kol-hā'ām yaḥdāw wayyō'm^{e}rû, kōl '^{a}šer dibber YHWH na'^{a}śeh.*

In the opening address the editor has abstracted what he considered to be of central significance in the Horeb event, namely, the promulgation of the decalogue (*d^{e}bārîm*) and its acceptance by the community. Exodus 24.3 adds the detailed legal stipulations (*mišpāṭîm*), since the ceremony as described here includes the public reading of the 'book of the covenant' (*sēper habb^{e}rît*, 24.7).[33] The complex ceremony at the foot of the mountain consists in the building of an altar and setting up of 12 *maṣṣēbôt* for the 12 tribes, implying that what is to follow is a pan-Israelite ceremony; sacrifices are offered by *n^e'ārîm*,[34] and there is a blood ritual uniting the people with the altar (i.e. the deity). The public reading of and assent to the lawbook precedes the blood ritual by means of which the significance of the act as covenant is given solemn

33. In the context, the *sēper habb^{e}rît* (24.7) must refer to Exod. 20.22–23.19. The preferred term for the Deuteronomic law in Deuteronomic writings is *sēper hattôrāh* (Deut. 28.61; 29.20; 30.10; 31.26; Josh. 1.8; 8.34; 2 Kgs 22.11) or *sēper tôrat mōšeh* (Josh. 8.31; 23.6; 2 Kgs 14.6; 22.8); *sēper habb^{e}rît* occurs only in the account of Josiah's reform (2 Kgs 23.2, 21). Perlitt (*Bundestheologie*, p. 191) makes the point that 24.3 anticipates 24.7 in the same way that 19.7-8 anticipates the Sinai event as a whole, though 'words' (*d^{e}bārîm*) are mentioned only at 24.3. On the passage as a whole see Nicholson, *God and his People*, pp.164-78.

34. Usually translated 'young men', but *na'ar* also occurs as a synonym for *m^{e}šārēt*, meaning 'cult official'; see Exod. 33.7-11 (Joshua), 1 Sam. 2.18, 24 (Samuel), 2 Kgs 9.4 (Gehazi, Elisha's acolyte).

ritual expression. Much of this is in accord with Deuteronomic theory: the public reading of the law at a prescribed pan-Israelite assembly (Deut. 31.10-13), the people's assent to it (5.27) and Moses as inscriber of the decalogue (31.9).[35] The same basic pattern is detectable in Josiah's covenant (2 Kgs 23.1-3), obviously a crucial juncture for the Dtr historian. The more archaic elements that have survived in Exod. 24.3-8 are reminiscent of certain features of the Shechem covenant-making ceremonial, which belongs in some obscure way to the prehistory of Deuteronomy (it is alluded to, significantly, immediately before and after the Deuteronomic law, Deut. 11.26-32 and 27.1-26). These archaisms include the erection of large stones on which the laws were inscribed (cf. Deut. 27.2-4, 8; Josh. 8.32), the setting up of an altar and sacrifices (cf. Deut. 27.5-7; Josh. 8.30-31; Gen. 35.3), probably also the ritual with the blood of the sacrificed animal, though this is not explicitly attested, and the public reading of the laws (Josh. 8.34-35; cf. the reading of the curses in Deut. 27.15-26). A closer study of this fragmentary tradition would be worth undertaking, but it lies outside of the scope of this essay.

The scenario involving Moses and Joshua, his *mešārēt*, the sojourn on the mountain for 40 days and nights, the delivery to Moses of the stone tablets, and the role of Aaron as *locum tenens* to Moses below the mountain (3), has the sole purpose of leading into the Golden Calf incident and the breaking and remaking of the covenant (24.12-15a, 18b; 31.18–34.35). That this extended account runs so closely parallel to Deuteronomy is readily explained if we recall the fundamental importance of *covenant violation* in the Deuteronomic scheme of things in general and as an interpretive principle in the history. Perlitt argued that chs. 32–34, the breaking and remaking of the tablets introduced in this third strand, is a distinct and fairly homogeneous narrative composed by a Levitical-Deuteronomic author during the reign of Josiah subsequent to the destruction of Bethel.[36] I agree with the main lines of Perlitt's source-critical argument, though a comparison of chs. 32–34 with the relevant and at times closely parallel narrative material in the Deuteronomic corpus will suggest a later date. This takes us on to the next stage of our inquiry.

35. Also Exod. 34.27-28. Much more frequently attested, however, is the alternative tradition that the decalogue was written by God himself (Deut. 4.13; 5.22; 9.10; 10.2, 4; cf. Exod. 24.12; 31.18; 32.15-16; 34.1).

36. Perlitt, *Bundestheologie*, pp. 203-32.

Moses on the Mountain Receives the Stone Tablets
(Exodus 24.12-15a, 18b, [31.18])

These verses introduce the account of the breaking and remaking of the covenant and covenant tablets, an account that is in effect a considerably expanded variant of Deuteronomy 9–10 (where the incident is one of several 'rebellions' in the wilderness) and one that, though it can be read as forming a structural unity with Exodus 19–24 (the making, breaking and remaking of a relationship), is not closely linked with these chapters. These verses, in fact, provide what linkage there is.[37] The resumptive *wayya'al 'el hāhār* (v. 18aβ), taking up from w*ayya'al mōšeh 'el-hāhār* (v. 15a), was required by the addition of Moses' admonition to the elders (v. 14) and the splicing in of the longer and later P version of Moses' encounter on the mountain (vv. 15b-18a). The sequence of events is straightforward: Moses is told to go up the mountain to take delivery of the two stone tablets inscribed by God; he does so forthwith in the company of Joshua, his acolyte, after conferring judicial authority on Aaron and Hur in his absence; in the course of a 40-day sojourn on the mountain he receives the stone tablets.

The Exodus narrative resembles the account in Deut. 9.9-11 in focusing on the law tablets (*lûḥôt*),[38] but describes them differently. They are *luḥôt hā'eben* (cf. the Deuteronomic *lûḥôt hā'ᵃbānîm*) or *lûḥôt hā'ēdut* (also at Exod. 32.15 and 34.29), a Priestly designation absent from Deuteronomy. The description of these artifacts in Exodus and Deuteronomy coincides only in the account of the remaking of the tablets (Exod. 34.1, 4 cf. Deut. 9.9-11; 10.1, 3). The two versions therefore have much in common: stone tablets written by God, indeed by the finger of God (Exod. 31.18; Deut. 9.10), emphasis on instruction (Exod. 24.12; Deut. 4.14), the mountain sojourn of 40 days and nights (Exod.

---

37. We might allow for the possibility, occasionally alluded to in the commentary tradition, that Exod. 32–34 provide in some of the narrative detail an intentional antithesis to chs. 19–24, e.g. the erection of an altar followed by sacrifices and meal of the apostates (32.5-6) contrasted with the same events at the sealing of the covenant (24.1-11).

38. Perlitt points out how the stone tablets, greatly emphasized in the Deuteronomic narrative (Deut. 4.13; 5.22; 9.9-11, 15, 17; 10.1-4), serve to unify the Exod. 32–34 account. They are variously designated *luḥôt hā'eben* (Exod. 24.12; 31.18), *lûḥôt hā'ᵃbānîm* (34.1, 4), *luḥôt hā'ēdût* (31.18; 32.15; 34.29) or simply *lûḥôt* (32.15-16; 34.1, 19, 28). See Perlitt, *Bundestheologie*, p. 207.

24.18b; Deut. 9.9, 11, 18; 10.10). As a link verse, moreover, 31.18 ('when God had finished speaking with him on Mount Sinai, God gave Moses the two tablets of the testimony, stone tablets written with the finger of God') is problematic and reads more like the conclusion to the P material immediately preceding. So far in this source God has not spoken; the reaction of the crowd described in the following verse (32.1) makes a better sequel to 24.18b recording Moses' long absence than to 31.18; the phrase *lûhôt hā'ēdût* is Priestly rather than Deuteronomic; and *har sînay* also suggests a P or at least a non-Deuteronomic context.[39]

The Making of the Golden Calf (Exodus 32.1-6)

The narrative of the event in Deuteronomy refers to the cult object in question in practically the same way as here (*massēkâ*, *'ēgel massēkâ*, Deut. 9.12, 16) and is even more negative with respect to Aaron (9.20). The delay and its sequel play out what is only implicit in Deut. 9.11-12—the 40-day absence of Moses on the mountain. However, Deuteronomy has no corresponding account of the manufacture of the calf icon as a precondition for the new cult and the new *ad hoc* polity centered on Aaron as cult leader (*yiqqāhēl hā'ām 'al-'ah^arōn*, Exod. 32.1).[40] The parallelism at this point shifts from Deuteronomy to Dtr's account of Jeroboam's cult establishment in the Northern Kingdom

---

39. *har sînay* occurs in the description of the theophany (19.11, 18, 20, 23) of uncertain provenance; in connection with the divine effulgence (*kābôd*) in 24.16 (P); in the preparation for the rewriting of the tablets (34.2, 4), also uncertain but betraying affinity with the initial theophany (34.3 cf. 19.13); and in the transfiguration episode (34.29, 32), probably one of the latest additions to the Sinai-Horeb narrative; cf. also *midbar sînay* in 19.1-2.

40. Since *qhl* (ni.) with *'al* can also connote hostile intent, specifically with reference to the Israelite throng in the wilderness (Num. 16.3; 17.7; 20.2), I would leave open the strong possibility that this is one of several indications of a rather half-hearted or inept attempt to mitigate Aaron's guilt. The acclamation and sacrifice are assigned to the people in MT as opposed to LXX (vv. 4, 6), and Aaron's own explanation for the calf icon (v. 24), inconsistent as it is with the account of its manufacture (v. 4), may not have sounded as ludicrous then as it does to us. Moreover, during the interrogation by Moses the latter assumes that Aaron was coerced by the mob into making it (32.21-22). See G.W. Coats, *Rebellion in the Wilderness: The Murmuring Motif in the Wilderness Traditions of the Old Testament* (Nashville: Abingdon Press, 1968), pp. 24-25.

(1 Kgs 12.26-32), which speaks of *'eglê zāhāb* (12.28), has the same acclamation (12.28; cf. Exod. 32.4, 8), the building of an altar and sacrifices offered on it (12.32, cf. Exod. 32.5, 6, 8), and the institution of a new festival (12.32-33, cf. Exod. 32.50)—all of which is too well known and acknowledged to require further elaboration.[41] Together with the interrogation of Aaron, his unconvincing and disingenuous self-exoneration, which contradicts the account of the manufacture of the calf icon, and the subsequent mass execution carried out by the 'sons of Levi' (32.21-29), this part of the narrative seems, therefore, to have been composed, with very considerable elaboration, on the basis of Dtr rather than of Deuteronomy.[42] Another indication is the use of gold in the manufacture of the icon, referred to in the Exodus version (32.2-4, 24, 31) and in Dtr (1 Kgs 12.28; 2 Kgs 10.29) but not in Deuteronomy. Also, as noted earlier, Deuteronomy always speaks of YHWH 'bringing out' rather than 'bringing up' from Egypt. In a manner quite typical of Pentateuchal narrative, Exod. 32.1-6 encodes concerns and polemics arising in the course of the history of Israel; in this instance, polemic directed against the Aaronid branch of the priesthood and the sanctuary of Bethel with which the Aaronids were associated and which retained its significance long after the fall of the kingdom of Samaria and probably also after its (alleged) destruction by Josiah.[43] So far, then, terminological and thematic indications favor the

41. The reader is therefore referred to the previously mentioned commentaries and to M. Auerbach and L. Smolar, 'Aaron, Jeroboam and the Golden Calves', *JBL* 86 (1967), pp. 129-40, who identified 13 points of similarity between the 2 texts.

42. Exod. 32.25-29 is no doubt meant to recall Jeroboam's appointment of non-Levitical priests (1 Kgs 12.31), but it is also a narrative elaboration on the basis of Deut. 10.8-9, which traces the Levitical office to the wilderness period at the time of the Horeb event (*bā'ēt hahî'*, Deut. 10.8-9; cf. 33.8-9).

43. The animus against the sanctuary of Bethel and its cultic officiants, as reflected in 1 Kgs 12 and 13, continued to the time of Josiah (see especially 13.2-3) and beyond. The (polemical) use of the designation *kōhⁿnîm hallᵉwiyîm* in Deuteronomy and the fact that the one allusion to Aaron in Deuteronomy is disparaging (Deut. 9.20) may be taken to point in the same direction. In 'The Judean Priesthood during the Neo-Babylonian and Early Achemenid Periods: A Hypothetical Reconstruction', *CBQ* 60 (1998), pp. 25-43, I revive and revise the old argument that Aaronid priests profited by the destruction of the Jerusalem temple to get a foothold in Judah, probably at a sanctuary at or near Bethel connected with the nearby administrative center of Mizpah. Something more will be said about this interpretive option at a later point of the paper.

chronological priority of Deuteronomy and Dtr to the Exodus version of
the breaking and remaking of the covenant. I assume, therefore, as a
point of departure, that Exodus 32 postdates not only the cultic inno-
vations of Jeroboam, assuming that they actually happened as described
or at all,[44] but also the actual composition of Dtr in the Neo-Babylonian
period.[45] We shall see whether this is borne out by a close reading of
the rest of the chapter.

Reaction to the Idolatrous Cult (Exodus 32.7-35)

In the opening paragraph Moses is alerted to what had transpired in his
absence at the foot of the mountain (32.7-10), although this does not
prevent him from expressing surprise and outrage when he comes upon
the scene (32.18-19). The synopsis (see Appendix) will show the close
affinity of this passage with Deut. 9.12-14, even though it would be
difficult to establish relative priority solely on the basis of lexical or
stylistic features. The expression $q^e\check{s}\bar{e}h$ '$\bar{o}rep$ (stiff-necked) and the
related verb form are, however, at home in Deuteronomic writings, and
I noted earlier how the replacement of $h\hat{o}\d{s}\bar{e}'t\bar{a}$ ('brought out') with
$he^{'e}l\hat{e}t\bar{a}$ ('brought up') fits a well-established pattern of usage. One
might be inclined to read the Exodus version as an attempt to simplify
Deut. 9.12-14, placing the intercessory prayer where we would expect
it, immediately after the threat of annihilation in 32.9-10. However, the
narrative logic is not perspicuous in either version. The expansive
account in the Exodus version of the Golden Calf and its cult, the sacrifices and acclamation (v. 8b), is intelligible on the assumption that at
this point the narrator is elaborating on the basis not of Deuteronomy
but of Dtr (1 Kgs 12.28-33).

---

44. Van Seters (*The Life of Moses*, pp. 295-99) argues that the incident is a
fictional composition of Dtr, the purpose of which was to provide an interpretive
framework for the history of the Northern Kingdom. This is saying more than we
know, especially since the Northern Kingdom did have its distinctive cult. But Jeroboam's cultic innovation is, in fact, presented as Israel's 'original sin' (1 Kgs
12.30; 13.34; 2 Kgs 17.21-23) transmitted and replicated in each successive reign,
as Dtr monotonously insists (*ḥt'* [hi.]). It is also paradigmatic for the moral and
religious failure of Judah, that imitated 'the customs which Israel introduced'
(2 Kgs 17.19 cf. 21.3, 11, 16).

45. Perlitt (*Bundestheologie*, pp. 207-208) dates the account of the manufacture
and destruction of the calf icon to the time of Josiah, the last third of the seventh
century, when the Bethel temple was destroyed.

The Exodus version continues with the intercession of Moses also paralleled, though not so closely, in Deuteronomy (Exod. 32.11-14; Deut. 9.25-29). Here, too, the indications favor the priority of the Deuteronomic version. Placating (literally: softening the face, *ḥlh* [pi.]) with respect to God occurs in Dtr (1 Sam. 13.12; 1 Kgs 13.6; 2 Kgs 13.4) and in the D-edited account of Jeremiah's temple sermon (Jer. 26.19). The term *'ebed* as an honorific title attached to great and holy figures in the tradition, Moses and David in particular, is strongly characteristic of Deuteronomic usage,[46] even if it is seldom used of the three ancestors. Abraham is, however, YHWH's servant in Gen. 26.24 (cf. also Ps. 105.42) in the context of the ancestral blessing, a characteristic feature of Deuteronomic editing. It may therefore be worth noting that, in the Exodus version, appeal to the three great *'ăbādîm* of YHWH is followed immediately by the promise of descendants as numerous as the stars, a typically Deuteronomic formulation.[47] Also Deuteronomic is the hostile attribution of evil intent to YHWH in bringing about the exodus from Egypt, expressed in direct quotation (cf. Deut. 1.27). The idea of YHWH changing his mind about punishing (with *nḥm* [ni.], as in Exod. 32.12, 14) is not characteristically Deuteronomic, but it is not attested elsewhere in texts earlier than Deuteronomy.[48]

The parallel versions continue with Moses' descent from the mountain, discovery of the aberrant cult activity, and destruction of both the newly inscribed tablets and the calf (Exod. 32.15-20; Deut. 9.15-17, 21). The versions agree in essentials: the discovery by Moses of the cultic transgression, the breaking of the tablets, and destruction of the cult object. Here and throughout, the Exodus version pays greater attention to the specific features of the calf cult that Deuteronomy refers to only in the abstract as one of a series of Israel's offences and 'turnings aside' in the wilderness. Exodus also focuses attention much more on Aaron (Exod. 32.21-24), whereas Deut. 9.20 makes no attempt to

---

46. With reference to Moses: Deut. 34.5; Josh. 1.2; 9.24; prophets: 1 Kgs 15.29; 2 Kgs 9.7, 36; 10.10; 14.25; 17.13, 23; 21.10; 24.2; Jer. 7.25; 25.6; 26.5; 29.19; 35.15; 44.4; David: 2 Sam. 3.18; 1 Kgs 8.24-26; 2 Kgs 19.34 (= Isa. 37.35); Jer. 33.21-22, 26.

47. Deut. 1.10; 10.22; 28.62; cf. Gen. 15.5-6; 22.17; 26.4-5—the last three occur in the context of a promise conditional on obedience.

48. Jer. 18.8; 26.3, 13, 19; 42.10; Joel 2.13; Jonah 3.10; 4.2. The only possible exception would be 2 Sam. 24.16.

exculpate him, merely stating that the intercessory prayer of Moses saved him from the death he deserved. One of the most salient differences, however, is in the designation of the tablets. *lûḥôt habbᵉrît* (Deut. 9.15) corresponds to *lûḥôt ha'ēdût* (Exod. 32.15; also 31.18 and 34.29), a term that occurs primarily in P contexts. In spite of the proposed Ugaritic parallel of the burning, grinding and scattering of the *disiecta membra* of Baal by his sister Anat, the account of the destruction of the icon points to a later rather than earlier date of composition.[49] The closest and perhaps the only biblical analogy to drinking contaminated water in a ritual context is the ordeal imposed on a wife suspected of sexual irregularity, a standard metaphor for religious apostasy (Num. 5.11-28 P). Here, too, the Exodus version looks like an elaboration on the basis of both Deuteronomy and Dtr.[50]

For our purpose little need be said about the discovery of the cultic activity at the foot of the mountain in which Joshua, the only companion of Moses on the mountain (24.13), is finally given a speaking role in the action, if a rather minor one (32.17-19a). It has no counterpart in Deuteronomy, is reminiscent in some respect of the curious account of the defeat of Amalek in which Joshua and Aaron also participate (Exod. 17.8-16),[51] and may be read as one of several narrative elaborations in the Exodus version.

The difficulty we experience in fitting the interrogation of Aaron by Moses and his rather lame self-exculpation (32.21-24) into the narrative

49. See, in addition to the commentaries, F.C. Fensham, 'The Burning of the Golden Calf and Ugarit', *IEJ* 16 (1966), pp. 191-93; S. Loewenstamm, 'The Making and Destruction of the Golden Calf', *Bib* 48 (1967), pp. 481-90; 56 (1975), pp. 330-43.

50. C.T. Begg ('The Destruction of the Calf [Exod 32,20 and Deut 9,21]', in N. Lohfink [ed.], *Das Deuteronomium: Entstehung, Gestalt und Botschaft* [Leuven: Leuven University Press, 1985], pp. 208-51) argued that Deut. 9.21 is a more detailed and elaborate version of Exod. 32.20. In defending the chronological priority of Deut. 9.21 against Begg, Van Seters (*The Life of Moses*, p. 307) makes a good point that 'the surface of the water' on which the ground-down calf was scattered (Exod. 32.20) finds its explanation in 'the stream coming down from the mountain' in Deut. 9.21.

51. Suggested by the overriding threat of annihilation, the same vocabulary for victory and defeat (*gbr*, *ḥlš*), and the use of rhythmic prose. See R.W.L. Moberly, *At the Mountain of God: Story and Theology in Exodus 32–34* (JSOTSup, 22; Sheffield: Sheffield Academic Press, 1983), pp. 111-12; Van Seters, *The Life of Moses*, p. 315.

as a whole is due to our ignorance of the historical circumstances behind the text. According to the Deuteronomic account of the apostasy Aaron was saved from sentence of death by the intercession of Moses (9.20), but we are not told that he made the idolatrous cult object. Taking off from this starting point, the Exodus version presents a decidedly unflattering, though not wholly condemnatory, view of Aaron's participation in the aberrant cult activity, and we would like to know why. Van Seters, who attributes the passage to his exilic Yahwist, rejects the still common connection of 32.1-6, 21-24 with an ancient cult tradition about Bethel and its alleged Aaronid clergy.[52] If, however, we could entertain the possibility that the Aaronid connection with Bethel was still a live issue in the province of Judah between the destruction of the first and construction of the second temple the situation would look rather different.[53]

The same conclusion finds support in the following episode, also without parallel in Deuteronomy, in which Levites earn their ordination (the 'filling of their hands') by exterminating 3000 of the transgressors (32.25-29; the number is intriguing, but I shall let it pass). Here, too, the author may have developed, somewhat after the manner of midrash, the notice in Deut. 10.8-9 about the appointment of Levites to a role of special responsibility vis-à-vis the ark of the covenant, combining it with a fairly transparent allusion to the Mosaic oracle on Levi (Deut. 33.8-11). The writer will also have had in mind the notice about Jeroboam's non-Levitical clergy (1 Kgs 12.31-32), which the historian (Dtr) may have added in view of contemporaneous strife between priestly factions.[54]

After the overtly Deuteronomic passage about guidance into the land (33.1-6), discussed earlier, several incidents illustrative and explanatory

52. Van Seters, *The Life of Moses*, p. 311.
53. See n. 43. It is interesting to observe that Noth (*Exodus*, pp. 244-45), who regarded the conversation between Moses and Aaron as 'evidently an addition', seemed to be moving in the same direction by proposing a situation prior to Aaronid hegemony (as attested in P) when Aaronid clergy were under attack for dubious cult practice.
54. Other expressions reminiscent of Jeroboam's cult establishment: the *'elōhê zāhāb* (32.31, also 32.2-4, 24 cf. 1 Kgs 12.28; 2 Kgs 10.29); the description of the act as a *hattā'āh gedōlāh* (32.21, 30-31); cf. 2 Kgs 17.21 and the numerous occasions in Dtr where Jeroboam's cult establishment is referred to as sinful and an occasion of sin for both kingdoms. See Perlitt, *Bundestheologie*, p. 209; Van Seters, *The Life of Moses*, pp. 315-17; Moberly, *At the Mountain of God*, pp. 54-56.

of the unique status of Moses have been imported into the Sinai-Horeb narrative complex (33.7-11, 12-16, 17-23; 34.29-35). Though incorporating other themes, especially that of guidance, these read like a series of short *midrašîm* on the phrase *pānîm 'el pānîm*, referring to Moses' unique relationship with the Deity.[55] They are without direct parallel in the Deuteronomistic literature, are probably among the latest expansions of the Sinai-Horeb story, and though of great intrinsic interest do not call for discussion in this essay.

The Remaking of the Covenant (34.1-28)

Here once again the Exodus narrative runs parallel to Deuteronomy at least initially (see the last section of the synopsis). YHWH tells Moses to carve two tablets like the former ones and declares his intention to inscribe on them the 'words' that were on the ones Moses smashed; Moses is told to go up (again!) in the morning, and he obeys both commands (Exod. 34.1-4; Deut. 10.1-3). YHWH then inscribes the decalogue on the tablets (Exod. 34.28b; Deut. 10.4a).[56] A synoptic reading at once brings out the differences. In the Deuteronomic version Moses is told to make a wooden chest for the tablets and to put them in it, which he does. Failure to mention the *'arôn* as depository of the tablets in Exodus may simply correlate with the postponed allusion to YHWH inscribing the decalogue; if they were not yet written they could not be deposited. The Exodus author instead includes ritual prescriptions to protect the sanctity of the *temenos*, the holy mountain, similar to the preparation for the theophany in 19.12-15: no one is to come up with him, and all human beings and livestock are to keep their distance (cf.19.12-13, 23). Both theophanies, the first public, the second private,

---

55. Since it was axiomatic that to see the face of God was to die, this kind of unmediated relationship called for explanation. Hence the cloud column (*'ammûd he'ānān*), the effulgence (*kābôd*) and the back or retro (*'aḥôr*), all theologoumena elaborating and attempting to explain Moses' face-to-face knowledge (Exod. 33.7-11, 12-23; 34.29-35).

56. The dubiety as to who is the subject of *wayyiktōb* (Exod. 34.28b) has occasioned a great deal of discussion that cannot be documented and evaluated here. It seems to me that the confusion has arisen through an editorial conflation of Moses writing the stipulations of the covenant immediately preceding (note the *inclusio* of vv. 10 and 27 both of which therefore refer to the bracketed stipulations) and YHWH writing the decalogue. The core text common to both Exod. 34.28b and Deut. 10.4a runs as follows: *wayyiktōb 'al-hallūḥōt 'et 'aśeret haddebārîm.*

take place in the morning (19.10, 16; 34.2 cf. 24.4).

Recent commentary on 34.6-7 has tended to reject Noth's view of this seven-member self-predication of YHWH as a *Zusatz*, a piece of bricolage put together out of 'customary, stereotyped phrases'.[57] If, as seems likely, it is in fact aboriginal to this context, it remains to be determined whether it derives directly from a liturgical source,[58] a sapiential milieu,[59] an exilic Yahwistic writer[60] or a member of the Deuteronomic school.[61] The sapiential affinities catalogued by Dentan and emphasized by Van Seters are certainly noteworthy, but so are the points of contact with Deuteronomic narrative and rhetoric, and the terms 'sapiential' and 'Deuteronomic' are not mutually exclusive. The liturgical expression *'ēl raḥûm wᵉḥannûn*, of frequent occurrence,[62] does not appear in Deuteronomy, but *'ēl raḥûm* does (4.31), as do also the related substantive and verb (13.18; 30.3; also 2 Kgs 13.23). The language of v. 7 is practically identical with the motive clause in the decalogic prohibition of image-making (Deut. 5.9-10; Exod. 20.5-6), and the presence of similar expressions elsewhere in Deuteronomy (e.g. 7.9) and in D-edited texts[63] would seem to suggest Deuteronomic affinity of some kind.

In his response to this private manifestation, which parallels the initial public theophany and, like it, leads to the making of a covenant, Moses introduces once again the guidance on the journey theme and does so in familiar Deuteronomic terms (34.8-9). This is the case not only with the description of the hapless Israelites as 'stiff-necked' (Deut. 9.6, 13; 31.27 cf. Exod. 32.9; 33.3, 5) but also with the idea of this same people as YHWH's *naḥᵃlâ,* expressed (by means of the substantive rather than the verb as here) in the longer intercessory prayer discussed earlier (Deut. 9.26, 29 cf. *'am naḥᵃlâ,* 4.20). The presentation

57. Noth, *Exodus*, p. 261.

58. A *Bekenntnisformel* according to J. Scharbert, 'Formgeschichte und Exegese von Ex. 34.6f.', *Bib* 38 (1957), pp. 130-50.

59. See R.C. Dentan, 'The Literary Affinities of Exodus XXXIV 6f.', *VT* 13 (1963), pp. 34-51.

60. See Van Seters, *The Life of Moses*, pp. 346-51.

61. See Perlitt, *Bundestheologie*, pp. 213-15.

62. Pss. 86.15; 103.8; 111.4; 112.4; 145.8; Joel 2.13; Jon. 4.2; Neh. 9.17, 31; 2 Chron. 30.9.

63. Van Seters (*The Life of Moses*, pp. 349-50) points to the frequent occurrence of *pqd*, 'punish', with God as subject, in D-edited passages in Jeremiah. This would indicate a late-Deuteronomic formulation in Exod. 34.

of Moses in the prophetic role of intercessor is one of the more prominent features of the Sinai-Horeb narrative as a whole.

The remade covenant is clearly identified as such by the inclusio of vv. 10 and 27: 'I am about to make a covenant... I have [just] made a covenant with you and with Israel'. The stipulations ($d^e\bar{a}r\hat{\imath}m$) enclosed within the _inclusio_, numbering anywhere from seven to eleven, are not part of our agenda. On the much debated subject of their function within the Sinai-Horeb context it will suffice to say that, if we are correct in viewing the framework and essence of the narrative as Deuteronomic, they do not constitute a new and distinct covenant; this will be effected only later, in Moab, just before entry into Canaan (Deut. 28.69). It is also worth noting that the only comment appended to the stipulations, following the requirement that adult males appear three times a year at the sanctuary, is couched in transparently Deuteronomic language (34.24).[64]

The entire passage 34.10-28 provides a poignant illustration of the dilemmas and dubieties attending the quest for source-critical certainty. It will be neither necessary nor profitable to rehearse all the options proposed. During the heyday of the Documentary Hypothesis, and still residually today, the preferential option was for J with D additions where parallels with distinctively Deuteronomic language could hardly be gainsaid.[65] But it seems clear today that this decision was based not on positive linguistic criteria but rather on the requirements of the hypothesis itself and specifically the need to identify a Yahwistic version of the covenant and decalogue to match the Elohist in chs. 19–24.

Now that this requirement is no longer binding, we do not find it surprising that the paranetic passages in the Sinai-Horeb pericope (19.3-6; 23.20-33; 33.1-4; 34.11-16) provide the clearest indications of a distinctively Deuteronomic rhetorical style, thematic and turn of phrase. Nowhere is this clearer than in the last of these (34.11-16), a fairly

---

64. _kî 'ôrîš gōyîm mippānêkā_ cf. Deut. 4.38; 9.3-5; 11.23; 18.12; Josh. 3.12; 23.9, 13, etc; _hirḥabtî 'et-g^ebûlekā_ cf. Deut. 12.20; 19.8. The rather obvious danger involved in the requirement that adult males appear three times a year at the sanctuary, namely, loss of or damage to property during these scheduled absences, is countered by reference to the decalogic prohibition of coveting (Exod. 20.17; Deut. 5.21).

65. See Noth, _Exodus_, p. 262, and for a brief review of opinions J.I. Durham, _Exodus_ (WBC, 3; Waco, TX: Word Books, 1987), pp. 458-59.

close, sometimes verbatim, parallel to Deut. 7.1-5.[66] We need look no further for the source of the preceding statement attached to the announcement of a covenant (34.10), a statement of great theological interest. The appeal to experience, reminiscent of 19.3-6, points in this direction. So also the marvellous deeds (*niplā'ôt*) of YHWH, whether performed in the past or announced for the future, whether in judgment or salvation (Josh. 3.5; Judg. 6.13; cf. Deut. 11.7; Exod. 3.20). Use of the verb *br'* (create) in connection with these deeds unfolding in the history of the people is also Deuteronomic (Deut. 4.31) and calls to mind the language of the exilic Isaiah.[67] The awe-inspiring nature of the divine activity (*nôrā'*, Deut. 10.21; 2 Sam. 7.23), as of the divine essence expressed in the Name (Deut. 7.21; 10.17; 28.58), is also a distinctively Deuteronomic theme that stands here as a climax to the covenant announcement.

Final, but Not Definitive, Reflections

The predominance of parenesis in our pericope would by itself lead us to suspect a debt to Deuteronomy, that most homiletic of books known to Philo under the title of *The Protreptics*. The closer but selective and by no means exhaustive scrutiny that (building on the work of many predecessors) I have dedicated to the language and idiom of the Sinai-Horeb pericope seems to confirm this suspicion. The Sinai-Horeb episode is of obvious importance, since it incorporates the interpretative principles according to which the past is constructed and the course of the future projected. It is the hinge on which the reminiscence of the Deuteronomic Moses turns. It seems to me likely that, just as the predictive element in the discourse of Moses in Deuteronomy is filled out in the history (Dtr), so the reminiscence (from Egypt to Canaan) dictates the scope and intent of a particular stage in the story of ethnic origins. But verification of this proposal awaits further detailed study of other parts of the narrative in Genesis, Exodus and Numbers.

We need hardly insist that the kind of history favored by these

66. On the characteristically Deuteronomic *šᵉmor-lᵉkā*, *hiššāmer* and other linguistic features of the passage, see F. Langlamet, 'Israël et "l'habitant du pays": Vocabulaire et formules d'Ex XXXIV,11-16', *RB* 76 (1969), pp. 321-50. Perlitt (*Bundestheologie*, p. 221) noted how the notorious Deuteronomic *Numeruswechsel* also appears in this passage (vv. 11-12, 14-16 singular, v. 13 plural).

67. Pointed out by Van Seters, *The Life of Moses*, p. 354, with reference to earlier works.

Deuteronomists is paradigmatic and expressive of situations and concerns of contemporaneous relevance. Unfortunately, however, the task of identifying the situation in which the history was produced is beset by numerous problems, not least of which is dating the successive stages in the composition of Deuteronomy. Converging considerations seem to me to point to the Neo-Babylonian or early Persian period (from the destruction of the first to the construction of the second temple) as the most likely time-frame for the composition of the Deuteronomic account of Sinai-Horeb, and therefore probably the Deuteronomic history of origins in general. One of these indications, affinity with prophetic texts from the exilic and early postexilic periods, would appear to merit closer scrutiny. At several points these texts evince a situation of bitter religious factional struggle, including strife between priestly factions, and the same situation is reflected in the Deuteronomic Sinai-Horeb paradigmatic history, which remains true even if Aaron is not depicted in the guise of a priest. This is consistent with what we know or can surmise was going on in Judah in the half century or so following the fall of Jerusalem, including the struggle to re-establish a central cult in Jerusalem, counter-claims from other quarters probably involving priests associated with Bethel past or present, accusations of apostasy exchanged between Judeo-Babylonians and Palestinians, the adherents of different priestly 'houses', and so forth.

It is difficult, and perhaps unwise, to attempt further determination of the origin and authorship of this historical construct beyond its evident dependence on Deuteronomy and Dtr, both in circulation (but with whom and where?) in the neo-Babylonian period. While I agree with much of Van Seters's careful analysis of the relevant texts, I do not see the point of keeping the title Yahwist for the author. Respect for continuity in the scholarly *diadoche* is all well and good, but the title is not only descriptively inappropriate, a case of *obscurum per obscurius*, but misleading. Even if one accepts the former quasi-consensus on the broad extent of the Yahwistic work, which Van Seters appears to do, one cannot simply lift a historical narrative out of the tenth or ninth century and relocate it unchanged and intact in the sixth century BCE. I therefore prefer to refer to the work we are envisaging as 'the Deuteronomic account of national origins' or something of the sort, leaving open the question whether it is the work of authors or editors, of an individual, a committee or a school.

APPENDIX:
SYNOPSIS OF DEUTERONOMY AND EXODUS VERSIONS

Deuteronomy 9.12-14

YHWH said to me, 'Arise, go down quickly from here, for your people that you brought out from Egypt has corrupted itself; they have turned aside quickly from the way I commanded them; they have made for themselves a molten image.

YHWH said to me, 'I have seen that this people is a stiff-necked people. Now let me alone, so I may destroy them and wipe out their name from under heaven. But I will make you into a nation more powerful and numerous than they are.'

Deuteronomy 9.25-29

I lay prostrate before YHWH these forty days and forty nights,[68] for YHWH had thought to destroy you. I prayed to YHWH saying, 'Lord YHWH, do not destroy your people and your inheritance which you redeemed by your greatness, whom you brought out from Egypt with a mighty hand! Remember your servants Abraham, Isaac and Jacob; do not regard the stubbornness of this people, or their wickedness, or their sin,

Exodus 32.7-10

YHWH spoke to Moses, 'Go down for your people that you brought up from the land of Egypt has corrupted itself; they have turned aside quickly from the way you commanded them; they have made for themselves a molten calf. They have bowed down to it and sacrificed to it, and they have said, 'These are your gods, O Israel, who brought you up from the land of Egypt.'

YHWH said to Moses, 'I have seen that this people is a stiff-necked people. Let me alone, that my anger may blaze against them and I may consume them. But I will make you into a great nation.

Exodus 32.11-14

Moses placated YHWH his God, saying, 'YHWH, why should your anger blaze against your people whom you brought out from the land of Egypt with great power and with a mighty hand?
[13]Remember Abraham, Isaac and Israel your servants to whom you swore by your own person, saying to them, "I will increase your descendants like the stars in the sky, and all this land which I said I would give to your descendants they will inherit forever."

68. *wā'etnappal lipnê YHWH 'et 'arbā'îm hayyôm wᵉ'et-'arbā'îm hallaylâ* takes up the narrative line from 9.18 after the interposition of 9.22-24, dealing with different incidents, and takes it further, especially by giving the text of Moses' prayer.

lest the land from which you brought us out should say, "Because YHWH was unable to bring them to the land which he promised them, and out of hatred for them, he brought them out to slay them in the wilderness." For they are your people and your inheritance whom you brought out by your great power and your outstretched arm.'

[19b]YHWH heeded me that time also.

[12]Why should the Egyptians say, "With evil intent he brought them out to kill them on the mountains, and to wipe them off the face of the earth?" Turn from your fierce anger and repent of this evil against your people!'

[14]YHWH repented of the evil which he said he would do to his people.

Deuteronomy 9.15-17, 21

[15]Then I turned and came down from the mountain, and the mountain was burning with fire; and the two tablets of the covenant in my two hands.

Exodus 32.15-20

[15]Moses turned and came down from the mountain
and the two tablets of the testimony in his hand; tablets written on both sides, on this side and on that they were written. [16]The tablets were the work of God, and the writing was the writing of God engraved on the tablets. [17]When Joshua heard the sound of the people as they shouted, he said to Moses, 'there is a sound of warfare in the camp.' [18]He said, 'It is not the sound of shouting for victory, nor the sound of the cry of defeat; it is the sound of revelry that I hear.'

[16]I saw that you had sinned against YHWH your God, making for yourselves a molten calf. You had turned aside quickly from the way that YHWH had commanded you.

[19]As soon as he approached the camp and saw the calf and the dancing, Moses was very angry.

[17]So I seized the two tablets and threw them from my two hands and smashed them in your sight.

He threw the tablets from his hand and smashed them at the foot of the mountain.

[21]I took your sinful object you had made, the calf, and burnt it with fire. I crushed it, grinding it very thoroughly until it was as fine as dust, and I threw its dust into the stream coming down from the mountain.	[20]He took the calf they had made and burnt it with fire. He ground it until it was fine, and scattered (it) on the surface of the water and made the Israelites drink (it).

Deuteronomy 10.1-3	*Exodus 34.1-4, 28b*
[1]At that time YHWH said to me, 'hew for yourself two tablets of stone like the former ones.	[1]YHWH said to Moses: 'hew for yourself two tablets of stone like the former ones; and I will write on the tablets the words which were on the former tablets which you smashed. [2]Be ready in the morning, and come up in the morning to Mount Sinai, and present yourself to me there on the mountain top. [3]Let no one come up with you, let no one be seen on all the mountain, and let no flocks or herds pasture in front of that mountain.'
Come up to me on the mountain and make for yourself a wooden ark; [2]I will write on the tablets the words which were on the former tablets which you smashed, and you shall put them in the ark.'	
[3]So I made an ark of acacia wood, and I cut two tablets of stone as formerly and went up the mountain, the two tablets in my hand. [4]He wrote on the tablets, like the former writing, the ten commandments.	[4]He cut two tablets of stone as formerly. Moses rose early in the morning and went up Mount Sinai as YHWH had commanded him. He took in his hand the two tablets of stone like the first... [28b]He (YHWH?) wrote on the tablets the words of the covenant, the ten commandments.

THE DEUTERONOMISTS AND THE FORMER PROPHETS, OR WHAT
MAKES THE FORMER PROPHETS DEUTERONOMISTIC?

A. Graeme Auld

It may be that my colleagues contributing chapters about the
Deuteronomists and Torah or Latter Prophets or Writings know what—
or who—they are talking about. And, if that is so, then they are doubly
more fortunate than I am. Not only do I become less and less sure that I
know *what* the Deuteronomists did in respect of the composition of the
Former Prophets, I also wonder more and more with my British colleague Richard Coggins[1] *whether* whoever-did-what should be called
'Deuteronomists'. The title 'The Deuteronomists and the Former Prophets' may be read as assuming too much. I prefer the alternative
title—a question with more of an edge: 'What Makes the Former Prophets Deuteronomistic?' I am inclined to answer: 'Are the Former
Prophets in fact Deuteronomistic?' But perhaps I should first unpack
the question a little further.

1. Are the Former Prophets in their Entirety Deuteronomistic?

The title and much of the practice of the Deuteronomistic History Section of the Society for Biblical Literature would appear to agree. And
the work of Robert Polzin[2] affirms this although he, I think, would not
be very comfortable in much of the work of that section. The first
mention of the Deuteronomistic History in his *Samuel and the*

---

1. R. Coggins, 'What Does "Deuteronomistic" Mean?', in Jon Davies, Graham
Harvey and Wilfred G.E. Watson (eds.), *Words Remembered, Texts Renewed:
Essays in Honour of John F.A. Sawyer* (JSOTSup, 195; Sheffield: Sheffield Aca-
demic Press, 1995), pp. 135-48; reprinted as the first essay in the present volume.
2. R. Polzin, *Moses and the Deuteronomist* (New York: Seabury, 1980); *idem*,
Samuel and the Deuteronomist (San Francisco: HarperSanFrancisco, 1989); *idem*,
David and the Deuteronomist (Bloomington: Indiana University Press, 1993).

Deuteronomist[3] is to blame Miller and Roberts for not setting the ark story in the context of the climactic end of the monarchy. And he goes on to blame 'Noth's picture of how the history came to be written'[4] for 'mostly fail[ing] to account for its artful construction';[5] and Van Seters[6] for the failure of his attempt to 'provide "evidence" concerning what belongs to Dtr's history (much more than previously thought), what predates it (much less than originally maintained), and what was later added to it (much more than anyone had realized)'.[7] Polzin is critical of scholars who are or would have been at home in that section for not taking sufficiently seriously the equation of Former Prophets, or at least Deuteronomy plus Former Prophets, with Deuteronomistic History.

And yet, are the books Joshua–Kings 'an entirety'? *Every Promise Fulfilled* (L.D. Hawk),[8] *Together in the Land* (G. Mitchell),[9] *Joshua and the Rhetoric of Violence* (L.L. Rowlett),[10] *A Functional Discourse Grammar of Joshua* (N. Winther-Nielsen)[11]—that clutch of recent final form readings of just one book within the Former Prophets—tend in a direction both similar to and different from Polzin's 'x and the Deuteronomist' series. The authors of these readings of Joshua evince little interest in the other Former Prophets or in Deuteronomy. How like Polzin are they? Polzin's strength is the brilliantly attentive reading of the whole text before him. Yet, as soon as that is said, we have to ask whether his approach leads him to avoid having to face some big questions. By discussing the premonarchic story, with all of Deuteronomy to

3. Polzin, *Samuel*, p. 8.
4. M. Noth, *Überlieferungsgeschichtliche Studien* (Tübingen: Max Niemeyer, 3rd edn, 1967).
5. Polzin, *Samuel*, p. 10.
6. J. Van Seters, *In Search of History: Historiography in the Ancient World and the Origins of Biblical History* (New Haven: Yale University Press, 1983).
7. Polzin, *Samuel*, p. 14.
8. L.D. Hawk, *Every Promise Fulfilled: Contesting Plots in Joshua* (Literary Currents in Biblical Interpretation; Louisville, KY: Westminster/John Knox Press, 1991).
9. G. Mitchell, *Together in the Land: A Reading of the Book of Joshua* (JSOTSup, 134; Sheffield: JSOT Press, 1993).
10. L.L. Rowlett, *Joshua and the Rhetoric of Violence: A New Historicist Analysis* (JSOTSup, 226; Sheffield: Sheffield Academic Press, 1996).
11. N. Winther-Nielsen, *A Functional Discourse Grammar of Joshua: A Computer-Assisted Rhetorical Structure Analysis* (ConBOT, 40; Stockholm: Almqvist & Wiksell, 1995).

Judges subsumed under the figure of Moses, separate from his discussion of Samuel and David and whoever follows, Polzin never actually has the whole text before him. We shall have to decide, once we have his whole text before us, whether he has convincingly described a single author (actual or implied), let alone a single Deuteronomist.

Any strong definition of the Former Prophets as '*the* Deuteronomistic History' implies comprehensive attention to the entirety of Joshua–Kings, possibly more than Joshua–Kings, but at least as much as Joshua–Kings. However, 'Deuteronomistic History/Historiography', without a definite article, is currently preferred by several scholars. It is a more tolerant term; you might fairly expect to find such an approach to history differently manifested in Jeremiah and in Kings, and as differently in Joshua or Samuel as in Kings or Jeremiah. And yet, if the term becomes too tolerant, then we will all find ourselves where I acknowledge I already am: not being sure what we are talking about.

2. *The State of the Question Sketched*

Of course Noth never was where Polzin and all final-form critics think he should have been. He detected a work constructed by one author, whose contents were not identical with the set of finished books, and whose main parts did not correspond with the present division between these books. But was there ever such a work? And should its authorship have been attributed to one or more Deuteronomists?

We have been talking for over 20 years of Smend and Cross and their disciples, of German and American schools disagreeing over Noth's inheritance, and taking their start from single articles by Smend (1971)[12] and Cross (1968)[13] to which Noth was no longer able to respond. I make no comment on America, but order seems to have broken down in the world of German-speaking *Deuteronomismus*. After a prolific career of scholarship on many Old Testament topics, Claus

---

12. R. Smend, 'Das Gesetz und die Völker: Ein Beitrag zur deuteronomistischen Redaktionsgeschichte', in H.W. Wolff (ed.), *Probleme biblischer Theologie: Gerhard von Rad zum 70. Geburtstag* (Munich: Chr. Kaiser Verlag, 1971).

13. F.M. Cross, 'The Structure of the Deuteronomic History', *Perspectives in Jewish Learning* (Annual of the College of Jewish Studies, 3; Chicago, 1968), pp. 9-24; republished in revised form in *Canaanite Myth and Hebrew Epic: Essays in the History of the Religion of Israel* (Cambridge, MA: Harvard University Press, 1973), pp. 274-89.

Westermann[14] has doubted whether such a unified work ever existed: the stuff of which each of the books Joshua to Kings is made is quite varied; each book had its own development and was separately edited after Jerusalem's collapse. Then Ernst Würthwein, after completing a two-volume commentary on the books of Kings (1984)[15] which uses the DtrH-P-N terminology of the Smend school, has published a new paper[16] proposing Samuel, Judges and Joshua as later introductions to the royal story told in Kings; each succeeds the one before (or after) to tell a still earlier story. The issues before us have been very well addressed, and differently evaluated, in volumes published in 1996 from just outside the German language area.

Erik Eynikel's Flemish doctoral thesis of 1989 was revised and issued in English as *The Reform of King Josiah and the Composition of the Deuteronomistic History*.[17] Eynikel pays tribute to Westermann and agrees with him that 'the unique character of each book prevents seeing the books of the dtr history as parts of one historical work'. Yet his own solution seems even closer to Würthwein, whose late essay (1994)[18] was not available to him. He too proposes an earlier version of the story beginning with Solomon as the earliest Deuteronomistic or proto-Deuteronomistic work and he too reckons with two main subsequent redactional strata in Kings. However, whereas Würthwein sees Samuel, Judges and Joshua as successive and later introductions to the story of the kings, Eynikel follows his mentor, Brekelmans,[19] in proposing most of Joshua–1 Samuel 12 as the product of one main draft. Then the most recently published relevant Dutch dissertation[20] treats the account of

---

14. C. Westermann, *Die Geschichtsbücher des Alten Testaments: Gab es ein deuteronomistisches Geschichtswerk?* (TBü, 87; Gütersloh: Chr. Kaiser Verlag, 1994).

15. E. Würthwein, *Die Bücher der Könige* (ATD, 11.1-2; Göttingen: Vandenhoeck & Ruprecht, 1977–84).

16. E. Würthwein, 'Erwägungen zum sog. deuteronomistischen Geschichtswerk, Eine Skizze', in *idem, Studien zum deuteronomistischen Geschichtswerk* (BZAW, 227; Berlin: W. de Gruyter, 1994), pp. 1-11.

17. E. Eynikel, *The Reform of King Josiah and the Composition of the Deuteronomistic History* (OTS, 33; Leiden: E.J. Brill, 1996).

18. Würthwein, 'Erwägungen'.

19. C. Brekelmans, 'Joshua xxiv: Its Place and Function', in J.A. Emerton (ed.), *Congress Volume: Leuven 1989* (VTSup, 43; Leiden: E.J. Brill, 1991), pp. 1-9 (7-8).

20. P.S.F. Van Keulen, *Manasseh through the Eyes of the Deuteronomists* (OTS, 38; Leiden: E.J. Brill, 1996).

Manasseh in 2 Kgs 21.1-18 as a single composition and indeed finds
2 Kings 21–25 as a whole to be broadly unitary and of exilic origin.

The other very significant recent resource has been edited by Albert
de Pury, Thomas Römer and Jean-Daniel Macchi from the offerings by
15 contributors at 7 seminars or lectures held between January and June
1995 under the auspices of Switzerland's French-speaking Faculties of
Theology.[21]

The longest single piece is Römer and de Pury's comprehensive and
magisterial review of 'Deuteronomistic historiography'.[22] They ask at
the end: what about the connections that work just below the level of
the present books? Their own preference, like Noth's, is to locate Dtr
prior to or behind the present text! They are sympathetic to McKenzie's
account of 'Deuteronomistic History' in *The Anchor Bible Dictionary*.[23]
They are not persuaded by the rejection of a continuous Dtr History,
each on different grounds, by Westermann and Würthwein. Römer and
de Pury criticize Würthwein for saying nothing in his brief and
schematic essay about the relationship of Deuteronomy to this expanding corpus. And, in a footnote response to Eynikel's conclusion that 'at
best we can speak of a dtr redaction in which the historical books are
parenetically interpreted',[24] they complain: 'In what way is this pare-
netic interpretation opposed to the idea of a Dtr History?'[25] For me also,
these are two of the key questions, although I would rephrase the second: Is there a history if there are only separate books? I would also
rephrase their other question: Why do we continue to talk about
Deuteronomistic authors in or of Joshua to Kings if we do not make
plain just how Deuteronomy relates to these books?

In this Swiss volume, it is Ernst-Axel Knauf who issues the most out-
spoken rejection of a Dtr historical work.[26] Yet he too continues to use
the term 'dtr' and to consider it beyond question that the prophetic

21. A. de Pury, T. Römer and J.-D. Macchi (eds.), *Israël construit son histoire:
L'historiographie deutéronomiste à la lumière de recherches récentes* (MB, 34;
Geneva: Labor et Fides, 1996).

22. T. Römer and A. de Pury, 'L'historiographie deutéronomiste (HD): Histoire
de le recherche et enjeux du débat', in de Pury, Römer and Macchi (eds), *Israël
construit son histoire*, pp. 9-120.

23. S. McKenzie, 'Deuteronomistic History', *ABD*, II, pp. 160-68.

24. Eynikel, *The Reform*, p. 361.

25. Römer and de Pury, 'L'historiographie deutéronomiste', p. 84 n. 339.

26. E.-A. Knauf, ' "L'historiographie deutéronomiste" (DtrG) existe-t-elle?', in
de Pury, Römer and Macchi (eds.), *Israël construit son histoire*, pp. 409-18.

books, including the Former Prophets, had been edited in 'dtr' manner. He defines 'dtr' as a literary style and collection of theological ideas, both borrowed from Assyrian imperialism. Mischievously, I think, he concludes with a canonical observation:

> When we consider the Psalms, which present as a collection the systematic theology of the OT in the OT, we find no testimony to 'DtrG'. What we do find attested are: the Torah (Pss. 74; 95; 135), the Torah with Joshua as supplement (Pss. 105; 114; 136[?]), the 'former prophets' Joshua–2 Kings (Pss. 44; 66; 68; 129[?]) and the 'historical books' Genesis–2 Kings (Pss. 78; 80; 81[?]; 89; 102; 103[?]; 106; 136[?]). These divisions ought to suffice both for theology and for exegesis.[27]

Nicely done! No witness in the psalms to such an entity as Deuteronomy–2 Kings. But, if we lose the specific link between Deuteronomy and Joshua–Kings, must we not also give up the term 'dtr' and find another term for Assyrian style and theology—like 'Assyrian' or 'Assyrian-influenced'?

Why has this work, or why have these books, been called 'Deuteronomistic'? Is it just that the story begins in Deuteronomy and continues on through successive books? Is it also, perhaps even more important, that the teaching of Deuteronomy is held to provide the categories and set the agenda? Dietrich and Mayes take different approaches to these issues in the Swiss volume. Dietrich[28] notes that when you start reading the history at the beginning (with Deut. 1) you are *not* unprepared for the conflicts in Judges and 1 Samuel on the relative merits of judges and kings as leaders. He admits that the judges about whom Moses legislates in Deut. 16.18–17.13 and the deliverer/rulers of Judges and 1 Samuel hardly represent the same office; and he admits too that Deut. 17.14-20 on the king has been supplemented from 1 Samuel 8. Yet an earlier version of Deuteronomy had provided categories relevant not just to reading but also to writing the story of the move to monarchy. Mayes,[29] however, supports the argument advanced in a series of publications by Lohfink and Braulik that Deuteronomy's law

---

27. Knauf, '"L'historiographie deutéronomiste"', p. 418.

28. W.L. Dietrich, 'Histoire et loi: Historiographie deutéronomiste et loi deutéronomique à l'example du passage de l'époque des Juges à l'époque royale', in de Pury, Römer and Macchi (eds.), *Israël construit son histoire*, pp. 297-323.

29. A.D.H. Mayes, 'De l'idéologie deutéronomiste à la théologie de l'Ancien Testament', in de Pury, Römer and Macchi (eds.), *Israël construit son histoire*, pp. 477-508.

of the king is entirely a Deuteronomistic supplement, that the constitutional heart of Deuteronomy in chs. 16–18 is secondary or Deuteronomistic. Their case had been further elaborated by Schäfer-Lichtenberger in her discussion of the laws on king and prophet as capstones of the dtr constitution for Israel.[30]

I need at this point to make one of the key questions more precise. 'Deuteronomistic' was coined to describe material which, though not Deuteronomic because not part of the book of Deuteronomy, was dependent on Deuteronomy or decisively influenced by it. The influence was seen to be flowing *from* Deuteronomy *to* the narrative books. If we now recognize the flow as going in the opposite direction, or even mainly in the other direction, then we must give up on the adjective 'Deuteronomistic'. Moreover, if we still find it appropriate to stress a link between Deuteronomy and the Former Prophets, we should talk about the latter as pre- or proto-Deuteronomic. Of course that will not make the *Former* Prophets any earlier; rather, a much later Deuteronomy would be implied than commonly supposed. Römer helpfully reminded those attending the 1993 SBL celebrations of Noth's work that covenant and election are pre-Deuteronomic usages, but applied to the king and not to Israel.[31] Here the so-called 'dtr' literature of the Former Prophets shares the language of the Psalms. One of the results of the later Deuteronomic democratization of this language is that there was little place left for a king in that later book. We have to change our terminology so that it more obviously 'goes with the flow', and 'Deuteronomistic', meaning influenced *by* Deuteronomy, is no longer appropriate.

Another issue which the Swiss volume keeps returning to is: which text is the dtr text? Schenker[32] attractively focuses on the Masoretic treatment of Jeroboam and Ahijah in 1 Kings 11 and 14, which is not only significantly longer than the LXX, but is often said to be

30. C. Schäfer-Lichtenberger, *Josua und Salomo: Eine Studie zu Autorität und Legitimität des Nachfolgers im Alten Testament* (VTSup, 58; Leiden: E.J. Brill, 1995), pp. 69-106. Dietrich takes issue with her ('Histoire et loi', p. 321).

31. T. Römer, 'The Book of Deuteronomy', in S.L. McKenzie and M.P. Graham (eds.), *The History of Israel's Traditions: The Heritage of Martin Noth* (JSOTSup, 182; Sheffield: Sheffield Academic Press, 1994), pp. 201-202.

32. A. Schenker, 'Jéroboam et la division du royaume dans la septante ancienne: LXX 1 R 12, 24 a-z,TM 11-12; 14 et l'histoire deutéronomiste', in de Pury, Römer and Macchi (eds.), *Israël construit son histoire*, pp. 193-236.

significantly more Dtr. In a recent related article,[33] he criticizes Willis and McKenzie, who have defended the MT in 1 Kgs 12.2 on the basis of homoeoteleuton diagnosed between *mṣrym* and *'prym*. Knauf[34] talks of several dtr schools with their own texts up to the third and second century BCE: quite appropriate for what till the second century had been deuterocanonical texts. Fernandez Marcos has reminded us of some of the literary implications of the fluidity of our texts in ancient times.[35] In my own 1995 SBL paper, 'What Makes Judges Deuteronomistic?',[36] I drew attention to arguments from text criticism and literary history for judging that the first two-and-a-half chapters of Judges are not part of, but depend on, material widely reckoned late Dtr. Much of the redactional study of the so-called Deuteronomistic History pays too little attention to the head-breaking complexity of the textual data. (I admit that the recent contributions on the text of Joshua by Svensson[37] and Winther-Nielsen[38] have been arguing in the opposite direction.)

3. *Hints Toward a Solution?*

My own preference too, increasingly, is to read the influence backwards from Kings, not forwards from Deuteronomy: backwards from the story of the Kings, through Samuel, and on to Deuteronomy. If I return to my alternative title for this paper, give it another spin, and ask again, in the light of what I am researching at the moment, 'What makes the Former Prophets Deuteronomistic?', I must answer: 'Just some further steps down the same road'.

I have been cross-checking and extending my results published a couple of years ago as *Kings without Privilege*,[39] and I find myself both in and out of sympathy with the trends I have been describing. Some

33. A. Schenker, 'Un cas de critique narrative au service de la critique textuelle (1 Rois 11,43–12,2-3,20)', *Bib* 77 (1996), pp. 219-26.

34. Knauf, ' "L'historiographie deutéronomiste" ', pp. 413-14.

35. N. Fernández Marcos, *Scribes and Translators: Septuagint and Old Latin in the Books of Kings* (VTSup, 54; Leiden: E.J. Brill, 1994).

36. A.G. Auld, 'What Makes Judges Deuteronomistic?', in *idem, Joshua Retold: Synoptic Perspectives* (Edinburgh: T. & T. Clark, 1998), pp. 120-26.

37. J. Svensson, *Towns and Toponyms in the Old Testament* (ConBOT, 38; Stockholm: Almqvist & Wiksell, 1994).

38. Winther-Nielsen, *A Functional Discourse Grammar of Joshua*.

39. A.G. Auld, *Kings without Privilege: David and Moses in the Story of the Bible's Kings* (Edinburgh: T. & T. Clark, 1994).

critical readers of *Kings without Privilege* have properly noted that the texts which Samuel–Kings and Chronicles share, the synoptic portions of these books, do not exhaust the links between the two works. Chronicles certainly, and Samuel–Kings possibly, allude to material in the other which they do not transcribe, and they also offer quite different information about characters from the other. Since much of this relates to prophetic figures, I am studying the narratives about divine intermediaries that both works present, as well as the reports and notes that are found only in one book or the other.

In the text shared by Samuel–Kings and Chronicles—what I am currently calling 'the Book of Two Houses' (the houses being those of David and of Yahweh, not of Judah and of Israel)—a great deal of the evaluation rests on the shoulders of the not-very-many prophetic stories that shared book contains: Nathan and the promise of two houses, Gad and David's census-test, Ahijah and Shemaiah and the division of the kingdom, Micaiah and a first attempt at common action after the division, Isaiah and Hezekiah, and Huldah and Josiah. Crucially important as they are for the understanding of the book, most of these intermediary stories report royal initiative in consulting the deity through them.

I find it significant that, as Samuel-Kings extend and build on this shared inheritance, the prophetic role becomes primary—Samuel right at the beginning, Nathan in the stories relating to Bathsheba and Solomon, and Elijah dominating the middle of Kings—all of these giants now take the initiative and confront. The title 'Prophets' or 'Former Prophets' now reflects those who are leading figures more accurately than the title 'Kings'. This shift is of course clearest in the case of Nathan. In 2 Samuel 7, material shared with 1 Chronicles 17, Nathan is consulted by the king. But in 2 Samuel 12 and 1 Kings 1, both within material unique to Samuel–Kings, Nathan takes the same sort of confrontational initiative over against David as we are familiar with in stories about Samuel or Elijah.

This classic, which I am calling the Book of Two Houses, not only underlies Samuel–Kings and Chronicles but has influenced many other biblical texts. David's sin over the census, far from being a late supplement to the books of Samuel, provides the categories for stories as diverse as the numberings in the wilderness, the opening of the book of Job, and the three-headed Philistine commando-force that punishes Saul for counting his people after not waiting for Samuel in 1 Samuel 13.

Other elements too of Saul stories have 'already' appeared in the record of David. The divine spirit, which makes mischief of Saul, has already led Ahab astray in the Micaiah story. The opening presentation of Samuel owes not a little to the Nathan oracle in 2 Samuel 7. It is because the foreign queen of Sheba has already been so amazed at Solomon in my Book of Two Houses, copied in both Kings and Chronicles, that 'there was no more spirit in her' that the foreign Rahab could apply the same words to her people's reaction to Israel's reputation (Josh. 2.11). The transition from Moses to Joshua is adapted from the transition from David to Solomon; as David did not built the holy 'place', so Moses did not enter the land. The troubled period of Israel under the Judges follows on the Moses-Joshua story as the troubled story of Northern Israel follows on David-Solomon. An earlier story was built by redeveloping the classic story of Jerusalem's kings.

And it was from this growing, developing story that important elements of Deuteronomy were also drawn. My preliminary results here interest and puzzle me. I am aware that the old picture of a legislative core in Deuteronomy 12–26, encased in encouragement in 5–11 and 27–30, and set finally in an outer narrative frame, is too simple as a history of how Deuteronomy was composed. Indeed I was referring earlier to the 'Deuteronomistic' affiliations of the constitutional chs. 16–18 at the very heart of the book. However, I am surprised to find the language shared by Deuteronomy and the Book of Two Houses clustering in the opening 11 chapters, more precisely in Deuteronomy 1, 4 and 9–11, while parallels with the language added to that book in the writing of Samuel-Kings appear in Deuteronomy 16–18 and 27–30.

Writing in *The Anchor Bible Dictionary*, McKenzie suggested that 'a more fruitful approach to the question of the composition of the DH may be found not in late redactions (a task that has preoccupied many researchers), but in the search for sources and redactions preceding the edition of Dtr 1' and also that 'Polzin has failed to show how his approach may interact with historical criticism'.[40] My remarks on 'Rereading Samuel [historically]' could serve as a response to both McKenzie and Polzin, and as mediation between them.[41]

---

40. McKenzie, 'Deuteronomistic History', p. 166.

41. A.G. Auld, 'Re-Reading Samuel (historically): "Etwas mehr Nichtwissen"', in V. Fritz and P.R. Davies (eds.), *The Origins of the Ancient Israelite States* (JSOTSup, 228; Sheffield: Sheffield Academic Press, 1996), pp. 160-69.

I am increasingly persuaded that we should direct more of our attention to extant texts and comparisons between them: between MT and
Qumran; between Hebrew and Greek; between the LXX of Alexandria
and of Antioch; between Samuel–Kings and Chronicles. Dietrich[42] took
the obvious link between Joshua's curse of Jericho in Josh. 6.26 and the
report of Hiel's building work there in 1 Kgs 16.34 as straightforward
proof that there had been a DtrG stretching from Joshua to Kings for
DtrP to supplement. Conroy has just published a masterly short study
that shows synchronically how well the verse has been crafted to link
16.29-33 on Ahab to the Elijah material beginning in 1 Kings 17, and
he highlights the diachronic implications of its absence from the
Lucianic LXX. 'A final-form examination of the text, carried out primarily for its own sake, can nonetheless make a contribution to the subsequent diachronic phase of study by pointing out features that have not
usually been included among the clues for arriving at a probable hypothesis about the origins of the text.'[43] It is equally true that text-critical
and other comparative examination of varied 'final forms' can contribute both to synchronic appreciation of each and to diachronic study
of earlier forms of the text.

42. W. Dietrich, *Prophetie und Geschichte: Eine redaktionsgeschichtliche
Untersuchung zum deuteronomistischen Geschichtswerk* (FRLANT, 108; Göttingen: Vandenhoeck & Ruprecht, 1972), p. 112.
43. C. Conroy, 'Hiel between Ahab and Elijah-Elisha: 1 Kgs 16,34 in its Immediate Literary Context', *Bib* 77 (1996), pp. 210-18.

THE DEUTERONOMISTS AND THE LATTER PROPHETS

Robert A. Kugler

The question of deuteronomic influence on the Latter Prophets has long been a matter of debate. Opinion ranges from the view that some prophets and the editors of their books were merely influenced by deuteronomic theology to the notion that a Deuteronomistic group systematically edited prophetic works to reconcile them to their theological program. This failure to achieve consensus is due in part to a failure of definition and criteria. The differences between the terms 'deuteronomistic' and 'deuteronomic' remain notoriously unclear.[1] Likewise, criteria for discerning the various degrees of 'deuteronomism' in the Latter Prophets are inadequate. Where basic issues like these remain unsettled confusion is sure to reign.[2] Increasing the difficulty of ascertaining deuteronomic influence is the trend toward viewing the prophetic books' compositional history not as a series of discrete redac-

---

1. For a recent attempt to attend to this issue, see R. Coggins, 'What Does "Deuteronomistic" Mean?', in Jon Davies, Graham Harvey and Wilfred G.E. Watson (eds.), *Words Remembered, Texts Renewed: Essays in Honour of John F.A. Sawyer* (JSOTSup, 195; Sheffield: Sheffield Academic Press, 1995), pp. 135-48; reprinted as Chapter 1 in this volume.

2. J.R. Porter, 'The Supposed Deuteronomic Redaction of the Prophets: Some Considerations', in R. Albertz *et al.* (eds.), *Schöpfung und Befreiung: Für Claus Westermann zum 80. Geburtstag* (Stuttgart: Calwer Verlag, 1989), pp. 69-78; and E. Ben Zvi, 'A Deuteronomistic Redaction in/among "The Twelve"? A Contribution from the Standpoint of the Books of Micah, Zephaniah and Obadiah', in K. Richards (ed.), *Society of Biblical Literature 1997 Seminar Papers* (Atlanta: Scholars Press, 1997), pp. 433-59, deny there was any deuteronomic redaction of prophets. Contrast J. Nogalski, *Literary Precursors to the Book of the Twelve* (BZAW, 217; Berlin: W. de Gruyter, 1993); *idem, Redactional Processes in the Book of the Twelve* (BZAW, 218; Berlin: W. de Gruyter, 1993), who claims there was a separate Deuteronomistic corpus of some of the Minor Prophets; along the same lines, see also M. Alvarez Barredo, *Relecturas deuteronomísticas de Amós, Miqueas y Jeremías* (Murcia: Instituto Teológico Franciscano, 1993).

tional moments (one or more of which might be identified as 'deutero-nomic') but as a continuous process of literary development among the prophets' followers.

There is reason to be concerned whether there was a deuteronomic transformation of the Latter Prophets. Just as some doubt that there was such a redaction, others entertain the notion that there was never a 'Deuteronomistic movement' besides.[3] Apart from the scholarly con-struct itself and the material in Deuteronomy to 2 Kings from which we infer its existence, there is little to support the notion of such a social movement. But proving a systematic deuteronomic revision of the Lat-ter Prophets—books not included in the 'deuteronomic canon'—would go a long ways toward confirming the existence of a social movement that actively promoted that theological outlook. To appreciate this claim, consider the view of prophecy in Deuteronomy and the Deuter-onomistic History: true prophets speak law and promote its keeping as a means of escaping impending doom (Deut. 18.15-22); they are subject to the law like anyone else (1 Kgs 13.8-9, 16-25); and they are known to lie (1 Kgs 13.18). Contrast that with the characteristic speech of Jere-miah, the prophetic contemporary of the rise of the deuteronomic worldview: there is only doom for the people of Judah for their failure to treat each other with common decency and properly to worship their God (Jer. 8.23–9.8 [Heb.]), and those who say that observing a written law delivers one from the impending fate are the true liars (Jer. 8.8-9). With such contrasting positions, it is hard to imagine that if there were a Deuteronomistic movement during the exile and beyond, it would not have edited the literary remains of the prophets to convert them to their perspective; thus a clear Deuteronomistic redaction of the Latter Pro-hets would provide much-needed external evidence for the notion of a Deuteronomistic movement. Likewise, the absence of a systematic adjustment of the prophetic voice, though not negating the hypothesis of a Deuteronomistic social movement, would commend caution in its pursuit.

The following article has the modest goal of selectively assessing the evidence usually cited in favor of the notion of a Deuteronomistic revi-sion of the Latter Prophets. Its contribution lies in making that assess-

---

3.   See N. Lohfink, 'Gab es eine deuteronomistische Bewegung?', in W. Gross (ed.), *Jeremia und die 'deuteronomistische Bewegung'* (BBB, 98; Weinheim: Beltz Athenäum, 1995), pp. 313-82 reprinted in an abridged and translated version as the second essay in this volume; see also Ben Zvi, 'A Deuteronomistic Redaction'.

ment with the aid of clear definitions and consistently applied criteria. This survey is by no means comprehensive, but it is hoped that examination of part of the evidence suggests the shape of the rest of it.

Definitions and Criteria

Previous discussions of deuteronomism in the prophets provide direction in establishing definitions and criteria. There are four rough categories of evidence usually cited in favor of a deuteronomic redaction of the Latter Prophets.

- *Category 4* evidence are passages improperly associated in past scholarship with deuteronomic themes, content or style. None of this indicates deuteronomic influence or revision. For examples of this sort of evidence, see the discussion below of texts in First Isaiah.
- *Category 3* evidence are passages that do address a theme or concept known only from the deuteronomic canon but that do not exhibit its peculiar diction or language. Where this is integrated with the surrounding context it indicates deuteronomic influence; where it is contradictory it indicates redaction. For examples of this sort of evidence, see the discussion below of Amos 2.4-5; 5.25-27.
- *Category 2* evidence are passages that lack obviously deuteronomic concepts or ideas but do exhibit the distinctive literary traits of the deuteronomic tradition.[4] Like category 3 evidence, this indicates influence where it complements the surrounding text and redaction where it is contradictory. Examples of this sort of evidence are discussed below in the section on Third Isaiah.
- *Category 1* evidence are passages that contain notions and literary traits typical of the deuteronomic tradition. Where these passages support the surrounding material they indicate deuteronomic influence; as in the case of category 2 and 3 evidence; when they contradict the surrounding material they suggest redaction. Some category 1 evidence appears in Amos 3.7; 5.4-5, 14-15.

---

4. Characteristically deuteronomic linguistic elements are listed by M. Weinfeld, *Deuteronomy and the Deuteronomic School* (Oxford: Clarendon Press, 1972), pp. 320-65.

Only when there is a pattern of widespread and systematic deutero-nomic redaction may one posit a Deuteronomistic redaction of the Lat-ter Prophets, that is, an intentional effort by a group to promote the theology of Deuteronomy at the expense of the theology and ideology of the books they edit.[5]

What are the measures of deuteronomic vocabulary, diction and style? The use in a narrow context of two to three words peculiar to the tradition is probably sufficient indication of influence, redaction or lit-erary dependence. With respect to diction, it is probably sufficient to find one instance of the stereotyped deuteronomic phrasing (e.g. עבדיו הנביאים) to assume influence. With respect to style, the hortatory or homiletic tone of the speeches in the deuteronomic corpus must be pre-sent, but it must also distinguish itself from the surrounding text since style is extrinsic and noticeable only in contrast with surrounding material.

Prophetic Books that Escaped the Deuteronomic Imprint: Joel, Obadiah, Jonah, Nahum and Habakkuk

Coggins has rightly said of Nahum and Habakkuk that they are entirely free of deuteronomic influence or redaction; the same may be said of Obadiah.[6] So Cothenet acknowledges that even though the polemic against idols in Hab. 2.5-20 echoes Deut. 4.28; 7.25, its presence does not mean the book was influenced or redacted along the lines of deuteronomic thought, since the same theme appears elsewhere in the Hebrew Bible.[7] And while M. Johnson's suggestion that Habakkuk was himself a Deuteronomist frustrated by the failure of Josiah's reforms is interesting, there is no evidence of deuteronomic influence or redaction

---

5. With the exception of the standard scholarly designation 'Deuteronomistic History', the word 'Deuteronomistic' is used here only for a social group and its activities; otherwise 'deuteronomic' will be used to denote a theological outlook, the texts that witness to it, its influence, or activities associated with it (such as redaction).

6. R. Coggins, 'An Alternative Prophetic Tradition?', in R. Coggins *et al.* (eds.), *Israel's Prophetic Tradition: Essays in Honour of Peter R. Ackroyd* (Cambridge: Cambridge University Press, 1982), pp. 77-94; on the non-deutero-nomic character of Obadiah, see also E. Ben Zvi, *A Historical-Critical Study of the Book of Obadiah* (BZAW, 242; Berlin: W. de Gruyter, 1996).

7. E. Cothenet, 'Prophètes: Habacuc', *DBSup*, VIII, pp. 796-97.

in the book.[8] There is also little or no evidence for deuteronomic influence on Joel. J. Bourke asserted that Joel's theme of 'return' (2.12-13) reflects an awareness of the deuteronomic tradition,[9] and Wolff says that the 'authority for such a call to return can find its legitimation...primarily in the deuteronomic-deuteronomistic curse oracles';[10] but the use of the verb שוב hardly constitutes evidence of influence much less redaction, since it is used in this sense more widely than Deuteronomy.[11] As for Jonah, its unique character within the prophetic corpus permits one to exclude it from this sort of investigation, although it should be noted that the tale is built from the memory of one of the prophets actually mentioned in the Deuteronomistic History (2 Kgs 14.25).

Deuteronomism in the Late-Exilic and Early-Postexilic Prophets: Second and Third Isaiah, Haggai, Zechariah and Malachi

The theology, ideology and diction of the deuteronomic tradition clearly influenced the late exilic and postexilic prophets; given the conventional dating of the deuteronomic canon and of the prophets in question this is hardly surprising. Thus while we find plenty of complementary category 1, 2 and 3 evidence, there is no sign of Deuteronomistic redaction among these books.

Critics have long noted that the so-called Second and Third Isaiah exhibit their authors' awareness of the deuteronomic conceptual and rhetorical world. The deuteronomic tradition is echoed in the phrases 'against whom we have sinned' (Isa. 42.24; Deut. 8.6; 10.12; 11.22; 19.9; 26.7; 28.9; 30.16) and 'dispossess the nations' (Isa. 54.3; Deut. 4.38; 7.22; 9.3, 4, 5; 11.23) and in the notions that the people belong to the Lord (Isa. 63.9; Deut. 9.29; 1 Kgs 8.51), the Lord is father (Isa. 63.16; 64.8; Deut. 32.6), God is in heaven (Isa. 63.15; 66.1; Deut. 26.15; 1 Kgs 8.30, 32, 34, 36, 39, 43, 45, 49) and the temple is a house of prayer for all peoples (Isa. 56.7; 1 Kgs 8.27-53). The placing of

8. M. Johnson, 'The Paralysis of Torah in Habakkuk I 4', *VT* 35 (1985), pp. 257-66.

9. J. Bourke, 'Le jour de Yahvé dans Joël', *RB* 66 (1959), pp. 5-31, esp. 15-16, 191-212, 206-208.

10. H.W. Wolff, *Joel and Amos* (Hermeneia; Philadelphia: Fortress Press, 1977), p. 11.

11. J.L. Crenshaw, *Joel* (AB, 24C; Garden City, NY: Doubleday, 1995), pp. 133-39.

God's word in people's mouths (Isa. 59.21; Deut. 30.14; Josh. 1.8), the theology of history in 63.7-14 and the prayer in 66.1-2 (cf. 1 Kgs 8.27) also seem to reflect acquaintance with the deuteronomic tradition.[12] But none of these parallels amounts to anything more than complementary category 2 or 3 evidence; at most they suggest their authors' acquaintance with deuteronomic language and thought.

Haggai and Zechariah 1–8 present a similar situation. There are a few hints of rhetorical and ideological contact between the two prophets and the deuteronomic tradition, but because they all contribute to the prophets' agenda they only indicate deuteronomic influence.[13] Haggai's insistence that a rebuilt temple and restored sacrifices will cause God to grant prosperity to Judah recalls the retributive justice of deuteronomic thinking (Hag. 1.7-11). Deuteronomic influence is perhaps indicated by the use of the divine epithet יי אלהיהם in 1.12, 14 as a way of referring to a covenantal relationship.[14] There is also a possible connection between Deuteronomy and Haggai in the practice of seeking a תורה from the priests (Hag. 2.10-14; Deut. 17.9, 11; cf. Lev. 10.10-20). In Zech. 1.1-6 there are two supposed deuteronomic turns of phrase: the reciprocal use of שוב and the phrase עבדי הנביאים.[15] Zechariah 8.16 is thought by some intentionally to mimic Deut. 1.1 to suggest that what follows is an epitome of covenantal law.[16] And like Haggai (and Malachi) this work is suffused with the general notion that keeping God's law and observing God's will brings prosperity, while the failure to do so leads to a harvest of sorrow.

Malachi presents a similar situation. Critics agree that many elements

12. See R.N. Whybray, *Isaiah 40–66* (NCB; Grand Rapids: Eerdmans, 1978) on the named passages from Isaiah.

13. For the rhetorical connections and their implications for conceptual acquaintance, see C.L. Meyers and E.M. Meyers, *Haggai, Zechariah 1–8* (AB, 25B; Garden City, NY: Doubleday, 1987), pp. 45-46.

14. Nevertheless, one must not attribute too much meaning even to this, since the person of the suffix is not the same as is usually the case in Deuteronomy; see H. Ringgren, 'elohim', *TDOT*, I, pp. 277-78.

15. J. Blenkinsopp, *A History of Prophecy in Israel* (Louisville, KY: Westminster/John Knox Press, 2nd edn, 1996), p. 204; yet the שוב connection is very loose at best, and the phrase עבדי הנביאים is only partly explained by reference to the more typical deuteronomic phrase עבדיו הנביאים (and the related phrase הנביא [name of the prophet] עבדו). Only several times does עבדי הנביאים actually appear in the deuteronomic corpus; see, e.g., 2 Kgs 17.13, but also v. 23!

16. Meyers and Meyers, *Haggai, Zechariah 1–8*, p. 426.

of this book betray acquaintance with and appreciation of the deutero-nomic tradition; see, for example, the use of phrases like 'love of the Lord' (Mal. 1.2; Deut. 7.7-8), 'the name of the Lord' (Mal. 1.6, 11, 14; 2.2; Deut. 12.5), the themes of the father–son relationship (Mal. 1.6; 2.10; 3.17; Deut. 1.21; 32.5-6), the Lord as One God (Mal. 2.15; Deut. 6.4), tithing (Mal. 3.10; Deut. 18.1-8) and the general view that blessing derives from the keeping of God's law.[17] Furthermore, at least Mal. 2.2-3 and 3.7 exhibit some characteristics of deuteronomic style.[18] But inasmuch as these phrases, themes and stylistic traits are integral to the book's own ideology and rhetoric they probably result from the author's appropriation of a general deuteronomic linguistic and religious ethos.

Meyers's and Meyers's apt critique of Raymond Person's claim to see Deuteronom(ist)ic composition and redaction in Second Zechariah leads to a similar conclusion.[19] They agree with Person that there is deuteronomic language in Zechariah 9–14, but they add that the language of other biblical texts appears here as well.[20] So rather than assume that a Deuteronom(ist)ic school shaped Second Zechariah, one suspects the author composed an 'intertextual' work that reused existing traditions and thought-worlds for new purposes. Research on Mal. 2.4-7 suggests the same compositional strategy was at work there; it combines elements of Genesis 34; Exod. 32.25-29; Num. 25.6-13; and Deut. 33.8-11 to create an ancient covenant with Levi not mentioned otherwise in the Bible.[21]

Deuteronomism in First Isaiah, Amos, Hosea, Micah, Zephaniah, Jeremiah and Ezekiel

These books offer the most interesting material relative to the issue at hand. All but one of them bears an ostensibly deuteronomic superscrip-

17. Blenkinsopp, *A History of Prophecy*, p. 211; A. van Hoonacker, 'La rapprochement entre le Deutéronome et Malachie', *ETL* 59 (1983), pp. 86-90.

18. Blenkinsopp, *A History of Prophecy*, pp. 211-12.

19. R.F. Person, Jr, *Second Zechariah and the Deuteronomic School* (JSOTSup, 167; Sheffield: JSOT Press, 1993).

20. C.L. Meyers and E.M. Meyers, *Zechariah 9–14* (AB, 25C; Garden City, NY: Doubleday, 1993), pp. 39-43, 57.

21. R.A. Kugler, *From Patriarch to Priest: The Levi-Priestly Tradition from Aramaic Levi to Testament of Levi* (SBLEJL, 9; Atlanta: Scholars Press, 1996), pp. 9-22.

tion, and to varying degrees each is thought to have undergone additional deuteronomic redaction. Examination of the evidence using the criteria set out above suggests that only Jeremiah and Amos provide dissonant category 1, 2 or 3 passages that suggest deuteronomic redaction.

Isaiah

J. Vermeylen and O. Kaiser hold the most liberal view regarding deuteronomic influence on Isaiah. Both say that either deuteronomistic circles or the prophets' deuteronomically influenced schools shaped the prophet's words.[22] Yet other scholars find virtually no deuteronomic influence on the formation of First Isaiah.[23] A sampling of the evidence usually cited supports the latter position, providing nothing more than category 4 evidence.

Because Isa. 1.1 matches the style of the superscriptions to Jeremiah, Hosea, Amos, Micah and Zephaniah, and that of 2 Kgs 14.23; 15.1 (and because ch. 2 begins with a fresh heading), it is often termed a 'deuteronomic' addition. However, as Ben Zvi has noted, the phrase 'בימי X' appears elsewhere in the Hebrew Bible and may not be deemed a strictly deuteronomic characteristic.[24] Thus this half verse is category 4 evidence; although it echoes a deuteronomic convention, it does not use uniquely deuteronomic diction.

The remainder of Isaiah 1 is also thought to evince deuteronomic influence.[25] Some hear in 1.2 (שמעו שמים והאזיני ארץ) an echo of Deut.

---

22. O. Kaiser, *Isaiah 1–12: A Commentary* (OTL; Philadelphia: Westminster Press, 2nd edn, 1983); *idem, Isaiah 13–39: A Commentary* (OTL; Philadelphia: Westminster Press, 1974); J. Vermeylen, *Du prophète Isaïe à l'apocalyptique* (2 vols.; Paris: J. Gabalda, 1977–78).

23. See C. Brekelmans, 'Deuteronomistic Influence in Isaiah 1–12', in J. Vermeylen (ed.), *The Book of Isaiah/Le Livre d'Isaïe: Les oracles et leurs relectures unité et complexité de l'ouvrage* (Leuven: Peeters, 1989), pp. 167-76; and L. Perlitt, 'Jesaja und die Deuteronomisten', in V. Fritz *et al.* (eds.), *Prophet und Prophetenbuch: Festschrift für Otto Kaiser zum 65. Geburtstag* (Berlin: W. de Gruyter, 1989), pp. 133-49.

24. Ben Zvi, 'A Deuteronomistic Redaction'.

25. Vermeylen, *Du prophète Isaïe*, I, pp. 37-112; Kaiser, *Isaiah 1–12*, pp. 1-23; R. Kilian, *Jesaja 1–12* (Würzburg: Echter Verlag, 1986), p. 26; and L. Ringnell, 'Isaiah Chapter 1: Some Exegetical Remarks with Special Reference to the Relationship between the Text and the Book of Deuteronomy', *ST* 11 (1957), pp. 140-58.

4.26; 30.19; and 32.1.[26] Yet only 32.1 resembles Isa. 1.2, and Deuter-onomy 32 has a lengthy compositional history that precludes it from being a particularly good representative of the deuteronomic idiom.[27] Similarly, Kaiser argues that in 1.4b the sentence 'they have forsaken the Lord, despised the Holy One of Israel' is a deuteronomic addition meant to raise the stakes on Israel's sin;[28] but the diction of the sentence is not that of Deuteronomy but of Isaiah who calls God קְדוֹשׁ יִשְׂרָאֵל (Isa. 1.4; 5.19, 24; 10.17, 20). More generally, commentators see in Isaiah 1 a covenant lawsuit, which implies the deuteronomic cove-nant,[29] and they claim it is deuteronomic to blame exile on the worship of foreign gods and a failure to trust in the Lord.[30] But if the passage were a covenant lawsuit some mention of covenant would also be expected,[31] and disgust for the worship of foreign gods is hardly con-fined to the deuteronomic perspective.

Isaiah 30.19-26 is also thought to evince deuteronomic influence, or even to be a deuteronomic insertion.[32] Suspected deuteronomic themes include the giving of rain (Isa. 30.23; Deut. 11.11, 14, 17; 28.12, 24; 32.2), increased agricultural production (Isa. 30.23-24; Deut. 14.22, 28; 16.15; 22.9), cattle (Isa. 30.23-24; Deut. 3.19), idolatry (Isa. 30.22; Deut. 9.12, 16; 21.15; Judg. 17.3, 4), and movement to the left and to the right (Isa. 30.21; Deut 2.27; 5.32; 17.11; 1 Sam. 6.12); and the shift in number of second-person address is a deuteronomic stylistic trait.[33] Yet none of these lexical, stylistic and thematic characteristics is unique to the deuteronomic tradition and is thus nothing more than category 4 evidence. Further analysis of First Isaiah merely repeats this pattern.[34]

---

26. Ringnell, 'Isaiah Chapter 1', pp. 141-42.

27. See P. Sanders, *The Provenance of Deuteronomy 32* (OTS, 37; Leiden: E.J. Brill, 1996).

28. Kaiser, *Isaiah 1–12*, p. 18.

29. Vermeylen, *Du prophète Isaïe*, I, pp. 65-66.

30. Kaiser, *Isaiah 1–12*, p. 70.

31. Brekelmans, 'Deuteronomistic Influence', p. 170.

32. See, for instance, L. Laberge, 'Is 30,19-26: A Deuteronomic Text?', *Eglise et Théologie* 2 (1971), pp. 35-54; M. Sweeney, *Isaiah 1–39* (Grand Rapids: Eerd-mans, 1996), pp. 396-97.

33. Sweeney, *Isaiah*, pp. 396-97.

34. Chs. 36–39 present a special case. They are probably a late insertion from Kings to create a bridge between the Assyrian and Babylonian periods addressed by the book; on this see Clements, *Isaiah 1–39*, pp. 277-80.

Amos

Since Werner Schmidt's landmark study in 1965 no other prophetic book apart from Jeremiah has earned such broad acclaim as a work shaped by deuteronomic redaction.[35] Yet a critical survey of the evidence all but reverses that view.

Among the passages attributed to deuteronomic redaction there are a few that are only category 4 evidence. Because the diction of the superscription has been shown (in discussion of Isa. 1.1) to lack deuteronomic distinction, Amos 1.1 falls into this category as well. The oracles against Tyre and Edom (1.9-12) are associated with the addition of the Judah oracle (2.4-5), which is usually thought to be a deuteronomic contribution;[36] yet there is nothing uniquely deuteronomic in their style, diction or vocabulary, much less their content, and they are likely nothing more than sixth-century updates of the prophet's words.[37] Many also assign Amos 2.10-12 and 3.1-2 to a deuteronomic redaction.[38] However, the verb used in both passages to describe the Israelites' escape from Egypt is not the hiphil of יצא, which is typical of the deuteronomic exodus tradition but the hiphil of עלה, the verb used in other pre-deuteronomic prophetic references to the exodus.[39] As for the recollection of the exodus tradition, a memory as vague as this is widespread and cannot be attributed solely to deuteronomic influence. Moreover, the supposed parallel between Amos 3.2b and deuteronomic election theology is also illusory; the verb used for God's relationship to Israel is ידע, not the usual deuteronomic בחר.[40] The references to

35. W.H. Schmidt, 'Die deuteronomistische Redaktion des Amosbuches', *ZAW* 77 (1965), pp. 168-93.

36. Wolff, *Joel and Amos*, pp. 158-60.

37. S. Paul ('A Literary Reinvestigation of the Authenticity of the Oracles against the Nations of Amos', in M. Carrez *et al.* [eds.], *De la Torah au Messie* [Paris: Descleé de Brouwer, 1981], pp. 189-204), defends the authenticity of all the oracles; for yet another view, see B. Goss, 'Le recueil d'oracles contre les nations du livre d'Amos et l'histoire deutéronomique', *VT* 38 (1988), pp. 22-40. For the view that the oracles are merely sixth-century updates, see Porter, 'The Supposed Deuteronomic Redaction', p. 76.

38. Schmidt, 'Die deuteronomistische Redaktion', pp. 169-73, 179-83.

39. See Deut. 1.27; T.R. Hobbs, 'Amos 3 1b and 2 10', *ZAW* 81 (1969), pp. 384-87.

40. S. Paul, *Amos* (Hermeneia; Philadelphia: Fortress Press, 1991), p. 101 (cf. Deut. 10.15).

Bethel as a place of worship in 3.14 and 5.6 need not be assigned deuteronomic status either.[41] Deuteronomy does eschew worship in any place but Jerusalem, but to assume that others did not also condemn the practice—especially a prophet to the north from the south—is unreasonable. Anyway, in the case of 3.14 the diction is decidedly non-deuteronomic: פקד על does not appear in deuteronomic texts. Finally, the claim that 7.10-17 is a deuteronomic story wherein Amos refers to himself with the image of the plumbline as well as the view that most of 9.8-15 comes from late deuteronomic redactors may be rejected.[42] There are no distinctive deuteronomic literary traits or content in these passages.

Amos 5.25-27 is a complementary category 3 text. While the explicit presumption that there were no sacrifices in the early period of Israel's history *is* found otherwise only in a deuteronomic portion of Jeremiah (7.21-23), the diction and vocabulary of this passage are not deuteronomic, apart perhaps from the hiphil of גלה in v. 27; but even this single word is not peculiar to the deuteronomic tradition. Another complementary category 3 passage is Amos 2.4-5, the oracle against Judah. Though the theme echoes deuteronomic notions, all of the supposedly deuteronomic terminology in these verses appears in pre-deuteronomic texts as well.[43]

There are some category 1 texts in Amos that are also disruptive in their context. Amos 3.7 breaks the flow of the text in 3.6, 8 and uses a boiler-plate deuteronomic phrase, עבדיו הנביאים.[44] Much the same may be said of Amos 5.4-5 and 14-15. Typical deuteronomic language and diction (e.g. דרשו יי; Deut. 4.27-31) appears out of nowhere to offer a message of hope for salvation in the midst of surrounding material that announces only unrelenting doom.[45] These category 1 texts stand out in

---

41. On 5.6, see, for example, Wolff, *Joel and Amos*, p. 240.

42. H.G.M. Williamson, 'The Prophet and the Plumb-Line', in A. van der Woude (ed.), *In Quest of the Past: Studies on Israelite Religion, Literature and Prophetism* (Leiden: E.J. Brill, 1988), pp. 101-21; and U. Kellerman, 'Der Amos-schluß als Stimme deuteronomistischer Heilshoffnung', *EvT* 29 (1969), pp. 169-83; see also P. Weimar, 'Der Schluß des Amos-Buches: Ein Beitrag zur Redaktions-geschichte des Amos-Buches', *BN* 18 (1981), pp. 80-100.

43. Wolff, *Joel and Amos*, pp. 264-66, makes the latter observation, yet still attributes this to a deuteronomic hand.

44. Blenkinsopp, *A History of Prophecy*, pp. 75, 268 n. 48.

45. Blenkinsopp, *A History of Prophecy*, p. 76.

their context, and so they indicate a deuteronomic redaction of the book, light though it may be.[46]

Hosea

Hosea presents special problems for those curious about deuteronomic influence. Some who assign Deuteronomy an Israelite provenance see Hosea, a northern prophet of the eighth century, as an immediate predecessor or contemporary of Deuteronomy's formation; thus sorting out the direction of influence between the two is particularly vexing.[47]

Most agree that Hosea influenced Deuteronomy in its concern for אלהים אחרים (cf. Deut. 5.7; 6.14; 7.4), its focus on the אהב יי (cf. Deut. 6.5; 11.1) and the theme of deliverance from Egypt (Deut. 7.8; 9.26). More difficult to determine are the passages thought to reflect deuteronomic influence or redaction in Hosea. Some discern little more than a sprinkling of redactional touches,[48] while others say a deuteronomic

46. See, in contrast, Vermeylen, *Du prophète Isaïe*, II, pp. 519-69, who defends the view that Amos underwent extensive deuteronomic redaction; for different understandings of the relationship between the deuteronomic outlook and Amos, see F. Crüsemann, 'Kritik an Amos in deuteronomistischen Geschichtswerk', in H.W. Wolff (ed.), *Probleme biblischer Theologie: Gerhard von Rad zum 70. Geburtstag* (Munich: Chr. Kaiser Verlag, 1971), pp. 57-63; and H.-H. Krause, 'Der Gerichtsprophet Amos, ein Vorläufer des Deuteronomisten', *ZAW* 50 (1932), pp. 221-39.

47. See, for example, N.P. Lemche, 'The God of Hosea', in E. Ulrich *et al.* (eds.), *Priest, Prophets and Scribes: Essays on the Formation and the Heritage of Second Temple Judaism in Honour of Joseph Blenkinsopp* (JSOTSup, 149; Sheffield: JSOT Press, 1992), pp. 241-57, who argues for the contemporaneous formation of the prophetic book and the deuteronomic material; H.W. Wolff, 'Hoseas geistige Heimat', *TLZ* 91 (1956), pp. 83-94; and *Hosea* (Hermeneia; Philadelphia: Fortress Press, 1974), p. xxxi, who argues that Hosea shaped the Deuteronomistic movement (see also J. Day, 'Pre-Deuteronomic Allusions to the Covenant in Hosea and Psalm LXXXVIII', *VT* 45 [1986], pp. 1-12; H. Lusczyk, 'Die Bundesurkunde: Ursprung und Wirkungsgeschichte des Deuteronomiums', in C. Brekelmans and J. Lust [eds.], *Pentateuchal and Deuteronomistic Studies* [Leuven: Peeters, 1990], pp. 167-70; and H.J. Zobel, 'Hosea und das Deuteronomium: Erwägungen eines Alttestamentlers zum Thema "Sprache und Theologie"', *TLZ* 110 [1985], pp. 14-23); and L. Perlitt, *Bundestheologie im Alten Testament* (WMANT, 36; Neukirchen–Vluyn: Neukirchener Verlag, 1969), pp. 141-49, who argues that Hosea underwent deuteronomic redaction (see also R. Clements, *Prophecy and Tradition* [Oxford: Oxford University Press, 1975], pp. 41-44).

48. See Blenkinsopp, *A History of Prophecy*, pp. 85-90; and Wolff, *Hosea*, p. xxxi.

reworking turned the symbol of marriage into a deuteronomic allegory for Israel and God in covenant together,[49] and still others insist that the book conforms to a deuteronomically imposed pattern shared with three other Minor Prophets.[50] The last two views are based entirely on category 4 evidence, and so may be summarily dismissed,[51] and examination of the claims for deuteronomic influence on Hos. 6.7 and 8.1 supports the view that it was Hosea who shaped the deuteronomic vision.

Hosea 6.7 refers to a covenant כאדם breached by human action, which is thought by some to be a deuteronomic reference.[52] While the concept of a ברית violated (עבר) is characteristic of the deuteronomic corpus, it is not unique to it; nor does the verse exhibit any other distinctively deuteronomic content, style, diction or language.[53] Hosea 8.1 is the most widely acknowledged candidate for evidence of a deuteronomic redaction in the book. The words ברית and עבר appear together, and תורה appears as well. However, the inflected forms of the two nouns, תורתי and בריתי, do not appear together in the deuteronomic corpus, but do occur in tandem in Ps. 78.10, which is widely recognized to be pre-exilic and close in age to Hosea.[54] So Hos. 6.7; 8.1 are category 4 texts and are probably best understood as having shaped Deuteronomy.[55]

49. For an explanation of this idea, see Zobel, 'Hosea und das Deuteronomium', *passim.*

50. Nogalski, *Literary Precursors*; see also G. Renaud, 'Le livret d'Oseé: Un travail complexe d'édition', *RSR* 56 (1982), pp. 159-78; but as in the case of Isa. 1.1; Amos 1.1, the style and diction of the superscription (Hos. 1.1), though different from that of the rest of the book, is not uniquely deuteronomic, and is only category 4 evidence.

51. For instance, those who speculate that the marriage theme is a metaphor for the covenantal relationship have no adequate parallels in Deuteronomy or the Deuteronomistic History that would support their imaginative suggestion.

52. Covenants that are clearly international treaties appear in 10.4; 12.2; cf. Wolff, *Hosea*, pp. 175, 211.

53. See Day, 'Pre-Deuteronomic Allusions', pp. 3-7; contrast Perlitt, *Bundestheologie*, pp. 141-44, who escapes the question by saying that the reference is to a treaty; but see the use of עבר for a violation of the covenant (Deut. 17.2; Josh. 7.11, 15; 23.16. etc.), not פדה, which occurs for treaties.

54. Day, 'Pre-Deuteronomic Allusions', pp. 7-11.

55. See Porter, 'The Supposed Deuteronomic Redaction', p. 77, who critiques the claim that there is also in Hosea a Judean redaction that may or may not be associated with Deuteronomic traditions (cf. 3.4-5; 4.15; 5.5; 6.11; 8.14); Day notes that these additions are inconsistent in their apparent intention and may not be attributed to a single hand.

Micah

Micah's relationship to the deuteronomic tradition is also difficult to sort out. Like Hosea, the solutions range from assuming Micah's influence on Deuteronomy to positing various deuteronomic reworkings of Micah.[56] And also like Hosea there is nothing in Micah that rises above complementary category 3 evidence, suggesting that those who posit Micah's influence on Deuteronomy are correct.[57]

Certainly Blenkinsopp is correct in saying that references to the removal of landmarks (Mic. 2; Deut. 19.14), usury (Mic. 2.8, 9a; Deut. 24.6, 10-13), defense of the poor (Mic. 3.1-2; 6.10; Deut. 15.4), the corruption of the justice system (Mic. 3.9; Deut. 16.18-20), bribery (Mic. 3.11; Deut. 16.18-20) and weights and measures (Mic. 6.10-11; Deut. 25.13-16) make Micah sound deuteronomic.[58] But he is also correct in saying that, given our knowledge of Micah's date and setting, these interests can just as easily indicate Micah's inspiration of the authors of Deuteronomy.[59] Whatever the case, there is nothing here that is deuteronomic in character *and* contradictory of the surrounding material; thus nothing supports a deuteronomic redaction of Micah.

Zephaniah

Also introduced by the 'deuteronomic' superscription, Zephaniah is thought to have been composed around the time of Josiah's reign.[60] So

56. A.S. van der Woude, 'The Classical Prophets: Amos, Hosea and Micah', in Coggins *et al.* (eds.), *Israel's Prophetic Tradition*, pp. 32-57 (52-53), suggests that Deuteronomists brought chs. 1–5 and 6–7 of Micah together by redactional glosses in 1.5c, 7ab and perhaps the last words of 6.16a and b; Nogalski, *Literary Precursors, passim*, suggests that there is a Deuteronomistic Micah corpus that includes chs. 1–3 and 6; e.g. 1.2-7 applies Samaria's experience to Judah and the polemic against Jerusalem in ch. 6, as well as in 2.12-13, 4.1-4, and 7.8-13 are Deuteronomistic eschatological redactions; see also S. Cook, 'Micah's Deuteronomistic Redaction and the Deuteronomists' Identity', in this volume.

57. The superscription in Mic. 1.1, though the most commonly cited evidence of deuteronomic influence, has the same value as those found in Isa. 1.1; Amos 1.1; Hos. 1.1 (see above).

58. Blenkinsopp, *A History of Prophecy*, p. 265 n. 19.

59. Blenkinsopp, *A History of Prophecy*, p. 120; Blenkinsopp suggests that Micah was a conserving dissident force like the Deuteronom(ist)ic movement.

60. A. Berlin, *Zephaniah* (AB, 25A; Garden City, NY: Doubleday, 1994), pp. 43-47; but see the contrary view articulated by E. Ben Zvi, *A Historical-Critical Study of the Book of Zephaniah* (BZAW, 198; Berlin: W. de Gruyter, 1991). On the non-deuteronomic character of the superscription, see the discussion of Isa. 1.1

caution is again required in the search for evidence of a deuteronomic redaction, since similarities may only be a matter of a shared linguistic and ideological-theological horizon. In fact, even without using the stringent criteria applied here, all of the passages usually cited from Zephaniah are explicable apart from recourse to a theory of deuteronomic influence or redaction. For instance, the phrase לקח מוסר in 3.2, 7 appears again in Jer. 2.30; 5.3; 7.28; 17.23; 32.33; 35.13; Prov. 8.10; 10.3; 24.32.[61] In 1.3 God announces the intent to cut off (hi. of כרת) God's people from the face of the earth, but in parallel deuteronomic passages the verb is the hiphil of שמד (e.g. Deut. 6.15; 1 Kgs 13.34).[62] צבא השמים in 1.5, though known in the deuteronomic corpus (Deut 4.19; 17.3; 2 Kgs 17.10), also appears in Neh. 9.6 and in a related form in Gen. 2.1. Also in 1.5 the reference to worship on rooftops, while found in some deuteronomic passages (2 Kgs 23.12; Jer. 19.13; 32.29), uses non-deuteronomic language to describe the practice (which was anyway no doubt observable to more than those who saw the world in deuteronomic terms). Zephaniah 1.13 echoes the futility curse known from Deut. 28.30, but a similar form occurs also in Amos 5.11, Mic. 6.14-15, Hag. 1.6, and in at least one ancient Near Eastern parallel.[63] And 2.7 and 3.20, using forms of the phrase שב שבות (cf. Deut. 30.3) only suggest a shared horizon between Deuteronomy and Zephaniah.[64] Finally N. Mendecki has argued that part of the late material in 3.9, 14-20 is deuteronomic and postexilic, but his arguments founder on the passage's lack of significant deuteronomic diction or language.[65]

above; in contrast, see Blenkinsopp, *A History of Prophecy*, p. 113, who suggests that the deuteronomic influence is especially apparent in the superscription's genealogical references, which he thinks are meant to overcome the hint of the prophet's foreign extraction ('Cushi'); Berlin, *Zephaniah*, p. 67, rejects this view.

61. Only three of the Jeremiah passages are 'deuteronomic texts'. For a critique from within the Zephianic context of the deuteronomic associations made for the phrase, see Ben Zvi, *Zephaniah*, pp. 184-219, 315-18.

62. But see 1 Kgs 9.7, where the verb is the hi. of כרת; it is worth noting that Amos, with which Zephaniah may have some relationship, also uses שמד in the same phrase (9.8).

63. See line 19 of the Aramaic text in T. Muraoka, 'The Tell-Fekherye Bilingual Inscriptions and Early Aramaic', *Abr-Nahrain* 22 (1983–84), pp. 79-117.

64. See Berlin, *Zephaniah*, pp. 14-15, for more on the notion that many of the intersections between the two books amount to a common intellectual milieu.

65. N. Mendecki, 'Deuteronomistische Redaktion von Zef 3,18-20?', *BN* 60 (1991), pp. 27-32; but see Berlin, *Zephaniah*, p. 15, who appreciates the connection

Jeremiah

Time and space limitations permit only general comments on Jeremiah.[66] Little more is necessary, since this prophetic book provides
overwhelming evidence for some sort of 'deuteronomic redaction'.

While at least W. Holladay thinks that the book of Jeremiah escaped
deuteronomic revision,[67] most understand the work's present form to be
either the result of a severely modifying deuteronomic redaction of
Jeremiah's words[68] or the outcome of a long process of composition
that in some way included substantial deuteronomic influence.[69] There
are undeniable *differences* of style and content between the poetry and
certain parts of the prose in Jeremiah, just as there are clear *connections*
between much of the prose and the deuteronomic corpus; the sermon on
keeping the covenant in Jer. 11.1-4 closely resembles homilies found
throughout the deuteronomic canon, and at the same time it differs radically from the rhetoric of Jer. 8.23–9.8 (Heb.), where doom is relent-
lessly proclaimed as the people's only fate.[70] From this perspective a
deuteronomic revision of Jeremiah's words seems impossible to reject.

between Zeph. 3.19-20 and Deut. 30.3-4 but once more attributes the connections to
a shared theological and intellectual horizon.

66. For a recent set of essays on the subject that capture much of the full spectrum of opinion and supply a bibliography, see Gross (ed.), *Jeremie und die
'deuteronomistische Bewegung'*; an older collection that provides the classical
entries on the question of Jeremiah and the deuteronomic worldview is L.G. Perdue
and B.W. Kovacs (eds.), *A Prophet to the Nations: Essays in Jeremiah Studies*
(Winona Lake, IN: Eisenbrauns, 1984).

67. W. Holladay, *Jeremiah 1: A Commentary on the Book of the Prophet Jeremiah Chapters 1–25* (Hermeneia; Philadelphia: Fortress Press, 1986); and *Jeremiah
2: A Commentary on the Book of the Prophet Jeremiah Chapters 26–52* (Hermeneia; Philadelphia: Fortress Press, 1989).

68. See the most prominent representative of this view, W. Thiel, *Die deuteronomistische Redaktion von Jer 1–25* (WMANT, 41; Neukirchen–Vluyn: Neukirchener Verlag, 1973); and *idem, Die deuteronomistische Redaktion von Jer 26–
45* (WMANT, 52; Neukirchen–Vluyn: Neukirchener Verlag, 1981); see more
recently, D.R. Jones, *Jeremiah* (NCB; Grand Rapids: Eerdmans, 1992), pp. 18-28.

69. See especially W. McKane, *A Critical and Exegetical Commentary on Jeremiah I–XXV* (ICC; Edinburgh: T. & T. Clark, 1986); and *idem, A Critical and Exegetical Commentary on Jeremiah XXVI–LII* (ICC; Edinburgh: T. & T. Clark, 1996).

70. See, however, Weippert's well-known observation that the prose carries
over some elements from the poetry (H. Weippert, *Die Prosareden des Jeremiabuches* [BZAW, 132; Berlin: W. de Gruyter, 1973]); nevertheless, much of the
prose remains unquestionably deuteronomic in character.

Whether such a revision was accomplished by opponents of Jeremiah who wrote from a deuteronomic perspective to coopt the prophet's words for their own aims, or whether it was undertaken by his own disciples who had been converted to a deuteronomic way of thinking, is difficult to determine. This is especially the case if McKane's hypothesis that Jeremiah developed as a 'rolling corpus' is on target.[71] So even here we must confess ignorance as to whether we have genuine evidence of a Deuteronomistic redaction—an effort carried out by a group representing the deuteronomic outlook—or just another example of deuteronomic influence.

Ezekiel

Scholarship on Ezekiel tends toward attributing differences within the book to an Ezekiel school's gradual modification of its mentor's words;[72] thus most embrace the idea that deuteronomic notions in Ezekiel come from Ezekiel's followers who were influenced or persuaded by the deuteronomic message as well as by the perspectives of the Priestly Work and the Holiness Code.[73] Still, some hew to the line that Ezekiel underwent a deuteronomic redaction.[74] Their view is difficult to maintain when measured against the criteria proposed here. Two brief examples suffice.

The covenantal concerns in Ezek. 34.25-30 are taken by some as a sign of deuteronomic redaction.[75] However, the passage lacks deutero-

---

71. McKane, *Jeremiah I–XXV*, pp. l-lxxxiii. See also M. Brettler's contribution to this volume; his suggestion that Jeremiah, deuteronomically revised, influenced late developments in Deuteronomy in turn, is a natural outgrowth of such a view of Jeremiah. Further such possible connections should be investigated.

72. See the survey of recent scholarship by K. Pfisterer Darr, 'Ezekiel among the Critics', *CR:BS* 2 (1994), pp. 9-24.

73. See, for example, W. Zimmerli, *Ezekiel 1: A Commentary on the Book of the Prophet Ezekiel, Chapters 1–24* (Hermeneia; Philadelphia: Fortress Press, 1979); and *Ezekiel 2: A Commentary on the Book of the Prophet Ezekiel, Chapters 25–48* (Hermeneia; Philadelphia: Fortress Press, 1983); others who take this view are discussed by Darr, 'Ezekiel among the Critics', *passim*; and by F.-L. Hossfeld, 'Ezechiel und die deuteronomisch-deuteronomistische Bewegung', in Gross (ed.), *Jeremie und die 'deuteronomistische Bewegung'*, pp. 272-79.

74. The first full defense of this view is to be found in S. Herrmann, *Die prophetischen Heilserwartungen im Alten Testament* (BWANT, 85; Stuttgart: Stuttgarter, 1965).

75. See B. Willmes, *Die sogenannte Hirtenallegorie Ez 34* (BBET, 19; Frank-

nomic language, diction and style and is no more than a category 4 text. The term ברית does occur here, but its pairing with שלום recalls a Priestly passage rather than a deuteronomic notion (Num. 25.12), and the divine epithet יי אלהיהם, though a typical deuteronomic way of naming God, misses the mark, since in Deuteronomy the suffixal form of אלהים is almost always second person.[76] Anyway, this passage's concept of covenant lacks a conditional character, an undeniable hallmark of deuteronomic thought.[77] A second test passage, Ezek. 36.26-27 (par. 11.19-20) also fails to meet the criteria for being labeled deuteronomic.[78] The phrase והייתם לי לעם in v. 28 recalls Deut. 4.20; 7.6; 14.2; 26.18; 27.9, but it also echoes Zech. 2.15; 8.8 and other portions of Ezekiel not given the deuteronomic imprimatur. And the end of v. 27, thought to resemble deuteronomic diction, has more in common with Lev. 26.3 of the Holiness Code.[79]

Conclusion

This very selective test of the evidence often cited for a Deuteronomistic redaction of the Latter Prophets has yielded negative results. The isolated hints of deuteronomic redaction found in Amos 3.7; 5.4-5, 14-15 hardly indicate the existence of a school of thought. The large-scale redaction of Jeremiah's words, though certainly intriguing, is just as easily explained by positing the conversion of Jeremiah's disciples to a deuteronomic outlook as it is by imagining that a separate 'Deuteronomistic' group edited his legacy with hostile intent. Does this require that the hypothesis of a Deuteronomistic school be abandoned? By no means. It does, however, urge caution, for it remains true that only Deuteronomy and the Deuteronomistic History permit the hypothesis the little vitality it has.

---

furt: Lang, 1984), pp. 471-44; and H.F. Fuhs, *Ezechiel II* (Würzburg: Echter Verlag, 1988), pp. 194-95.

76. See n. 14 above.

77. Zimmerli (*Ezekiel 2*, p. 220) also notes the passage's close connections to the Holiness Code.

78. See Fuhs, *Ezechiel*, pp. 204-205.

79. For bibliography of works that deal more extensively with the ostensible deuteronomic influence on or redaction of Ezekiel, see Hossfeld, 'Ezechiel und die deuteronomisch-deuteronomistische Bewegung', pp. 294-95.

THE DEUTERONOMIST AND THE WRITINGS

James L. Crenshaw

While writing this paper I found it necessary to resist a strong sense of *déjà vu*. Thirty years ago a pan-sapientialism infected much research relating to the Hebrew Bible, as if to make up for years of ignoring or worse, disdaining, wisdom literature because of the prevailing theological interest in 'salvation history'. The prophets Isaiah and Amos were said to have been educated in wisdom circles—the first within the royal court, the second in wisdom of the clan—and the same general background, the court, was posited for the story of human origins in Genesis 1–11 and the narrative about Joseph in Genesis 37–50. In 1968 I suggested to my class that the next logical step would be to view the so-called Succession Document as a product of the sages. Before the quarter ended, R.N. Whybray proposed precisely that, arguing that the episodes in 2 Samuel 9–20 and 1 Kings 1–2 reinforce the moral lessons found in aphorisms within the book of Proverbs. This tendency to posit wisdom influence throughout canonical literature seemed out of control, so that even such an unlikely candidate as the book of Esther was coopted for the sages. Within a decade few books of the Hebrew Bible had escaped the claim of sapiential influence—one thinks of Deuteronomy, Ruth, Jonah, Psalms, Micah, Habakkuk, Song of Songs, and various textual units elsewhere. I determined to resist this trend on methodological grounds, at the same time launching a career in wisdom literature.[1] If now, considerably older, I continue that resistance,

1. J.L. Crenshaw, 'Method in Determining Wisdom Influence upon "Historical" Literature', *JBL* 88 (1969), pp. 129-42, reprinted in J.L. Crenshaw, *Urgent Advice and Probing Questions: Collected Writings on Old Testament Wisdom* (Macon, GA: Mercer University Press, 1995), pp. 312-25. S.L. Harris, *Proverbs 1–9: A Study of Inner-Biblical Interpretation* (SBLDS, 150; Atlanta: Scholars Press, 1995) has reversed the process, arguing on the basis of Prov. 1.8-19; 1.20-33; and 6.1-19 that the author used the Joseph narrative and Jeremiah, among other earlier

although on a new playing field, you will not be surprised.

The similarities between the two trends, pan-sapientialism and pan-Deuteronomism, are astonishing. Lacking adequate controls or agreed-on criteria, scholars make their cases by appealing to: (1) phraseological similarities; (2) thematic considerations; (3) social location; (4) creative adaptation; and (5) oppositional ideology.[2] The reasoning, overwhelmingly circular, convinces only those who have already subscribed to the theory. The strongest argument, linguistic parallels, loses force when one considers the paucity of written material from ancient Israel that remains. We simply do not know what literature was available to ancient authors, for we cannot assume that all of it survived as the biblical canon. Seldom does anyone examine the underlying assumptions, particularly with respect to the extent of literacy in ancient Israel and the availability of exemplars of canonical texts.[3]

Some observations about terminology seem appropriate at this juncture. The distinction between Deuteronomic and Deuteronomistic should be retained, the former pointing to an original source and the latter to subsequent works in the same vein. The terms 'Deuteronomistic movement' and 'Deuteronomistic school' are more problematic, as is also 'Deuteronomism'.[4] Movements and schools imply definite social

canonical texts. Harris relies on 'the transposition of words from another context, the anthological combination of vocabulary adapted to a new sapiential context, key words and phrases, virtual citations, and allusive language' (p. 22) to relate biblical texts to one another. One must be careful, however, not to seize upon accidental similarities in language resulting from a limited vocabulary and common topics as evidence of actual reflection on a given canonical text.

2.   See the discussions in R. Coggins, 'What Does "Deuteronomistic" Mean?', in Jon Davies, Graham Harvey and Wilfred G.E. Watson (eds.), *Words Remembered, Texts Renewed: Essays in Honour of John F.A. Sawyer* (JSOTSup, 195; Sheffield: Sheffield Academic Press, 1995), pp. 135-48, reprinted as Chapter 1 in this volume, and N. Lohfink, 'Gab es eine deuteronomistische Bewegung?', in W. Gross (ed.), *Jeremia und die 'deuteronomistische Bewegung'* (BBB, 98; Weinheim: Beltz Athenäum, 1995), pp. 313-82, reprinted in an abridged and translated version as the second essay in this volume.

3.   Lohfink, 'Gab es eine deuteronomistische Bewegung?', recognizes the problems involved in ascertaining the extent of literacy in postexilic Yehud. Jews in exile had seen the importance of written texts in the Babylonian culture, but on returning to Yehud they possessed limited resources and met with considerable difficulty, both politically and economically.

4.   Coggins, 'What Does "Deuteronomistic" Mean?', asks a significant question: who were these Deuteronomists? He lists the different responses within schol-

locations and specific language, perhaps even their own literature.[5] Evidence is lacking for any of these. Josiah's early death must surely have crushed the brief national-cultic reform movement, and the next sustained movement in Yehud was inaugurated by the Maccabees. Neither the scribal activity of Hezekiah's men nor the reforms of Ezra–Nehemiah amount to a movement. Similarly, no real Deuteronomistic school, in the institutional sense, existed, and no Deuteronomistic 'school of thought' can reasonably be postulated on the basis of the evidence.[6]

The task of assessing the relationship between the Deuteronomist and the Writings would be quite different if Deuteronomy actually arose in wisdom circles, as Moshe Weinfeld has endeavored to demonstrate.[7] His argument rests on too many improbabilities to carry conviction— turning the dating of the proverbial collections upside down, with no justification;[8] assuming an exclusive ownership among sages for com-

arly literature: Levites (G. von Rad), heirs to the prophetic tradition (E. Nicholson), wisdom schools (M. Weinfeld), and reformers (R. Clements). Perhaps one should also inquire as to the meaning of school, which is preceded by the adjective Deuteronomistic. Presumably, the reference is to a particular kind of thinking based on the book of Deuteronomy rather than an institution consisting of professional teachers and students.

5. P. Dutcher-Walls, 'The Social Location of the Deuteronomist: A Sociological Study of Factional Politics in Late Pre-Exilic Judah', *JSOT* 52 (1991), pp. 77-94, uses the research of G. Lenski and T.F. Carney on related agrarian societies in her effort to understand the social tiers and conflicts in Israel. Consciously ignoring apologetic or polemic in Deuteronomistic texts, she hopes to arrive at unbiased description, itself problematic. Deuteronomists, in her view, cut across the various social groupings and roles making up the highest class of society in Yehud. They comprised 'a mixed elite grouping of priests, prophets, scribes, court officials and gentry' (p. 93). Specific groups within North American society illustrate the manner in which discourse comes to be specific to a particular segment of the population. Athletes, for example, talk of 'making history' through breaking a record of victories or the like; they speak about 'coming to play' and 'giving one hundred and ten percent' of effort to the game.

6. No institution, given the absence of an identifiable social entity to bestow vitality and endurance. No 'school of thought', because of the broken character of the 'Deuteronomistic ideology' from generation to generation—as indicated by its sporadic outcroppings in canonical literature.

7. M. Weinfeld, *Deuteronomy and the Deuteronomic School* (Oxford: Clarendon Press, 1972).

8. Weinfeld considers the Sayings of Agur in Prov. 30.1-14 to be early, but a

mon concepts in the ancient world;[9] attributing all scribal activity to sages;[10] and ignoring significant differences between Deuteronomy and wisdom literature.[11] Nevertheless, his list of verbal links between Deuteronomy and wisdom literature provides a point of departure for this discussion.[12]

virtual scholarly consensus has placed this text at the end of the compositional process in the book of Proverbs. Its meaning continues to baffle interpreters, who cannot agree on its length and sense. R.C. van Leeuwen ('The Background to Proverbs 30:4a', in M.L. Barré [ed.], *Wisdom, You Are my Sister: Studies in Honor of Roland E. Murphy, O. Carm., on the Occasion of his Eightieth Birthday* [CBQMS, 29; Washington: The Catholic Biblical Association of America, 1997], pp. 102-21) provides the latest in a long line of investigations into the meaning of this difficult text. He emphasizes the antiquity of the *topos* about heavenly ascent and descent by gods and quasi-divine figures. R.N. Whybray (*The Book of Proverbs: A Survey of Modern Study* [Leiden: E.J. Brill, 1995], pp. 86-91) discusses the different scholarly views about the sayings of Agur.

9.   The belief in reward and retribution was widespread among various professionals—prophets, priests, sages—and probably represented the view of the populace at large. The claim that a sensitive or humane concern for the defenseless (whether animal, fowl or human) was peculiarly sapiential begs the question. Presumably, sensitive persons belonged to most, if not all, ranks of life.

10.   Priestly and royal interests probably enlisted the service of most scribes. Sages did not restrict their activity to the written word. They taught and learned largely through oral pedagogy, and the verb 'to write' occurs only five times (once in Sirach) in canonical wisdom. The oral nature of Israelite society has been highlighted by S. Niditch, *Oral World and Written Word: Ancient Israelite Literature* (Louisville, KY: Westminster/John Knox Press, 1996).

11.   Particularism, collections of laws, curses, narratives exalting the deity, and a host of similar features place Deuteronomy in a different world from wisdom literature.

12.   Weinfeld, *Deuteronomy and the Deuteronomic School*, pp. 320-65 (Appendix A). In the preface, Weinfeld insists that this appendix is 'a vital part of the work, since style is the only objective criterion for determining whether a biblical passage is Deuteronomic or not'. Just how objective the material really is remains questionable. The conclusions drawn from similarities in phraseology are highly subjective. L. Stulman (*The Prose Sermons of the Book of Jeremiah: A Redescription of the Correspondences with Deuteronomistic Literature in the Light of Recent Text-Critical Research* [Atlanta: Scholars Press, 1986], p. 44) views the phrase *qr' wl''nh* as similar to Deuteronomic language although it never occurs in Deuteronomy! The expression appears in Prov. 1.28 (*'az yiqrā'unnî wᵉlō' 'eᵉneh*).

The Deuteronomist and Wisdom Literature

I turn first to suggested affinities between Deuteronomy and the book of Proverbs. In Deut. 4.2 the following prohibition occurs: 'Do not add to the word that I command you, nor take away from it' (cf. Deut. 13.1 [Eng. 12.32], 'Do not add to it or take from it'). The sayings of Agur in Prov. 30.1-14 contain this warning: 'Do not add to his words lest he rebuke you and you be made a liar'. The first text concerns divine commands, the other palpably human reflections; one gives no rationale, the other specifies the reason underlying the warning. One uses the negative particle *lō'*, the other has *'al*. One balances the warning, giving both a positive and a negative; the other does not mention taking away from something.[13] Moreover, the expression in its balanced form is at home in treaty curses and scribal colophons, which suggests that others besides the author of Deuteronomy used it.[14] Which is more likely? That a foreign sage knew and quoted Deuteronomy, or that he used language from ancient Near Eastern treaty formulation and scribal remarks about faithful renderings of a text?[15]

The injunction in Deut. 19.14 against removing a neighbor's landmark finds a parallel in Prov. 23.10, 'Do not remove a widow's land-

---

13. J.L. Crenshaw, 'Prohibitions in Proverbs and Qoheleth', in E. Ulrich *et al.* (eds.), *Priests, Prophets, and Scribes: Essays on the Formation and the Heritage of Second Temple Judaism in Honour of Joseph Blenkinsopp* (JSOTSup, 149; Sheffield: JSOT Press, 1992), pp. 115-24, and in Crenshaw, *Urgent Advice and Probing Questions*, pp. 417-25. On the sayings of Agur, see J.L. Crenshaw, 'Clanging Symbols', in D.A. Knight and P.J. Paris (eds.), *Justice and the Holy* (Philadelphia: Fortress Press, 1989), pp. 51-64, and in Crenshaw, *Urgent Advice and Probing Questions*, pp. 371-82.

14. Weinfeld concedes this fact (*Deuteronomy and the Deuteronomic School*, p. 262). He claims that a new concept of wisdom emerged during the time of Hezekiah, 'which marked the beginning of Deuteronomic literary activity' (p. 255). 'The Deuteronomist no longer conceived of "wisdom" as meaning cunning, pragmatic talent, or the possession of extraordinary knowledge, but held it to be synonymous with the knowledge and understanding of proper behaviour and with morality.' In Weinfeld's opinion, an ideological conflict resulted: human wisdom was no longer knowledge of nature and human nature but expressed itself in fear of God.

15. See the perceptive remarks on colophons by M. Fishbane, *Biblical Interpretation in Ancient Israel* (Oxford: Clarendon Press, 1985), pp. 27-32.

mark or encroach on the fields of orphans'.[16] The differences in the language stand out: *lō'* versus *'al*, *rē'ᵃkā* instead of *'ôlām* or *'almānāh*. The typical Deuteronomic rhetoric ('in your inheritance which you will hold in the land Yahweh your God gives you to possess') is lacking in Proverbs. The ancient curse in Deut. 27.17 has a participle (*massîg*); here the oath particle functions as negation and the pronominal suffix is third-person plural rather than second-person singular. Between Prov. 23.10 and these texts only two words agree: *tassēg gᵉbûl*.[17] Can anyone imagine that only the author of Deuteronomy worried about this treachery in an agrarian economy? An Egyptian parallel to this injunction suggests otherwise.[18] Egyptian usage also readily explains the phrase, 'abomination of Yahweh', in Proverbs (3.32; 11.1, 20; 12.22; 15.8, 9, 26; 16.5; 17.15; 20.10, 23), for this idea belongs to wisdom circles as well as to legal texts.[19] There is nothing exclusively Deuteronomistic about *tô'abat YHWH*; the whole society understood certain acts as repulsive to the deity.

The author of Deuteronomy urged a visually stimulating practice to assure the preservation of divine statutes: binding them on parts of the body (the hand and the forehead) and on entry ways (doorposts and gates, 6.7-9; 11.18-20). At the same time, the people must keep the commandments on the heart always, teaching children on rising, during the day and at bedtime. In Prov. 6.20-22 the father tells the son to bind parental teaching on the heart and to tie the instruction around the neck so that it will protect him during all circumstances. The differences are important: divine commandments as opposed to parental teaching, literal verbs of binding and writing over against figurative language (cf.

16. This translation assumes an original balanced parallelism of *'almānāh* and *yᵉtômîm* (cf. the Instruction of Amenemopet 6, *ANET*, p. 422).

17. Fishbane, *Biblical Interpretation in Ancient Israel*, *passim*, has shown how extraordinarily gifted editors were in handling older traditions, but such practice obscures relationships between texts. With minimal affinities between a supposed original and its adaptation, one comes up against the strong possibility that the overlap in expression is purely accidental.

18. Amenemopet 6 ('Do not carry off the landmark at the boundaries of the arable land, Nor disturb the position of the measuring-cord; Be not greedy after a cubit of land, Nor encroach upon the boundaries of a widow' [*ANET*, p. 422]).

19. Instructions from ancient Egypt use the expression, 'an abomination of the gods', quite freely (cf. Amenemopet 13, 'Do not confuse a man with a pen upon papyrus—the abomination of the god'; Amenemopet 10, 'Do not talk with a man falsely—the abomination of the god' [*ANET*, p. 423]).

Prov. 7.3, 'tablet of your heart'). From time immemorial parents have encouraged their children to put their teachings into practice, and the prominence of this admonition in ancient wisdom outside the Bible suggests that the author of Prov. 6.20-22 did not need to be instructed by the book of Deuteronomy.[20]

The other supposed borrowings from Deuteronomy within the book of Proverbs have even less claim to credence. These include the warning in Prov. 30.10 against slandering one's slave in the presence of his master, which has absolutely nothing in common with Deut. 23.15-16 (a legal injunction against returning an escaped slave to his master); the expression 'to show partiality in judgment' in Deut. 1.17 and 16.19 and in Prov. 24.23b (cf. 28.21); the words 'pursue justice' in Deut. 16.20 and Prov. 21.21; and 'inherit the land' in Prov. 2.21-22 and 10.30, frequently in Deuteronomy.[21] One must explain the change from prohibitive to participial assertion in Prov. 24.23, as well as the sequel, replacing the merism, small and great, with *bal tôb*. The prophet Amos, among others, understood the intimate connection between the pursuit of justice and life. This was no secret lore known only to the author of Deuteronomy. As for the reference to dwelling on the land in Prov. 2.21-22 and 10.30 (cf. Job 15.19; 22.8), the idea has nothing to do with the concept of divinely promised inheritance in Deuteronomy. The sages merely meant that decent people will have land to occupy (*škn*) as reward for virtue.[22]

To sum up, resemblances in phraseology between Deuteronomy and Proverbs do exist, but always amid notable differences. When using a text, an author can make alterations, but once this occurs, later readers cannot determine whether or not borrowing actually took place.

When one moves beyond linguistic similarities to broad concepts,

20. One difference between Egyptian wisdom and similar texts in Mesopotamia and the Bible is noteworthy. In the former, the address, 'my son', occurs at the beginning, with a single exception. Sumerian and biblical sages intersperse the expression, 'my son', throughout the teaching.

21. Here I disagree with Weinfeld, *Deuteronomy and the Deuteronomic School*, pp. 44-81.

22. The importance of land to anyone in Israel during the biblical period seems obvious, inasmuch as most people's survival depended on its yield. They harvested grain, grapes, olives, figs, cucumbers and similar crops, and their small cattle (sheep and goats) required enough land to survive the hostile environment. On the role of various members of an Israelite family, see L.G. Perdue *et al.*, *Families in Ancient Israel* (Louisville, KY: Westminster/John Knox Press, 1997).

does the situation change? Three ideas have been said to indicate wisdom influence on Deuteronomy or vice versa: the fear of the Lord, theodicy, and reward.[23] Not every instance of the concept, fear of Yahweh, in Deuteronomy comes under the category of a covenantal relationship, otherwise how could the author accuse Amalek, a foreigner, of lacking this quality (25.18)?[24] Nevertheless, that falls far short of asserting that the fear of Yahweh constitutes the first principle and impetus of all knowledge. The author of Deuteronomy makes a similar point quite differently: foreigners will recognize that keeping the divine statutes is the people's wisdom and understanding (4.6). Moreover, the notion of fearing God is not even unique to Deuteronomy within the Pentateuch, for it looms large in contexts normally attributed to an Elohistic writer.

If the concept of theodicy were unique to Deuteronomy and Proverbs, one could reasonably argue that the two books are somehow related. Unfortunately, theodicy pervades the thinking of the ancient world, leaving virtually nothing untouched.[25] Its centrality to thinkers everywhere makes it pointless to claim that a special relationship exists between Deuteronomy and Proverbs, or Job, for that matter. Belief that deserving persons had a secure future (*'aḥᵃrît*) and that their hope would not be cut off (Prov. 23.18; 24.14; cf. Ps. 37.38; 73.17) characterized prophets, priests, sages and apocalyptists in the ancient world. Reward and punishment belong to this nexus of thought. The idea was so widespread that none could escape its influence, even when reacting strongly against the concept (cf. the book of Job). What about specific applications of the theory such as the claim that Yahweh disciplines the one he loves just as a father reproves the son who pleases him (Prov. 3.12)?[26] When Deuteronomy makes a similar point, the language differs

23. Weinfeld, *Deuteronomy and the Deuteronomic School*, pp. 274-81 (fear of God), pp. 316-19 (theodicy), pp. 307-13 (reward).

24. Weinfeld, *Deuteronomy and the Deuteronomic School*, pp. 274-75, acknowledges that the concept of fear of the god has no national limitations.

25. J.L. Crenshaw (ed.), *Theodicy in the Old Testament* (Philadelphia: Fortress Press; London: SPCK, 1983). The importance of this concept to the author of Gen. 18 has recently claimed my attention ('The Sojourner Has Come to Play the Judge: Theodicy on Trial', in T. Linefelt and T.K. Beal (eds.), *God in the Frey: A Tribute to Walter Brueggemann* [Minneapolis: Fortress Press, 1998], pp. 83-92).

26. The presence of harsh discipline in pedagogical settings makes a saying such as 'Without love there can be no instruction' stand out all the more. It is not clear precisely what this Egyptian saying implies: that learning requires love for the subject matter, love for the student, love for the teacher, or all the above. Mutuality

significantly: a form of the verb *yāšar* instead of *yākaḥ*, *'îš* for *'āb*, and no indication that the son pleases the father (Deut. 8.5). In Proverbs the analogy moves from the divine to the human, whereas Deuteronomy argues the other way around—Yahweh behaves in the same way humans do. Strikingly, the author of Prov. 3.12 stresses divine love, missing in Deut. 8.5.

Deuteronomy and Qoheleth

Two contexts in Qoheleth require comment: 5.1-5 and 12.13-14. The author of Deuteronomy observes three things about vows: (1) when you make one, be sure to carry it out; (2) abstaining from making a vow is acceptable conduct; and (3) Yahweh keeps track of promises and requires a full reckoning (Deut. 23.22-24 [Eng. 21-23]). In the context of warning against hasty speech, presumably of a religious nature, Qoheleth points to the vast gulf separating Elohim from humankind, one that invites reticence in speech. Qoheleth then turns to the topic of vows, after deprecating loquacity. He urges prompt payment of religious vows, inasmuch as the deity has no particular fondness for fools. Repeating the advice to pay the vow, this time in those exact words, Qoheleth expresses the opinion that abstaining from such promises is preferable to making them and subsequently failing to carry them out. He goes on to warn against any conduct that places the body in jeopardy; as a precaution against danger, he urges fear of Elohim, which apparently means exactly that rather than a mild notion of religious devotion. The importance of vows in Israelite society can be seen from the fact that even Qoheleth comments on the practice, and this daily occurrence, not the book of Deuteronomy, shaped the advice in Qoh. 5.15. Admittedly, both Qoheleth and Deuteronomy use virtually the same vocabulary at one juncture: 'When you vow an oath...do not put it off' (*kî-tiddōr neder...lo't^e'aḥēr l^ešall^emô* in Deut. 23.22, *ka'^ašer tiddōr neder...al-t^e'aḥēr l^ešall^emô* in Qoh. 5.3), but the idiom was a common one.[27]

The second epilogue to Qoheleth sums up matters quite simply—fear

of interest must surely be present before learning takes place.

27. Qoheleth represents a distancing from the deity, both with respect to the designation for God (Elohim in Qoheleth, Yahweh in Deuteronomy) and in the avoidance of a personal pronoun attached to the word for deity. On the text, see J.L. Crenshaw, *Ecclesiastes* (Philadelphia: Westminster Press, 1987), pp. 116-17.

Elohim and keep his commandments—although completely at odds with the overwhelming sentiment of the book.[28] The moderating effort to negate the impact of Qoheleth's skepticism may come from traditional Yahwism, but that does not result in a personalizing of the deity, who retains the general name Elohim here. Furthermore, this author envisions a final judgment when every secret thing will be exposed. The author of Deuteronomy also reflects on secret things, but they belong to the special knowledge of Yahweh as opposed to the revealed things in the Mosaic legislation (29.29).

Deuteronomy and Late Liturgical Prayers

Liturgical prayers in the ninth chapters of three books—Ezra, Nehemiah and Daniel—use occasional language reminiscent of the book of Deuteronomy. Two reasonable explanations for this phenomenon come to mind. The several books reflect a special religious discourse[29] or they indicate conscious imitation of an original religious document, probably Deuteronomy.[30] The balance of probability goes to the first explanation for this phenomenon, although editorial activity cannot be ruled out. The conservative nature of piety encourages the use of traditional language, but the reservoir from which the worshiper draws is fed by more than one stream.[31] Similarities with Deutero-Isaiah and prose

28. G.T. Sheppard, 'The Epilogue to Qoheleth as Theological Commentary', *CBQ* 39 (1977), pp. 182-89; and *idem, Wisdom as a Hermeneutical Construct* (BZAW, 151; Berlin: W. de Gruyter, 1980). C.-L. Seow, ' "Beyond Them, My Son, Be Warned": The Epilogue of Qoheleth Revisited', in Barré (ed.), *Wisdom, You Are my Sister*, pp. 125-41, does not consider the epilogue to be alien to the teachings of the rest of the book ('Only vv. 13b-14 may be regarded as secondary, but like vv. 9-13a, the content of these verses is not contrary to the rest of the book', p. 141). The perspective is not far different, Seow writes, from that expressed in Deut. 4.6.

29. J. Bright (*Jeremiah* [AB, 21; Garden City, NY: Doubleday, 1965]) and A. Weiser (*The Psalms* [OTL; Philadelphia: Westminster Press, 1962]) have rightly recognized the presence of a liturgical mode of discourse in the time of Jeremiah and later, a style that resembles didactic expressions in Deuteronomy. If they are right, one need not assume that a biblical book, specifically Deuteronomy, shaped the language and style.

30. Weinfeld, *Deuteronomy and the Deuteronomic School*, passim.

31. J.L. Crenshaw ('The Restraint of Reason, the Humility of Prayer', in *idem, Urgent Advice and Probing Questions*, pp. 206-21) traces the development of prayer in sapiential circles, particularly in Sirach.

passages in the book of Jeremiah quickly come to mind.[32]

The relevant expressions in Ezra 9 include 'thy servants the prophets' and 'as at this day', together with the idea that Israelites must not intermarry with their neighbors (Deut. 7.3). The prayer in Nehemiah 9 adds the concept of Yahweh's uniqueness and mentions the importance of divine reputation ('thou alone' and 'acquired a name'). To these expressions Daniel 9 adds an allusion to the curse recorded in Deut. 28.15-45, while reiterating such language as 'his servants the prophets' and 'acquired a name'. These prayers remind God, and indirectly the reader, of a host of experiences in the wilderness, but the episodes are not unique to Deuteronomy. The closest resemblance comes in the rhetoric, often wordy, but even here one finds more restraint than in Deuteronomy (cf. Dan. 9.15, where 'with a mighty hand' stands alone without the balancing 'and a strong arm').

The matter becomes enormously complicated when one considers the relationship between Deuteronomy and the Psalter. To be sure, the same words appear here and there in both books, but one expects such overlap in similar discourse. Didacticism punctuates certain psalms (e.g. Ps. 34) in the same way it shapes discourse in aphorisms and instructions, on the one hand, and Deuteronomy, on the other hand. For this reason, Weinfeld's assembling of common words in Psalms and Deuteronomy carries little weight—even the emphasis on Yahweh's uniqueness (Pss. 83.19 [Eng. 18]; 86.10), the necessity of acting 'with all one's heart' (Pss. 119.10, 34, 69), and the indication of allegiance, cleaving to Yahweh (Ps. 63.9 [Eng. 8]) or to his testimonies (Ps. 119.31).[33] Such resemblances between Deuteronomy and a torah Psalm occasion little surprise.

The remaining books in the Writings operate in different realms of discourse from Deuteronomy—Song of Songs with its erotic lyrics, Lamentations with its heavy emotional distress, Ruth's idyllic story, Esther's realistic politics and the Chronicler's revisionist history.[34] If Deuteronomistic editors really existed as late as the period from Nehemiah to the Maccabean revolt,[35] why did they overlook Esther, a

32. The ancestry of religious language in Deutero-Isaiah probably includes royal boasts from Mesopotamia as well as lyrical texts.

33. Weinfeld, *Deuteronomy and the Deuteronomic School*, Appendix A.

34. Space does not permit a detailed discussion of these biblical books.

35. R.F. Person, Jr (*Second Zechariah and the Deuteronomic School* [JSOTSup, 167; Sheffield: JSOT Press, 1993], pp. 146-75) thinks a Deuteronomic school con-

book that invites a different understanding of divine activity than that offered, one that identifies human actions as the determinant of the nation's fate?[36] The absence of distinct Deuteronomistic ideas in these books raises the issue of selectivity.[37] Why would redactors ignore a book that cried out for alternative interpretations of reality?[38] Did the editors not know Esther?

Some Methodological Observations

Having examined the linguistic connections between Deuteronomy and the Writings, I want to close with some comments about the assumptions underlying the current pan-Deuteronomism. First, several types of argument lack cogency: those based on a common social location (e.g. that both Deuteronomy and X derive from the Northern kingdom) and those that set two books over against each other (e.g. that the author of Job was reacting to the teachings of Deuteronomy).[39] Similarly, the approach that explains differences in phraseology between Deuteronomy and other books as developments in the linguistic expression of Deuteronomistic redactors seems inadequate. The same goes for attempts to attribute different themes to changing socio-economic situations. Such arbitrary claims make it impossible to establish controls over one's logic, which changes to suit the occasion. Languages do change, but this fact makes it impossible to establish literary dependence when the two expressions differ noticeably.

tinued in the exile, returning to Yehud with Zerubbabel and later becoming disenchanted with Ezra because of his ties with the Achaemenids. Person views the increase in eschatology as one result of their disappointment. He also senses a change in Deuteronomic language over the years (p. 98) and a vigorous interpretive community (p. 103).

36. A sharper contrast with Deuteronomy's preoccupation with Yahweh's 'hands-on' approach to governing the chosen people can scarcely be imagined.

37. The choice of texts to annotate almost never expresses itself in such a way as to reveal the rationale behind it. Some texts seem to have cried out for editorial revision, but none occurred; others appear to have been dragged, kicking and screaming, through a process of virtual reformulation.

38. Worldviews may have clashed in this instance, as the scholarly discussion about the absence of any reference to God in the book of Esther indicates rather emphatically.

39. Person (*Second Zechariah and the Deuteronomic School*) relies heavily on social setting and linguistic affinities.

Second, most people in Israel and Judah were illiterate, even as late as the second century.[40] One wonders how Deuteronomistic redactors could have gotten access to exemplars of the individual scrolls of the Writings.[41] Only the wealthy could afford scrolls, and individual libraries probably did not exist.[42] Even if exiled Judeans were introduced to literature, they lacked the means of becoming literate.[43] The few scribal guilds probably guarded their craft,[44] and writing was incidental to learning, even for Ben Sira.[45] Those scholars who think Deuteronomistic redactors persisted from the sixth century onwards seem to think of a literate society with accessible libraries and copious manuscripts. The exceptional situation at Qumran[46] should not be read back into earlier centuries in Yehud. Apocalyptic understandings of reality produced entirely new ways of thinking about written texts;[47] so did *pešer*

40. I examine the evidence for literacy in ancient Israel in *Education in Ancient Israel: Across the Deadening Silence* (ABRL; New York: Doubleday, 1998).

41. Lohfink, 'Gab es eine deuteronomistische Bewegung?'.

42. The first Greek private library seems to date from the third century BCE.

43. W.V. Harris (*Ancient Literacy* [Cambridge, MA: Harvard University Press, 1989]) mentions the various factors that made literacy possible on a wider scale. These include the invention of the printing press, the availability of cheap paper, Protestantism's emphasis on reading the Bible, the invention of eye glasses, the industrial revolution with its need for literate supervisors, philanthropy, and density of population. An agricultural economy in Israel presented a natural hindrance to formal education, for children were needed to assist in the almost endless tasks associated with farming.

44. The Instruction for Duauf (Satire of the Trades) from ancient Egypt offers an example of scribal elitism and disdain for other trades, whereas the similar text in Sir. 38.24–39.11 states that society cannot exist without the services of such workers.

45. J.L. Crenshaw, 'The Primacy of Listening in Ben Sira's Pedagogy', in Barré (ed.), *Wisdom, You Are my Sister*, pp. 172-87.

46. Lohfink ('Gab es eine deuteronomistiche Bewegung?') states that, besides Essene writings, Qumran has yielded 33 exemplars of the Psalter, 27 of Deuteronomy, 20 of Isaiah and 16 of *Jubilees*.

47. In Mesopotamia omen texts played a central role in predicting the future, and access to crucial documents belonged to a few knowledgeable scribes. Esotericism thrived in Jewish apocalyptic circles, and conscious efforts at concealing data by means of coded language came to prominence. In addition, apocalyptic authors wrote under the names of well-known figures from the distant past. For such deception to succeed, their followers claimed that the texts had been hidden among the faithful for generations.

readings, which elevate a sacred text almost to the numinous.[48] Finally, if Deuteronomistic redactors were so active in late canonical texts, why did they ignore Sirach with its numerous possibilities?[49]

48. The sacred word was thought to have been invested with profound meaning that had to be interpreted by discerning students. Those who searched out the right interpretation (*pešer*) of a text became convinced of its awesome mystery (*raz*).

49. L. Schrader (*Leiden und Gerechtigkeit: Studien zu Theologie und Text-geschichte des Sirachbuches* [BBET, 27; Frankfurt: Peter Lang, 1994]) reckons with minor textual additions during the Maccabean era but does not find evidence of extensive redaction by Deuteronomistic scribes.

Part III

PAN-DEUTERONOMISM: CASE STUDIES

IS THERE EVIDENCE OF A DTR REDACTION
IN THE SINAI PERICOPE (EXODUS 19–24, 32–34)?

John Van Seters

The presence of a deuteronomistic (dtr) redaction in the Pentateuch outside of Deuteronomy has become a highly complex and much discussed topic in the last few years.[1] I have addressed this issue on previous occasions, advocating the view that it is incorrect to speak of a dtr redaction of the Tetrateuch.[2] Recent discussion, however, has raised a new set of issues, so I will take up the matter again, and here I will deal primarily with the Sinai pericope (Exod. 19–24, 32–34) since that has become a focal point in the current debate.[3]

Before engaging in a review of this debate, it is important to be clear about the object of our search, a dtr redaction, so that we know what we are looking for. By 'deuteronomistic' I understand the term to mean a piece of literature that is closely related to the recognized work of the Deuteronomist within the corpus of Deuteronomy and Deuteronomistic History (DtrH) and that reflects a set of theological and social concerns

---

1. See the recent review of the problem and the literature in M. Vervenne, 'The Question of "Deuteronomistic" Elements in Genesis to Numbers', in F. García Martínez *et al.* (eds.), *Studies in Deuteronomy in Honour of C.J. Labuschagne on the Occasion of his 65th Birthday* (VTSup, 53: Leiden: E.J. Brill, 1994), pp. 243-68.

2. 'The So-Called Deuteronomistic Redaction of the Pentateuch', in J.A. Emerton (ed.), *Congress Volume: Leuven 1989* (VTSup, 43; Leiden: E.J. Brill, 1992), pp. 58-77; *Prologue to History: The Yahwist as Historian in Genesis* (Louisville, KY: Westminster/John Knox Press, 1992), pp. 227-45; 'The Deuteronomistic Redaction of the Pentateuch: The Case Against It', in M. Vervenne and J. Lust (eds.), *Deuteronomy and Deuteronomic Literature: Festschrift C.H.W. Brekelmans* (Leuven: Peeters, 1997), pp. 301-20.

3. See the numerous articles on this unit in M. Vervenne (ed.), *Studies in the Book of Exodus* (BETL, 126; Leuven: Peeters, 1996).

that are most characteristic of this editorial hand.[4] It is not enough that an author merely shares some of the same terminology if its use is quite different from Deuteronomy and DtrH. I understand the term 'redaction' to mean a limited editorial activity of collecting or combining written materials. When a writer's own contribution is extensive then we are dealing with an author and have every right to expect those marks of authorship that have otherwise been expected of 'sources'. It is a serious abuse of the concept of redactor to attribute to such a person a rather heterogeneous collection of written materials because one has difficulty associating them with a reconstructed source of the Pentateuch.

Lothar Perlitt

The point of departure for much of the present discussion about a dtr redaction of the Tetrateuch is the renewed effort to find the oldest basis for the Sinai-Horeb tradition and the time and circumstances under which the law (*Torah*) became associated with it. The question is present in the earlier treatments of Wellhausen, von Rad and Noth, among others, but comes to the fore particularly with L. Perlitt.[5] It is he who argues that the oldest tradition of Sinai was a theophany (Exod. 19) accompanied by a ritual (Exod. 24) and that the association of law and covenant with Sinai is to be connected with a dtr movement of the seventh century BCE. Perlitt finds the presence of a dtr redaction in Exod. 19.3b-8 and in the additions of covenant making to the ritual of 24.3-8 but especially within chs. 32–34. Perlitt regards both the Decalogue and the Covenant Code as secondary units within the original Sinai tradition, but he does not attempt his own literary analysis of Exodus 19–24 in terms of the older Documentary Hypothesis.[6]

Since the work of Perlitt, however, there has been a strong tendency by many scholars to identify an early pre-exilic theophanic tradition

---

4.   This is a very brief summary of the position of N. Lohfink to which I heartily subscribe. See his 'Gab es eine deuteronomistischen Bewegung?', in W. Gross (ed.), *Jeremia und die 'deuteronomistische Bewegung'* (BBB, 98; Weinheim: Beltz Athenäum, 1995), pp. 313-82, reprinted in an abridged and translated version as the second essay in this volume.

5.   L. Perlitt, *Bundestheologie im Alten Testament* (WMANT, 36; Neukirchen–Vluyn: Neukirchener Verlag, 1969), pp. 156-238.

6.   Perlitt, *Bundestheologie*, pp. 157-58. See esp. p. 158 n. 3.

associated with Sinai that was secondarily modified by a dtr redactor to include the giving of the law. I will now look somewhat selectively at recent developments of this thesis.

Erhard Blum

Following the attack on the Documentary Hypothesis in the mid-1970s, E. Blum advocated the thesis of two major literary compositions within the Pentateuch/Tetrateuch: a *D-Komposition* (KD) followed by a *P-Komposition* (KP).[7] Within the Sinai pericope it is easy for Blum to take over Perlitt's view of the dtr redaction of the Sinai tradition as his KD with its incorporation of older traditions, including the Covenant Code.[8] Blum is uncommitted about whether the Decalogue (20.1-17) belongs to this compositional phase or not.

Frank Crüsemann

F. Crüsemann, in a recent work, *The Torah*,[9] likewise follows the view that law (the Decalogue and the Covenant Code) is not original to the Sinai tradition.[10] He adopts Blum's model of literary analysis but with some significant modifications. In particular, Crüsemann reverses the order of KD and KP and construes the dtr shaping of the Sinai pericope as a reaction to a priestly formation of Sinai that already existed. In his view the filling out of the earlier Sinai pericope of Exodus 19–24 goes back to a post-P dtr expansion that he calls the Pentateuchal Redaction, to which he also attributes the connection between the Tetrateuch and Deuteronomy, some time in the Persian period. Exodus 19–24 was used by this redactor as a counter-balance to the body of priestly legislation.

Crüsemann considers Sinai to be originally a tradition of deliverance not theophany, so that the law's first connection with it is as an act of salvation, part of their deliverance from Egypt. He points to the early

---

7.   E. Blum, *Studien zur Komposition des Pentateuch* (BZAW, 189; Berlin: W. de Gruyter, 1990).

8.   Blum, *Studien*, pp. 45-99.

9.   F. Crüsemann, *The Torah: Theology and Social History of Old Testament Law* (Minneapolis: Fortress Press, 1996; a translation from the German, *Die Tora: Theologie und Sozialgeschichte des alttestamentlichen Gesetzes* (Munich: Chr. Kaiser Verlag, 1992). Citations will be to the English edition.

10.   For what follows see Crüsemann, *The Torah*, pp. 27-57.

poetic references to Sinai (Judg. 5.4-5; Deut. 33.2; Ps. 68.8-9) and to
the Elijah story (1 Kgs 19) to argue for a pre-dtr understanding of Sinai-
Horeb that fits this view. He also draws on Exodus 3 with its
announcement of deliverance to support his position. His dating of both
1 Kings 19 and Exodus 3, however, is problematic.[11]

It is, however, in his view of Exodus 32–34 that Crüsemann really
parts company with Blum and even Perlitt. Crüsemann understands this
unit as a narrative created in response to the fall of the Northern Kingdom. The golden calf story reflects the Northern state's bull cult, the
cause of their defeat, which is here used both as a warning to the Southern Kingdom and as a promise of Israel's survival through loyalty to
Yahweh. In 34.11-27 the regulation of such loyalty and correct worship
of God is set down on stone tablets, which Moses rewrote to replace
those he had broken and to reflect a covenant renewal. This 'ritual
code' and not the Decalogue is the original content of the stone tablets.
The substitute of the Decalogue for the content of the tablets is a later
dtr revision. Crüsemann sees behind the story an actual series of political events in which a set of destroyed texts from a northern sanctuary
(Hos. 8.12) was renewed in the South in the late eighth century.

Crüsemann believes that Exodus 32–34 was a self-contained narrative (missing its beginning) that made the first connection between
divine instruction and the divine mountain originally associated with
God's deliverance from Egypt (Exod. 3). How is it that such a story
about a religious crisis of the late eighth century was placed in this
early period and at this mountain? Crüsemann sees the connection
between Jeroboam's state cult and the exodus event in 1 Kgs 12.28 as
the basis for its placement after God's deliverance from Egypt. The
account of divine forgiveness after apostasy in Exodus is understood as
an offer of deliverance from the Assyrian disaster after the Northern
Kingdom's apostasy, and for this reason it is set in the time and place of
the mountain of deliverance The level of unsupported speculation is
very high at this point, especially if the account of Jeroboam's state cult
in 1 Kgs 12.26-33 and its association with the Northern Kingdom's dis-

---

11. Blum (*Studien*, p. 40) considers Exod. 3.1–4.18 as all part of his postexilic
KD. See also J. Van Seters, *The Life of Moses: The Yahwist as Historian in Exodus–Numbers* (Louisville, KY: Westminster/John Knox Press, 1994), pp. 36-63. On
the lateness of 1 Kgs 19 see S.L. McKenzie, *The Trouble with Kings* (VTSup, 42;
Leiden: E.J. Brill, 1991), pp. 81-86.

aster in 2 Kgs 17.7-23 are viewed as the work of DtrH.[12]

From this narrative stage (Exod. 32–34) to the later full-blown development of the Sinai pericope there are two steps. According to Crüsemann, the first is the construction of the priestly tabernacle text around Exodus 32–34. P also includes the Holiness Code in the Sinai event, thereby laying the basis for the present-day association of Sinai as the place where both the cult and justice were founded. Second, the passages in dtr style, the incorporation of the Decalogue and the Covenant Code within Exodus 19–24 and the composition of Deuteronomy 5 and 9–10 with their Horeb-Covenant conception are all part of a Pentateuchal redaction of the pre-existing P Sinai conception. It is this that creates the integration of the priestly Tetrateuch with Deuteronomy and its lay theology. Prior to this, *Torah* in D was not connected with Horeb-Sinai but with the exodus and the preparation for the conquest. This is why Sinai is not part of the historical credos until very late (Neh. 9.13-14).

Without going into detail on Crüsemann's treatment of individual texts, I will mention only four issues. First, it is doubtful that Crüsemann can maintain the understanding of Exodus 32–34 as a self-contained narrative independent from Exodus 19–24. Both E. Zenger[13] and Blum[14] have been critical of him on this point and have offered many instances of the interconnection. In addition, the strong evidence that Exodus 32 is later than and dependent upon Deuteronomy 9–10 cannot be ignored or dismissed by Crüsemann.[15] Second, the theme that the golden calves are the 'great sin' that destroyed the Northern Kingdom (1 Kgs 12.26-32; 2 Kgs 17) is the invention of DtrH. Exodus 32 is entirely dependent upon this scheme and on the specific account of the apostasy in 1 Kgs 12.26-32. Third, to include within the same redactor's work both versions of the Decalogue (Exod. 20 and Deut. 5) and two

---

12. See J. Van Seters, *In Search of History: Historiography in the Ancient World and the Origins of Biblical History* (New Haven: Yale University Press, 1983), pp. 313-14.

13. E. Zenger, 'Wie und wozu die Tora zum Sinai kam: Literarische und theologische Beobachtungen zu Exodus 19–34', in Vervenne (ed.), *Studies in the Book of Exodus*, pp. 265-88.

14. E. Blum, 'Das sog. "Privilegrecht" in Exodus 34, 11-26: Ein Fixpunkt der Komposition des Exodusbuches?', in Vervenne (ed.), *Studies in the Book of Exodus*, pp. 347-66.

15. See Van Seters, *The Life of Moses*, pp. 290-318.

parallel but different accounts of the Sinai/Horeb event does not seem to me in the least likely. Fourth, there is no attempt at a serious literary critical analysis of Exodus 19–20, 24 with its clear evidence of two literary layers in the text.

Erich Zenger

E. Zenger, for his part, advocates a three-stage development of the Sinai pericope.[16] In the first stage he proposes a basic text that contains an account of a theophany in ch. 19, a ritual in ch. 24, the golden calf apostasy story of ch. 32 and the 'law of religious obligations' of 34.6-7, 12-26. This source, which he characterizes as a *'Jerusalemer Geschichtswerk'*, a proto-dt work that extended from Genesis 12–Numbers 32, is associated with the early Manasseh period. The next stage of development of the Sinai pericope is a dtr reworking (*Bearbeitung*), which construes the event as a covenant making in chs. 19–24, a covenant breaking in ch. 32 and a covenant renewal in chs. 33–34. It is this dtr redactor who is responsible for the incorporation of the 'old and highly respected Book of the Covenant' within the Sinai event, which is made analogous to the Deuteronomic Code (Deut. 12–26, 28) by means of the dtr references in 24.3-8 to these laws as the 'Book of the Covenant' and the 'words and commandments' of God. This dtr redactor opens the Book of the Covenant with a version of the image prohibition (Exod. 20.23) to anticipate the violation of this law in ch. 32 as a covenant breech, followed by the covenant renewal by the gracious covenant God in chs. 33–34. The renewal of the stone tablets in 34.1, 4 is combined with the 'law of obligations' of 34.11-26 as a recapitulation of the Covenant Code reshaped with the use of dtr language (cf. the dtr epilogue of Exod. 23.20-33). This dtr treatment of covenant breech and covenant renewal is associated with the crisis of the exile.

The third revision of the Sinai Pericope is attributed to a post-P pentateuchal redactor who incorporated a priestly version of the Decalogue into the Sinai event to stand alongside of the Covenant Code on the analogy of Deuteronomy with its Decalogue and law code.

My problems with this analysis are threefold: (1) Apart from the *a priori* conviction that there must be a pre-D source in the Sinai pericope, I can find no clear arguments in Zenger for distinguishing his proto-dt JG (=Jehovist) source from his dtr redaction. They belong

16. See especially the work cited in n. 13 above.

together as a continuous narrative. (2) The idea that a dtr redactor would set aside both the Decalogue and the D code and replace it with another law code and then label it the 'Book of the Covenant', using the same term that is used for the D Code, is not credible. DtrH and DtrJer always mean the D Code when they refer to the covenant law or the laws of Moses. Furthermore, the suggestion in Exod. 24.12 and 34.11-28 that the content of the tables of the law was not the Ten Commandments but a different set of laws is another serious contradiction of both Deuteronomy 4 and 5. And why would a dtr redactor add an old, outmoded law (the Covenant Code) when it had been replaced, so we are told, by Deuteronomy? Why did he not merely add the Decalogue, which could have served his purpose of anticipating ch. 32 just as well. (3) Finally, there seems to me to be little point in adding yet another Pentateuchal redactor to introduce 19.20-24; 20.1-17 (the Decalogue) into the final version when the P author will do just as well. The unit is clearly an addition between 19.19 and 20.18 and belongs together with the rest of the P material in 24.15b-18a. The only reason that it is given to a redactor is to try to preserve the independence of P at all costs since 19.20–20.17 can only be understood as a supplement to a pre-existing text.

Eckart Otto

For E. Otto, the study of the evolution of Israelite law and its integration into the narrative framework is said to be the key to solving Pentateuchal literary problems. It would seem, therefore, that the Sinai pericope and its compositional history should be central to this task. His proposed analysis, however, appears to be a patchwork of the suggestions made previously by Crüsemann and Zenger.[17]

Otto takes his point of departure from Crüsemann in proposing a post-P Pentateuchal redactor who was the first to integrate the legal material of the Decalogue and Covenant Code into the Sinai pericope and to make the connection between the priestly Tetrateuch and the D corpus. This is similar to Zenger, except that Otto has combined Zenger's dtr redactor and a post-P Pentateuchal redactor into one level. Thus, in his diachronic analysis of the Sinai pericope Otto discusses

17. These remarks will focus on Otto's recent article 'Die nachpriester-schriftliche Pentateuchredaktion im Buch Exodus', in Vervenne (ed.), *Studies in the Book of Exodus*, pp. 61-111.

three levels of development: (1) the latest (and most extensively treated) is the post-P Pentateuchal redaction (= Zenger's dtr redactor + a post-P redaction); (2) prior to this was the P corpus; and (3) alongside of P and independent from it was the pre-P theophany tradition (= Zenger's earliest stage). I will consider his proposed analysis in reverse order:

1. The pre-P level, that is, Exod. 19.2b, 3a, 10-20; 34.(11a), 18-23, 25-27. This is hardly much of a narrative. Its beginning is very weak: 'And Israel encamped before the mountain, and Moses went up to God'. As the start of a narrative it makes no sense. The separation from 19.2a, which gives the statement of travel and arrival, is arbitrary.[18] Furthermore, there is no reason to exclude v. 9 from what follows, since it announces the theophany and what will happen in it, namely, that the people will witness God speaking with Moses, which is what happens in the climax in v. 19. This theophany is continued in 20.18, as commentators have long noted, so that what follows in 19.20-24; 20.1-17 is all secondary. Nor is 19.10-19 a unit. Verses 12-13a contradict the whole point of consecrating the people (vv. 10-11) so that they can approach the deity. These verses are closely connected to 19.20-24 and belong to the same source (P).[19]

Otto does follow Zenger in retaining an old legal code in 34.18-27, but Blum's most recent study of the whole of 34.11-27 as a late text makes this problematic.[20] Furthermore, this law code does not follow as a continuation of the narrative in 19.10-20, as he suggests. Otto's early theophanic source must be rejected as incoherent and inconsistent.

2. P, that is, Exod. 19.1, 2a; 24.15b-18aα; 25-31; 35.1–Lev. 9.24. This hardly constitutes a self-contained P narrative. Particularly difficult is the radical break between 31.17, where Moses is on the mountain with God, and 35.1, where he is down with the people, with no accounting for the transition. Even if one combined P with Otto's pre-P source it would still not make any difference in solving this problem. It is obvious that P is an addition to chs. 32–34, but such a view would upset Otto's whole scheme.

---

18. This splitting of v. 2 could perhaps be justified by the old Documentary Hypothesis on the notion that such fragments could be combined by a redactor. But if Otto has given up the old source theory then he cannot use the same division of text.

19. See my discussion in *The Life of Moses*, pp. 248-52.

20. Blum, 'Das sog. Privilegrecht', pp. 290-318.

3. Pentateuchal Redactor (consisting of the following blocks): narrative additions, namely, Exod. 19.3b-9; 20.18-21; 24.3-8, 12-15aα, 18b; 32–34*; addition of the Covenant Code, that is, Exod. 20.22–23.33, to which the redactor made the following expansions: 20.22 23; 21.1; 22.19b, 20aβb, 21, 23, 24b, 30; 23.9, 13, 14-19 (20-33); addition of the Decalogue, namely, Exod. (19.21-24) 20.1-17. Let us look at these blocks in stages:

(a) First we may dismiss Exod. 19.20-24; 20.1-17, since it has no connection with the rest of the material under discussion. It is clearly Priestly and interrupts the continuity of 19.19 and 20.18.[21]

(b) The supposed expansions to the Covenant Code are nothing of the kind.[22] The humanitarian laws in 22.20-24 are generally considered late, because they betray prophetic and Deuteronomic influence. And since Otto regards the cultic laws of 34.18-26* as pre-P and original, he must view those of 23.14-19 as secondary. Yet why did the redactor make 34.18-26 the content of the stone tablets if he also included the Decalogue, and if Deuteronomy 9–10, which was his source for Exodus 32–34, told him that the content of the tablets was the Decalogue? The whole editorial activity of Otto's redactor is so erratic that it does not make any sense.

(c) Once there is no longer any need to find an early source within the Sinai pericope, then texts such as 19.3b-8(9) and 20.18-23 fit very smoothly within the whole sequence of 19.2-19 (excluding vv. 12-13a); 20.18-23 and lead easily into the Covenant Code without break or tension.

Otto's efforts to make this source post-P in date appears rather forced at times. An example is his suggestion that 19.3b with its use of the parallelism 'house of Jacob' and 'sons of Israel' reflects P terminology. It is true that in *one* instance in P (Gen. 46.27) the term 'household of Jacob' occurs where it refers to all the members of Jacob's household, literally, who migrated with him to Egypt. But that is a different use of the term and it is *never* used as a parallel for the 'sons of Israel', which is P's regular term for the people. Furthermore, the divine speech in

21. Already Blum expressed some confusion on these texts, and this muddle is repeated by Crüsemann and Otto. For Zenger they belong to a separate post-P redactor.

22. See my study, 'Cultic Laws in the Covenant Code and their Relationship to Deuteronomy and the Holiness Code', in Vervenne (ed.), *Studies in the Book of Exodus*, pp. 319-45.

19.3b-6 has the form of a prophetic oracle with a certain amount of parallelism. The same parallelism of Jacob/Israel occurs frequently in the Balaam oracles (Num. 23–24), and it is very common in a wide range of prophetic literature, including the use of the term 'house of Jacob' as a parallel for Israel. The influence of this text is from prophecy, not from P.

Nor is it at all likely that the phrase 'kingdom of priests' results from any P influence. On the contrary, it is part of the whole perspective of this source to understand all of the people of Yahweh as having a priestly function, to which they are duly consecrated in 24.3-8 in radical distinction from the priesthood of P. The idea that it reflects the perspective of the '*Jerusalemer Tempelgemeinde*' of the Persian period is beyond comprehension. Once one properly distinguishes non-P from P, there is nothing in the former that reflects P.

Furthermore, Otto's post-P redactor is responsible for putting into the Pentateuch a long out-dated Covenant Code (with some minor additions) and setting it alongside of and in contradiction to Deuteronomy (although he is a Deuteronomist) and for incorporating the Holiness Code into the Pentateuch in order to produce still further contradictions. He is further responsible for parts of Deuteronomy, such as Deuteronomy 4, which parallels but contradicts his own composition of the Sinai theophany in Exodus 19–20. This post-P redaction, as a literary work, has neither coherence nor consistency nor any degree of literary integrity. It therefore has nothing left to commend it and may be dismissed from further consideration.

I have laid out my own approach to the Sinai Pericope in my book, *The Life of Moses*, and cannot begin to repeat all of that here. Basically there are only two sources, a post-Dtr J source with a P supplement.[23] I part company with Perlitt and all of those who followed him in the development of the notion of a dtr redaction of an earlier Sinai theophany tradition. Let me summarize briefly my own view of the development:[24]

1. There was an early theophany tradition associated with the worship of Yahweh, but it is not to be found in Exodus 19–20. The notion of theophany, so common throughout the Near East, is at home in association with Yahweh within the Zion tradition, quite independent from any

---

23. *J*: Exod. 19.2-11, 13b-19; 20.18–23.33; 24.3-8, 12-15a, 18b; 31.18; 32-34.
P: Exod. 19.1, 12-13a, 20-24; 20.1-17; 24.1-2, 9-11, 15b-18a; 25.1–31.17; 35-40.
24. See my remarks in *The Life of Moses*, pp. 286-89.

exodus/wilderness connection. In some early poetry Yahweh is spoken of as coming in theophanic splendor from the southern desert region of Seir, Edom, Paran and Sinai (Judg. 5.4-5; Deut. 33.2) but this was not a departure from a particular theophanic mountain nor did it have any direct connection with the exodus. It is Deuteronomy that creates, for the first time, the idea of a theophany experience at a mountain in the wilderness in a region that is vaguely named Horeb (= 'barren'). The theophany is simply used by D to enhance the 'ten words' that the people hear God speak. To have God speak the whole of the D code at one time would hardly do, so the law code is given privately to Moses as their go-between.

2. J takes over both the combination of theophany at the mountain and the giving of the law from D *and from nowhere else*. However, he modifies it in two important respects. First, the theophany is not for the purpose of the people hearing the Decalogue but in order that they may witness God's voice speaking to Moses, which sounded like a loud blast of the *shofar*, and in this way legitimate Moses' special role as intermediary. Thus, in J's version of the lawgiving at Sinai, all the laws are given to Moses alone at the same time, both those that are parallel to the Decalogue and those that correspond to the D code; all are in just one 'Book of the Covenant'. That is a radical shift from the very essence of the dtr perspective. Second, J identifies this vague 'Horeb' with the location of Sinai, a name derived from the early theophanic poetry but not previously the location of any special event.

3. There are no early laws in either the Covenant Code (Exod. 20.22–23.33) or the religious obligations law of Exod. 34.11-27.[25] They are all the work of J and therefore post-D, so a dtr redactor is not necessary. When J therefore uses dtr terminology, such as 'Book of the Covenant', it is quite clear from the context that he means something very different from the lawbook in D or dtr. Such theological transformations of dtr concepts and perspectives is so ubiquitous and deliberate in J that it is the fundamental mark of his theology and the reason why, in my view, it is a mistake to characterize him as a dtr redactor or his work as a 'D composition'. There is, therefore, no dtr redaction in the Tetrateuch.

25. See my 'Cultic Laws in the Covenant Code'.

PREDESTINATION IN DEUTERONOMY 30.1-10

Marc Zvi Brettler

Unlike many of the other contributions to this volume, I am not going to present a new proposal concerning Deuteronomistic influence on a biblical book or corpus, nor will I offer a programmatic analysis of the relationship between two works like Jeremiah and Deuteronomy, whose connections are generally acknowledged. Instead, I will focus on a short pericope from the end of Deuteronomy, namely 30.1-10, and on certain prophetic texts that are allied with it. This analysis will raise certain questions that deserve further exploration as we consider the issue of pan-Deuteronomism.

Deuteronomy 30.1-10 is usually understood as a rather typical Deuteronomistic sermon, from the exilic period or later.[1] Although I agree that it is a late text, I would challenge almost every other aspect of the consensus: it is not a sermon, it is not Dtr, and it is not typical.[2] I will question the established reading of this passage by focusing on its central v. 6, by re-opening the question of the unit's genre and by offering a new understanding of the syntax of the unit's initial and final verses. Reflexes of this passage in early Jewish literature will be used to buttress my interpretation. Finally, I will probe the implications of this new understanding for the question under consideration: the relation between Deuteronomy and the prophetic corpus. I will ultimately suggest that we have a likely case where Jeremiah has influenced Deuteronomy.

---

1.   See, e.g., A.D.H. Mayes, *Deuteronomy* (NCB; Grand Rapids: Eerdmans, 1987), pp. 367-68.

2.   Some of the unique aspects of Deut. 30.1-10 have been appreciated by others; see, e.g., G. Braulik, 'The Development of the Doctrine of Justification in the Redactional Strata of the Book of Deuteronomy', in *idem, The Theology of Deuteronomy: Collected Essays of Georg Braulik, O.S.B.* (trans. Ulrika Lindblad; North Richland Hills, TX: Bibal, 1994), pp. 87-164 (162-64).

The central v. 6 reads:

> ומל יהוה אלהיך את־לבבך ואת־לבב זרעך לאהבה את־יהוה
> אלהיך בכל־לבבך ובכל־נפשך למען חייך:

YHWH your God will circumcise your heart and the heart of your children to love YHWH your God with all your heart and all your being so
you may live.[3]

As many commentators have noted, this verse is really far from
straightforward when considered within the broader framework of
Deuteronomy in all of its levels.[4] It would seem that Deut. 10.16, in the
middle of a typical Dtr sermon calling for obedience, is similar:

> ומלתם את ערלת לבבכם וערפכם לא תקשו עוד:

you should circumcise the foreskin of your heart, and should harden your
neck no longer.

Yet, in Deuteronomy 10, the Israelites are supposed to do the
'circumcising'; this fits in with a wide variety of texts elsewhere in
Deuteronomy that note that the individual has free choice, and must
choose wisely.[5] Although there are some striking similarities between
Deut. 30.6 and 10.16-17, this should not obscure the fundamental difference between them:[6] ch. 10 fits the typical Deuteronomic and
Deuteronomistic ideology, which emphasizes free choice, while
Deuteronomy 30, as it were hiding behind all of the typical Dtr terminology,[7] suggests that it is YHWH who will determine Israel's positive
behavior:

---

3.   All translations from the Hebrew are my own.
4.   See, e.g., Gerhard von Rad, *Deuteronomy* (trans. Dorothea Barton; OTL;
Philadelphia: Westminster Press, 1966), p. 184, 'Thus the situation of Israel is very
different when compared with that in earlier parts of Deuteronomy'.
5.   See, e.g., Deut. 30.19-20. Indeed, whether or not we use the term 'wisdom'
influence in relation to Deuteronomy, it cannot be doubted that Deuteronomy typically attempts to persuade the Israelite to follow the norms that the authors believe
are correct, and free will stands at the very basis of this choice.
6.   This difference is highlighted most recently in J.H. Tigay, *Deuteronomy*
(The Jewish Publication Society Torah Commentary; Philadelphia: Jewish Publication Society of America, 1996), p. 285.
7.   The implication of this non-Dtr idea dressed in Dtr terminology will be
explored below.

ומל יהוה אלהיך את־לבבך ואת־לבב זרעך

YHWH your God will circumcise your heart and the heart of your children.

Some scholars downplay the existence of editorial layers in Dtr, even in reference to the issue under discussion; for example, Moshe Weinfeld suggests that 'There is apparently no significant difference between God's circumcising the heart of Israel and Israel's circumcising their heart'.[8] Weinfeld's point is unlikely and follows his general disposition for minimizing the editorial layers within the Dtr corpus; I follow the majority position that sees as significant the fact that YHWH is the subject of ומל in ch. 30, and posits that this verse must be connected to various prophetic passages, particularly to the well-known 'new covenant' passage in Jer. 31.31-34 and a similar idea in 32.37-41, passages that do not agree with typical Deuteronomic notions.[9]

The similarity between Deut. 30.1-10 and Jeremiah 31 was first noted to the best of my knowledge by Nachmanides, the Jewish Spanish exegete active in the thirteenth century, who, as we shall later see, also raises certain intriguing possibilities concerning the syntax of the unit's introduction:

> But in the messianic age, the desire to choose what is good will be a natural urge, and the heart will not desire to do what is improper, will not desire it at all. This is the reference to circumcision that we have here, since coveting and desiring are a foreskin of the heart, and circumcising the heart means that one will no longer covet or desire. Humanity will return at that time to what he was like before the sin of Adam [*Urzeit ist Endzeit!*], who naturally did what should be done, and did not have in his mind to do something and its opposite, as I explained in Genesis (2.9). This is what the text in Jeremiah (31.30-31) means when it says: 'See, days are coming—the utterance of YHWH—and I will make a new covenant with the house of Israel and the house of Judah...not like the covenant that I made with their ancestors...'[10]

8. M. Weinfeld, 'Jeremiah and the Spiritual Metamorphosis of Israel', *ZAW* 88 (1976), pp. 17-56 (35 n. 63).

9. See esp. H.D. Potter, 'The New Covenant in Jeremiah XXXI 31-34', *VT* 33 (1983), pp. 347-55 (350), who notes that the verses in Jeremiah 'are a deliberate contrast to Deuteronomy, not a complement to it, or a restatement of it'.

10. The translation follows the text printed in C.D. Chavel, *The Torah Commentary of Rabbi Moses Son of Nachman (Nachmanides)*, II (Jerusalem: Mossad Harav Kook, 1959), p. 480. I would note parenthetically that even those critical scholars who otherwise show some interest in the usefulness of medieval interpretation for

The parallels between Jer. 31.31-34 and Deut. 30.1-10 are striking.[11] In content, Jer. 31.32, which refers to the old type of covenant, finds its parallel in Deut. 30.1a, which refers to הברכה והקללה. Verse 33 describes the new covenant, which finds its parallel in Deut. 30.6, though the language of the latter is not explicitly covenantal, a point that is worth noting, since ברית is mentioned so often in Dtr.[12] Jeremiah 31.34abα,

ולא ילמדו עוד איש את־רעהו ואיש את־אחיו לאמר דעו את־
יהוה כי־כולם ידעו אותי למקטנם ועד־גדולם נאם־יהוה

They will no longer teach one another nor say to one another, 'Know YHWH', for they will all know me, from youngest to oldest—the utterance of YHWH,

explicitly notes that all will be pre-programmed or 'firmwired' to follow YHWH.[13] Given the other similarities between Jeremiah 31 and Deuteronomy 30, might we not expect the conclusion of the Deuteronomy pericope to make a similar point? I will return to this question later, when I explore the syntax and meaning of Deut. 30.10.[14]

Most commentators see only v. 6 of our unit as exceptional within the typical theology of Deuteronomy. This is because they understand vv. 1-2 as a protasis describing Israel's complete repentance, which finds its apodosis in vv. 3-9, which describes YHWH's reaction to this apodosis. Thus, a measure-for-measure understanding of שוב is often

modern study of the Bible typically ignore Nachmanides. In many ways, this is not surprising, since his Hebrew is somewhat more difficult than that of Rashi's, and a significant number of his comments are mystical in nature. Yet, he often adduces extremely useful and original insights, and elsewhere I have shown the usefulness of his observations on typology for understanding Gen. 12–50; see my *The Creation of History in Ancient Israel* (London: Routledge, 1995), pp. 52-53.

11. See Pierre Buis, 'La nouvelle alliance', *VT* 18 (1968), pp. 1-15 (13).

12. The word ברית appears 27 times, more than once per thousand words, in Deuteronomy. This high distribution alone does not fully signify the importance of ברית in that book; for additional aspects of covenant in Deuteronomy, see the summary of E.W. Nicholson, *God and his People: Covenant and Theology in the Old Testament* (Oxford: Clarendon Press, 1986), pp. 60-68.

13. I have taken this term from M.A. Carasik, 'Theologies of the Mind in Biblical Israel' (PhD dissertation, Brandeis University, 1997), p. 132.

14. There are, however, some differences between these two passages; see D.T. Olson, *Deuteronomy and the Death of Moses: A Theological Reading* (OBT; Minneapolis: Fortress Press, 1994), p. 154.

posited: when Israel שוב‎s twice (vv. 1-2), then YHWH will שוב‎ twice (v. 3).[15] In the words of the recent short commentary by Thomas W. Mann: 'The people need to know that God will accept them if they return—this is the purpose of the chapter. But their return is also part of the overall movement of restoration, and without it, God's return, as it were, cannot happen.'[16] For most interpreters, including Mann, God's beneficent act of circumcising Israel's heart (v. 6) will only happen after they begin the process of change as reflected in vv. 1-2. While this interpretation is possible, it is not likely. An investigation of the syntax of the unit, its genre, its knowledge of other biblical texts and its earliest interpretations suggests that an alternative understanding of the unit is preferable.

I would like to question the predominant assumption that the protasis of the conditional clause extends through vv. 1-2, while the apodosis may be found only in vv. 7-9. The following four sentences, which share the syntax of our unit, clarify the underlying issue: all have כי‎ followed by an imperfect (as in Deut. 30.1a כי-יבאו‎) and then by a converted perfect (as in Deut. 30.1b והשבת‎). I begin with Deut. 23.10 (example A), a completely straightforward verse:

כי-תצא מחנה על-איביך ונשמרת מכל דבר רע:

Here, the כי‎ followed by the imperfect introduces the protasis, while the converted imperfect of ונשמרת‎ introduces the apodosis. In fact, Joüon calls the *waw* of words like ונשמרת‎ 'the *waw* of apodosis'.[17] The fact that there are only two verbs in this sentence makes it quite clear that one belongs to the protasis, while the other belongs to the apodosis. Since both the protasis and the apodosis are 'simple' in the sense that they each have one verb, the verse is quite straightforward and must be translated something like: 'When you establish a camp against your enemy, you must be careful concerning every evil thing'. Contrast the

15. On measure for measure in biblical literature, see S. Loewenstamm, 'Measure for Measure', *Encyclopaedia Biblica*, IV, pp. 840-46 (Hebrew) and the analogous study of early postbiblical literature in Y. Amir, 'Measure for Measure in Talmudic Literature and in the Wisdom of Solomon', in H.G. Reventlow and Y. Hoffman (eds.), *Justice and Righteousness: Biblical Themes and their Influence* (JSOTSup, 137: Sheffield: Sheffield Academic Press, 1992), pp. 29-46.

16. T.W. Mann, *Deuteronomy* (Louisville, KY: Westminster/John Knox Press, 1995), p. 157.

17. P. Joüon and T. Muraoka, *A Grammar of Biblical Hebrew*, II (Subsidia Biblica, 14; Rome: Pontifical Biblical Institute, 1991), p. 646 (§176).

following three examples:

Gen. 32.18-19 (example B)

‫18 ויצו את־הראשׁון לאמר כי יפגשׁך עשׂו אחי‬
‫ושׁאלך לאמר למי־אתה ואנה תלך ולמי אלה לפניך: 19 ואמרת‬
‫לעבדך ליעקב מנחה הוא שׁלוחה לאדני לעשׂו והנה גם־הוא אחרינו:‬

Exod. 1.10 (example C)

‫10 הבה נתחכמה לו פן־ירבה והיה כי־תקראנה מלחמה ונוסף גם־הוא‬
‫על־שׂנאינו ונלחם־בנו ועלה מן־הארץ:‬

Gen. 12.12 (example D)

‫והיה כי־יראו אתך המצרים ואמרו אשׁתו זאת והרגו אתי ואתך יחיו:‬

These examples are complex in the sense that there are two or more
converted perfects after the initial ‫כי‬ plus imperfect. Context determines
whether the first converted perfect falls in the protasis or in the apodosis. In example B, it is context that determines that ‫ושׁאלך לאמר‬, 'and
he asks you, saying' belongs to the protasis, while context determines
that ‫ונוסף‬, 'then he will join' of example C opens the apodosis. In other
words, in example B the converted perfect belongs to the protasis,
while in example C the first of two converted imperfects already
belongs to the apodosis. Example D is more complex, and actually is
quite similar to what we find in the opening verses of Deuteronomy 30:
where does ‫ואמרו אשׁתו זאת‬ belong? Should we translate: 'When the
Egyptians see you [end of protasis and beginning of apodosis] *then* they
will say she is his wife and they will kill me and allow you to live' or
'When the Egyptians see you and say she is his wife [end of protasis
and beginning of apodosis] *then* they will kill me and allow you to
live'? The cantillation marks suggest the latter,[18] but this is not decisive.
Returning to Deuteronomy 30, I would suggest that from the syntactic
perspective, the clause structure of vv. 1-9 is similar to example D and
is ambiguous. In such cases, extra-syntactic considerations must be
considered to resolve the ambiguity. Most scholars seem to be unaware
of this ambiguity and have simply assumed that the apodosis in
Deuteronomy 30 begins in v. 3. This would allow the passage to fit the
predominant notions found elsewhere in Deuteronomy, but I will
adduce reasons why we might not want to make this passage agree with

18. Note the *'athnah* under the word ‫זאת‬.

other Deuteronomic passages. Although the syntactic parsing of the typical reading *might* be the more usual one,[19] example C shows quite clearly that the first waw may be the waw of apodosis, so the typical reading is certainly not the only one possible. If that typical reading is rejected, the passage would read very smoothly, and the theology of v. 6 would permeate all of it. It would be saying that once the blessing and curse are fulfilled (1a), the following will happen: you will return (vv. 2-3); YHWH will return and will return you to the land (vv. 3-5), he will then circumcise your hearts (v. 6) and punish your enemies (v. 7); you will indeed[20] return (v. 8), and YHWH will bless you (v. 9). A similar reading of v. 2 may be found in Nachmanides' gloss: 'The meaning of ושבת עד־יהוה אלהיך ושמעת בקלו ככל אשר־אנכי מצוך היום אתה ובניך is that you will return (שתשוב) to YHWH with all of your heart and all of your being, and you will accept upon you and your children forever to fulfill everything that I am commanding you today'. I would emphasize again that the reading of Mann and most others is plausible grammatically, particularly within the broader context of Deuteronomy, the first biblical book, canonically speaking, to place such an emphasis on שוב ing or תשובה (repentance). However, as shown by v. 6 and its affiliation with the quite undeuteronomistic sentiments that are allied to Jer. 31.31-34, we should not automatically read Deut. 30.1-10 within the broader context of Deuteronomy. Other ways in which Deut. 30.1-10 is exceptional will further indicate that it should *not* be automatically considered within the purview of other texts in Deuteronomy.

Before developing this idea further, let me turn briefly to another syntactic issue concerning the end of the unit. Verse 10 twice uses כי followed by an imperfect; these are usually seen as temporal or causal clauses, in other words, as parallel summary statements which clarify that all that is being discussed in vv. 1-9 will transpire *when* or *because* the Israelites heed (כי תשמע) or return (כי תשוב). But in my reading, these כיs are emphatic or asseverative.[21] There is no internal syntactic

---

19. I know of no studies on this issue; the major works of syntax do not treat it, and it is notoriously difficult to collect and analyze the necessary data.

20. On this understanding of כי, see below.

21. See *HALOT*, II, p. 470, and B.K. Waltke and M. O'Connor, *An Introduction to Biblical Hebrew Syntax* (Winona Lake, IN: Eisenbrauns, 1990), §39.3.4e. T. Muraoka (*Emphatic Words and Structures in Biblical Hebrew* [Jerusalem: Magnes Press, 1985], pp. 158-62) somewhat disagrees, but mentions (pp. 162-63) 'the use

reason why a temporal or causal כִּ is preferable to an asseverative כִּ,
and there are extra-syntactic reasons for preferring the asseverative
sense. I would thus translate v. 10: 'You will indeed heed YHWH your
God to observe his commandments and ordinances that are written in
this book of teaching; you will indeed return to YHWH your God with
all of your heart and all of your being' This verse then precisely parallels the idea of Jer. 31.34: כִּי־כוּלָם יֵדעוּ אוֹתִי, 'for they will all know
me'. If this is correct, the author of Deut. 30.10 would be using Dtr
clichés in quite unusual ways in each half of the concluding verse of the
pericope in Deuteronomy. The phrases לִשְׁמר מצוֹתיו וחקתיו and וּבכל־
נפשך בכל־לבבך elsewhere typically refer to human initiative at following the law, as in the famous Deut. 6.5:

ואהבת את יהוה אלהיך בכל־לבבך ובכל־נפשך ובכל־מאדך:

> you shall love YHWH your God with all your heart and all your being
> and all your might.[22]

It is far from obvious, however, that we should subsume Deuteronomy
30, with its radically different v. 6, into this prevalent notion. Phrased
differently, had we found the כִּ phrases of v. 10 elsewhere in
Deuteronomy, we would have read them as conditional and have understood the following imperfects as reflecting volition. It thus seems again
that Dtr clichés have been intentionally used, but with a twist. It is quite
significant that a different type of twist is found on this same phrase in
Jer. 32.39-41, a text which, as von Rad has pointed out, shares much
with our passage and with other parts of Jeremiah 32.[23] I refer
specifically to Jer. 32.41b, which reads:

ונטעתים בארץ הזאת באמת בכל־לבי ובכל־נפשי

> I will plant them in this land in truth, with all my heart and all my being,

where the לב and נפש are YHWH's, rather than the Israelite's.
My understanding of the syntax of vv. 1-9 and of v. 10 allows the
entire unit to be understood in a new way, one that has not been suggested in modern biblical scholarship. Von Rad comes closest when he
notes:

of *ki* in a climactic construction', which could fit Deut. 30.10 as well.

22. לִשְׁמר מצוה is used very frequently in Deuteronomy to reflect human intiative in following the law; it is found, for example, in the introduction to Deuteronomy in: 4.2, 40; 5.10, 29; 6.2, 17, 25; 7.9, 11; 8.1, 2, 11; 10.13; 11.1, 8, 22.

23. Von Rad, *Deuteronomy*, p. 184.

In fact, our text can no longer be called an exhortation; it contains no admonitions, but with regard to Israel's future, simple affirmative propositions, that is, it is clothed altogether in the style of prophetic predictions.[24]

However, in his ATD volume, which includes a new translation of Deuteronomy, he does not follow the logical conclusion of his observation and instead translates the verbs in vv. 1b-2 as part of the protasis and v. 10 as a temporal clause.[25]

As noted, certain aspects of my understanding of Deut. 30.1-10 have been anticipated by the pre-modern commentator Nachmanides. He is not, however, the first to understand Deut. 30.1b-2 as a prediction of YHWH's beneficence rather than as a precondition for YHWH's restoration. Various late biblical and early postbiblical texts that interpret Deuteronomy 30 reflect this same understanding, with only Deut. 30.1a comprising the protasis of the promise.

The opening of Deuteronomy 30 is clearly reflected in 4QMMT, which has become one of the most controversial and significant texts discovered among the Dead Sea Scrolls.[26] Section C lines 13-22 are clearly based on the text of Deut. 30.1-3.[27] The passage opens with a quotation of our passage, which is blended with Deut. 4.30. It continues by noting that the time of blessings and curses (see Deut. 30.1a) has already transpired—blessings during the period of Solomon and curses from Jeroboam to Zedekiah (ll. 18-19). The text continues:[28]

ואנחנו מכירים שבאוו מקצת הברכות והקללות שכתוב בספר מושה
וזה הוא אחרית הימים שישובו בישראל[29]לתמיד

24. Von Rad, *Deuteronomy*, p. 183.
25. G. von Rad, *Das fünfte Buch Mose Deuteronomium* (ATD, 8; Göttingen: Vandenhoeck & Ruprecht, 1964), p. 130.
26. On 4QMMT, see the collection of essays by J. Kampen and M.J. Bernstein (eds.), *Reading 4QMMT: New Perspectives on Qumran Law and History* (SBL Symposium Series, 2; Atlanta: Scholars Press, 1996).
27. I have cited 4QMMT from E. Qimron and J. Strugnell, *Qumran Cave 4 V: Miqsat Ma'ase ha-Torah* (DJD, 10; Oxford: Clarendon Press, 1994).
28. I have not marked cases where the text is slightly broken; there are no major uncertainties in the readings.
29. This is partially restored; I follow the restoration of the editors, which is very likely, and is accepted by F. García Martínez, *The Dead Sea Scrolls Translated: The Qumran Texts in English* (trans. W.G.E. Watson; Leiden: E.J. Brill, 1994), p. 79.

and we are aware that the range[30] of blessings and curses that are written in the Book of Moses have transpired, and this is the end of days when those of Israel will return forever.

The author of 4QMMT is thus understanding 30.1b-2

והשבת אל־לבבך בכל־הגוים אשר הדיחך
יהוה אלהיך שמה: ² ושבת עד־יהוה אלהיך ושמעת בקלו ככל
אשר־אנכי מצוך היום אתה ובניך בכל־לבבך ובכל־נפשך:

not as the pre-condition for restoration, but as part of אחרית הימים, 'the end of days', a state in which God will force the people to return to him. According to this text, Deut. 30.1b is not some vague option for the future, but reflects a time pre-ordained by God, a time in which the author of this document believed he was living—'this is the end of days when Israel will return (forever)'.

4QMMT is not the only text that was significantly influenced by Deut. 30.1-10. Estelle (Esther) Glickler Chazon has shown that this Deuteronomic text has been very influential on other biblical texts as well as on early Jewish texts known from Qumran and elsewhere.[31] It was used by the author of Neh. 1.6-11, who understood the passage in the way that I am advocating. In a plea for forgiveness and for YHWH to listen to his prayer, Nehemiah notes (vv. 8-9):

⁸ זכר־נא את־הדבר אשר צוית את־משה עבדך
לאמר אתם תמעלו אני אפיץ אתכם בעמים: ⁹ ושבתם אלי
ושמרתם מצותי ועשיתם אתם אם־יהיה נדחכם בקצה השמים משם
אקבצם והבואתים [והביאותים] אל־המקום אשר בחרתי לשכן את־שמי שם:

Remember the promise[32] which you commanded to your servant Moses, 'If you transgress, I will disperse you among the nations. You will return to me, and heed my commandments and fulfill them...'[33]

---

30. This is the best translation of קצה in this document; cf. *BDB*, p. 892 קצה 3.

31. See her 'A Liturgical Document from Qumran and its Implications: "Words of the Luminaries" (4QDibHam)' (Hebrew) (PhD dissertation, Hebrew University, 1991). The observations in the following paragraphs are based on pp. 277-79 of that dissertation. I would like to thank Professor Chazon for sending me these pages and discussing this issue with me.

32. This is a frequent use of דבר, most especially in Dtr language and contexts, to which this passage is referring; cf., e.g., Deut. 9.5; 1 Kgs 2.4; 6.12.

33. Contrast, however, the use of Deut. 30.1-10 in the exilic section of Solomon's prayer (1 Kgs 8.46-50), which has the 'standard' understanding of the passage. On the dating of this passage, see my 'Interpretation and Prayer: Notes on the Composition of 1 Kings 8.15-53', in M. Brettler and M. Fishbane (eds.), *Minhah le-*

This idea is even more explicit in a liturgical text found at Qumran, the Words of the Luminaries (דברי המאורות), which notes:[34]

> בגוים ותחון את עמכה ישראל בכול
> הארצות אשר הדחתם שמה להשיב
> אל לבבם לשוב עודך ולשמוע בקולכה
> ככול אשר צויתה ביד מושה עבדכה

> ...among the nations. You had compassion on your nation Israel in all the of lands where you dispersed them, making them take [it] to heart to return to you and to heed your voice just as you had commanded through your servant Moses.

This text is most likely not sectarian,[35] and the interpretation of Deuteronomy 30 that it develops should not be seen as sectarian or peripheral.

This idea is even more explicit in Bar. 2.27-35:[36]

> Yet you have treated us, O Lord our God, with all your goodness and great mercy, as you promised through your servant Moses on the day when you commanded him to write your Law in the presence of the children of Israel, saying: 'If you do not obey me, this very great multitude will be reduced to a small number among the nations where I shall banish them. For I know that they will not obey me—because they are a stiffnecked people—but in the land of their captivity they will repent, acknowledging that I am the Lord their God. I shall give them a heart and ears that hear, and they will praise me in the land of their captivity and will remember my name, and they will turn from their stubbornness and wickedness because they will remember what became of their ancestors who sinned against the Lord. I shall then bring them back to the land which I swore to give to their forefathers, Abraham, Isaac and Jacob, and they will take possession of it; I shall increase their number and they will not be diminished. And I shall make an everlasting covenant with them

Nahum (JSOTSup, 154; Sheffield: Sheffield Academic Press, 1993), pp. 17-35. However, given the main purpose of Solomon's prayer, the effectiveness of the Temple (site) in effecting repentence, this interpretation is hardly surprising.

34. M. Baillet, *Qumrân Grotte 4 III (4Q482–4Q520)* (DJD, 7; Oxford: Clarendon Press, 1982), p. 145 (col. V, 1–2 recto, 11-14). Some noncontroversial, minimal restorations and unclarities are not marked here; see the edition.

35. E.G. Chazon, 'Prayers from Qumran and their Historical Implications', *DSD* 1 (1994), pp. 265-84 (278-79).

36. I quote from the edition of E. Tov, *The Book of Baruch: Also Called I Baruch (Greek and Hebrew)* (Texts and Translations, 8; Pseudepigrapha Series, 6; Missoula, MT: Scholars Press, 1975), pp. 1-26 (24).

> that I shall be their God and they will be my people, and I shall no more
> uproot my people Israel from the land which I have given to them.'

Both 4Q504 and Baruch suggest explicitly that it is YHWH's grace
that causes him to make Israel return or repent. As they are reading the
biblical text, Deut. 30.1b begins the apodosis and is not part of the protasis. Especially when seen in contrast to the typical modern critical
readings of the biblical passage, this early Jewish reading seems odd. It
is even stranger when we consider the historical contexts of these passages, which would not suggest that Israel is in a state of forced repentance. This further bolsters the likelihood that the reading suggested
here is not merely a modern one, taking advantage of various complex
syntactic possibilities opened up through contemporary scholarship, but
is ancient, and might reflect the original meaning of Deut. 30.1-10. This
passage thus describes a one-step, not a two-step process: as in Jeremiah 31 and 32, there is no need for Israel to return of its own initiative
before YHWH steps in.

Having made these various suggestions about the syntax and meaning of this unit, let me briefly turn to its genre. As noted earlier, many
consider Deut. 30.1-10 to be a sermon. For reasons that are outside the
purview of this essay, I am generally quite uncomfortable with that
form-critical label;[37] I am particularly uncomfortable with it in this case
for a quite simple reason: the unit is very bookish, and does not share
the oral features that one might expect in a true sermon. It does not
open with the typical markers that appeal to the senses, like ראה or
שמע. Given its content, it would be silly as a sermon, whose main goal
is persuasion: if there is ultimately no free choice, there is no need to
persuade. Finally, and I believe most significantly, the unit is embedded
in Deuteronomy in a very unusual way, alluding to, indeed assuming,
texts found in the previous chapters. Thus, it should be contrasted with
sermons, which are typically more self-contained. The dependence of
ch. 30 on other material in Deuteronomy is most obvious in the opening
words of the chapter,

---

37. In brief, 'sermon' is a quite Protestant term that suggests an exposition of a
central biblical text by a particular type of religious functionary. This situation does
not fit the book of Deuteronomy very well. See the discussion in R. Mason,
Preaching the Tradition: Homily and Hermeneutics after the Exile (Cambridge:
Cambridge University Press, 1990), pp. 142-43.

והיה כי־יבאו עליך כל־הדברים האלה הברכה והקללה אשר נתתי לפניך

when all of these things, the blessing and the curse which I have set
before you come to pass',

which assume the great תוכחה or rebuke of ch. 28.[38] Several scholars
have noted additional connections between these chapters, and have
even suggested that ch. 30 was the original continuation of ch. 28.[39]
However, given the clear dependence of this unit on ch. 28, it is quite
striking that 30.7 refers to the covenant curses using the word אלה,
'curse', which is not present in ch. 28. The term אלה is found, however,
five times in ch. 29, in vv. 11, 13, 18, 19 and 20. Deuteronomy 29.20b,

ככל אלות הברית הכתובה בספר התורה הזה

according to all of the curses of the covenant which is written in this
Torah book,

the only place in that chapter to use אלה in the plural, is very close to
30.10ab:

לשמר מצותיו וחקתיו הכתובה בספר התורה הזה

to observe his commandments and laws which are written in this Torah
book.[40]

It thus seems probable that 30.1-10 is not at all sermonic, that is, related
to an originally oral genre, but is a learned written addition, very well
integrated into, and thus subsequent to, the previous two chapters.

In addition to those connections between ch. 30 and the previous two

---

38. Indeed, v. 9 of our chapter also returns to ch. 28; 9a והותירך יהוה אלהיך בכל
מעשה ידך בפרי בטנך ובפרי בהמתך ובפרי אדמתך לטובה is reminiscent of 28.4a:
ברוך פרי־בטנך ופרי אדמתך ופרי בהמתך, and 9b כי ישוב יהוה לשוש עליך לטוב
והיה כאשר־שש יהוה עליכם להיטיב clearly recalls 28.63aα: כאשר־שש על־אבתיך:
אתכם ולהרבות אתכם. Additional points of contact have been noted by D.E.
Skweres, *Die Rückverweise im Buch Deuteronomium* (AnBib, 79; Rome: Biblical
Institute Press, 1979), p. 70, and A. Rofé, *Introduction to Deuteronomy* (Jerusalem:
Akademon, 1988), p. 189 (Hebrew) and Rofé, 'The Covenant in the Land of Moab
(Deuteronomy 28:69–30:20): Historico-Literary, Comparative, and Form-critical
Considerations', in D.L. Christensen (ed.), *A Song of Power and the Power of
Song: Essays on the Book of Deuteronomy* (Sources for Biblical and Theological
Study, 3; Winona Lake, IN: Eisenbrauns, 1993), pp. 269-80 (271-72).

39. See Rofé, *Introduction to Deuteronomy*, p. 189, esp. n. 45.

40. On the problem of grammatical agreement of הכתובה see the commentaries
and *BHS* note a.

chapters, scholars have often noted connections between Deut. 30.1-10
and ch. 4. Though they are of different genres, there is truth to the
observation that 30.1-10, in the words of S.R. Driver, 'may be regarded
as an expansion of 4[29-31]'.[41] Indeed, Robert Polzin, in his literary study
of Deuteronomy, has shown how Deuteronomy 30 extends the message
of ch. 4, moving from (4.30bβ): ושבת עד־יהוה אלהיך ושמעת בקלו, 'you
will return to YHWH your God and will heed his voice' (30.8) to
ואתה תשוב ושמעת בקול יהוה ועשׂית את־כל־מצותיו אשר אנכי מצוך היום:,
'You will return and will heed the voice of YHWH, and will fulfill all
of his commandments which I am commanding you today'.[42] This
observation further supports the bookish, exegetical nature of our passage.[43] Additionally, it shows that the author of 30.1-10 is not slavishly
dependent on his sources, but expands the ideas of his base text—
exactly the process, in a more radicalized fashion, that I am suggesting
has transpired throughout the passage.

A final indication of the bookishness of this unit is the use in v. 10 of
the phrase לשׁמר מצותיו וחקתיו הכתובה בספר התורה הזה, 'to observe his
commandments and laws which are written in this Torah book'. I would
stress that this use of בספר התורה in the Torah as referring to a large
body of law is quite unusual: elsewhere in chs. 28 and 29 it is used of a
limited scroll containing curses;[44] only 31.26 might share the same
usage. Nowhere else in Deuteronomy is ספר התורה clearly a comprehensive book, containing מצותיו וחקתיו rather than covenant curses. It is
difficult to determine exactly when this term began to be used in that
broad sense, which is particularly well attested in Nehemiah and
Chronicles.[45] The comparison to these late books is apposite given the

41. S.R. Driver, *Deuteronomy* (ICC: Edinburgh: T. & T. Clark, 1895), p. 328.
42. R. Polzin, *Moses and the Deuteronomist: A Literary Study of the Deuteronomic History*. I. *Deuteronomy, Joshua, Judges* (New York: Seabury, 1980), p. 70.
43. For a different understanding of the literary relationship between these two
blocks of material, see E. Otto, 'Deuteronomium 4: Die Pentateuchredaktion im
Deuteronomiumsrahmen', in T. Veijola (ed.), *Das Deuteronomium und seine Quer-
beziehungen* (Helsinki: Finnische Exegetische Gesellschaft, 1996), pp. 201-209.
44. See 28.61 and 29.20.
45. Neh. 8.1, 3, 8, 9, 18; 9.3; 2 Chron. 17.9; 34.14. On the use of this term in
Nehemiah, see the discussion in J. Blenkinsopp, *Ezra–Nehemiah* (OTL; Philadelphia: Westminster Press, 1988), pp. 152-58. On Chronicles, see J.R. Shaver, *Torah
and the Chronicler's History Work: An Inquiry into the Chronicler's References to
Laws, Festivals, and Cultic Institutions in Relationship to Pentateuchal Legislation*
(BJS, 196; Atlanta: Scholars Press, 1989), esp. p. 75.

suggestion of Mendecki and others that Deut. 30.1-10 contains other signs of postexilic authorship.[46] It is furthered by the suggestion of several recent studies that the work of Dtr continued into the postexilic period.[47]

Let me begin to tie together the various pieces of my argument and reflect on how they connect to the broader issue of pan-Deuteronomism. Deuteronomy 30.1-10 has an important, largely unnoticed role within Deuteronomy. Other scholars have brought ch. 30 into the mainstream of Deuteronomic thought by noting connections to the seminal ch. 4;[48] a closer look shows that ch. 4 does not share the major point of 30.1-10, lack of free choice, nor does 30.1-10 share the major interests of ch. 4: the belief in a transcendent God and the linking of covenant faith and wisdom.[49] Their styles are also remarkably different: in contrast to 30.1-10, ch. 4 attempts to persuade, and uses expressions like ועתה ישראל שמע and ראה (vv. 1, 5). Yet Deut. 30.1-10 is saturated, perhaps even over-saturated, with Dtr vocabulary. But affiliation to a school must be judged on the basis of ideology combined with phraseology, and v. 6 is distinct within the purview of Dtr ideology. As a text that almost gets it right, Deut. 30.1-10 is similar to compositions that we would call archaistic rather than archaic in the sense that it is imitating something else and almost capturing its essence, but it contains certain clues that it is not part of the block it is attempting to imitate. Thus, our passage, which looks Dtr, is really pseudo-Deuteronomic,[50]

---

46. N. Mendecki, 'Dtn 30,3-4—nachexilisch?', *BZ* 29 (1985), pp. 267-71; for others, cf. A. Cholewinski, *Heiligkeitgesetz und Deuteronomium: Eine vergleichende Studie* (AnBib, 66; Rome: Biblical Institute Press, 1976), p. 313 n. 4, and N. Lohfink, 'Der Bundesschluß im Land Moab: Redaktionsgeschichtliches zu Dt 28,69–32,47', *BZ* 6 (1962), pp. 32-56 (41-42). Given the strong stylistic connections to the prose of Jeremiah, Ezekiel and Second Isaiah, it is prudent to consider Deut. 30.1-10 as exilic.

47. See R.F. Person, Jr, *Second Zechariah and the Deuteronomic School* (JSOTSup, 167; Sheffield: JSOT Press, 1993), esp. pp. 1-78 and 146-205, and T.C. Römer, 'Transformations in Deuteronomistic and Biblical Historiography: On "Book-Findings" and Other Literary Strategies', *ZAW* 109 (1997), pp. 1-11.

48. See e.g., Polzin, *Moses and the Deuteronomist*, p. 70.

49. See S.A. Geller, 'Fiery Wisdom: Logos and Lexis in Deuteronomy 4,' *Prooftexts* 14 (1994), pp. 103-41, reprinted in a revised form in his *Sacred Enigmas: Literary Religion in the Hebrew Bible* (London: Routledge, 1996), pp. 30-61.

50. This term was suggested to me by analogy to Dead Sea Scroll material by Professor E.G. Chazon.

while being anti-Dtr. If this is correct, and if the use of the phrase התורה בספר and other linguistic evidence is significant for determining the date of the passage, this may very well be one of the latest sections within Deuteronomy. I return to what seems to be the excessive use of Dtr vocabulary and wonder if a later editor wanted to sneak an innovative idea into the text by dressing it—even over-dressing it—with Dtr phraseology. Here we must remember the various uses of terms like כמשפט in the postexilic corpus[51] and אלהיך כאשר צוך יהוה in Deuteronomy,[52] terms that suggest continuity when presenting innovation, thereby masking the newness of their proposals. The over-use of Dtr terminology here is similar—it reveals an author imitating Deuteronomy in order to introduce an idea that is quite radical relative to the corpus in which it is imbedded. Yet this passage is not Dtr, as seen in the theology of v. 6, which is very non-Dtr, and the lack of mention of ברית, which is so central to Dtr, and would have fitted so neatly into this passage. It is quite possible that the author of this passage did not fully appreciate that by integrating his ideas into the book of Deuteronomy, their theological innovation, namely that YHWH will assure Israel's repentance, might be lost, as this passage would be read within the purview of standard Deuteronomic theology. This is indeed what seems to have happened within modern biblical scholarship.

The nature and date of Deut. 30.1-10, when considered in relation to Jeremiah 31 and 32, allow for two possibilities. The usual position is that the passages from Jeremiah that sound like Jeremiah are Dtr, having been influenced by Deut. 30.1-10 and their ilk.[53] However, at least

51. See M. Fishbane, *Biblical Interpretation in Ancient Israel* (Oxford: Oxford University Press, 1985), pp. 135-37, 210.

52. See B.M. Levinson, *Deuteronomy and the Hermeneutics of Legal Innovation* (New York: Oxford University Press, 1997).

53. For a summary, see W. McKane, *A Critical and Exegetical Commentary on Jeremiah XXVI–LII* (ICC; Edinburgh: T. & T. Clark, 1996), pp. 823-25, though he ultimately rejects this position, as does W.L. Holladay, *Jeremiah 2: A Commentary on the Book of the Prophet Jeremiah Chapters 26–52* (Hermeneia; Philadelphia: Fortress Press, 1989), p. 197, who considers 31.31-34 to be authentic to Jeremiah, though he too claims that it was influenced by Deuteronomy. Especially relevant to the reconstruction I am proposing is the observation of R.P. Carroll, *A Critical and Exegetical Commentary on Jeremiah XXVI–LII* (OTL; Philadelphia: Westminster Press, 1986), p. 613, 'Deuteronomistic influence must be acknowledged in the passage, but in view of the fact that the Deuteronomists do not themselves at any point in their writings propose a new covenant, not even in the late piece on the

as I understand it, Deut. 30.1-10 is likely quite late and is *sui generis* within Deuteronomy in terms of its ideology, though not in terms of its phraseology. I cannot pretend that I know the chronological range of the Dtr reworking of Deuteronomy versus the Dtr reworking of Jeremiah, though given the evidence, it seems quite possible, even likely, that Deut. 30.1-10 may be later than the exilic Dtr revision of Jeremiah, and thus the Deuteronomy passage has been influenced by Jeremiah. This explains, for example, why Deut. 30.1 uses the root נדח in the hiphil of dispersing Israel, a usage which is not found in Deuteronomy, but is typical of the prose of Jeremiah.[54] Similarly, the combination שוב שבות and רחם are found in v. 3, and in Jer. 3.26 and 12.15, as well as Ezek. 39.25. The same verse in Deuteronomy uses the root קבץ in the piel to refer to YHWH gathering the dispersed Israel; this is a unique usage in Deuteronomy, though it is well attested in Jeremiah and Ezekiel.[55] The unusual phrase שוש על is shared by v. 9 and Jer. 32.41,[56] a verse which, as we saw, has the idea that a new heart will be implanted in Israel, releasing them from free choice. Returning to YHWH with all your heart, found in v. 10, is also uniquely found here in Deuteronomy, though it occurs in Jer. 3.10 and 24.7.[57] The fact that several of the phrases shared by Jeremiah and Deut. 30.1-10 are characteristic of Jeremiah rather than Deuteronomy or Dtr significantly bolsters the suggestion that in this case, Deuteronomy has been influenced by Jeremiah rather than vice versa.

The general model that I am suggesting is certainly complicated, but I would argue, quite reasonable—textual history is rarely as straightforward as one would like: Deuteronomy influenced Jeremiah, but once

restoration of Israel in Deut. 30.1-10, it must be questioned whether they are responsible for this addition to the cycle'.

54. The hiphil of נדח is used in a different sense in Deuteronomy, in connection to apostasy (13.6, 11, 14). The linguistic connection to Jeremiah was made by Driver, *Deuteronomy*, p. 329, who cites the 11 cases of its use in Jeremiah. He does not, however, draw the same implications from this similarity of phraseology. Note especially Deut. 30.1: בכל־הגוים אשר הדיחך יהוה אלהיך שמה, and Jer. 29.18 בכל־הגוים אשר הדחתים שם: and 46.28 בכל־הגוים אשר הדחתיך שמה.

55. These observations follow Driver, *Deuteronomy*, p. 329.

56. This is noted in Driver, *Deuteronomy*, p. 330.

57. See M. Weinfeld, *Deuteronomy and the Deuteronomic School* (Oxford: Clarendon Press, 1972), p. 335 n. 11. It is also found in 1 Kgs 8.48 and 2 Kgs 23.25, which are both late texts. Thus, contrary to Weinfeld, this is not really a Deuteronomic phrase at all.

this happened, the 'new' book of Jeremiah had in some sense become Deuteronomic, and influenced Deuteronomy.

The theme of this book of essays is the influence of Deuteronomy on other biblical texts. I am only suggesting that we have at least one likely case of dependence in the other direction, where the text of Jeremiah has influenced a text that has found its way into Deuteronomy. It may not be accidental that this text is found towards the end of a biblical book, a place that is perceived to be particularly open to editorial additions.[58] I leave it to others to see how convincing this example is, whether it is totally exceptional, or indicative of a broader phenomenon, which, once observed, may be outlined more extensively, complicating yet further our understanding of Deuteronomy, its spheres of influence, and its interconnections with other biblical books.

58. See for example the conclusions of Jeremiah, Amos and Malachi.

HOW DID JEREMIAH BECOME A CONVERT TO DEUTERONOMISTIC IDEOLOGY?

Thomas C. Römer

The Confusing State of Current Research
on the Book of Jeremiah

The relationship between the book of Jeremiah and the so-called Deuteronomistic History (DH) had been noticed, at least partially, a long time before the DH as a scholarly theory came into existence. The Talmud (*b. B. Bat.* 14b-15a) indeed describes Jeremiah as the author of the books of Kings. This might be due to the fact that Jeremiah is contemporaneous with the last events related in 2 Kings 25, but we may also ask if the rabbis had some intuitions about stylistic and theological parallels between these books.

In modern research, it was Bernhard Duhm who first claimed that most of the book of Jeremiah should be ascribed to dtr redactors, who might easily be identified by their repetitious style and theological platitudes. According to Duhm, there was no systematic dtr redaction of the book. Rather, it grew like a jungle until the first century BCE.[1] But some 50 years later, when Old Testament scholarship became more interested in *Redaktionsgeschichte*, the commentaries by Rudolph and Hyatt,[2] which appeared about the same time as Noth's 'Dtr History',[3] argued for a coherent dtr redaction of the book of Jeremiah. According to Hyatt, 'the "school" of writers we call the Deuteronomists' edited DH as well as chs. 1–45 of Jeremiah.[4] This position became dominant and

1. B. Duhm, *Das Buch Jeremia* (KHAT, 11; Tübingen: J.C.B. Mohr, 1901), p. xx.
2. W. Rudolph, *Jeremia* (HAT, 1.12; Tübingen: J.C.B. Mohr, 1947); J.P. Hyatt, 'The Book of Jeremiah', IB, V, pp. 775-1142.
3. M. Noth, *Überlieferungsgeschichtliche Studien* (Halle: Max Niemeyer, 1943).
4. J.P. Hyatt, 'The Deuteronomic Edition of Jeremiah', in L.G. Perdue and

was reinforced by Thiel's work, which established convincingly the
links between DH and the dtr redaction of Jeremiah.[5]

Nevertheless, other explanations for the 'Deuteronomistic' character
of Jeremiah have been offered. John Bright, Helga Weippert and
William L. Holladay claimed that we should not glibly speak of dtr
redaction in Jeremiah,[6] since what seems to be dtr is just the characteristic rhetorical prose of the seventh/sixth centuries. This thesis seems
quite difficult to uphold, because it fails to explain why some texts in
the book of Jeremiah do appear with this style and others do not. If
there was a *Kunstprosa* (a common artistic prose style) in the seventh/
sixth century why does it not recur in other books from the same period
as, for instance, Isaiah or Zephaniah? Therefore it seems quite reasonable to admit one or more dtr redactions in Jeremiah.

But then there is another question that arises particularly regarding
the pluses of the MT. Most of these pluses, which may be dated from
the third or second century BCE sound very 'dtr'.[7] This is not surprising
at all, since the dtr style is very easy to imitate. But does this mean that
we should return to Duhm who denied any coherent redactional composition of the book? This is indeed the position of Carroll who states
that 'so few of the elements constituting the book are datable, and the
social background of many of them equally obscure, that the book may
represent many and various political movements from the fall of
Jerusalem to the Graeco-Roman period'.[8] The recent commentary of
McKane agrees, considering the formation of the book of Jeremiah as a
'rolling corpus'. He refuses to speak of composition since it would

B.W. Kovacs (eds.), *A Prophet to the Nations: Essays in Jeremiah Studies* (Winona
Lake, IN: Eisenbrauns, 1984), pp. 247-67.

    5.   W. Thiel, *Die deuteronomistische Redaktion von Jeremia 1–25* (WMANT,
41; Neukirchen–Vluyn: Neukirchener Verlag, 1973).

    6.   J. Bright, 'The Date of the Prose Sermons in Jeremiah', in Perdue and
Kovacs (eds.), *A Prophet to the Nations*, pp. 193-212; and H. Weippert, *Die
Prosareden des Jeremiabuches* (BZAW, 132; Berlin: W. de Gruyter, 1973); W.L.
Holladay, *Jeremiah 1: A Commentary on the Book of the Prophet Jeremiah Chap-
ters 1–25* (Hermeneia; Philadelphia: Fortress Press, 1986).

    7.   Cf. H.-J. Stipp, *Das masoretische und alexandrinische Sondergut des
Jeremiabuches: Textgeschichtlicher Rang, Eigenarten, Triebkräfte* (OBO, 136;
Freiburg: Universitätsverlag; Göttingen: Vandenhoeck & Ruprecht, 1994); P. Pio-
vanelli, 'La condamnation de la diaspora égyptienne dans le livre de Jérémie (JrA
50,8–51,30 / JrB 43,8–44,30', *Trans* 9 (1995), pp. 35-49.

    8.   R.P. Carroll, *Jeremiah* (OTG; Sheffield: JSOT Press, 1989), p. 107.

mean attributing to the redactors 'a degree of planning and thoughtfulness which they do not possess'.[9] Again, this seems to be a return to Duhm's position.

There is still another problem: Those who admit a dtr redaction in Jeremiah are often puzzled by the fact that the prophet Jeremiah is not mentioned in the DH. Some scholars, especially in Germany, claim that the dtr milieu consists of two different 'parties': the Deuteronomists of the DH and the Deuteronomists of Jeremiah. If we believe Albertz and others, the Deuteronomists of the DH were traditionalists and 'hardliners' compared to their more open-minded colleagues who edited Jeremiah.[10] So, were there 'republicans' and 'democrats' in the dtr school? If this was the case why should we label them both 'dtr'?

This confusion in the current state of research on Jeremiah suggests two questions: (1) How should the dtr redaction of Jeremiah (if there was any) be described? (2) What is the relationship between the dtr redactors of Jeremiah and those of the historical books?

The Profile of the (First) Dtr Redaction of Jeremiah

Recent discussion on deuteronomism has shown that there is no consensus regarding the characteristics that make a text deuteronomistic. In order to avoid a sort of pan-Deuteronomism, which is not very helpful, we should try to combine the evidence of language, style, compositional techniques and ideology, even if the last criterion is very difficult to handle.

As for the book of Jeremiah, these criteria apply best to the so-called 'prose sermons' or discourses. This was observed by Mowinckel,[11] and

---

9. W. McKane, *A Critical and Exegetical Commentary on Jeremiah I–XXV* (ICC; Edinburgh: T. & T. Clark, 1986), p. lxii.

10. R. Albertz, 'Die Intentionen und Träger des deuteronomistischen Geschichtswerks', in R. Albertz *et al.* (eds.), *Schöpfung und Befreiung: Für C. Westermann zum 80. Geburtstag* (Stuttgart: Calwer Verlag, 1989), pp. 37-53; C. Hardmeier, 'Die Propheten Micha und Jesaja in Spiegel von Jeremia xxvi und 2 Regnum xviii–xx: Zur Prophetie-Rezeption in der nach-josianischen Zeit', in J.A. Emerton (ed.), *Congress Volume: Leuven 1989* (VTSup, 43; Leiden: E.J. Brill, 1991), pp. 172-89; H.-J. Stipp, 'Probleme des redaktionsgeschichtlichen Modells der Entstehung des Jeremiabuches', in W. Gross (ed.), *Jeremia und die 'deuteronomistische Bewegung'* (BBB, 98; Weinheim: Beltz Athenäum, 1995), pp. 225-62.

11. S. Mowinckel, *Zur Komposition des Buches Jeremia* (Kristiania: Jacob Dybwad, 1914).

so is nothing new. What is more important is that some of these discourses are clearly interrelated. This is especially the case for chs. 7, 25 and 35 (according to the Masoretic order[12]), which mark important divisions in the book: 7–24 and 26–35 with 25.1-13 being a sort of 'hinge'. Both parts start with the temple speech of Jeremiah (chs. 7 and 26) and end with a word of comfort to a restricted group (ch. 24: the deportees of 597; ch. 35: the Rechabites[13]).

Chapters 7, 25 and 35 are linked to each other in different ways. First of all, the topic of the land as a gift from Yhwh to the fathers is typically dtr in terminological and ideological concerns. In the book of Jeremiah this topic occurs for the first time in Jer. 7.7, 14 and for the last time in Jer. 35.15. In these verses the maintenance of the land given to the fathers depends on the amendment of the addressee's ethical and theological behavior. The same formulation found in Jer. 35.15 is in Jer. 25.5: 'turn again now every one from his evil way, and from the evil of your doings':

כי אם־היטיב תיטיבו את־דרכיכם ואת־מעלליכם	Jeremiah 7.5
שובו־נא איש מדרכו הרעה ומרע מעלליכם	Jeremiah 25.5
שבו־נא איש מדרכו הרעה והיטיבו מעלליכם	Jeremiah 35.15

There are many other parallels between chs. 7 and 25,[14] such that Jeremiah 25 is partially a summary of ch. 7, but displays at the same time links with ch. 35 (esp. 25.3-6 and 35.14-15[15]). Thus there are clear indications that these three chapters function as a literary vault. This observation weakens the idea that the book of Jeremiah does not represent a compositional project. There are many other links between the

---

12. For convenience I will refer to the Masoretic order. If the order of the Septuagint is to be preferred this does not affect the remarks on the dtr structure of the book, since the oracles to the nations do not seem to have been edited by the Deuteronomists.

13. According to C. Levin (*Die Verheissung des neuen Bundes in ihrem theologiegeschichtlichen Zusammenhang ausgelegt* [FRLANT, 137; Göttingen: Vandenhoeck & Ruprecht, 1985], p. 158) and H. Cazelles ('La production du livre de Jérémie dans l'histoire ancienne d'Israël', *Masses Ouvrières* 343 [1978], pp. 9-31 [24-25]), ch. 35 was the final of an exilic edition of the book of Jeremiah.

14. T. Römer, *Israels Väter: Untersuchungen zur Väterthematik im Deuteronomium und in der deuteronomistischen Tradition* (OBO, 99; Freiburg: Universitätsverlag; Göttingen: Vandenhoeck & Ruprecht, 1990), pp. 458-60.

15. Thiel, *Die deuteronomistische Redaktion von Jeremiah 1–25*, pp. 265-67.

discourses that cannot be enumerated here. Still I would like to pay some attention to the relationship between Jeremiah 11 and 31.31-34*, which present the two poles of the dtr covenant theology in Jeremiah:

...להוציאם מארץ מצרים	31.32 לא כברית אשר כרתי את־אבותם
ביום הוציאי־אותם מארץ־מצרים (11.4)	11.10 את־בריתי אשר כרתי את־אבותם
	31.32 אשר־המה הפרו את־בריתי
	11.10 הפרו...את־בריתי

Jeremiah 31.32 clearly refers to ch. 11: 'not according to the covenant that I made with their fathers in the day that I took them by the hand to bring them out of the land of Egypt; when they broke my covenant...' (cf. 11.10: 'they have broken my covenant that I made with their fathers' and 11.4: '...in the day that I brought them out of the land of Egypt'). The link between these texts also explains the quite unusual designation of the fathers in 11.10 as *ri'šōnîm*, since this prepares for the announcement of the *berît ḥªdāšāh* in 31.31 (the pair *ri'šon-ḥādāš* is quite common in prophetic oracles of the exilic period).[16]

Structuring the book by discourses that relate to each other is exactly the same compositional technique observed by Noth for the DH. Thus, we can conclude that there is a coherent dtr redaction of Jeremiah. Perhaps the first dtr redaction of Jeremiah only encompassed chs. 7–35. Indeed, ch. 7 contains the first and ch. 35 the last of the prose discourses which, according to Nicholson, display the same structure.[17] This may even be confirmed by some statistics. L. Stulman,[18] following Weinfeld,[19] has compiled lists of dtr vocabulary in Jeremiah and the DH that show that about 75 per cent of the dtr terms common to the two works occur between Jeremiah 7 and 35. This first dtr redaction of Jeremiah is well organized and related to the DH, as I shall now try to show.

16. T. Römer, 'Les "anciens" pères (Jér 11,10) et la "nouvelle" alliance (Jér 31,31)', *BN* 59 (1991), pp. 23-27.

17. E.W. Nicholson, *Preaching to the Exiles: A Study of the Prose Tradition in the Book of Jeremiah* (Oxford: Basil Blackwell, 1970), p. 34.

18. L. Stulman, *The Prose Sermons in the Book of Jeremiah: A Redescription of the Correspondences with Deuteronomistic Literature in the Light of Recent Text-Critical Research* (SBLDS, 83; Atlanta: Scholars Press, 1986), pp. 33-44.

19. M. Weinfeld, *Deuteronomy and the Deuteronomic School* (Oxford: Clarendon Press, 1972).

The Relationship between the Deuteronomists of Jeremiah
and the Deuteronomists of the DH

According to Stipp there is 'a deep gap between the authors of the DH and the authors of the dtr texts in Jer.',[20] and quite a lot of scholars agree. But are there really different *dtr* ideologies in both corpora? Stipp, Albertz and others claim that the rejection of the temple in Jeremiah 7 is to be understood as opposition to the temple ideology of the DH.[21] Personally, I cannot find any rejection of the temple in Jeremiah 7. The dtr redactors do denounce a magical and popularist comprehension of the temple. They want to explain in their setting after 587 why the temple has been destroyed, and in the first part of the speech (vv. 2-7) they put forward the conditions under which it would have been possible to live in the *māqôm*, which alludes to the temple as well as to the land. There is no contradiction at all with the view of the temple in the DH.[22] We may go even further and argue that Jeremiah 7 functions as a parallel to the temple speech in the DH, namely the inauguration of the temple by Solomon in 1 Kings 8. Both texts envisage and explain the catastrophe of the exile. The formulation of the 'land given to the fathers' appears in the DH for the first time in 1 Kings 8, and in the book of Jeremiah in ch. 7. 1 Kings 8.36 as well as Jer. 7.3, 5 mention the 'good way' in which the audience should walk. The possibility of deportation, which is the topic of Solomon's last prayer (8.46-53), is confirmed by the announcement of judgment in Jeremiah's discourse (7.15). It seems quite clear that both texts are related to each other, and we may assume, following Lohfink, that the dtr redactors of the historical books and those of Jeremiah tried to establish cross-references between the two corpora.[23] Many other links could be observed. Rendtorff has stated that Jer. 25.1-13 'displays clear connections with

20. Stipp, 'Probleme des redaktionsgeschichtlichen Modells', p. 232.

21. Stipp, 'Probleme des redaktionsgeschichtlichen Modells', p. 232; Albertz, 'Die Intention', pp. 345-47.

22. See also T. Seidl, 'Jeremias Tempelrede: Polemik gegen die joschijanische Reform? Die Paralleltraditionen Jer 7 und Jer 26 auf ihre Effizienz für das Deuteronomismusproblem in Jeremia befragt', in Gross (ed.) *Jeremiah und die 'deuteronomistische Bewegung'*, pp. 141-79 (175).

23. N. Lohfink, 'Gab es eine deuteronomische Bewegung?', in Gross (ed.), *Jeremia und die 'deuteronomistische Bewegung'*, pp. 313-82 (360).

the summary Deuteronomistic interpretation of the history of Israel in II Kings 17'.[24] The covenant speech in Jeremiah 11 could also have been given by Moses in the book of Deuteronomy. The idea in 11.3-4 that Yhwh commanded his *b^{e}rît* to the fathers (for the same expression, see Judg. 2.20) at the very time he brought them out of Egypt is also to be found in the DH (Deut. 29.24 and 1 Kgs 8.21). The Mosaic covenant which, as Gary Knoppers has recently emphasized,[25] is important to the Deuteronomists, provides another link between DH and the book of Jeremiah. It is indeed easy to show that the author of Jeremiah 11 is quoting from Deuteronomy (compare 11.4-5 to Deut. 7.8 and 8.18). In the DH as well as in the dtr redaction of Jeremiah, God's promise is presented as on oath (*nišba'*), and as John Van Seters has convincingly shown, in both corpora 'the oath to the fathers represents the divine promise to the exodus generation'.[26] We may also recall the end of the vision of the good and bad figs (Jer. 24.9-10)[27] which is clearly related to the curses of Deuteronomy 28 (esp. 28.25, 63). There are no ideological problems between the Deuteronomists of Jeremiah and those of the DH. The problems that exist occur on another level.

How Did Jeremiah Become a Convert to Dtr Ideology?

The problem is the absence of Jeremiah in the DH. How does one explain this *Prophetenschweigen*, which also concerns Amos and Hosea,[28] and which is quite astonishing, since the books of these prophets sound very deuteronomistic? One suggestion is that these

24. R. Rendtorff, *The Old Testament: An Introduction* (London: SCM Press, 1985 [1983]), p. 204.

25. G.N. Knoppers, *Two Nations under God: The Deuteronomistic History of Solomon and the Dual Monarchies*, II (HSM, 52; Atlanta: Scholars Press, 1993), p. 160.

26. J. Van Seters, *Prologue to History: The Yahwist as Historian in Genesis* (Zürich: Theologischer Verlag, 1992), p. 235; see also Römer, *Israels Väter*, *passim*.

27. It is questionable, however, whether this chapter belongs to the first dtr edition of Jeremiah. Cf. G. Wanke, *Jeremia* (ZBK, 20; Zürich: Theologischer Verlag, 1995), pp. 222-23.

28. K. Koch, 'Das Profetenschweigen des deuteronomistischen Geschichtswerks', in L. Perlitt and J. Jeremias (eds.), *Die Botschaft und die Boten: Festschrift für Hans Walther Wolff zum 70. Geburtstag* (Neukirchen–Vluyn: Neukirchener Verlag, 1981), pp. 115-28.

prophets announced an irrevocable disaster that did not suit dtr ideology. This solution is hypothetical as far as both the message of the 'historical' Jeremiah and the ideology of the DH are concerned. But there are indeed tensions between the non-dtr texts in Jeremiah and the DH. The purchase of a field by Jeremiah in Jer. 32.1-15, which is normally not considered dtr material,[29] makes the following point: 'Houses, fields, and vineyards[30] will still be acquired in this land' (15b).[31] This text clearly expresses hope for an ongoing life in Judah. The restoration will take place in Palestine, not Babylon. It seems then that those left in the land after 597/587 were envisioned.[32] This hope is also visible in the non-dtr parts of Jeremiah 37–44. According to 39.14 and 40.2-6 the prophet chooses to remain with the non-exiled population in the land, refusing the offer of Nebuzaradan to accompany him to Babylon. These texts legitimate the idea that God is on the side of the remnant community in the land. According to 40.12 the government of Gedaliah, who is assisted by Jeremiah (40.6), produces welfare for the people: 'they harvested an abundance of wine and summer fruit'. It is not astonishing that this statement is missing in the parallel account in 2 Kgs 25.22-26, which, according to Seitz, seems to 'downplay the potential rule of Gedaliah'.[33]

The vision of a non-dtr 'biography' of Jeremiah in chs. 37–44 contradicts indeed the perspective of the exilic edition of the DH which states at its conclusion: 'So Judah was deported away from her land' (2 Kgs 25.21). We may conclude that the DH does not mention Jeremiah because there was a Jeremiah tradition that strongly supported the views of the remaining population in Judah. This view is found in the primitive version of chs. 37–44, which Christopher Seitz has characterized as a 'scribal chronicle'. According to Seitz, this chronicle was written by a member of the post-597 Judean community[34] and

---

29. For instance W. Thiel, *Die deuteronomistische Redaktion von Jeremia 26–45* (WMANT, 52; Neukirchen–Vluyn: Neukirchener Verlag, 1981), p. 29.

30. 'Houses' and 'vineyards' may have been added secondarily (cf. Holladay, *Jeremiah*, pp. 210-11) but this does not affect the sense of the oracle.

31. According to the very critical Levin (*Die Verheissung*, p. 159), this reflects the message of the historical Jeremiah.

32. Cf. W. McKane, *A Critical and Exegetical Commentary on Jeremiah XXVI–LII* (ICC; Edinburgh: T. & T. Clark, 1996), p. 841.

33. C.R. Seitz, *Theology in Conflict: Reactions to the Exile in the Book of Jeremiah* (BZAW, 176; Berlin: W. de Gruyter, 1989), p. 217.

34. Seitz, *Theology*, p. 285.

presents 'a profile of this community that is not unsympathetic'.[35] This perspective is excluded from DH and the Ezekiel traditions.[36] When this scribal chronicle came to Babylon (following Seitz this happened during the third deportation in 582) it was reworked from an exilic and dtr perspective. Jeremiah 43.5-7, which states that 'all the remnant of Judah...every person whom Nebuzaradan had left with Gedaliah... came into the land of Egypt, for they did not obey the voice of Yhwh', stresses a picture of wholesale evacuation, which corresponds to the end of DH.

We can imagine the 'deuteronomization' of the Jeremiah tradition in the following way: The exilic redactors of the DH conflicted with a chronicle telling the last days of Jeremiah and of the kingdom of Judah. Since this chronicle revealed a positive attitude of Jeremiah towards the 'autochthonous', the population who had not been deported, the redactors of the DH were not eager to mention Jeremiah at the end of their historiography. Two centuries later the Chronicler would include Jeremiah at the end of his story, because, as Sara Japhet has shown,[37] he had, in opposition to the DH, a more autochthonous vision of Israel, playing down the impact of exile and exodus. But let us go back to the Deuteronomists. Even if they did not like Jeremiah they could not ignore him. So they edited a dtr version of Jeremiah, in Jeremiah 7–35*. It would be interesting to explore the hypothesis that such dtr editing of Jeremiah was carried out at the same time as the dtr redaction of Amos and Hosea. If this were true we would then have a kernel of a 'dtr' prophetic canon. Such a hypothesis could eventually explain why the historical books and the prophetic books were bound together.

Turning back to Jeremiah 7–35, we have seen that this first dtr edition is very close to the DH in vocabulary, compositional techniques and theology. In this edition Jeremiah speaks as if he were a member of the dtr party. But when the scribal chronicle, as identified by Seitz, came to Babylon, it was integrated into a second dtr edition of the book of Jeremiah. This second edition usurped the scroll containing chs. 37–44 as well as the collection of oracles in Jeremiah 2–6, in which, as Mark

---

35. Seitz, *Theology*, p. 287.

36. Seitz, *Theology*, p. 286.

37. S. Japhet, 'L'historiographie post-exilique: Comment et pourquoi?', in A. de Pury, T. Römer and J.-D. Macchi (eds.), *Israël construit son histoire: L'historiographie deutéronomiste à la lumière de recherches récentes* (MB, 34; Geneva: Labor et Fides, 1996), pp. 123-52.

Biddle has shown,[38] the dtr redaction is quite different from chs. 7–35. This second edition is framed by chs. 1 and 45,[39] as well as by the idea of the disobedience of the fathers (Jer. 2.5 and 44.9). At the end of this new edition, chs. 43–44 present a very harsh criticism of the Egyptian diaspora, which seems very well established. So we should date this second edition not earlier than the end of the exilic period, or, better, at the beginning of the Persian period. There seems to be a certain evolution of the vocabulary in this edition since about 55 per cent of Stulmann's 'dtr' or 'C' diction not attested in the DH is found in chs. 1–6 and 36–45. Moreover, in the revised dtr edition the expression 'the land given to the fathers' has been changed into 'the Torah given to the fathers' (44.10). This may indicate that the return to the land became less important and that the Babylonian redactors of Jeremiah 1–45 transformed the *golah* into diaspora. For them there was no urgency to return to *eretz yisrael* since the Torah had become the new land in which Yhwh fully could be worshiped.

The importance of the written word of Yhwh appears quite clearly in the story of the re-edition of the burnt scroll in Jeremiah 36. This story, which is in many respects linked to 2 Kings 22–23, legitimates the new edition of the book of Jeremiah (v. 32) and offers a new interpretation for the 'chronicle' contained in chs. 37–44. At first, the oracle 'quoted' in 36.29 says that the king of Babylon will empty the land, cutting off from it man and beast, which gives an *interpretatio babylonica* to the following story. But the point of ch. 36 is to appeal to the audience not to behave as did king Jehoiakim, in showing them that the written prophetic word transcends time and place and does not depend on any institution. As Carroll puts it, 'committed to writing, the word has a permanence...and can survive even the absence of its original bearer'.[40] In other words: the conversion of Jeremiah into a dtr preacher was suc-

---

38. M.E. Biddle, *A Redaction History of Jeremiah 2.1–4.2* (ATANT, 77; Zürich: Theologischer Verlag, 1990).

39. Jer. 1 is a mixture of dtr and postexilic prophetic terminology (see S. Herrmann, *Jeremia* [BKAT, 12.1; Neukirchen–Vluyn: Neukirchener Verlag, 1986], pp. 52-55). Jer. 45 is linked to Jer. 1 (cf. 1.10 and 45.4, see R.P. Carroll, *Jeremiah* [OTL; London: SCM Press, 1986)], p. 746). We cannot discuss here the addition of Jer. 52. As W. Brueggemann has shown, Baruch is a cipher for the Babylonian community of Jews and functions as a counterpoint to the Egyptian Jews who are condemned in chs. 43–44 (*To Build, to Plant: A Commentary on Jeremiah 26–52* [ITC; Grand Rapids: Eerdmans, 1991], pp. 204-208).

40. Carroll, *Jeremiah*, p. 668.

cessful, because those redactors bound sermons, oracles and stories together into a book. This book as it stands is marked by dtr ideology, but since it also integrates other conceptions of 'Israel' and God, it offers the possibility for different trends of Judaism to find room inside this new homeland, which is the book.

PAN DEUTERONOMISM AND THE BOOK OF EZEKIEL

Corrine L. Patton

Identification of deuteronomic redaction in books outside of Deuteronomy and the Deuteronomistic History has increased dramatically in recent years. The wide range of redactional activity in these texts has raised several methodological issues, such as the use of the terms 'deuteronomic' and 'deuteronomistic', the linguistic criteria by which such identifications are made, and the existence of a defined and identifiable social group responsible for such widespread scribal activity. These methodological questions become particularly acute in the discussion of possible deuteronomistic redaction in the book of Ezekiel, where too little attention is paid to the complexity of reconstructing the setting in which such redaction could have occurred.[1]

---

1. For a review of recent attempts to delineate deuteronomistic influence, see the summary provided by F.-L. Hossfeld, 'Ezechiel und die deuteronomisch-deuteronomistische Bewegung', in W. Gross (ed.), *Jeremia und die 'deuteronomische Bewegung'* (BBB, 98; Weinheim: Beltz Athenäum, 1995), pp. 272-77. He reviews S. Herrmann, *Die prophetischen Heilserwartungen im Alten Testament: Ursprung und Gestaltwandel* (BWANT, 85; Stuttgart: W. Kohlhammer, 1965); R. Liwak, 'Überlieferungsgeschichtliche Probleme des Ezechielbuches: Eine Studie zu postezechielischen Interpretationen und Komposition' (PhD dissertation, University of Bochum, 1976); F.-L. Hossfeld, *Untersuchungen zur Komposition und Theologie des Ezekechielbuches* (FzB, 20; Würzburg: Echter Verlag, 1977); B. Willmes, *Die sogenannte Hirtenallegorie Ez 34* (BBET, 19; Frankfurt: Peter Lang, 1984); D. Baltzer, 'Literarkritische und literarhistorische Anmerkungen zur Heilsprophetie im Ezechielbuch', in J. Lust (ed.), *Ezekiel and his Book* (BETL, 74; Leuven: Leuven University Press, 1986), pp. 166-81; H.F. Fuhs, *Ezechiel* (2 vols.; NEB, 7, 22; Würzburg: Echter Verlag, 1984–88); T. Krüger, *Geschichtskonzepte im Ezechielbuch* (BZAW, 180; Berlin: W. de Gruyter, 1989); F. Sedlmeier, *Studien zu Komposition und Theologie von Ez 20* (SBB, 21; Stuttgart: Katholisches Bibelwerk, 1990); S. Ohnesorge, *Jahwe gestaltet sein Volk neu: Zur Sicht der Zukunft Israels nach Ez 11, 14-21; 20, 1-44; 36, 16-38; 37, 1-14, 15-28* (FzB, 64; Würzburg: Echter Verlag, 1991); F. Fechter, *Bewältigung der Katastrophe: Untersuchungen zu*

Several methodological problems with identifying deuteronomistic
activity in general have been spelled out most recently by Coggins and
Lohfink.[2] Both caution about the ambiguity of the terms 'deuteronomic'
and 'deuteronomistic', as well as the means by which scholars identify
the presence of dtr redaction in texts not generally attributed to the
deuteronomist. In light of these cautions, let me first clarify my use of
the terms. I use the term 'deuteronomic' or D to refer to the pre-exilic
source of the *Kern* of the book of Deuteronomy. Obviously this author
could have contributed nothing to the book of Ezekiel. I use the term
'deuteronomistic' or Dtr to refer to the exilic redactors of the final form
of both Deuteronomy and the Deuteronomistic History, who possibly
redacted portions of Jeremiah. I do not deny that there may have been
intermediate redactors or authors of this deuteronomistic corpus, but the
one redactor we are sure existed is the one who brought the history of

ausgewählten Fremdvölkersprüchen im Ezechielbuch (BZAW, 208; Berlin: W. de
Gruyter, 1992); and K.-F. Pohlmann, *Ezechielstudien: Zur Redaktionsgeschichte
des Buches und zur Frage nach den ältesten Texten* (BZAW, 202; Berlin: W. de
Gruyter, 1992). See also W. Zimmerli, *Ezekiel 1: A Commentary on the Book of the
Prophet Ezekiel, Chapters 1–24* (Hermeneia; Philadelphia: Fortress Press, 1979),
pp. 21-23, 43-46; *idem, Ezekiel 2: A Commentary on the Book of the Prophet
Ezekiel, Chapters 25–48* (Hermeneia; Philadelphia: Fortress Press, 1983), p. xv;
R.R. Wilson, *Prophecy and Society in Ancient Israel* (Philadelphia: Fortress Press,
1980), pp. 282-86; J. Pons, 'Le vocabulaire d'Ezéchiel 20: Le prophète s'oppose à
la vision deutéronomiste de l'histoire', in Lust (ed.), *Ezekiel and his Book*, pp. 214-
33; P. Joyce, *Divine Initiative and Human Response in Ezekiel* (JSOTSup, 51;
Sheffield, JSOT Press, 1989); B. Halpern, 'Jerusalem and the Lineages in the Seventh Century BCE: Kinship and the Rise of Individual Moral Liability', in B.
Halpern and D.W. Hobson (eds.), *Law and Ideology in Monarchic Israel*
(JSOTSup, 124; Sheffield: JSOT Press, 1991), pp. 11-18; N. Mendecki, 'Post-
deuteronomistische Redaktion von Ez 28, 25-26?', *BN* 73 (1994), pp. 66-73, and F.
Sedlmeier, '"Deine Brüder, deine Brüder..." Die Beziehung von Ez 11,14-21 zur
dtn-dtr Theologie', in Gross (ed.), *Jeremia und die 'deuteronomistische Bewegung'*,
pp. 297-312. Greenberg also posits deuteronomistic influence throughout his commentary, but does not devote a separate section to discussing it (*Ezekiel 1–20* [AB,
22; New York: Doubleday, 1983]).
    2. R. Coggins, 'What Does "Deuteronomistic' Mean?", in Jon Davies, Graham
Harvey and Wilfred G.E. Watson (eds.), *Words Remembered, Texts Renewed:
Essays in Honour of John F.A. Sawyer* (JSOTSup, 195; Sheffield: Sheffield Academic Press, 1995), pp. 135-48, reprinted as the first essay in this volume, and N.
Lohfink, 'Gab es eine deuteronomistische Bewegung?', in Gross (ed.), *Jeremia und
die 'deuteronomistische Bewegung'*, pp. 313-82, reprinted in an abridged and translated version as the second essay in this volume.

Israel to its close with the fall of Jerusalem. I assume that both D and Dtr have similar ideologies, since it appears that Dtr judged Israel's history by the laws contained in D.[3] As opposed to Person,[4] I view the majority of deuteronomistic activity as pre-dating the Persian period and the later texts that exhibit deuteronomistic influence as doing so independently by their authors' own conscious appropriation of deuteronomistic ideology.[5] Even within such chronological confines, parallels between Ezekiel and 'Ephraimite' prophetic texts,[6] such as Jeremiah and Hosea, complicate any attempt to identify a given text in Ezekiel as the result of conscious deuteronomistic editing.

Attempts to identify a deuteronomistic redaction of or deuteronomistic influence on the sporadic texts that exhibit close parallels between Ezekiel and Jeremiah illustrate the methodological difficulties of any such enterprise.[7] The question of the exact or relative dates of

3. It appears that this author came from a group that did not have access to either royal or Zadokite positions in Judah (they may or may not have had access to power in the North), yet were clearly learned, and distinguishable by their narrow definition of what constitutes legitimate worship of Yahweh. As such they were xenophobic, believed in the strict limitation of royal power, especially in religious matters, and in the efficacy of the prophetic word. They appear to have had access to literary works, archives, documents, etc., and to have been able to put forth their ideas primarily through the 'power of the pen' (or stylus), but not through direct control of economic, political or religious institutions, at least in monarchic Judah. As such, if there was a scribal group that worked independently or interdependently of kings, priests, judges, and the like, then I would look for the deuteronomists there. There is only scant evidence of a 'school', but more likely the views in the variety of texts that show deuteronomistic redaction come from a group that shared an ideology (a 'school of thought'), rather than a profession. As such, then, only some of the 'members' of this group would need to be scribes. For other representative reconstructions of the deuteronomists, see the review of positions in Lohfink, 'Gab es eine deuteronomistische Bewegung?', pp. 313-17.

4. R.F. Person, Jr, *Second Zechariah and the Deuteronomic School* (JSOTSup, 167; Sheffield: JSOT Press, 1993).

5. The use of the DtrH by Chronicles shows its quick, widespread influence in the Persian period.

6. Ephraimite refers to the northern prophetic tradition that continues in the south after 722. For the use of this term, see Wilson, *Prophecy and Society*, pp. 17-18.

7. Scholars who stress the connection between Ezekiel and Jeremiah include Fuhs, Fechter, Wilson, Joyce and Halpern, as well as J.W. Miller, *Das Verhältnis Jeremias und Hesekiels sprachlich und theologisch Untersucht* (Assen: Van Gorcum, 1955), and D. Vieweger, *Die literarische Beziehungen zwischen den Büchern*

the deuteronomistic redactor, the final form of Jeremiah and the final form of Ezekiel too often serve as the backdrop for various reconstructions, rather than as their vanguard. Most scholars who see the parallels as reflecting an authorial connection posit either a late deuteronomistic redaction of both prophetic texts or Ezekiel's knowledge of and influence by Jeremiah and/or the deuteronomists. Yet a deuteronomistic redaction of the book as a whole is highly improbable. Even the most optimistic identification of deuteronomistic redaction limits its presence to isolated additions.[8] Moreover, most of these additions do not show a 'pure' deuteronomism but are often 'mixed' with a kind of priestly perspective characteristic of the whole book of Ezekiel. Finally, the additions do not appear consistently throughout the book framing older material in a way that changes how it is read—a feature of deuteronomistic redaction in the Deuteronomistic History and, possibly, Jeremiah.

Scholars such as Herrmann and Hossfeld, who envision a redaction by an identifiable deuteronomistic editor, equate this figure with the deuteronomistic editor of Jeremiah. I assume that they envision that this redactor set out to edit prophetic texts, devoting more energy to the revision of Jeremiah, a text more readily supplemented by a deuteronomistic perspective than Ezekiel. In Ezekiel the redactional work was limited primarily to visions of restoration, rather than reconfiguring the whole text. This reconstruction explains the parallels between the last layers of these two texts but does not address the fact that these parallels are not identical. Instead, as will be shown, these additions serve the prevailing ideology of each of these two prophetic works.

More often, however, scholars shy away from identifying the redactor of Ezekiel with the deuteronomistic redactor, but instead speak of a redactor who exhibits deuteronomistic 'influence'. Presumably, what is meant by this is that the redactor is not a member of an identifiable social group that we would call the deuteronomists but is someone who is familiar with this group's ideology and, for the most part, assents to it. This redactor's ideology is distinct from that of the author of 'proto-Ezekiel' but may also be in some way distinct from the deuteronomists. This view takes a variety of forms. Ohnesorge asserts the presence of a

---

Jeremia und Ezechiel (BEATAJ, 26; Frankfurt: Peter Lang, 1993).

8. The only possible exception may be Liwak's unpublished dissertation, summarized by Zimmerli, *Ezekiel,* II, pp. xiv-xv.

later redactor influenced by the deuteronomists.[9] Wilson suggests that
the author of Ezekiel, and not some later redactor, was influenced by
'Ephraimite' views, since these views are present at all levels of the
text.[10] Joyce allows that these texts may come either from a deuteronomistic redactor, or from deuteronomistic influence on Ezekiel himself.[11]
Greenberg often points to deuteronomistic parallels in Ezekiel but shies
away from an independent insertion that changes the book.[12] In the first
volume of his commentary, Zimmerli suggests that deuteronomistic
features actually reflect pre-exilic prophetic traditions held in common
by the deuteronomists and the author of Ezekiel,[13] while in volume 2 he
merely asserts that the question requires further study.[14]

Finally, several scholars deny any modifications of the message of
Ezekiel by a deuteronomistic redactor or someone influenced by the
deuteronomists, instead positing that any parallels with deuteronomistic
material stem from texts whose ultimate view explicitly opposes those
cited. Pons suggests that the elders in ch. 20 represent a deuteronomistic
ideology that Ezekiel explicitly rejects,[15] while Pohlmann sees more
affinities between Ezekiel 20 and Second Isaiah than with any deuteronomistic text.[16] Halpern, on the other hand, believes that Ezekiel and
Jeremiah represent two rival parties that both critique the deuteronomistic view.[17]

Little attempt has been made recently to trace possible influence of
Ezekiel's text on either the book of Jeremiah or, even more, on the
deuteronomistic history. The prevailing presumption has been that the
influence flows in one direction. I will examine those terms and ideas
most commonly attributed to deuteronomistic and/or Jeremianic influence, such as the outline of Israel's history in Ezekiel 16, 23 and 20,[18]

9.   Ohnesorge, *Jahwe gestaltet sein Volk neu*, pp. 31-33.
10. Wilson, *Prophecy and Society*, p. 283.
11. Joyce, *Divine Initiative*, pp. 21-32.
12. Greenberg, *Ezekiel 1–20*.
13. Zimmerli, *Ezekiel 1*, pp. 43-46.
14. Zimmerli, *Ezekiel 2*, p. xv.
15. This is the main point of Pons' article 'Le vocabulaire d'Ezéchiel 20'.
16. Pohlmann, *Ezechielstudien*, esp. pp. 154-77.
17. Halpern, 'Jerusalem and the Lineages in the Seventh Century BCE', pp. 14-15.
18. See Wilson, *Prophecy and Society*; Pons, 'Le vocabulaire', and Liwak, 'Überlieferungsgeschichtliche Probleme'.

the covenant, especially in Ezekiel 34 and 37,[19] the explanation of the fall of Jerusalem as punishment for Israel's cultic violations, especially in ch. 6,[20] the terms for idols and rebellion used by Ezekiel, and the language of the new heart in chs. 11 and 36,[21] in order to determine whether they give evidence of a secondary, contradictory or modifying redaction of the book of Ezekiel, Ezekiel's own appropriation of deuteronomistic theology, or an independent reflection of terms common in the exile. These possibilities can be summarized as follows: (1) a secondary addition by a deuteronomistic redactor; (2) a secondary addition by a redactor influenced by and assenting to the deuteronomistic position; (3) Ezekiel's own influence by deuteronomistic ideology; (4) Ezekiel's manipulation and critique of deuteronomistic ideology; or (5) Ezekiel's own terms that are then later taken up by a redactor of Jeremiah and the Deuteronomistic History.

Ezekiel as a Manipulative Author

Ezekiel is known to manipulate well-known texts and motifs.[22] The creative and theological freedom with which this author turns and extends traditions extant in earlier literature marks him as brilliantly creative. Most of this manipulation serves Ezekiel's larger theological concerns in the book: the preservation of God's power and control as well as the defense of God's right to destroy the temple and Jerusalem. The most obvious example of this literary manipulation can be found in the texts describing Israel as wife and whore.[23] As Galambush has

19. See Joyce, *Divine Initiative*; and Ohnesorge, *Jahwe gestaltet sein Volk neu*. This is critiqued by A.S. Kapelrud, 'The Prophets and the Covenant', in W.B. Barrick and J.R. Spencer (eds.), *In the Shelter of Elyon: Essays on Ancient Palestinian Life and Literature in Honor of G.W. Ahlström* (JSOTSup, 31; Sheffield: JSOT Press, 1984), pp. 175-83.

20. See Zimmerli, *Ezekiel 2*; Wilson, *Prophecy and Society*; and Joyce, *Divine Initiative*.

21. See Joyce, *Divine Initiative*; Ohnesorge, *Jahwe gestaltet sein Volk neu*; and Sedlmeier, *Studien*.

22. Most scholars have to admit that places that contain deuteronomistic language in Ezekiel mix this language with material closer to H (= the Holiness Code; Lev. 17–26) and P. See, for instance, Hossfeld, 'Ezechiel und die deuteronomisch-deuteronomistische Bewegung'.

23. See Miller, *Das Verhältnis Jeremias und Hesekiels*; W. Zimmerli, *The Law and the Prophets: A Study of the Meaning of the Old Testament* (New York: Harper

shown,[24] Ezekiel takes a literary figure well known in Israelite tradition and extends it to its most graphic expression. In the process of this expansion, Ezekiel adapts the motif to illustrate the book's view of the essential result of Israel's sins: the defilement of God's holy home, leading to the justified abandonment of this land/bride. The motif easily expresses the text's prevailing answer to the theological problem of the exile: Israel never deserved God's devotion and has no defense to counter Yahweh's divorce proceedings.[25]

Ezekiel's retelling of Israel's history in these chapters, as well as in ch. 20, also illustrates the author's conscious shaping of earlier traditions to suit the text's purposes.[26] The outline of Israel's history in ch. 20 shows clear familiarity with the Exodus traditions: the sojourn in Egypt (vv. 5-8), the deliverance by Yahweh (vv. 9-10), the two generations in the wilderness (vv. 10-25), the giving of law in the wilderness (vv. 11-13 and 25-26) and the entry into the land (v. 28). The purpose of the passage is clearly polemical: rather than reviewing the mighty acts of God, the emphasis is on the pervasiveness of Israel's sin. The scheme certainly matches historical reviews present and presumed in deuteronomistic texts, including the historical review in Deuteronomy 1–11, the speech of Solomon in 1 Kings 8 and the speech of Joshua in Joshua 24. These parallels have led both Liwak and Wilson to use ch. 20 as evidence for deuteronomistic influence or redaction. However, all of the deuteronomistic materials outside of Ezekiel emphasize the

& Row, 1965), pp. 80-86; K.W. Carley, *Ezekiel among the Prophets* (SBT, 31; Naperville, IL: A.R. Allenson, 1974), pp. 49-57; T.M. Raitt, *A Theology of Exile: Judgement/Deliverance in Jeremiah and Ezekiel* (Philadelphia: Fortress Press, 1977), p. 74; R.M. Hals, *Ezekiel* (FOTL, 19; Grand Rapids: Eerdmans, 1989), p. 168; J. Blenkinsopp, *Ezekiel* (Interpretation; Louisville, KY: Westminster/John Knox Press, 1990), p. 101; and B. Uffenheimer, 'Theodicy and Ethics in the Prophecy of Ezekiel', in H.G. Reventlow and Y. Hoffman (eds.), *Justice and Righteousness: Biblical Themes and their Influence* (JSOTSup, 137; Sheffield: Sheffield Academic Press, 1992), pp. 200-27.

24. J. Galambush, *Jerusalem in the Book of Ezekiel: The City as Yahweh's Wife* (SBLDS, 130; Atlanta: Scholars Press, 1992).

25. See also Uffenheimer, 'Theodicy and Ethics', pp. 200-27, and Joyce, *Divine Intiative*, pp. 76-77 and 126-29.

26. See Sedlmeier, *Studien*, Ohnesorge, *Jahwe gestaltet sein Volk neu*, Hossfeld, 'Ezechiel und die deuteronomisch-deuteronomistische Bewegung', as well as C.L. Patton, ' "I Myself Gave Them Laws that Were Not Good": Ezekiel 20 and the Exodus Traditions', *JSOT* 69 (1996), pp. 73-90.

role of Moses and the location of the giving of the law at Horeb/Sinai, traditions consistently absent in Ezekiel. In fact, Ezekiel's assertion that in the wilderness Yahweh gave Israel laws that would lead them to defile themselves so that God could punish them with integrity (vv. 25-26) clearly shows that this historical review has also been adapted to serve the larger theme of justifying God's non-involvement in the fall of Jerusalem. The manipulation also expands the limits of the prophet's own powers: by declaring the laws of the wilderness 'no good', the book sets up the reader to accept the new laws of chs. 40–48.

Less obvious points of Ezekiel's manipulation of given traditions can also be detected. Twice in the book Ezekiel quotes a *māšāl* which he then twists to suit his purpose. The most noted of these is the one also quoted in Jeremiah: a father eats sour grapes and his children's teeth are set on edge. Ezekiel explicitly refutes the implications of such a saying, not allowing the present generation to escape responsibility for the fall of Jerusalem by blaming it on their parents.[27] In chs. 17 and 24 Ezekiel offers his own *mešālîm*, and in ch. 21 he is called the maker of *mešālîm*. So again, the rejection of given traditions leads directly to the prophet's creative activity, now not as lawgiver but as riddlemaker.

Finally, the cultic violations of ch. 6 can also be read as Ezekiel's manipulation of received traditions. Certainly the sins of the high places, worshiping idols and offering incense to foreign gods permeate the deuteronomistic literature. In particular, both Wilson and Joyce connect this chapter with deuteronomistic views, seen most plainly in the laws of the book of Deuteronomy. This would mean that the author of Ezekiel is influenced not necessarily by dtr, but possibly by D, known especially through the Josianic reform in Judah. Once again, however, Ezekiel does not merely adopt the earlier tradition as it stands but makes it his own. The terms he uses for the cultic installations are not those most common in D: the idols are *gillûlîm*; the incense altars are *ḥāmān*, a term never found in deuteronomic or deuteronomistic literature. The reference to worship under every tree finds its closest parallels in Hosea and Leviticus. In fact, parallels with the Holiness Code, especially in Leviticus 26, permeate this chapter. Both of these chapters refer to Israel's sin as the worship of *gillûlîm* by the lighting of fires on a *ḥāmān*. The punishment for these sins in both texts is the heaping of Israel's corpses on top of or in front of these idols. These

27. See especially, Joyce, *Divine Initiative* and G.H. Matties, *Ezekiel 18 and the Rhetoric of Moral Discourse* (SBLDS, 126; Atlanta: Scholars Press, 1990).

parallels place Ezekiel 6 closer to H than to D.[28] In addition, once
again, Ezekiel's use of cultic violations serves the larger purpose of
justifying God's punishment as well as Ezekiel's larger purpose: so that
they shall know that '1 am Yahweh'.[29] Ezekiel, then, freely uses concepts found in pre-exilic texts such as D and Hosea, and adapts them to
suit the purposes of the book.

Ezekiel and Language of the Exile: Cases of Mistaken Identity

While the above section focuses on Ezekiel's propensity to manipulate
early deuteronomic and Ephraimite concepts, it must also be noted that
certain elements in the book that are prominent in deuteronomistic literature are not necessarily known to Ezekiel exclusively through this
tradition.[30] In order to identify Ezekiel's appropriation of concepts such
as Israel's rebellion and the idea of the covenant as reflecting the
deuteronomists it has to be shown that Ezekiel's language depends on
their particular use of these terms.

Ezekiel characterizes Israel's sin as rebellion, $m^e r\hat{\imath}$. In the Pentateuch,
while the root appears in Numbers 14, 17, 20 and 27, the use there is
quite different from Ezekiel's: either the people rebel against Moses
(17.25; 20.10), or the texts describe Moses' own sin that keeps him out
of the Land (20.24 and 27.14). However, the word appears seven times
in Deuteronomy to refer to the sin of the people as a whole (1.26, 43;
9.7, 23, 24; 21.18, 31.27), sin that often leads to death (21.18), or
exclusion from the land (1.26). While this suggests that Ezekiel's use of
the term reflects that of the deuteronomist, outside of the Pentateuch the
term is used in a wide variety of texts in the way Ezekiel uses it, from
Isaiah and Nehemiah to Proverbs and Psalms.[31] Therefore, the notion of
rebellion cannot provide evidence of an exclusive deuteronomistic
editor.

One of the most common assertions of deuteronomistic influence

---

28. This does not necessitate H preceding Ezekiel, however; see, especially,
Patton, ' "I Myself Gave Them Laws" ', p. 84. For an overview of parallels between
Ezekiel and various legal traditions see Zimmerli, *Ezekiel 1*, pp. 46-52.

29. W. Zimmerli, ' "Ich bin Jahwe" ', in W.F. Albright (ed.), *Geschichte und
Altes Testament: Albrecht Alt zum 70. Geburtstag dargebracht* (BHT, 16; Tübingen: J.C.B. Mohr [Paul Siebeck], 1953), pp. 179-209.

30. Certainly this caution must be noted for Ezekiel's review of Israel's history.

31. See, e.g., the use of the noun in Pss. 78 and 106, Lam. 1 and Zeph. 3.11.

stems from Ezekiel's use of the term 'covenant', especially in the oracles of salvation.[32] However, of the more than 16 occurrences of the
word *bᵉrît* in Ezekiel, the vast majority are used in ch. 16 to refer to the
marriage between Israel and God and ch. 17 to refer to a treaty with
Babylon. The broken covenant of 44.7 is equated with the desecration
of the temple, a covenant closer to the Davidic covenant than to the
Mosaic. The covenants of peace in 34.25 and 37.26 clearly refer to the
Davidic covenant, while the reference to the new covenant in 20.37 is
ambiguous. In fact, there is no clear reference to a Mosaic or Sinaitic
covenant in the book of Ezekiel. The term characteristic of covenant
loyalty in D and Dtr, *ḥesed*, is also missing in Ezekiel. God's covenant
in no way depends on Israel's behavior, and, therefore, when present, is
unconditional; when absent, never deserved. Further, as Batto has
pointed out,[33] the covenant of peace in chs. 34 and 37 stems from
ancient Near Eastern concepts of covenant that stress the deity's
promise not to destroy a *rebellious* humankind,[34] not because they are
no longer inherently rebellious, but simply because the deity chooses
not to do so. The language that typifies the deuteronomistic covenant,
then, is absent here, replaced by an exclusive non-deuteronomistic view
of the term, a use much better suited to Ezekiel's overall theology and
purpose.

Ezekiel as Shaping the Traditions

The above arguments assume that the deuteronomistic material precedes or is coterminous with those sections of Ezekiel and that no
influence from Ezekiel on these texts can be seen. Yet serious consideration of dating possibilities has not been factored in. To be sure, postmonarchic, pre-Persian texts are essentially contemporary, but this does
not mean only one line of influence can be drawn, especially in light of
redactional additions posited within texts such as Jeremiah, the Deuteronomistic History and Ezekiel. We know that the text of Jeremiah, for
instance, is multi-layered,[35] as is the deuteronomistic history, so that

32. For a general discussion of Ezekiel's use of the term, see Kapelrud, 'The
Prophets and the Covenant', pp. 175-83.
33. B. Batto, 'The Covenant of Peace: A Neglected Ancient Near Eastern
Motif', *CBQ* 49 (1987), pp. 187-211.
34. Emphasis mine.
35. See most recently H.-J. Stipp, 'Probleme des redaktionsgeschichtlichen

when one posits deuteronomistic influence on Ezekiel the question still remains: to which deuteronomist are we referring? The most obvious instances of 'deuteronomistic influence' can be found in both the concept of the new heart, found almost verbatim in both Jeremiah and Ezekiel, and the use of the *gillûlîm* for idols, seen almost exclusively in Ezekiel and Kings.

It has been shown that the term *gillûlîm* characterizes Ezekiel. Outside of the book it appears once in Jeremiah 50, part of the oracles against the nations, to refer to the idols of Babylon, once in the curses of the Holiness Code (Lev. 26.30), once in Deut. 29.6 and six times in Kings. It is completely absent in Chronicles. Such use might suggest that Ezekiel borrows this term from deuteronomistic literature. However, all of the uses of this term in Kings are in the last layer of the text, the summary statements of the kings' reigns. It appears nowhere else in the Deuteronomistic History nor outside of the summary statements where the more common term *šiqqûṣîm* appears. Similarly, the appearance in Deuteronomy is in the last layer of the text, the summary speech of Moses, which serves as the frame to the older law. All uses of the term outside of Ezekiel are in exilic texts concerned with religious activity associated with Babylon. This suggests one of two options for understanding the term. Either it is a technical term from that period to denote Babylonian cult statues, or it is a term coined by Ezekiel but taken up by a later deuteronomistic redactor as that which typifies Israel's apostasy. The term is more at home in Ezekiel where it is used more consistently there and more pervasively than in any other text. Its 'home' then fits the exilic prophet better than a Palestinian prophet or historian.

The remaining connection between Ezekiel and deuteronomistic literature is the question of the restoration depicted as a new heart given to the people, a motif present in Ezek. 11.19; 36.26; and Jer. 32.37-41. Although these passages are very similar to one another, each shows slight variations. In Ezekiel 11, the shorter version of the motif, Israel will get 'one heart' and 'a new spirit', following the MT literally, and its heart of stone will be turned into a heart of flesh. The direct result of this will be Israel's ability to follow God's statutes. Similarly, in 36.26 they will get a *new* heart and a new spirit. The result here will be loathing and shame for their past behavior. In ch. 11 the passage

Modells der Entstehung des Jeremiabuches', in Gross (ed.), *Jeremia und die 'deuteronomistische Bewegung'*, pp. 225-62.

immediately precedes the departure of God's presence from Israel, a departure forced by Israel's defilement of the temple, so graphically described in ch. 8. This connection is emphasized in 11.21, when it states that after they receive this heart of flesh they will no longer go after the 'detestable and abominable things' that is, things that defile. The passage closes with a depiction of the death of Pelatiah, which represents the death of the whole nation.[36] The heart of stone, then, is associated with death, the heart of flesh with life; that is, they are associated with the overriding effects of following the law that characterize Ezekiel.[37]

These themes are furthered in ch. 36. First, the passage immediately precedes the depiction of the dead bones, and their return to life. The heart of stone/heart of flesh, then, is an alternate image of death to life. Here the giving of the heart is the end process of a ritual cleansing of Israel, a ritual cleansing she must undergo in order to be eligible to return to the land. This ritual cleansing is performed not by Israel but by God, who will sprinkle her with water, remove impurity and then give the new heart. This association is reiterated in v. 29, where God speaks of saving Israel from its uncleanness, and in v. 31 where Israel will loathe her 'abominable deeds'.

The motif of the new heart answers a problem about the restoration that Ezekiel's ideology poses: if Israel has never in the past been able to follow the laws that would have protected it from God's holiness, then how will restoration help? Or from a different perspective, how does the rebuilding of the temple according to Ezekiel's law in chs. 40-48 guarantee the proper personnel, proper offerings and the avoidance of 'abominable acts'? Ezekiel still maintains that Israel, on its own, is unworthy and unable to avoid 'abominable acts'; the concept of the restoration in chs. 11 and 36 addresses this. Just as Israel was cleansed at her birth by God (ch. 16), so too she will be cleansed at her rebirth. But this cleansing will not be just a surface washing like the first one

---

36. Although Sedlmeier, ' "Deine Brüder, deine Brüder" ' does not see the death of Pelatiah as original to this passage, I would argue that even if it is secondary the language of the new heart still connects the heart of stone with death.

37. W. Zimmerli, ' "Leben" und "Tod" im Buche des Propheten Ezechiel', *TZ* 13 (1957), pp. 494-508. Hossfeld, 'Ezechiel und die deuteronomisch-deuterono-mistische Bewegung', connects the language in Ezekiel to Jeremiah's reference to other gods in 2.27 and 3.9. Even if this is true, it does not negate the further parallel with death and life.

that failed, but an internal change of heart such that now Israel cannot help but follow these laws. God has sacrificed her free will to guarantee her life.

The use of the image in Jeremiah is far more abbreviated than this and appears only in a chapter replete with parallels to Ezekiel. To be sure, the use of the motif in Jeremiah is adapted to this prophet's theology. Jeremiah speaks of Israel receiving 'one heart and one spirit'. In Ezekiel the statement that 'Israel will be God's people, and Yahweh will be their God' is the result of the heart transplant; in Jeremiah this statement is the prerequisite for the transplant. In Jeremiah the image is never associated with life and death, stone and flesh. Instead, the result of the new heart will be fear of the Lord, a theme that permeates Deuteronomy. The statement sits in the midst of chs. 31–33, which show obvious signs of later redaction.[38] These are also the chapters with the most parallels to Ezekiel. Verse 31.29 contains the *māšāl* about the sour grapes.[39] Verses 31.31-34 talk about a new covenant written on the heart that cannot be transgressed, a covenant that makes Israel Yahweh's bride, and will result in Israel 'knowing' Yahweh (a slight variation on Ezekiel's terms that, similar to Hosea, highlights the sexual

38. For a recent review of scholarship on chs. 30–31, see W. McKane, 'The Composition of Jeremiah 30–31', in M.V. Fox *et al.* (eds), *Texts, Temples, and Traditions: A Tribute to Menahem Haran* (Winona Lake, IN: Eisenbrauns, 1996), pp. 187-94 (187-89). See also, R.E. Clements, *Jeremiah* (Interpretation; Atlanta: John Knox Press, 1988), p. 176; R.P. Carroll, 'Intertextuality and the Book of Jeremiah: Animadversions on Text and Theory', in J.C. Exum and D.J.A. Clines (eds.), *The New Literary Criticism and the Hebrew Bible* (JSOTSup, 143; Sheffield: JSOT Press, 1993), pp. 55-78, and G. Fischer, 'Aufnahme, Wende, und Überwindung dtn/r Gedankengutes in Jer 30f', in Gross (ed.), *Jeremia und die 'deuteronomistische Bewegung'*, pp. 129-39. Note that even J. Bright has to admit that these chapters exhibit much late material (*Jeremiah* [AB, 21; Garden City, NY: Doubleday, 1965], pp. 288-98). It must be noted, however, that some scholars still maintain a Jeremianic origin for these chapters. See, for instance, J.G. McConville, *Judgment and Promise: An Interpretation of the Book of Jeremiah* (Winona Lake, IN: Eisenbrauns, 1993) esp. pp. 30-33, 92-103 and 173-76.

39. W. Thiel asserts that both Jeremiah and Ezekiel reflect a common source but are not necessarily dependent on each other (*Die deuteronomistische Redaktion von Jeremia 26–45* [WMANT, 52; Neukirchen–Vluyn: Neukirchener Verlag, 1981], pp. 22-23), while W.L. Holladay posits that Jeremiah's text, a secondary insertion, was composed after that of Ezekiel (*Jeremiah 2: A Commentary on the Book of the Prophet Jeremiah Chapters 26–52* [Hermeneia; Minneapolis: Fortress Press, 1989], p. 163).

aspect of knowledge).[40] As Krašovec points out,[41] this new covenant is depicted in Jeremiah as something wholly undeserved, granted even in the face of Israel's unfaithfulness, again a pattern that permeates Ezekiel's concept of Israel's initial and restored election.

After a biographical section about Jeremiah's sign act of buying a field, a large section with no parallels to Ezekiel, ch. 32 picks up again the question of intergenerational responsibility, at first asserting its legitimacy in v. 18 and then reaffirming its rejection in v. 9.[42] Verse 20 states that Yahweh made a name for 'himself' in Egypt and brought the people out of Egypt with an 'outstretched arm to a land of milk and honey', phrases seen not only in D, but also in Ezekiel 20 in vv. 33 and 34. Verses 26-35 list Israel's cultic violations: pouring libations on the roof, turning their backs to God, committing abominations in Yahweh's house (also seen in Ezekiel 8), and performing child sacrifice.[43] These actions, which defile Yahweh's presence in the temple, have gone on 'from her youth', a notion seen in Ezekiel 16 and 23. While Ezekiel claims that God gave them the law of child sacrifice to cause them to sin, Jeremiah's text explicitly refutes Ezekiel's depiction of the ritual, 'I did not commend them [to perform it], nor did it enter my mind that they should do this abomination, causing Judah to sin' (32.35). This text clearly knows of *someone* who contends child sacrifice was performed in the name of Yahweh, who wanted to cause them to sin, assertions clearly made in Ezek. 20.21-26. This chapter ends with a vision of return characterized by the one heart.

40. For secondary literature on this passage, see the bibliography provided by J. Krašovec, 'Vergebung und neuer Bund nach Jer 31, 31-34', *ZAW* 105 (1993), pp. 428-44 (428-29 n. 1), who also points out the parallels of this passage with Ezek. 34. Most scholars see this restoration as reflecting typical deuteronomistic language. See, for instance, Thiel, *Die deuteronomistische Redaktion*, pp. 23-28, and Clements, *Jeremiah*, pp. 189-92. However, only Ezekiel associates the new covenant with the restoration of the heart that results in Israel 'knowing' Yahweh.

41. Krašovec, 'Vergebung und neuer Bund', pp. 428-44.

42. Holladay (*Jeremiah 2*, pp. 208-209) also sees these verses as secondary. For more recent discussions of the compositional history of Jeremiah 32, see J.M. Oesch, 'Zur Makrostruktur und Textintentionalität von Jer 32', in Gross (ed.), *Jeremia und die 'deuteronomistische Bewegung'*, pp. 215-23, and H. Migsch, *Jeremias Ackerkauf: Eine Untersuchung von Jeremia 32* (ÖBS, 15; Frankfurt: Peter Lang, 1996).

43. See, e.g., Ezek. 16.20, 20.26 and 23.37. For a review of scholarship on these verses that regards them as late, see Holladay, *Jeremiah 2*, pp. 207-208.

Jeremiah 33 echoes further images of restoration found also in Ezekiel, including God's cleansing of Jerusalem (v. 8; Ezek. 36.25),[44] the restoration of the Davidic covenant with an eternal covenant (vv. 5-22; Ezek. 37.24-25) and renaming the city of Jerusalem (v. 16; Ezek. 48.35).[45] Finally, one last instance of a refutation of a concept found in Ezekiel occurs in Jeremiah 33. Along with the eternal covenant with David, God offers an eternal covenant with the Levites, so that they will be allowed always to offer sacrifices in God's temple. Verse 24 hints at the presence of 'those people' (*hā'ām hazzeh*) who reject the legitimacy of the Levites continuing as God's 'chosen' family, a position that the text strongly rejects by stressing the permanence of this covenant. Again, we find Jeremiah's foil in Ezekiel (44.10), an explicit rejection of the Levites as no longer worthy of serving as sacrificial priests in the temple because of their sins before the Fall.

The closest parallels between Ezekiel and Jeremiah, then, cluster in these three chapters, three chapters that end with an account of how this particular scroll, dictated to Baruch, came to be lost, a sign that it is a 'lost', that is, late teaching of Jeremiah. These chapters show knowledge and explicit refutation of ideology found in Ezekiel. I would argue, then, that although it is possible that Ezekiel knew a version of Jeremiah and borrowed language from it, the closest parallels to both Jeremiah and deuteronomistic literature show more evidence that these texts used Ezekiel than the other way around.[46]

44. Holladay calls this verse a secondary gloss unlike anything found in Jeremiah (*Jeremiah 2*, pp. 222-23).

45. On the secondary character of Jer. 33.14-16, see Holladay, *Jeremiah 2*, pp. 228-31. Several of these elements are also present in Jer. 23.1-8, a chapter with many parallels to Ezek. 34. Again, the motif in Jeremiah is far more abbreviated than in Ezekiel, and the connections or implications of this motif in the two prophetic texts serve different ends. For instance, Jeremiah stresses the judicial function of the king and connects the motif with the exodus. Ezekiel stresses God's judgment on the sheep, and the establishment of a covenant of peace, which focuses on God's protection against forces of chaos. It is possible, then, that Ezek. 34 knew the motif in Jer. 23 and manipulated it to suit the book's purpose. However, the redactor of Jer. 33 revised the material in Jer. 23 to address issues raised in other sections of Ezekiel.

46. For other passages in Jeremiah that may reflect influence from Ezekiel, see C.R. Seitz, *Theology in Conflict: Reactions to the Exile in the Book of Jeremiah* (BZAW, 176; Berlin: W. de Gruyter, 1989), pp. 223-28. For a recent argument explicitly denying any influence of Ezekiel on Jeremiah passages outside of these,

Conclusion

The book of Ezekiel utilizes motifs and traditions known from deuteronomistic tradition, both from the Deuteronomistic History and from the 'Ephraimite' prophets. Every use of these motifs serves the text's larger theological purpose of explaining the fall of Jerusalem without sacrificing an ounce of God's power or reputation. This is done by stressing Israel's unworthiness of God's presence or covenant both at her founding and in her return. God alone can make Israel worthy, cleanse her to meet God's glory, and keep her from further acts of abomination. God alone can give her a live heart that will loathe her idols, cure her rebellion and bring a covenant of peace that will finally alter her history. These images were so powerful that many were taken up by later redactors, who were also struggling with the theological implications of Israel's fall and restoration.

see Vieweger, *Die literarischen Beziehungen*, esp. pp. 76-84, 133-34 and 166-70.

MICAH'S DEUTERONOMISTIC REDACTION AND THE DEUTERONOMISTS' IDENTITY

Stephen L. Cook

The latest layers of Micah consist of a direct Deuteronomistic redaction of the book; indeed, they constitute an untapped but rich source of evidence about Deuteronomistic thought and literary activity, its nature and its provenance. The potential richness of this Mican evidence becomes excitingly clear when it is realized that these late layers of the book are not only products of Deuteronomistic redactors but also constituent parts of the tradition of Micah and his school. These links between late editorial activity and a pre-exilic prophetic circle point toward some definite hypotheses about the identity and social location of the Deuteronomists.

Deuteronomistic Redaction in Micah

That the biblical prophetic works underwent Deuteronomistic redaction is suggested by the presence of Deuteronomistic superscriptions, redactional material and shaping in these works. The nature of this redaction, which incorporated several of the Latter Prophets into an emerging Deuteronomistically shaped canon, has been investigated by several scholars, including D.N. Freedman and J. Blenkinsopp.[1] The latter

---

1. D.N. Freedman, 'The Law and the Prophets', in J.A. Emerton *et al.* (eds.), *Congress Volume: Bonn 1962* (VTSup, 9; Leiden: E.J. Brill, 1963), pp. 250-65; *idem*, 'The Formation of the Canon of the Old Testament', in E.B. Firmage *et al.* (eds.), *Religion and Law: Biblical, Judaic and Islamic Perspectives* (Winona Lake, IN: Eisenbrauns, 1990), pp. 315-31; J. Blenkinsopp, *Prophecy and Canon* (Notre Dame: University of Notre Dame Press, 1977). Cf. G.M. Tucker, 'Prophetic Superscriptions and the Growth of the Canon', in G.W. Coats and B.O. Long (eds.), *Canon and Authority: Essays in Old Testament Religion and Theology* (Philadelphia: Fortress Press, 1977), pp. 56-70.

scholar has argued that the Deuteronomistic collection included Micah
early on, along with First Isaiah, Jeremiah, Hosea, Amos and Zephaniah. Blenkinsopp's thesis has been accepted by many scholars, and
N. Gottwald has popularized a variation of it in his introductory text,
The Hebrew Bible.[2]

Despite these gains, much analysis remains to be done on the
specifics of the Deuteronomistic redactions of individual prophetic
works. H.W. Wolff has made one major case for a Deuteronomistic
redaction in Micah.[3] But Wolff himself describes some of his own work
on this aspect of Micah as tentative, and I believe he has overlooked
some significant evidence. As my own probe into the Deuteronomistic
redaction of Micah, I would like to examine two pericopes: Mic. 5.9-14
(Eng. 5.10-15) and Mic. 7.14-17, 18-20. These pericopes in Micah
arguably represent Deuteronomistic redaction that functioned to level
the incorporation of the book into the biblical canon.

Micah 5.9-14 (Eng. 5.10-15)
Redaction of Micah has rounded off the book's central section, Micah
3–5, with an insertion describing the eschatological purging of Israel.
The insertion is form-critically marked as an expanding addition by its
introductory clause, והיה ביום־ההוא ('And it will happen on that day').
This is a formula for introducing supplemental eschatological material
(cf. Ezek. 38.18; Zech. 14.6; Joel 4.18 [Eng. 3.18]). Beyond its form,
the passage is marked as late and redactional by its material content and
its closing perspective, which focuses on a stage of history after the
covenant curses of Deuteronomy have been endured.

More so than other parts of Micah, the pericope is aimed against
reliance on human means of national strength and against aberrant religious practices. These are the kinds of concerns reflected in the book of
Deuteronomy and in descriptions of Deuteronomic reforms, such as that
of Josiah.[4] By describing the eschatological stripping of Israel of military armament and false worship, the redactors stress the ideals embodied in the Josianic reform. Redaction here projects such ideals into the

2. N. Gottwald, *The Hebrew Bible: A Socio-Literary Introduction* (Philadelphia: Fortress Press, 1985), pp. 464-65.
3. H.W. Wolff, *Micah: A Commentary* (trans. Gary Stansell; Minneapolis:
Augsburg, 1990), pp. 18-19, 23, 26, 34, 42, 91-92, 96, 170.
4. Thus, Wolff is on target when he tentatively identifies those who invento-
ried the concerns listed here as 'Deuteronomistic' teachers (*Micah*, p. 154).

future in the face of post-reform regression and exilic punishment.[5]

The supplement's Deuteronomistic aversion to royal systems and standing armies appears in vv. 9-10 (Eng. vv. 10-11). As in Deut. 17.16, multiplication of and reliance on horses for military strength is condemned (cf. Hos. 14.4 [Eng. 14.3]). The ערי ארצך ('cities of your land') that the first colon of v. 10 (Eng. v. 11) says will be destroyed probably refer to state military fortifications and storage sites. These are a false source of security according to texts such as Jer. 5.17. This interpretation is supported in that the full bicolon achieves poetic effect here by splitting the phrase עיר (ו\ערי) (ה)מבצר ('fortified city[ies]'), which occurs in Jer. 4.5; 5.17; 8.14; and 34.7.

The remaining verses of the supplement describe Israel's purification from specific religious practices considered illegitimate by the Deuter-onomists. Verse 11 (Eng. v. 12) describes God's removal of 'sorceries' and 'soothsayers'. These same two Hebrew roots, כשף ('practice sor-cery') and ענן (pol.: 'practice soothsaying'), are used in Deut. 18.10 as part of the Deuteronomic polemic against what it views as abhorrent Canaanite religious practices (see also Jer. 27.9). According to Deut. 18.14, such practices lead to land dispossession. Micah 5.12-13 (Eng. vv. 13-14) goes on to describe God's cutting off of religious objects condemned by Deuteronomy: פסיל ('carved image', see Deut. 7.5, 25; cf. Hos. 11.2), מצבה ('sacred pillar', see Deut. 16.22; cf. Hos. 3.4; 10.1, 2), מעשה ('work [of hands]', see Deut. 4.28; cf. Hos. 14.4 [Eng. 14.3]; Jer. 1.16 [D]), and אשירה ('Ashera/sacred pole', see Deut. 7.5; 12.3; 16.21; cf. Jer. 17.2 [D]). The removal in particular of sacred pillars and Asherim brings to mind the Deuteronomic reforms of Hezekiah and Josiah, whom 2 Kgs 18.4 and 23.14 describe as taking exactly the same action.[6]

There are several indications that the final verses of the supplement in Mic. 5.9-14 (Eng. 5.10-15) go beyond the theme of purification to describe an eschatological reversal of the Deuteronomic covenant curse that involved Israel's dispossession of its inherited land. Thus, whereas in Deut. 29.26-27 (Eng. 29.27-28) and 1 Kgs 14.15 Yahweh 'uproots' Israel from their land because they abandon the covenant, worshiping

5.   Backsliding away from Josianic reforms is depicted in such texts as Jer. 44; 2 Kgs 23.32, 37; 24.9, 19; and 2 Chron. 36.14.

6.   See L.C. Allen, *The Books of Joel, Obadiah, Jonah, and Micah* (NICOT; Grand Rapids: Eerdmans, 1976), p. 358; J.L. Mays, *Micah: A Commentary* (OTL; Philadelphia: Westminster Press, 1976), p. 126.

Asherim and other gods, Mic. 5.13 (Eng. 5.14) reverses this state of affairs. Israel is back in its land and God instead 'uproots' the Asherim from among Israel. All three of these passages speak of 'uprooting' using the Hebrew root נתשׁ ('pull/pluck up'), a usage found especially in Jeremiah. Further, whereas in Deut. 29.27 (Eng. 29.28) Yahweh acts against Israel באף ובחמה ('in anger and fury'), in Mic. 5.14 (Eng. 5.15) God's anger, described using the same Hebrew phrase, is redirected against the foreign nations. (Note that this phrase is a Deuteronomic idiom, occurring in Deut. 29.22, 27 [Eng. 29.23, 28] and Jer. 21.5; 33.5 [cf. Deut. 9.19; Jer. 32.31, 37 (D); 42.18; 44.6]. Its appearance in Ezek. 5.15; 22.20; and Isa. 63.3 is probably due to Deuteronomic influence on these texts.)[7]

In my judgment, this closing perspective of Mic. 5.9-14 (Eng. 5.10-15) strongly buttresses the view that this Mican supplement is a Deuteronomistic redaction.[8] It must have originated from among the circles that also produced the Deuteronomistic prose oracle against Judah's neighbors found in Jer. 12.14-17.[9] As in Micah 5, this Jeremianic supplement also reverses Israel's fall by playing on the Hebrew root נתשׁ ('pull/pluck up'). After exilic punishment, Israel will be 'uprooted' from among the foreign nations and returned to its נחלה ('inheritance'). Further, in both Jer. 12.17 and Mic. 5.14 (Eng. 5.15) final punishment is executed on any nation not choosing to be 'obedient to Yahweh' (שׁמע).[10]

Micah 7.14-20
Next to be examined is Mic. 7.14-17, 18-20, an epilogue to Micah that prays for God's restoration of Israel from exilic punishment. My argument that the two strophes of this Mican epilogue are Deuteronomistic

7. Cf. Wolff, *Micah*, p. 160.

8. Note Wolff's comparable linking of the supplement's final verse to 'those conceptions of the Deuteronomistic school that reflect upon Israel's relation to the nations' (*Micah*, p. 160).

9. For the view that Jer. 12.14-17 is the work of the Deuteronomistic redactors who edited Jeremiah in exile, see W. Thiel, *Die deuteronomistische Redaktion von Jeremia 1–25* (WMANT, 41; Neukirchen–Vluyn: Neukirchener Verlag, 1973), pp. 162-68; E.W. Nicholson, *The Book of the Prophet Jeremiah, Chapters 1–25* (CBC; Cambridge: Cambridge University Press, 1973), pp. 26, 119.

10. For the idiomatic use of the verb here and its Jeremian-Deuteronomistic provenance, see 'שׁמע', *BDB*, p. 1034; Thiel, *Die deuteronomistische Redaktion*, pp. 290-95; Wolff, *Micah*, p. 161.

is not a common one. One minority scholarly position, however, does strongly suggest that these strophes represent Deuteronomism. This is the thesis of several scholars that the final pericopes of Micah exhibit strong similarities to Hosea and related proto-Deuteronomic writings of north Israel.

In 1926 the Cambridge scholar F.C. Burkitt presented the view that Micah 6 and 7 are 'northern prophecy'. Again in 1962 O. Eissfeldt interpreted Mic. 7.7-20 as a psalm stemming from the north. Eissfeldt's thesis was buttressed and further specified by J. Dus in 1965. Then, two years later in 1967, B. Reicke similarly identified all of Micah 7 as a north-Israelite liturgy. Finally in 1971 A.S. van der Woude, at first working without knowledge of these previous studies, reargued the position that Micah 6–7, which he distinguished as a 'Deutero-Micah', most probably forms a north-Israelite writing.[11]

In my view, scholars are mistaken in assigning a northern provenance to these texts near the end of Micah. They have rightly discerned the presence of Deuteronomism in this part of the book, but, based on presuppositions about Deuteronomism's northern roots, have been too quick to trace these sections to north Israel.[12] If one brackets the geo-

---

11. F.C. Burkitt, 'Micah 6 and 7: A Northern Prophecy', *JBL* 45 (1926), pp. 159-61; O. Eissfeldt, 'Ein Psalm aus Nord-Israel: Micha 7, 7-20', *ZDMG* 112 (1962), pp. 259-68; J. Dus, 'Weiteres zum nordisraelitischen Psalm Micha 7, 7-20', *ZDMG* 115 (1965), pp. 14-22; B. Reicke, 'Liturgical Traditions in Micah 7', *HTR* 60 (1967), pp. 349-67; A.S. van der Woude, 'Deutero-Micha: Ein Prophet aus Nord-Israel?', *NedTTs* 25 (1971), pp. 365-78. Also see A. van Hoonacker, *Les douze petits prophètes* (Ebib; Paris: J. Gabalda, 1908); O. Eissfeldt, *Der Gott Karmel* (SPAW; Berlin: Akademie Verlag, 1953), pp. 7-8; H.A. Ginsberg, 'Dqdwqym bšnym 'šr', *ErIsr* 3 (1954), pp. 83-84; J.T. Willis, 'A Reapplied Prophetic Hope Oracle', in G.W. Anderson *et al.* (eds.), *Studies on Prophecy: A Collection of Twelve Papers* (VTSup, 26; Leiden: E.J. Brill, 1974), pp. 64-76.

12. In addition to making arguments about proto-Deuteronomic motifs and diction, scholars sometimes cite references to northern geographical locales to demonstrate a northern provenance for these Mican texts (see Mic. 6.5; 7.14). The authentic interest of the southern prophet Micah in Samaria in Mic. 1.6-7 immediately belies the cogency of this approach. If, as is probable, Micah and his book's redactors held the Deuteronomistic view that despite their geography Yahweh's people are one community, they may certainly have had occasion to make reference to the geography, history, fate and possible future reoccupation of the north. D. Hillers is correct: 'Because we can locate the places [in some Mican texts], we must not imagine we have located the author!' (*Micah* [Hermeneia; Philadelphia: Fortress Press, 1984], p. 90).

graphical aspect of their interpretation, however, its general tenor has
much to commend it. The Mican epilogue does not stem from north
Israel, as Eissfeldt and van der Woude hold, but is nevertheless a genuinely Deuteronomistic addition to Micah, as I hope the following discussion of its details reveals.[13]

Verse 14 provides the first signal that vv. 14-17, the first half of the
Mican epilogue, is a Deuteronomistic composition. This verse longs for
the return of an idealized Israel, שֹׁכְנִי ('tenting') by itself, בָּדָד
('secluded') from other peoples. Wolff and others are incorrect to see
here a description of postexilic Jerusalem 'hemmed in and cut off' from
outlying fertile territory.[14] Verse 14, rather, uses clear Deuteronomistic
language of ideal Israel as a pastoral society, set apart by God's special
election. The combination of vocabulary that is used here is rare, so it is
highly significant that Deut. 33.28 has the identical diction. The verse
recalls a blessed Israel, which 'tented' in security, 'secluded' in a land
of grain and new wine. This language has proto-Deuteronomistic roots
in the E strand of the Pentateuch. In Num. 23.9, Balaam also describes
Israel as a people 'that tents secluded', that cannot be reckoned among
the nations. As many scholars accept, E stands prominently among the
Bible's proto-Deuteronomic traditions.[15]

The diction about tenting apart is not used elsewhere in the Hebrew
Bible. There is only a reminiscence of it in Jer. 49.31 amidst a prophecy

13. The defenders of the northern Micah thesis are wrong not only about the
geographical provenance of the ending of Micah but also about its dating. The epilogue is not the product of a north Israelite contemporary of Micah, the eighth-century prophet, but must be a later, post-586 appropriation of the Mican collection. As
shown below, Micah's redactional ending presupposes a late reading of the earlier
collection of Mic. 1.1–7.7, a reading that views the Mican threats, such as that of
Mic. 3.12, as fulfilled. Cf. Wolff's arguments that 7.14-20 was added to Micah as a
final step in the redaction of the book (*Micah*, p. 27).

14. Wolff, *Micah*, p. 226.

15. On the traditions of E as proto-Deuteronomic, see A.W. Jenks, 'Elohist',
ABD, II, p. 480, and *idem, The Elohist and North Israelite Traditions* (SBLMS, 22;
Missoula, MT: Scholars Press, 1977); S.D. McBride, Jr, 'Deuteronomium', *TRE*,
VIII, p. 538; T. Fretheim, 'Elohist', *IDBSup*, p. 261; E.W. Nicholson, *Deuteronomy
and Tradition* (Oxford: Basil Blackwell, 1967), pp. 60, 70. Landmark arguments for
this view were presented in 1965 by C. Brekelmans, 'Die sogenannten deuterono-
mistischen Elemente in Genesis bis Numeri: Ein Beitrag zur Vorgeschichte des
Deuteronomiums', in G.W. Anderson *et al.* (eds.), *Congress Volume: Geneva 1965*
(VTSup, 15; Leiden: E.J. Brill, 1966), pp. 90-96.

against Arabia. Jeremiah 49 sees Babylon's defeat of Arabian pastoral tribes as a presage of Israel's judgment.

A part of another of the Jeremianic prophecies against the nations, the prophecy against Babylon, is strongly akin to the hopeful picture of Mic. 7.14. Jeremiah 50.18-19 speaks of Israel as a flock pasturing in Bashan and Gilead, just as the Mican epilogue does. 'I am going to punish the king of Babylon and his land, as I punished the king of Assyria. I will restore Israel to its pasture, and it shall feed on Carmel and in Bashan, and in the hill country of Ephraim and in Gilead.' This Jeremianic oracle must be a post-586 BCE Deuteronomistic literary product. The text describes Nebuchadnezzar's destruction of Judah in v. 17, assuring a postexilic date, and Gilead and Bashan are grouped together elsewhere in the Hebrew Bible only in passages that belong to the Deuteronomistic History (Deut. 3.10, 12-16; 4.43; Josh. 20.8; 2 Kgs 10.33).

Micah 7.14 sharpens its vision of an ideal, future Israel using additional Deuteronomistic language about the ימי עולם ('olden days'). The olden days in question refer to the Mosaic period, when God first covenanted with tribal Israel. The Mican epilogue strongly echoes the Song of Moses in Deuteronomy here. Specifically, Deut. 32.7 recalls the same olden days spoken of in Mic. 7.14. Note how Deut. 32.9 speaks of God's people as his נחלה ('inheritance'), just as Mic. 7.14 does, and how the reference in Deut. 32.12 to Yahweh בדד ('alone') guiding Israel reverberates with Israel as a people who are set apart, 'alone', in the Mican verse.

Verse 15 of the Mican epilogue begins to describe Israel's restoration, which the epilogue is entreating, using images from the story of the exodus.[16] The language of this verse is straight from Deuteronomy. In the Hebrew Bible, only Deut. 16.3 has the exact same string of vocabulary. Deuteronomy enjoins Israel continually to focus on 'the day when you came out from the land of Egypt', the same focus held in Mic. 7.15. Three verses later, Deut. 16.6 again describes the exodus to Israel as 'your coming out from Egypt'. The 'marvelous acts' of redemption that God will show the people according to Mic. 7.15 are to be akin to those God wrought at the exodus. Asaphite Ps. 78.11 recalls these same acts using the same verbal forms as the epilogue does. This

---

16. On the emphasis that (proto-)Deuteronomistic traditions place on the exodus, wilderness and settlement themes, see van der Woude, 'Deutero-Micha', p. 369.

is significant, since the language and ideas of the Psalms of Asaph (Pss. 50, 73–83) bear a strong affinity to Deuteronomism.[17]

The prayer of supplication of Mic. 7.14-17 ends with Deuteronomistic language about the nations yielding to Israel when God restores the people to the land. The epilogue's language here of the nations losing heart and trembling out of their fortresses resonates strongly with David's song of praise in 2 Sam. 22.46. Then the supplication concludes with the string 'and they will be afraid of you', which appears elsewhere in the Hebrew Bible only in Deut. 28.10. This is the Deuteronomic verse that gives the covenant blessing that 'All the peoples of the earth shall see that you are called by the name of the Lord, and they shall be afraid of you'. As Wolff notes, the more general idiom here, which employs the verb ירא ('be afraid') with מן ('of'), is also Deuteronomistic.[18] Compare its occurrence in Deut. 1.29; 2.4; 7.18; 20.1; and Josh. 10.8.

Verses 18-20, which conclude the Mican epilogue, form a two-part psalm in praise of God. This praise inspires confidence that God will indeed restore the people. Here again, the epilogue reveals itself as a clearly Deuteronomistic redaction. Verse 18 praises God by applying to the present ancient covenant language about God's forbearance and faithful loyalty (Exod. 34.6-7; Num. 14.18). The verse terms present Israel the שארית נחלתו ('remnant of his inheritance'). This term for God's people occurs elsewhere in the Hebrew Bible only in the Deuteronomistic condemnation of Judah to exile in 2 Kings 21.[19] Micah 7.18 thus effectively reverses 2 Kgs 21.14, 'I will cast off the remnant of my inheritance, and give them into the hand of their enemies'.

Verse 19 continues the epilogue's expression of confidence that God will forgive the people. The language of this verse includes an idiom of 'casting away' of 'sin' into the watery depths. Clearly Deuteronomistic, this language occurs elsewhere only in Deut. 9.21. There the pulverized metallic calf, termed the people's חטאת ('sin'), is cast into the waters of the stream at the divine mountain.

Verse 20 brings the Mican epilogue to a close with two final Deuteronomistic expressions. The verse employs an idiom of 'giving

17. H. Nasuti has argued persuasively that the Asaphite psalms belong within the same stream of traditions as Deuteronomism (*Tradition History and the Psalms of Asaph* [SBLDS, 88; Atlanta: Scholars Press, 1988]).

18. See Wolff, *Micah*, p. 228.

19. See Wolff, *Micah*, p. 229.

truth' that occurs elsewhere in the Bible only in Josh. 2.12 (and in the
Septuagint of Jer. 14.13). Then the verse's concluding bicolon rounds
off the epilogue's expression of confidence by invoking God's oath to
the ancestors. Deuteronomy 26.15 is the only other place in the Hebrew
Bible that employs the identical string 'which you swore to our
ancestors'. The general idiom of the oath is much more common, of
course, and, as Wolff notes, it is typically Deuteronomistic.[20] (See Deut.
6.10, 23; 7.8, 12, 13; 8.18; 10.11; Josh. 1.6; 21.44; Judg. 2.1.)

The Coherence of Micah's Deuteronomistic Redaction and Mican Prophecy

Some prophetic books exhibit a Deuteronomistic redaction interjected
as foreign and discontinuous within its surroundings. Another type of
redactional activity, however, seems more promising for investigating
the Deuteronomists' identity. Some Deuteronomistic redaction in
prophetic texts is continuous with, and an outgrowth of, the composition and tradition history of the prophetic work in which it occurs.[21] It is
this second type of Deuteronomistic redaction that demonstrably occurs
in the book of Micah. The late layers of Micah that are being treated
here emerge under study as constituent parts of the tradition of Micah
and his school.[22] This can be shown best through another look at the
Mican epilogue.

Already at the beginning of the Mican epilogue, the ideal hope for
Israel that is presented closely resonates with the ideals expressed by

20. Wolff, *Micah*, p. 231.

21. The book of Jeremiah illustrates well the possibility of Deuteronomistic
redaction being in continuity with the compositional history of a prophetic text. On
the continuity of the Jeremiah tradition, see E.W. Nicholson, *Preaching to the
Exiles* (New York: Schocken Books, 1970), pp. 56, 134-38; T.W. Overholt,
'Remarks on the Continuity of the Jeremiah Tradition', *JBL* 91 (1972), pp. 457-62;
R.R. Wilson, *Prophecy and Society in Ancient Israel* (Philadelphia: Fortress Press,
1980), pp. 232-51.

22. An implication of establishing this thesis will be the identification of the
authentic Mican prophecies as proto-Deuteronomistic traditions. This would be a
significant advance in understanding Deuteronomism for, as K. Zobel has pointed
out, previous scholarly investigation of the prophetic precursors of Deuteronomism
has concentrated quite one-sidedly on the affinities between Hosea and Deuteronomy (*Prophetie und Deuteronomium: Die Rezeption prophetischer Theologie durch
das Deuteronomium* [BZAW, 199; Berlin: W. de Gruyter, 1992], p. 6).

eighth-century Mican prophecy. The eighth-century Mican oracles make a strong connection between God's election, or inheritance, of the Israelite people and their inheritance, in turn, of God's land. The Mican ideal is very close to the picture of Deut. 4.20-21 and 32.8-9, where the Israelites are elected as God's נחלה ('inheritance'), and where God in turn grants this people a territory as their נחלה.

Micah's concern focuses on Israel's use of God's land, specifically on the people's preservation of covenant-structures vested in the land's allotment. Micah upholds the right of permanent tenure of Israel's inherited land within the lineage categories of tribe, clan and family. Much of the burden of the book is to hold the ruling stratum of Jerusalem responsible for ignoring rights to permanent land tenure and for subjugating Judean country farmers and driving them off this inherited land (Mic. 2.2, 9; 3.3, 9-10). According to Mic. 2.1-5 the Jerusalem leaders will lose their estates, which they wrongfully amassed from others' family and clan inheritances. God will dispossess the lords; and their land will revert to presettlement conditions, the way made clear for its subsequent reapportionment among the country folk of Judah. Verse 5 of Micah 2 describes the procedure for this land reallotment.[23] The prospect of land reversion and reapportionment is then repeated in Mic. 3.12. This well-known verse threatens that Zion will be reduced to במות יער ('wooded heights'). This is precisely the condition the land exhibited before Israel's settlement. Joshua 17.18 thus tells the house of Joseph that they must clear the highlands of Canaan for settlement: 'the hill country shall be yours, for though it is a forest [יער], you shall clear it and possess it'.

The Mican epilogue is in continuity with these much earlier passages in Mic. 2.4-5 and Mic. 3.12. The epilogue's beginning, Mic. 7.14, pictures the land in the ideal state that is hoped for in the earlier sections of Micah. God's inherited, covenant people (נחלתך) are alone to be given God's land, a land described as a יער (a 'forest' or 'woodland'), as כרמל ('Carmel'), the mountain forest on the Mediterranean.[24] It is not

23. See A. Alt, 'Micha 2,1-5: ΓΗΣ ΑΝΑΔΑΣΜΟΣ in Juda', in M. Noth (ed.), *Kleine Schriften zur Geschichte des Volkes Israel* (3 vols.; Munich: Beck, 1959), III, pp. 377-81. Compare how Mays aptly relates the redistribution heralded by Mic. 2.5 to the pattern set in the settlement account of the Deuteronomistic History (*Micah*, p. 66).

24. On the possible connotations of 'Carmel' in Mic. 7.14, see Wolff, *Micah*, p. 226. Van der Woude correctly argues that Mic. 7.14 pictures God's land as a

merely a case of the epilogue artistically mirroring here the vocabulary of older passages in Micah, however. The epilogue and the two Mican passages share a deeper relationship. Their similarities and differences signal their common membership in a family of texts from the Deuteronomistic stream of tradition. This family of texts, when read together, presumes a definite picture of God's land. They picture God's land as inherited, as holy, as wooded and as hilly. Besides the Mican texts, the family members at issue include Exod. 15.17; Josh. 17.18; Asaphite Ps. 78.54; Jer. 17.3-4; and 50.19. These texts do not each share all of the ingredients of the picture of the land that I have listed but gravitate together in their shared overlappings.

Where v. 14 of the Mican epilogue displays a more straightforward redactional artistry is not in its picture of God's ideal land but in its mirroring of Mic. 3.12's threat. Micah 7.14 assumes as fulfilled the quintessential Mican threat that Jerusalem will be reduced to a יער ('forest'). As Wolff suggests, the term is 'intentionally chosen' by the redaction 'to make a connection with Micah's best-known prophecy'.[25] Micah 7.14 presupposes that postexilic Judah has, in effect, reverted to presettlement conditions. Given this clean slate, the Mican epilogue hopes for an ideal repetition of Israel's original settlement in the land.

Several further links in the Mican epilogue reflect its coherence with and intention to reflect upon Micah's earlier prophecies. The epilogue again connects itself to Mican prophecy in v. 16. The link here is to Mic. 3.7-8, the conclusion of Micah's judgment oracle against the false prophets. As part of the threat of the original oracle, Micah had declared that at the time of their judgment the seers ובשו ('will be ashamed') and that they would perform a gesture of covering their mouths. Then, in v. 8, Micah defiantly added that the real גבורה ('might') in his contemporary confrontation belonged not to his prophetic opponents but to himself as an authentic lineage-head of the people.

Redaction in v. 16 of the epilogue links up with all three of these features of Mic. 3.7-8. In the restoration prayed for by the epilogue the earlier punishment inflicted upon an inner-Judean group will now fall on the nations. God's original displacement at the exodus of the nations

forest in the midst of north-Israelite Carmel, but he is on tenuous ground in adopting Eissfeldt's view that the one dwelling on Carmel in the verse is YHWH rather than Israel ('Deutero-Micha', pp. 372-73).

25. Wolff, *Micah*, p. 226.

and his guidance of Israel into the land (Exod. 15.15-18) will be repeated now so that Israel may be restored. Just as with the earlier false prophets of Micah 3, the epilogue prays that the nations will now become ashamed. They will even repeat the gesture of covering their mouths that appeared in Mic. 3.7. Finally, the nations will also disavow their גבורה ('might'), just as the false prophets had, recognizing true might instead in God's chosen tribes.

The next clear evidence in support of my thesis of the coherence in Micah of Deuteronomistic redaction and original prophecy occurs in v. 18 of the epilogue. The first colon of the verse shouts out its link to Micah, exclaiming מי־אל כמוך ('Who is a God like you?'). This is a deliberate echo of מיכה, Micah's name. Then, the admission of פשע ('transgression') in the verse also picks up a catchword from Micah (Mic. 3.8; also Mic. 1.5, 13b; 6.7). Further, as Wolff and Hillers note, the term שארית ('remnant') in the verse forms an additional strong link to Micah's salvation promises (Mic. 2.12; 4.7; 5.6-8).[26]

A final feature of v. 18 also links it to Micah, but in an indirect way as in v. 14. Although Mican prophecy stresses חסד ('loyalty') in Mic. 6.8, it does not contain the epilogue's specific idiom that 'God delights in loyalty'. The epilogue here reverberates not in the first instance with Micah but more with Hos. 6.6 and Jer. 9.24, the only other two places in the Hebrew Bible that contain this specific idiom (חפץ + חסד). Hosea 6.6, however, connects in turn more closely to Mic. 6.8 rather than to the epilogue in other of its features.[27] Here again, strikingly, the epilogue finds its place among a small family of differing but overlapping Deuteronomistic texts that includes a Mican text. Thus, again, it betrays a coherence with Mican prophecy that runs deeper than a mere use of Mican catchwords.

As noted above, v. 20 invokes a typical Deuteronomistic expression, the oath to the ancestors. This Deuteronomistic reference also forms a final effusion of Mican tradition in the epilogue. As in v. 14, the epilogue here looks forward to the people's return to God's own land. The

26. Wolff, *Micah*, p. 229; Hillers, *Micah*, p. 91.

27. Hos. 6.6 and Mic. 6.8 both employ the term חסד ('loyalty') within a context of critiquing the sacrificial cult. Further, both texts are generically linked as summaries of the stipulations and values of the Deuteronomistic covenant. On the latter point, cf. Mic. 6.8 with Deut. 4.13; and see W. Beyerlin, *Die Kulttraditionen Israels in der Verkündigung des Propheten Micha* (FRLANT, 54; Göttingen: Vandenhoeck & Ruprecht, 1959), pp. 42-43, 50-51.

oath to the ancestors, as Wolff reminds us, had everything to do with God's gift of the land to the people.[28] (See, e.g., Exod. 13.5; Deut. 6.10, 23; 7.13; 10.11.) Both Mican prophecy and the Mican epilogue expect that the reallotment of this land will re-establish the ancient covenant and the old land-vested social networks that undergirded it. The Mican epilogue thus ends as it began, in continuity with the original Mican focus on the centrality of the land in God's covenant with Israel.

I want next to explore the implications for the Deuteronomists' identity of the fact that Micah's Deuteronomistic redaction coheres with the earlier Mican prophecy. It should be noted here, however, that demonstrating this coherence has also buttressed the case for Micah's final redaction as an authentically Deuteronomistic one. The epilogue has family relationships with earlier texts from within proto-Deuteronomistic tradition. These relationships mean that more is going on in the epilogue than merely the intertextual influence of Deuteronomism discretely conceived—the mere cross-fertilization and generalized spread of Deuteronomistic language in postexilic times. Family ties between texts and their traditions signal organic, diachronic relationships. The organic relationships of our text mean that the Mican epilogue represents the same sort of flowering of proto-Deuteronomistic tradition that we have in Jeremiah or in the Deuteronomistic History.

The Provenance of the Mican Circle and the Deuteronomists' Identity

The Mican epilogue provides valuable evidence about postexilic Deuteronomism, first because it transparently reflects Israelite communal prayer from after the fall of Jerusalem. In the prayers of Mic. 7.14-17, 18-20, the postdestruction community responds to Micah's message.[29] Several scholars have already suggested a link between Deuteronomism and such liturgical creations of the post-586 BCE period. The work of E. Janssen and O.H. Steck, for example, suggests that the public activity of the Deuteronomistic stream of tradition took the form of penitential prayer and preaching in the early postexilic period. Deuteronomism emerged postexilically partly within cultic genres, creating communal liturgy such as Asaphite Psalms 74 and 79.[30]

28. Wolff, *Micah*, p. 231.
29. Cf. Allen, *Micah*, pp. 251-52, 393; Wolff, *Micah*, pp. 25-27, 228.
30. E. Janssen's arguments for a postexilic, Judean origin for the

This partial link of Deuteronomism to the cult suggests the Levites as logical candidates in the quest to pinpoint the identity of the Deuteronomists. We know from 1 Chron. 6.24-28 (Eng. 6.39-43); 9.14-15 that the Asaphite authors of Psalms 74 and 79 were considered to be Levites in the postexilic period. In light of some strong reverberations that the epilogue of Micah has with these two psalms, the epilogue's Deuteronomism looks increasingly to me like the product of postexilic Levites. This Levitical identification of the Deuteronomists is corroborated by Chronicles' attestation to the Levites' dual involvement in psalmody and scribalism (2 Chron. 34.12-13; cf. 1 Chron. 9.26-27, 33).[31]

The idea suggested by study of the Mican epilogue that the postexilic Deuteronomistic redactors were Levites correlates well with Gerhard von Rad's proposal, in his monograph *Studies in Deuteronomy*, that country Levites were the original authors of the book of Deuteronomy. Von Rad wrote, 'The actual spokesmen of [the pre-exilic reform] movement were the country Levites, whom Deuteronomy presumes to be living here and there in the country towns. At any rate, the authors of Deuteronomy are to be sought amongst those Levites.'[32]

Deuteronomistic History, Lamentations and several psalms suggest a viable homeland community capable of substantial compositional activity (*Juda in der Exilszeit: Ein Beitrag zur Frage der Entstehung des Judentums* [FRLANT, 69; Göttingen: Vandenhoeck & Ruprecht, 1956]). On Pss. 74 and 79, see pp. 19-20, 60, 72. Janssen believes that the epilogue to Micah specifically was composed in the homeland, not the exile, and not too far into the Persian period (pp. 89-91). O.H. Steck, for one, specifically identifies Janssen's group of homeland texts with Deuteronomism ('Theological Streams of Tradition', in D. Knight [ed.], *Tradition and Theology in the Old Testament* [Philadelphia: Fortress Press, 1977], pp. 206-209).

31. On the central role of Levites and Levitical groups in postexilic liturgical and scribal activity, see M.S. Smith, 'The Levitical Compilation of the Psalter', *ZAW* 103 (1991), pp. 258-63. On the Levites' predilection for the type of historical and moral view of the cult and its liturgy seen in the Mican epilogue, see Gottwald, *Hebrew Bible*, pp. 462-63. Apparently, as part of the compromise among priestly groups that must be supposed to lie behind the postexilic restoration, the Levites were largely allowed the role of redacting the biblical canon. The Zadokites and Aaronids, in turn, retained dominant custody of the sacrificial cult. See Wilson, *Prophecy and Society*, pp. 305-306; cf. Gottwald, *Hebrew Bible*, pp. 462-65; S. Cook, 'Innerbiblical Interpretation in Ezekiel 44 and the History of Israel's Priesthood', *JBL* 114 (1995), pp. 193-208 (206).

32. G. von Rad, *Studies in Deuteronomy* (SBT, 9; London: SCM Press, 1953), p. 66, and cf. *idem, Deuteronomy: A Commentary* (OTL; Philadelphia: Westminster

In the same study, von Rad exposed another group of Deuteronomistic tradents, a group visible in the Kings' accounts of reforming
monarchs. It is fascinating that these tradents turn out to be the very
group that authored the original Mican prophecy, prophecy with which
the Mican epilogue is in continuity. Von Rad observed in texts such as
2 Kings 11 that a group known as the עם־הארץ ('the people of the
land') figured prominently in, and intervened in favor of, Deuteronomistic reform in Jerusalem, the capital. Von Rad conjectured that these
Judean country citizens bore proto-Deuteronomistic covenant traditions
and that the Deuteronomistic Levites were their representatives.[33] In
light of the subsequent discovery of scholars, such as H.W. Wolff, that
the prophet Micah and his original circle were elders of the land—kin-
group heads representing this self-same constituency in Jerusalem—the
above established coherence of Micah's redaction and Mican prophecy
emerges as fully natural.[34] One should have expected Micah's Deuteronomistic redaction to cohere with the prophecy of this elder, who
represented the people of the land.

Von Rad's thesis that the people of the land, groups such as Micah's
constituency, stand behind Deuteronomism correlates very well with
the organic connection that has been uncovered here between the Mican
prophecies and the Deuteronomistic Mican epilogue. This organic con-

Press, 1966), p. 25; Janssen, *Juda in der Exilszeit*, p. 58.

33. Von Rad, *Studies in Deuteronomy*, pp. 63-66; cf. Janssen, *Juda in der Exilszeit*, pp. 46, 49-54. For a summary of von Rad's thesis, see Nicholson, *Deuteronomy*, pp. 83-86. Note that von Rad's argument correctly suggests that the membership of the Deuteronomists in pre-exilic Judah encompassed more than one group
and role. The Deuteronomistic faction included both Levites and country gentry.
Pushing beyond von Rad, P. Dutcher-Walls has persuasively reconstructed the
Deuteronomists as a coalition of groups ('The Social Location of the Deuteronomists: A Sociological Study of Factional Politics in Late Pre-Exilic Judah', *JSOT*
52 [1991], pp. 77-94 [esp. pp. 91-93]). Her analysis provides a more comprehensive
view of the provenance of Deuteronomism than the various, modern proposals of
Clements, Nicholson and Weinfeld.

34. Micah's repeated reference to עמי ('my people') together with other evidence, such as his clan-based language (e.g. his funerary language), have suggested
to scholars that he was one of old (i.e. village-) Israel's lineage heads, an 'elder of
the land'. H.W. Wolff has argued this case in an especially convincing manner. As
Wolff states, 'Micah's active defense of those whom he calls "my people" is not the
concern of a solitary small landowner or even that of an (exceptionally) righteous
estate owner who has regard for the distress of the little people; rather, it is best
understood as that of an elder' (*Micah*, p. 7; cf. pp. 59, 75).

nection leads us back behind Deuteronomistic redaction to its social roots. The roots of Deuteronomism are to be found, in part at least, among certain leading clan elders of the land, such as those whom we now know comprised the original Mican circle.

These observations suggest the following reconstruction, which should be buttressed by a close linguistic study of the original Mican prophecies themselves. The evidence suggests that the members and forebears of the Mican group in the pre-exilic period were among those circles that affected Deuteronomistic reforms and bore the stream of tradition that eventuated in Deuteronomistic composition and redaction. These elders of the land shared their role of Deuteronomistic tradents with groups of Levites, some of whom joined with the elders as representatives of the עם־הארץ, the 'people of the land', as their spokespeople. After the fall of Jerusalem in 586 BCE, Levitical groups continued as tradents of Deuteronomism. Perhaps some members of this Levitical circle were exiled to Babylon while others remained in the homeland. These Levites, whose postexilic roles involved them in both liturgical and scribal activities, composed new liturgical material, replete with Deuteronomistic language and ideas, and continued the process of Deuteronomistic redaction of prophetic books such as Micah.

A DEUTERONOMISTIC REDACTION IN/AMONG 'THE TWELVE'?
A CONTRIBUTION FROM THE STANDPOINT OF THE BOOKS
OF MICAH, ZEPHANIAH AND OBADIAH*

Ehud Ben Zvi

1. *Introduction*

A renewed interest in the claim that the prophetic books underwent a substantial deuteronomistic redaction(s) is obvious in recent years. The works of Coggins, Nogalski and Alvarez Barredo,[1] to mention a few, as well as the lively discussions on this topic in the 1996 SBL Deuteronomistic History Section and some of the papers in the 1996 SBL Seminar on 'The Formation of the Book of the Twelve'[2] clearly attest to this development.[3]

*   Paper presented at the 1997 Seminar on 'The Formation of the Book of the Twelve', at the annual meeting of the Society of Biblical Literature held in San Francisco, November 1997.

1.   R.J. Coggins, 'What Does "Deuteronomistic" Mean?', in Jon Davies, Graham Harvey and Wilfred G.E. Watson (eds.), *Words Remembered, Texts Renewed: Essays in Honour of John F.A. Sawyer* (JSOTSup, 195; Sheffield: Sheffield Academic Press, 1995), pp. 135-48, reprinted as Chapter 1 in this volume; M. Alvarez Barredo, *Relecturas deuteronomísticas de Amós, Miqueas y Jeremías* (Murcia: Instituto Teológico Franciscano, 1993); J. Nogalski, *Literary Precursors to the Book of the Twelve* (BZAW, 217; Berlin: W. de Gruyter, 1993); and cf. A. Schart, *Die Entstehung des Zwölfprophetenbuchs* (Habilitationsschrift; Phillips-Universität Marburg, 1995).

2.   E.g. A. Schart, 'The Combination of Hosea, Amos, Micah, and Zephaniah on a Single Scroll: Unifying Devices and Redactional Intentions'. Paper presented at the 1996 Meeting of the Seminar on 'The Formation of the Book of the Twelve', 1996 SBL Annual Meeting, New Orleans.

3.   Almost opposite sides of the spectrum of ideas and approaches were represented by (1) R. Kugler, 'Prophets and Pan-deuteronomism' and (2) S.L. Cook, 'Micah's Deuteronomistic Redaction and the Deuteronomists' Identity' (both of these papers are included in this volume). Papers related to this debate were pre-

The reasons for this renewed interest are multiple. It is due in part to the implications that this position has (or may have) regarding the scholarly understanding of the composition and redaction of the prophetic books in general and the present debate about the redactional unity (or lack thereof) of 'The Twelve' (or a proto-Twelve corpus). From a larger perspective, the attention given to these issues reflects the clear intertwining of the debate about possible deuteronomistic redaction(s) or influence in these prophetic books and that about the scope, nature and even existence of a deuteronomistic corpus (or corpora) elsewhere in the Hebrew Bible, particularly in the (so-called) Deuteronomistic History. In turn, these debates are deeply related to those regarding the (historical) existence or lack thereof of a deuteronomistic movement or movements in ancient Israel. It goes without saying that the last of these issues has profound implications for the reconstruction of the history of ideas in ancient Israel.

It is obvious that a full discussion of these issues requires at least a lengthy monograph. However, it is the contention of this study that despite its inherent genre limitations, a book chapter may still shed some light on these issues, provided that it approaches them with a relatively narrow focus, such as the question of potential deuteronomistic redaction(s) and influences upon a few prophetic books. This study will focus on the books of Micah, Zephaniah and Obadiah.[4] The conclusions reached through this focused study will then be tentatively set within the larger framework of the current debate.

2. *General Considerations and the Basic Ground of the Hypotheses of Dtr Redaction(s)*

There is ample support in modern research for the claim that the prophetic books (i.e. those later included in the 'Latter Prophets' section of the HB) in general and those included in 'The Twelve' (e.g. Micah, Zephaniah) in particular underwent deuteronomistic redaction(s) or were edited under the influence of (or even by) the/a deuteronomistic movement. This claim is based, in the main, on:

sented also at the 1996 session of 'The Formation of the Book of the Twelve'.

4. Two of these books (Micah and Zephaniah) are often associated with a dtr redaction or redactions.

(a)   the construction of a deuteronomic/deuteronomistic corpus of
       literature (namely, Deuteronomy–Kings + the 'deuteronomic
       [or deuteronomistic] prose sermons of Jeremiah') that is set as
       a standard for 'deuteronomisticity' against which other cor-
       pora (or individual biblical books, or textual subunits within a
       book) may be compared;

(b)   the position that there was in ancient Israel a deuteronomistic
       movement/school or deuteronomistic group(s) (or tradents)
       that was clearly differentiated from all other contemporaneous
       groups/movements/schools by a distinctive set of language and
       ideas, that is, by the creation and development of a particular
       sociolect and theological discourse;

(c)   the claim that some theological ideas that are considered to be
       central to dtr thought are expressed in the relevant prophetic
       book (i.e. the one that is claimed to have been edited/redacted
       by a dtr group or under the influence of dtr thought);

(d)   the observation that some words or expressions appear in both
       the dtr corpus and in the text of the relevant prophetic book;
       and

(e)   the adoption of a set of redactional-critical hypotheses in
       regard to the formation of the relevant prophetic book, and of
       their necessary presuppositions.

This essay proceeds with a critical examination of each of the mentioned 'bases' on which the claim for a dtr redaction/edition rests.[5] This
examination will begin with the general redactional issues (i.e. point 'e'
above) and will then address the more particular issues referred to as
points 'c' and 'd'. It will focus next on the more general historical and
methodological issues that are involved in the (a–b) construction. The
analysis of the latter, within the contexts of the conclusions reached by
studying the former, will set the grounds for an alternative approach to
these issues within a larger frame (see section 6 below).[6]

---

5.   At least for the purposes and scope of this essay this approach seems preferable to the sequential and separate analysis of each textual unit or subunit that has
been associated with the dtr movement or dtr redaction/s.

6.   It is worth mentioning already at this stage that points (a) and (b) are closely
related, since the proposed existence of dtr groups/schools is an inference made
mainly on the basis of the literary corpus referred to in (a). Had Deuteronomy–
Kings been lost, no one would have advanced the idea of deuteronomistic groups.

3. *Redactional Issues: Some Considerations*

Since point (e) above raises critical questions that I have addressed on previous other occasions,[7] it suffices here to stress the following:

1. A claim for a deuteronomistic redaction implies by necessity not only that there was a text that existed before the redaction but that this text and the textual additions and transformations that came about due to the redaction can be reconstructed (at least, in the main), and accordingly, characterized (or even 'classified') in terms of, among other things, sociolect, authorship/redactionship and theology/ideology. This claim is (at least) debatable, and particularly so given the following two considerations.

2. Redactional claims tend to create and control their own 'textual evidence'. In other words, they tend to govern the way in which data are interpreted.[8] Thus, for instance, if a book such as Zephaniah contains, as it does, a relatively lengthy section that resembles a text in the book of Ezekiel (see Zeph. 3.3-4 and cf. Ezek. 22.25, 27, 28, 26, 29), this data will not be considered as strong evidence that an Ezekielian group/movement (i.e. a particular social group characterized by its use of Ezekielian language) redacted (or authored) the present book of Zephaniah, nor does the similarity between Zeph. 2.15 and Isa. 47.8 suggest to most scholars that (in addition to other groups, also) a (Deutero)Isaianic group redacted (or authored) Zephaniah. Yet the similarities between these texts are clearly much greater than those observed between texts in the standard dtr corpus and the books of Zephaniah and Micah (e.g. the use of לקח מוסר in Zeph. 3.2, 7 or פדה מבית עבדים in Mic. 6.4; on these and other examples see below).

---

7. See E. Ben Zvi, *A Historical-Critical Study of the Book of Obadiah* (BZAW, 242; Berlin: W. de Gruyter, 1996); *idem*, 'Twelve Prophetic Books or "The Twelve": A Few Preliminary Considerations', in P. House and J.W. Watts (eds.), *Forming Prophetic Literature: Essays on Isaiah and the Twelve in Honor of John D.W. Watts* (JSOTSup, 235; Sheffield: Sheffield Academic Press, 1996), pp. 125-56; *idem*, 'Studying Prophetic Texts against their Original Backgrounds: Pre-Ordained Scripts and Alternative Horizons of Research', in S.R. Reid (ed.), *Prophets and Paradigms: Essays in Honor of Gene M. Tucker* (JSOTSup, 229; Sheffield: Sheffield Academic Press, 1996), pp. 124-35.

8. To the point that 'textual evidence' is created or controlled by the assumptions that this 'evidence' is meant to support, the entire argument suffers from circularity.

Likewise the presence in the book of Zephaniah of a number of themes and precise language that appear in Psalms or Proverbs[9] is usually not interpreted in the same manner as similar features associated with deuteronomistic characteristics (for examples, see below), nor is the presence of the former weighed against that of the latter (see below) when claims about a deuteronomistic (as opposed to a 'Psalmic' or 'wisdom') redaction/influence are advanced.

Moreover, if a postexilic date for the *books* of Micah, Obadiah and Zephaniah is accepted—and accordingly one assumes that much of the dtr corpus was known to the authors of the text—then it seems reasonable to assume that both (a) the lack of significant typical deuteronomistic phraseology at places where it could have been easily used—see esp. section 6 below—and (b) the obvious preference for a unique language outweighs the presence of a few words that do appear in deuteronomistic texts.[10] Yet if one assumes a dtr redactional model, one may consider the same evidence as pointing to a social and historical process in which an earlier text that included no dtr elements was edited by a deuteronomistic group, and then by a post-deuteronomistic group. This inconsistency is usually due to some basic assumptions about the redactional history of the prophetic books. These assumptions govern the interpretation of the 'bare data', and thus create or control what is seen as 'textual evidence'.

3. Many of the redactional reconstructions of proposed dtr redactions are often based on questionable premises. Thus, for instance, according to Jörg Jeremias:

> The books of Amos and Hosea have much in common. This fact is not surprising but is to be expected since both prophets spoke in the northern kingdom which would soon come to an end. Naturally, they shared common convictions, and they condemned similar guilt and crime, and of course, the younger one, Hosea, knew the older one.

---

9. See, for instance, the situation in Zeph. 1.15; 2.3, 11; 3.9, which I have discussed elsewhere (see Ben Zvi, *A Historical-Critical Study of the Book of Zephaniah* [BZAW, 198; Berlin: W. de Gruyter, 1991], pp. 122-23, 144-49, 174-75, 225-26).

10. See, for instance, Zeph. 1.4-5 whose main 'idolatrous' terms (i.e. Baal, host of heaven and priestlings) are found in 2 Kgs 23, but whose text is unequivocally different from that in 2 Kgs 23 (or any of its subunits) and nowhere seems to imitate this text (cf. Ben Zvi, *Zephaniah,* pp. 78-79). Micah 6.16, which is discussed below, presents a similar case.

...I can understand these literary connections [i.e. those between the books of Amos and Hosea] on different levels only if *the pupils of Amos and the pupils of Hosea who handed down the message of the prophets* wanted to teach the readers that they could not grasp the ideas of these prophets by reading their books in complete isolation from one another.[11]

Jeremias's analysis obviously assumes (a) the existence of two social groups, namely the pupils of Amos and those of Hosea; and (b) that both books were written by the relevant pupils on the basis of the message of the prophet whom they have heard and followed. Clearly if either of these premises is wrong, then Jeremias's analysis will fall apart. But is the claim that Amos and Hosea had 'pupils' well supported by the evidence?[12] Moreover, even if for the sake of argument one grants that both of them had a group of disciples/pupils, is there any evidence that these groups continued to exist as separate social entities long after the death of their prophets/teachers?[13] Furthermore, even if one grants this assumption, is there any reason to assume that these groups consisted of the kind of literati necessary for the production of the books attributed to them, that is, books such as Amos and Hosea that imply a high level of literacy regarding both readership and authorship? Finally, are Amos and Hosea basically (a) two literary characters who are created and shaped within the world of their respective books and to whom the (re)readership of the books has access through their (re)reading of the relevant texts, but whose resemblance to historical figures who lived in the northern kingdom is largely unknown? Or are they (b) two historical prophets about whom so much is known that we may use their life, words and circumstances as the starting point for a *historical* analysis of the ideas and the production of literary texts in monarchic Israel?

It goes without saying that a full discussion of these issues is impossible within the content of this essay. It is worth stressing for the

11. J. Jeremias, 'The Interrelationship between Amos and Hosea', in House and Watts (eds.), *Forming Prophetic Literature*, pp. 171-86 (171); emphasis mine.

12. To be sure, Jeremias's proposal of 'pupils' is similar to the common references to 'tradents' if the latter are constructed as tradents of only one particular tradition, i.e. 'Isaianic tradents', 'Jeremianic tradents', and the like. On pre-ordained scripts governing research and its horizons see Ben Zvi, 'Studying Prophetic Texts'.

13. To be sure, the existence of the text itself is no proof for the existence of such a group. The reference to 'pupils' in the quoted text implies an understanding of prophet/teacher.

present, however, that much of the claim about deuteronomistic redaction(s) in the prophetic books is grounded in a set of particular redaction-critical constructions that rest on questionable grounds.

Thus, for instance, texts in Micah and Zephaniah that refer to the destruction of Jerusalem/Judah, the 'exile' and restoration are often considered secondary (or redactional) and therefore some of them (the hopeful passages are usually excluded[14]) are at least potential candidates for a deuteronomistic redaction on the basis that either (a) a historical prophet who lived several decades before the events could not have foreseen them or (b) these references are unlikely to be part of the books of Micah and Zephaniah that existed during the monarchic period. But if these two books were composed (as opposed to redacted[15]) in the postmonarchic period, then these considerations do not hold, and this being so, any argument about the 'redactional' or 'editorial' character of these texts that is based on such grounds falls apart.[16] If there is no convincing reason to assume that a certain text must be redactional, then there is no reason to assume that it must be part of a dtr redaction. There is no dtr redaction if there is no redaction.

An additional example, Nogalski's analysis of the composition of the Book of the Twelve, not only assumes the existence of such a book, but also makes his reconstruction of the putative stages of this corpus the

14. They are often considered later than the dtr redaction (e.g. Nogalski, *Literary Precursors*, p. 88). It is worth noting, however, that Deuteronomy itself contains references to the restoration that will come after the exile. In fact, its brightest promises refer to the situation that will obtain *after* the exile (see Deut. 30.1-10; and cf. Deut. 4.25-31). As Deurloo maintains, 'according to its setting, Deuteronomy is a book of restoration' (K.A. Deurloo, 'The One God and All Israel', in F. García Martínez *et al.* [eds.], *Studies in Deuteronomy in Honour of C.J. Labuschagne on the Occasion of his 65th Birthday* [VTSup, 53; Leiden: E.J. Brill, 1994], pp. 31-46 [33]).

15. Composition may involve sources—even written sources—but it is a very different activity from redacting or editing a received book. Thus, for instance, Chronicles is never considered a redacted/edited version of the books of Samuel and Kings, but a book in its own right. I discussed these issues in Ben Zvi, *Obadiah*.

16. Significantly, since the present text of these books is postmonarchic and since it shows textual coherence, the burden of proof falls on those who claim earlier dates. Yet in many cases, the whole interpretation of the book, or at least of some significant sections, rests on a default position that associates any text in the book with the figure and time of the personage identified in the superscription, unless proven otherwise. I criticized this approach in Ben Zvi, 'Studying Prophetic Texts'.

governing interpretive key for his textual analysis in general, and of the three books mentioned in the title of this essay, namely Micah, Zephaniah and Obadiah. Again, there is no need to reiterate my recent critique of his approach,[17] yet it is worth stressing that debatable claims such as that the Book of the Twelve and its hypothetical forerunners were treated (and redacted) as one unit do govern the range of allowed interpretations.[18]

In sum, claims that the books of Micah, Zephaniah or Obadiah underwent a dtr redaction(s) are necessarily based on redactional hypotheses that are at least questionable.

4. *Shared Words and Expressions*

a. *Introduction*

Points (c) and (d) (see above, section 2) are concerned with certain textual observations. The issue addressed in point (d) relates to words or expressions that appear in both the literature usually accepted as dtr

17. See Ben Zvi, 'Twelve Prophetic Books'. It may be mentioned that Nogalski, Jeremias, and other scholars who maintain the existence of a dtr redaction(s) in these books follow what I characterized in that paper as a 'Writer/Redactor or Production Centered Approach' as opposed to an 'Audience or Reception Centered Approach'. Regarding Obadiah, see also Ben Zvi, *Obadiah*.

18. For instance, Nogalski states: 'The mention of Samaria in Mic. 1.5, 6f. clearly does not *depend* upon traditions in Ezekiel and Obadiah. *The question remains* whether the use of Samaria in Micah lies closer to the other 8th century prophets Hosea and Amos, or whether this usage falls nearer the deuteronomistic polemic' (Nogalski, *Literary Precursors*, p. 133; emphasis mine). True, there is no reason to assume that the text of Mic. 1.5-7 depends upon any text in Ezekiel or Obadiah (nor vice versa). But if this is so do the two alternatives that Nogalski proposes comprise the entire range of possibilities? Probably yes, if one accepts Nogalski's reconstruction of the redactional processes and texts and his hypothesis regarding the Book of the Twelve. (For a critique, see Ben Zvi, 'Twelve Prophetic Books'.)

Incidentally, one may also notice that the following positions are taken for granted: (a) we know a substantial amount about the eighth-century prophets as historical personages; (b) there existed '*the* (not 'a') deuteronomistic polemic' against Samaria. Both claims are questionable. Significantly, the first one reflects certainty about the historicity of a certain shaping of the proposed historical figures (namely Hosea and Amos) that is based on a supposedly original (and likely oral) text, or better series of texts that are 'recovered' by scholars from admittedly much later texts.

and the prophetic books or certain sections of them, whereas that in point (c) has to do with shared ideas, though not necessarily expressed by the same language. Of course, these 'raw' observations provide 'data'; the question of whether these data furnish convincing evidence for a deuteronomistic redaction of prophetic books depends on the criteria used to analyze them.

b. *Citations or 'Closely Related Texts'*
Actual citations or the presence of closely related texts spanning several verses are the best diagnostic tool for some form of direct textual relationship among texts.[19] As is known, the books of Micah, Obadiah and Zephaniah neither quote any portion of Deuteronomy–Kings nor show any single verse that appears in a closely related, textual form within that corpus.[20] In sharp contrast, each of these prophetic books contains texts that are closely related to other texts in prophetic books (see Mic. 4.1-3 and cf. Isa. 2.2-4; Zeph. 3.3-4 and cf. Ezek. 22.25, 27, 28, 26, 29; Zeph. 2.15 and cf. Isa. 47.8; Obad. 1-7 and Jer. 49.7aα, 14-16, 9-10). Conversely, texts in the Deuteronomy–Kings corpus are quoted elsewhere, both within that corpus (see 2 Kgs 14.6 and cf. Deut. 24.16) and outside it, as in Chronicles,[21] but not in Micah, Zephaniah and Obadiah. This lack of citation of deuteronomistic texts along with the non-existence of closely related texts of any significant length is certainly *not* suggestive of a deuteronomistic redaction.

c. *Typical Deuteronomistic Phraseology*
Aside from citations or closely related texts, the best possible evidence for some form of relationship between the prophetic books discussed here and a deuteronomistic group of writers that is predicated on a particular language would be the presence of 'classical deuteronomistic

19. This relationship may take the form of one text depending on the other, or both depending on a common written source.
20. Some connections may be seen, however, between the books of Jeremiah and Zephaniah. The best example is Zeph. 3.2 and Jer. 7.28, but their relationship should not be interpreted in a void; it is to be contextualized by the presence of similar or stronger textual connections between Zeph. 3.1-5 (and its subunits) and other texts. On these verses, see Ben Zvi, *Zephaniah*, pp. 184-213, 315-17.
21. The last example clearly shows that from the citation of deuteronomistic texts it does not necessarily follow that the texts were written or redacted by a deuteronomistic group.

phraseology'. This being so, the present analysis has to address the amount of overlap (or lack thereof) between an inventory of 'classical deuteronomistic phraseology' that was not prepared with the books of Micah, Zephaniah and Obadiah in mind[22] and the actual language present in these prophetic books.[23]

There is probably no more comprehensive inventory for these purposes than the one compiled by M. Weinfeld.[24] This inventory includes 316 main entries, none of which—including all their subentries—is found in Obadiah. Only one is present in the book of Zephaniah, and only two are in the book of Micah. Moreover, the only entry that occurs in both Weinfeld's list and the book of Zephaniah is לקח מוסר which (1) is not a clear marker of deuteronomistic redaction/influence,[25] and (2) occurs within subunits that show no particular dtr style, and do not seem to consist of 'redactional' (as opposed to compositional) material.[26] Furthermore, the two entries found in Micah are in fact only one, פדה מבית עבדים (Mic. 6.4) which creates two 'hits' in Weinfeld's

---

22. So as to avoid *ad hoc* hypotheses and circular thinking.

23. Needless to say, should some overlap be found, the study should take into account not only mere occurrence of expressions but also the meaning(s) that they convey in their literary context. According to Weinfeld 'what makes a phrase deuteronomic is not its mere occurrence in Deuteronomy, but its meaning within the framework of deuteronomic theology'. See M. Weinfeld, *Deuteronomy and the Deuteronomic School* (Oxford: Clarendon Press, 1972), pp. 1-2; cf. M. Vervenne, 'The Question of "Deuteronomic" Elements in Genesis to Numbers', in García Martínez *et al.* (eds.), *Studies in Deuteronomy in Honour of C.J. Labuschagne*, pp. 244-68, esp. p. 268. One should note, however, that there is no single deuteronomistic theology. Cf. R. Albertz, *A History of Israelite Religion in the Old Testament Period*, II (trans. J. Bowden; Louisville, KY: Westminster/John Knox Press, 1994), pp. 382-83, and *passim*; E.-A. Knauf, ' "L'historiographie deutéronomiste" (DTRG) existe-t-elle?', in A. de Pury, T. Römer and J.-D. Macchi (eds.), *Israël construit son histoire: L'historiographie deutéronomiste à la lumière de recherches récentes* (MB, 34; Geneva: Labor et Fides, 1996), pp. 409-18 (410). On these issues see below.

24. Weinfeld, *Deuteronomy and the Deuteronomic School*, esp. pp. 398-404.

25. See below.

26. לקח מוסר also occurs once in Zeph. 3.2 within a unit (Zeph. 3.1-5) that is textually coherent with its literary environment and whose closest affinities are not with deuteronomistic literature. See Ben Zvi, *Zephaniah*, pp. 184-213, 315-17. The second occurrence of לקח מוסר is also within a context (Zeph. 3.6-7) that is not necessarily or even likely deuteronomistic (see Ben Zvi, *Zephaniah*, pp. 213-19 and esp. p. 318).

inventory, because the latter includes both פדה מבית עבדים and בית
עבדים.[27] Even if one includes as 'shared hits' three additional
expressions in Micah and one in Zephaniah that come close to those
included in Weinfeld's inventory of deuteronomistic phraseology,[28] the
fact remains that about 99 per cent of the typical deuteronomistic
phraseology compiled by Weinfeld is absent from Micah and
Zephaniah, and 100 per cent of it is absent from Obadiah.

Of course, these data do not support the idea that a group that is
identified by the use of deuteronomistic phraseology is responsible for
these books. Moreover, from these data one has to infer that these

27. See Weinfeld, *Deuteronomy and the Deuteronomic School,* pp. 326, 399,
403. There is one instance of שחת in the hiphil in Zeph. 3.7, but Weinfeld's list
includes this verbal form only when it is intransitive, which is not the case in Zeph.
3.7. See Weinfeld, *Deuteronomy and the Deuteronomic School*, pp. 340, 400 and
the examples there.

28. The expressions in Micah are:

(1) מעשה ידיך, referring to 'idols', occurs in Mic. 5.12 and in similar forms in dtr
texts (see Deut. 4.28; 2 Kgs 19.18//Isa. 37.19), but see also Isa. 2.8; Pss. 115.4;
135.15 (see above). Moreover, it appears in works that are not deuteronomistic but
are aware of deuteronomistic works (see 2 Chron. 32.19 not directly paralleled in
either Kings or Isaiah).

(2) באף ובחמה rather than באף ובחמה ובקצף גדול (see Weinfeld, *Deuteronomy
and the Deuteronomic School*, pp. 116, 348, 398) appears in Mic. 5.14. Still,
caution is warranted since the pair באף ובחמה is not necessarily a deuteronomistic
marker (see, for instance, Ezek. 5.15; 22.20; Pss. 6.2; 90.7; cf. Ezek. 25.14; and the
pair אף־חמה is relatively common; e.g. Nah. 1.6; Prov. 21.14; 22.24; 29.22); moreover, the third term in Mic. 5.14 (i.e. נקמ[ה]) is found in Ezek. 25.14, but does not
occur as a member of this triad in dtr literature.

(3) נתן לשרקה וחרפה appears in Mic. 6.16 (cf. Weinfeld, *Deuteronomy and the
Deuteronomic School*, pp. 348, 402). The closest expression to it is in Jer. 29.18,
but the differences are clear. Moreover, the choice of words in Mic. 6.16 seems to
point to a strong tendency to use unusual combinations (defamiliarize?) within
familiar territory. Thus one may note the rare occurrence of שמר חק(ה) with שמר in
the hitpael (rather than qal), and the choice of terms such as חקת עמרי and
מעשה בית אחאב that do not occur elsewhere. On this matter, see also E. Ben Zvi,
Micah (FOTL; Grand Rapids: Eerdmans, forthcoming).

The expression in Zephaniah is כל עובר עליה ישרק (Zeph. 2.15; cf. Weinfeld,
Deuteronomy and the Deuteronomic School, p. 402, which refers to 1 Kgs 9.8; Jer.
19.8; 49.17; 50.13). Yet all the mentioned expressions (except the one in Zeph.
2.15) include שם in the middle (as recognized by Weinfeld). A similar expression
without שם occurs in Lam. 2.15 and, more important, the text in Zeph. 2.15 is
closer to Isa. 47.8 than to any dtr text.

books do not show a wording that would lead rereaders[29] to associate them closely with the works included in the (standard) deuteronomistic corpus.[30] Moreover, the ease with which typical dtr language can be reused and imitated[31] makes it impossible to explain its lack in the

29. I am using the term 'rereaders' rather than 'readers' to draw attention to the fact that most of the reading of these texts was actually 'rereading'. The process of 'rereading' is not identical to that of 'reading' for the first time. Texts written so as to be continuously reread are much more likely to develop polisemy, potential and actual ambiguities and the like. On rereading from a (contemporaneous) literary perspective, see M. Calinescu, *Rereading* (New Haven: Yale University Press, 1993); from that of empirical studies see, for instance, P. Dixon, M. Bortolussi, L.C. Twilley and A. Leung, 'Literary Processing and Interpretation; Towards Empirical Foundations', *Poetics* 22 (1993), pp. 5-33; and in relation to Hebrew Bible studies, see Ben Zvi, *Obadiah*, p. 4 and *passim*; and *idem*, 'Micah 1.2-16: Observations and Possible Implications', *JSOT* 77 (1998), pp. 103-120.

30. In other, less precise words, the books of Micah, Zephaniah and Obadiah do not have the 'feeling' of the books (later) included in the corpus Deuteronomy–King nor that of the prose sermons of Jeremiah. For a discussion of the 'Audience or Reception Centered Approach' that is assumed here, see Ben Zvi, 'Twelve Prophetic Books'. This approach is significant at many levels of the discussion about dtr redaction(s) of the relevant prophetic texts. For instance, van der Woude has proposed that the present book of Micah represents a deuteronomistic and Josianic combination of the writings of two prophets, namely Micah of Moresheth and another prophet whose name 'may have been Micah as well', and who was from the northern kingdom of Israel and contemporaneous with Micah of Moreshet. Van der Woude attributes to the northern prophet—Deutero–Micah—chs. 6 and 7. See A.S. van der Woude, 'Three Classical Prophets: Amos, Hosea and Micah', in R. Coggins, A. Phillips and M. Knibb (eds.), *Israel's Prophetic Tradition: Essays in Honour of Peter R. Ackroyd* (Cambridge: Cambridge University Press, 1982), pp. 32-57 (50-51); cf. L. Alonso Schökel and J.L. Sicre Díaz, *Prophets*, II (Madrid: Cristiandad, 1980), pp. 1033-35, and F.C. Burkitt, 'Micah 6 and 7: A Northern Prophecy', *JBL* 45 (1926), pp. 159-61. Leaving aside for the sake of argument all the problems that this thesis faces, it is obvious that Mic. 1.1 does not tell its rereaders that such is the case; to the contrary, Mic. 1.1 asks the intended rereader to associate the entire book with the figure of Micah the Morashethite, which is to be expected since there is no prophetic book that is associated with more than one central prophetic figure (see Ben Zvi, 'Twelve Prophetic Books'). So even if one were to grant the likelihood of this hypothesis, it tells us nothing (or close to nothing) about the message of the book of Micah to its intended audience, nor about the social role/s and influences that the repeated reading and study of this book could have had. Needless to say, the latter are the most likely reasons for the composition of the book of Micah.

31. Cf. Dan. 9. See T. Römer, 'Y a-t-il une rédaction deutéronomiste dans le

books of Micah, Zephaniah and Obadiah in terms of supposed ('technical') difficulties. It is most reasonable to assume that the absence of typical dtr phraseology is neither the result of blind chance nor a necessity of the respective genre (i.e. prophetic book versus historical narrative or the like), as clearly proven by the case of the book of Jeremiah.[32] In other words, it is not an 'accident' that the books of Micah, Zephaniah and Obadiah do not have the 'feeling' of the books (later) included in the corpus Deuteronomy–Kings, but do possess their own feel. Possible explanations for this feature are advanced in section 6 below. But at this stage in the argument, other data regarding the wording of the books of Micah, Zephaniah and Obadiah and their relevance to the issue at stake should be examined.

d. *Randomly Chosen Shared Words and Short Expressions*
From the simple fact that a word appears in both a prophetic book and in the standard dtr corpus it does not follow that the prophetic book underwent a dtr redaction, nor that the particular unit in which the word appears represents a dtr addition. In fact, it does not follow from this observation per se that the prophetic text (or section thereof) is necessarily closer (or communicates a sense of particular closeness) to the dtr corpus than to other literary works that were later included in the Hebrew Bible. Not only is the (Hebrew) biblical vocabulary relatively circumscribed, but also Deuteronomy–Kings represents a very large section of the Hebrew Bible. By one count, Deuteronomy–Kings contains 83,682 words, which is more than 27 per cent of the total words in the Hebrew Bible (305,498) and far more than Genesis–Numbers (65,689), the books of Psalms (19,586), Proverbs (6915), Isaiah (16,933) or Jeremiah (21,835), to mention a few.[33] Thus if there were a completely random choice of words then it is about 12 times more

---

livre de Jérémie?', in de Pury, Römer and Macchi (eds.), *Israël construit son histoire*, pp. 419-41 (423-24) and the examples and bibliography mentioned there.

32. These observations are central to the argument that will be developed in section 6, below.

33. F.I. Andersen and A. Dean Forbes, 'What Did the Scribes Count?', in D.N. Freedman *et al.* (eds.), *Studies in Hebrew and Aramaic Orthography* (Biblical and Judaic Studies, 2; Winona Lake, IN: Eisenbrauns, 1992), pp. 297-318 (309). The count mentioned above is that of Andersen and Forbes. The slight differences between this and the other counts mentioned is irrelevant for the purpose of the argument advanced here.

likely that a word appearing in one of the prophetic books would also occur in Deuteronomy–Kings than in Proverbs, or about 4 times more likely than in Psalms. In other words, under these conditions, 12 shared occurrences between Deuteronomy–Kings and Micah (or Zephaniah or Obadiah) weigh as much as 1 between Proverbs and the same prophetic book. Significantly, since the standard dtr corpus is larger than Deuteronomy–Kings,[34] even these ratios tend to exaggerate deuteronomistic influence. If one were to restrict the reference group to Deuteronomy alone (14,294 words), which is not the usual practice, the probability of shared occurrences would still be larger than with Proverbs and about the same size as with the book of Isaiah (16,933).

In addition, given the sheer volume of the dtr standard corpus (i.e. Deuteronomy–Kings + Dtr Jeremiah) it is to be expected that several words and expressions would appear in a prophetic book and also occur one or two times in that vast corpus, but not elsewhere.[35] Thus the requirements for potentially 'diagnostic' repetitions must include more than the simple observation of one (or a very few) shared occurrences.

It is obvious that by these standards, the data do not point to a particularly close relationship between the books of Micah, Zephaniah or Obadiah on the one hand and the standard dtr corpus on the other.[36]

e. *Shared 'Clusters' or 'Expressions'*
Although the relevant prophetic books show no citations of dtr texts nor closely related texts of any significant length, nor do they contain any significant amount of 'typical' dtr phraseology, nor is the data from

---

34. It includes also the (deuteronomistic) prose sermons in the book of Jeremiah.

35. E.g. the occurrences of (a) שארית נחלה in 2 Kgs 21.14 and Mic. 7.18, and (b) אתנן זונה in Deut. 23.19 and Mic. 1.7, but nowhere else in the Hebrew Bible. Incidentally, similar instances with much smaller corpora of comparison do occur. For example, the expression עטה על שפם appears only in Lev. 13.45 and Mic. 3.7. (For other potential 'similarities' between the books of Micah and Leviticus, see Mic. 2.2 and cf. Lev. 19.13; Mic. 4.14 and cf. Lev. 26.26; Mic. 7.13 and cf. Lev. 26.32; of course, none of them should be reasonably used to claim a 'Leviticus [mini]redaction of Micah'.) Also in the book of Micah, as well as in Zephaniah, one may find an idiom that is not rare in the Hebrew Bible, but never occurs in Deuteronomy–Kings despite its size, namely מלא חמס (see Mic. 6.12 and Zeph. 1.9; and cf. Gen. 6.11; 13; Ezek. 7.23; 8.17; 12.9; 28.16; Ps. 74.20). But what can be learned from this observation?

36. Significantly, this holds true even if one uncritically focuses mainly or even only on the instances in which words or short expressions occur in both the

more or less randomly chosen words and short expressions supportive in any way of a particular textual relation between these books and the dtr corpus, one may still claim to demonstrate dependence on dtr texts by pointing to a substantial number of clusters of words or idioms that are clearly *peculiar* to the standard dtr corpus—though they may not fully qualify as 'typical' deuteronomistic phraseology—and that appear also in either Micah, Zephaniah or Obadiah.

prophetic book and the dtr corpus and disregards other expressions that are present in the text and that by the same standards would point to the closeness of other corpora (on these issues see below). To illustrate, the expression לקח מוסר occurs in Zeph. 3.2, 7 and also in Jer. 5.3; 7.28; 17.23; 32.33; 35.13 and Prov. 1.3; 8.10; Prov. 24.32. According to the parameters above, nothing can be learned from this distribution about the dtr character of the book of Zephaniah, or even the text of Zeph. 3.2, 7. Similarly, the expression בטח בה (which encapsulates one of the theological tenets usually associated with the deuteronomistic movement) occurs in 2 Kgs 18.5, 19.10 (//Isa. 37.10) and in Zeph. 3.2; but it appears also in Ps. 9.11; 21.8; 22.5, 6; 25.2; 26.1; 28.7; 32.10; 37.3; 40.4; 55.24; 56.5, 12; 62.9; 84.13; 91.2; 112.7; 115.9, 10, 11; 125.1; 143.8 and in Isa. 26.3, 4; Jer. 17.7; 39.18; Prov. 16.20, 29.25; 1 Chron. 5.20. Likewise the theologically significant לקרא בשם ה' in Zeph. 3.9 occurs in 2 Kgs 5.11 (cf. 1 Kgs 18.24), but also in Gen. 4.26, 12.8, 13.4, 21.33, 26.25; Exod. 33.19, 34.5; Joel 3.5; and Ps. 116.4, 13, 17.

The book of Micah provides additional examples. For instance, calls to 'hear', expressed by imperative forms of שמע not only appear in Mic. 1.2; 3.1 and 6.1, 2 but may mark the main structural or discursive sections in the book (cf. D.G. Hagstrom, *The Coherence of the Book of Micah* [SBLDS, 89; Atlanta: Scholars Press, 1988], pp. 11-27). They also appear in the standard dtr corpus, but not only there (see Deut. 6.4; Judg. 5.3; 2 Kgs 7.1; Isa. 1.2; 7.13; 48.1; Jer. 10.1; Amos 3.1; 4.1; 5.1; Mic. 3.1; Prov. 4.1; Job 34.2; and cf. the 'atypical' case of Lam. 1.18). In another example, the expression וישבו איש תחת גפנו ותחת תאנתו appears in 1 Kgs 5.5 (cf. 2 Kgs 18.31 // Isa. 36.16) and Mic. 4.4, but it also occurs in Zech. 3.10 and this is not unexpected given that גפן and תאנה constitute a common word-pair (e.g. Isa. 34.4; Jer. 8.13; Hag. 2.19; Ps. 105.33).

Finally, the same holds true for the book of Obadiah. For instance, ביום צרה occurs in Obad. 12 and in 2 Kgs 19.3 (//Isa. 37.3), but also in Prov. 25.19; Pss. 20.2; 50.15; 77.3; 86.7, among many other texts. Also ביום אידם is found in Deut. 32.35; 2 Sam. 22.19; Jer. 18.17; 46.21; Obad. 13; Ps. 18.19; Prov. 27.10; Job 21.30).

Of course, there are also a few cases like the idiom 'לאבת-X' (where X stands for a pronominal suffix) + שבע (niphal) which is found in Mic. 7.20 and appears in most of its occurrences in the Hebrew Bible in Deuteronomy–Kings. But still see Num. 11.12; 14.23 (cf. Exod. 32.13) and compare the size of the Deuteronomy–Kings corpus with Numbers. It should be stressed, however, that even if one grants for the sake of argument that the presence of the idiom in Mic. 7.20 reflects an awareness of its use in dtr material, it still does not mean that v. 20 is a

Leaving aside the issue of 'dependence'; that presupposes a direction and relative dates, it is possible (and probably heuristically correct) to assume that if two written texts show both a substantial number of potentially 'diagnostic' clusters of words in common, it *may be* that the two texts were interrelated in some way, even if the other features mentioned above are absent. Therefore, this study should address the issue of clusters and their possible meaning.

To open with a few methodological qualifications: The authors/ redactors wrote in biblical Hebrew, and they (as well as their rereadership) were conversant with the relevant religious literature and the literary (and theological) discourse(s) of their time. Thus one must not necessarily assume that every repetition of a single cluster must be the result of a conscious effort on the part of the authors/editors; such repetition may be due to the simple fact that the authors/redactors used biblical Hebrew and were surely able to activate linguistic expressions in their language according to grammar, genre, stylistic conventions and the general discourse (and world of knowledge) in which they lived.[37]

---

deuteronomistic verse, nor that it must have been written by a member of a particular dtr movement (as opposed to other movements) nor that its intended rereaders were supposed to relate the verse to Dtr texts or discourse particularly. Even a cursory analysis of the language of Mic. 7.20 shows (a) נתן אמת and נתן חסד occur only in Mic. 7.20 (the closest expressions to these are found in Josh. 2.12; Isa. 61.8; Pss. 115.1; Neh. 9.13); (b) אמת ליעקב is found in Mic. 7.20 and nowhere else in the Hebrew Bible, (c) חסד לאברהם occurs in Mic. 7.20 and nowhere else in the Hebrew Bible; and finally (d) the pair יעקב־אברהם (in that order) is very rare and appears elsewhere only once, in Isa. 41.8 (and cf. Isa. 21.22); and (e) ימי קדם is found besides Mic. 7.20 in 2 Kgs 19.25; Isa. 23.7; 37.26; 51.9; Jer. 46.26; Ps. 44.2; Lam. 1.7; 2.17 and is by no means a dtr expression. Significantly, the books of Micah, Zephaniah and Obadiah all contain numerous expressions that are unique to each of these books. As mentioned above it is important to weigh all the data and not only 'selected' items.

37. Of course, some of these conventions may have a long history and may appear in texts written in ancient Near Eastern languages other than Hebrew. For instance, the introductory phrase in Qoh. 1.12 is similar to the opening of several royal inscriptions (e.g. Kilamu[wa], Kil 1, Karatepe A I, 1 Mesha 1; on these issues see M.V. Fox, *Qohelet and his Contradictions* (JSOTSup, 71; Sheffield: JSOT Press, 1989), p. 174. This resemblance does *not* suggest that there ever was a Kilamu(wa)n (or the like) redaction of Qohelet, nor a specific influence of the language of the Mesha Inscription (or any other of the mentioned inscriptions) on Qohelet, nor even that the author of Qohelet had to be aware of any of these inscriptions in particular.

Therefore, whereas from a certain perspective one may correctly claim that most texts produced within a certain discourse show some degree of intertextuality, not much can be learned from that observation beyond the obvious fact that these people shared in the main a common language (which includes a common lexical register), symbolic system, literary repertoire and world of knowledge.[38] Most if not all of the examples discussed in sections 4c and 4d (and esp. in the relevant footnotes) can be explained in this way and do not require one to assume the existence of a particular social and intellectual group of writers distinct from all others, nor any hypothetical redactional history for any text.[39]

Thus our analysis of these additional clusters and idioms[40] should aim at potentially more rewarding conclusions. Since the issue at stake is whether a deuteronomistic group—which is known only by the written works attributed to it—redacted some prophetic books, the main questions are:

1. Is there convincing support for the proposal that the case of double occurrence was necessarily due to writers consciously copying or imitating a deuteronomistic written source at hand rather than by using the lexical repertoire that they possessed within their world of knowledge? (When one assesses this question one should take into account that

---

38. Significantly, most (if not all) of the biblical books that are discussed here were written at least in their final form in postmonarchic times and probably in Achaemenid Yehud. In any case, the number of literati who constituted both the authorship and rereadership of these books was severely limited, as was the capacity for developing significantly different literary repertoires and worlds of knowledge. I discussed these issues in Ben Zvi, 'The Urban Center of Jerusalem and the Development of the Literature of the Hebrew Bible', in W.G. Aufrecht *et al.* (eds.), *Aspects of Urbanism in Antiquity* (JSOTSup, 244; Sheffield: Sheffield Academic Press, 1997), pp. 194-209; and *idem, Micah*, pp. 260-67. On the possible implications of these considerations on the issues discussed in this paper, see esp. section 6 below.

39. Notice also that whereas the reference to פדה מבית עבדים in Mic. 6.4 may well be explained in terms of lexical items associated with the exodus myth (see below), and perhaps may reflect even some awareness of written representations of this myth in forms similar or identical to those in Deuteronomy, its presence does not require the hypothesis of a dtr redaction, any more than in similar instances of shared expressions with other texts (see above), nor does possible knowledge of a text included in the dtr corpus demand an explanation in terms of a dtr redaction (cf. with the case of Chronicles).

40. That is, additional to those already addressed in sections 4c and 4d.

people tend to associate certain lexical items with particular realms of discourse, and accordingly caution is required when two writers activate a similar set of terms in reference to similar events, stories, traditions and the like.[41])

2. Is there evidence that suggests that the text was written so as to draw the attention of the intended rereaders to a direct and interpretatively significant intertextuality between the text in the prophetic book and a particular section in one of the written works that are included in the standard dtr corpus, as opposed to simply assuming a rereadership that is aware of certain traditions and shares some basic theological tenets and a certain construction/(hi)story of their own past?[42]

If one accepts a relatively minimalist definition of a cluster as three (or more) words (not including particles) in close proximity,[43] then our analysis should deal with (a) whether such clusters appear in any of the three prophetic books discussed here (i.e. Micah, Zephaniah and Obadiah) and are also peculiar to, and widely found in the standard deuteronomistic corpus (regarding single occurrences, see above); (b) whether the presence of these shared clusters is more likely due to a process of copy or imitation of the dtr literature that was carried out by deuteronomistic groups than to any other literary process; and (c) whether the

---

41. To illustrate with a simple and contemporaneous example, it is not difficult to imagine a Jewish child today who has never read the Hebrew Bible (in any language), but who is required to write a composition for school in which the basic story of Passover is to be retold. Such a composition is likely to contain lexical terms that are not commonly activated by the child in other school compositions. Of course, the only thing that will be proved in this case is that this child accesses certain terms when she or he has to deal with certain topics. The situation would not be substantially different if a pastor, priest, rabbi or critical scholar is asked to retell the story of the exodus.

42. For instance, the tradition of the brotherhood of Esau and Jacob and their association with Edom and Israel is assumed to belong to the world of knowledge of the intended rereadership of the book of Obadiah and the exodus from Egypt to that of the book of Micah; the concept of YHWH as the God of Israel, the idea that wrongful behavior leads (or may lead) to divine punishment, and the particular role of Zion in the divine economy are all implied knowledge of the intended rereadership of Micah, Zephaniah and Obadiah.

43. Cf. R.A. Kugler, 'Prophets and Pan-deuteronomism', paper presented at the 1996 meeting of the Deuteronomistic History Section of the SBL, New Orleans (and included in this volume). Cf. A. Aejmelaus, 'Der Prophet als Klageliedsänger: Zur Funktion des Psalms Jes 63,7 – 64,11 in Tritojesaja', *ZAW* 107 (1995), pp. 31-50 (32).

intended rereadership of prophetic books is asked to understand their text in relation to a particular text in the standard dtr corpus rather than against their concepts and images within their general world of knowledge.

Before turning to the study of these questions it is worth stressing already that the analysis of some texts (e.g. Dan. 9)[44] may result in positive answers to some of these questions, but this is *not* the case in regard to Micah, Zephaniah and Obadiah. In fact, the task here is easier than expected, because the corpus of potential clusters to begin with is very reduced, as the studies of Kugler and others have shown.[45] In fact, Kugler's analysis concludes that none is present in Obadiah, and that a case can be made only for the superscriptions in Zephaniah and Micah.[46] Yet Kugler may be less cautious than usual here.[47]

For most scholars the crux of the matter in these cases seems not to be the reference to the written text of the book of Micah or Zephaniah as דבר ה׳ (i.e. YHWH's word).[48] After all Joel shows a title of the form דבר ה׳ אשר היה אל-X and is not considered an integral member of the proposed system of 'typical deuteronomistic' superscriptions that includes Hos. 1.1; Amos 1.1; Mic. 1.1; and Zeph. 1.1.[49] The truly crucial

44. See n. 31.

45. See Kugler, 'Prophets and Pan-deuteronomism'. Regarding Zephaniah one may consult also the quite extensive lists of 'parallel' expressions in M. Bolle, תרי עשר ב׳ עם פידוש דעה מקרא ספר צפניה) [Jerusalem: Mosad HaRab Kuk, 1970], pp. 7-9); significantly, none of these expressions points to a cluster peculiar to the dtr corpus. (Potentially relevant expressions in the book of Micah were discussed above.)

46. C.f. among others, Coggins, 'What Does "Deuteronomistic" Mean?', pp. 141-42.

47. Kugler has recently alerted me that he has changed his mind in this regard (personal communication).

48. דבר ה׳ is included in the title of these two books; it characterizes the ensuing text. On titles of prophetic books, and the importance of superscriptions, I have written elsewhere, see Ben Zvi, 'Studying Prophetic Texts', and *idem*, *Obadiah*, pp. 10-13. It is usually proposed that the title דבר ה׳ אשר היה אל-X belongs to one of the earliest stages of the redactional history of the book. See, for instance, Nogalski, *Literary Precursors*, pp. 127-28. But for a different approach, see H.W. Wolff, *Micah* (Minneapolis: Augsburg, 1990), pp. 33-34.

49. See Nogalski, *Literary Precursors*, pp. 76-78, 84-89, 127-28, 176-78, 181-87; cf. paper presented in the 1996 annual meeting of the seminar on 'The Formation of the Book of the Twelve' by A. Schart, 'The Combination of Hosea, Amos,

issue seems to be the temporal reference. To be sure, the super-scriptions instruct the intended rereadership of these books to approach them from a perspective that is temporally cued; that is, they are anchored in the circumstances that obtained at some time in the past of the rereadership as reconstructed/imagined by this rereadership.[50] The temporal references are presented here as usual in vague and general terms that stand in contrast to the more precise temporal references that tend to appear in books that ask their intended rereadership to associate them with the circumstances of monarchic Judah on the eve of its fall or in the period following it.[51] To be sure, there is nothing peculiar in organizing the past according to general regnal periods, particularly if no precise date is given. In fact, the precise expression in these super-scriptions, that is בימיX (X being the name of the ruler and accordingly, in relation to the monarchic period, the name of the king) is only to be expected (cf. Gen. 14.1; 26.1; Judg. 5.6; 1 Sam. 17.2; 1 Kgs 10.21; Isa. 1.1; 7.1; Jer. 1.2, 3; Zech. 14.5; Est. 1.1; Ezra 4.7; 1 Chron. 4.41, among others).[52] Neither the organization of time nor the particular ref-erence to it in terms of X בימי requires the assumption that Mic. 1.1 and Zeph. 1.1 were written by a deuteronomistic group or groups, nor that a deuteronomistic redaction has taken place. In fact, there is no strong reason to assume that these verses were added to the books at a later stage.[53]

Micah, and Zephaniah on a Single Scroll: Unifying Devices and Redactional Inten-tions'.

50. These superscriptions serve as textually inscribed, and very significant, interpretative keys for the community(ies) supposed to read and reread these books. (See Ben Zvi, 'Studying Prophetic Texts'; *idem, Micah; idem, Obadiah*, pp. 10-43.)

51. Cf. E.W. Conrad, 'The End of Prophecy and the Appearance of Angels/ Messenger in the Book of the Twelve', *JSOT* 73 (1997), pp. 65-79, and esp. pp. 67-69.

52. Significantly, these four books are not the only prophetic books whose superscription includes a temporal reference of this type (see Isa. 1.1 and cf. Jer. 1.2), nor are prophetic books the only books in which the intended rereadership is asked to understand the world of the text in relation to a period described at the very outset of the book as X בימי (see references above).

53. From the fact that these superscriptions do not display a syntagmatic rela-tionship to the ensuing text it does not follow that they are later additions. First, titles (as opposed to incipits) do not tend to show such a relationship (e.g. Obad. 1; Prov. 1.1), and second, lack of syntagmatic relationship per se is not a strong argu-ment for redactional character in any case. It is true that these superscriptions look at the prophetic characters as in the past of the rereading community, but this

It is to be granted, however, that these superscriptions assume and actually require the intended rereadership to activate their prior knowledge of the periods under discussion. Given that the books of Micah and Zephaniah (and Obadiah) are postmonarchic, it is likely that the world of knowledge of their rereaders included a construction of their past that either resembled or was based on that expressed and shaped by the books of Kings.[54] It is in this regard that one may say that both the

observation may serve as grounds for a redactional character only if one assumes that the books of Micah and Zephaniah were actually written by the historical prophets, which is at the very least a very questionable premise.

It is worth mentioning also that Mic. 1.1 show no synchronism between the kings of Judah and Israel (unlike Hos. 1.1, Amos 1.1, but like Isa. 1.1). If such a synchronism is considered a dtr feature, then it is not present here. (Zeph. 1.1 cannot show such a synchronism, because it associates the figure of Zephaniah with a time that follows the fall of the northern kingdom.) Moreover, if the exact choice of language is conducive to conclusions about the dtr character of Mic. 1.1 (and the related superscription), then one must take into account that (a) the name יחזקיה in reference to the king of Judah appears only in Hos. 1.1 and Mic. 1.1 (referring to another person in Ezra 2.16); and (b) the closely related form יחזקיהו, which is found in the temporal clause in Isa. 1.1, is the typical Chronicler's rendition of the name of the king consistently called חזקיהו/ in the book of Kings (except once, in 2 Kgs 20.10). (On these issues but from a different perspective, see Nogalski, *Literary Precursors*, p. 186.)

Finally, the proposed dtr emphasis on the positive figures of Hezekiah and Josiah in the books of Micah and Zephaniah is simply not present in the text, but is a secondary theoretical construction based on a particular reading of Hos. 1.1, Amos 1.1, Mic. 1.1 and Zeph. 1.1 in the light of the hypothesis of a dtr prophetic corpus comprising the relevant books and a proposed redaction history of the Book of the Twelve. Nowhere in the book of Micah is there a clear reference to Hezekiah (contrast to the book of Isaiah), nor is there any indication in the world of the text that YHWH's word (as presented by the text) is to be more associated with the period of Hezekiah than with those of Jotham and Ahaz. As for the book of Zephaniah, it is obvious that the circumstances that the text associates with the kingship of Josiah are not positive. In fact, the question of how this image of the period may square with that in Kings (and Chronicles) has been the focus of much debate (for one type of proposal, see J.J.M. Roberts, *Nahum, Habakkuk and Zephaniah* [OTL; Louisville, KY: Westminster/John Knox Press, 1991], p. 163; and see the discussion in A. Berlin, *Zephaniah* (AB, 25A; New York: Doubleday, 1994), pp. 43-47, 68-69). For a different approach, see, for instance, Nogalski, *Literary Precursors*, p. 87; and Schart, 'Combination'.

54. The writer(s) of Obadiah likely knew either the book of Kings or sections thereof. The writer(s) and rereadership of this book are also aware of the construction of a time in the past of the community that is associated with the period of the

writers of these books and their rereadership were likely influenced by texts included in the deuteronomistic corpus, but so were those of Chronicles and Ruth (cf. Acts 7, Stephen's speech). In other words, it is likely that their world of knowledge included a version of their own (hi)story about themselves in terms similar to those in Deuteronomy–Kings. This, of course, does not mean that either the writers or the primary rereaders for whom these texts were written had to be members of a deuteronomistic group (cf. the case of Chronicles and Ruth).

In sum, these superscriptions do not require one to hypothesize deuteronomistic redactor(s). They alert the intended rereadership of their prophetic books to reread them in a way that is informed by their construction of the past. It is likely that this image of the past was at least partially based on, or that it reflected texts in Deuteronomy–Kings.[55] Still it is important to recognize that the 'informed' rereading required by the superscription leads to the creation of a *tapestry of images* of the past (rather than simply mirroring the 'deuteronomistic' portrayal in Kings).[56] This tapestry involves the interweaving of the images of the past evoked by the prophetic book itself and those suggested by other texts in the world of knowledge of the rereadership, including (or perhaps mainly including) those associated with Deuteronomy–Kings. In any case, from these considerations, it does not follow that the mentioned prophetic books underwent a dtr redaction, nor that the superscription or its temporal clause is a redactional addition written by a member of a 'deuteronomistic movement' or someone who was active in a separate 'deuteronomistic group'.

5. *A Common Theology?*

The discussion above has demonstrated that (1) the language of the books of Micah, Zephaniah and Obadiah does not support the idea that they were composed or redacted by members of a deuteronomistic groups or of a dtr movement (which is characterized by the style of its written works; on this see below); and (2) the texts were not written so as to convey a sense of textual coherence or particular affinity with the

---

Judges. See Ben Zvi, *Obadiah,* pp. 17-19, 220-21, 223-29.

55. I explicitly advanced this claim regarding the books of Obadiah, Jonah, Zephaniah and Micah (see, for instance, Ben Zvi, *Obadiah*, pp. 14-19).

56. For significant differences in the portrayal of the past, see above.

works included in Deuteronomy–Kings.[57]

Yet the hypothesis of a dtr redaction of prophetic books is also based on claims of a shared theological approach. Redactions and dating based only on ideas are questionable because it is a well-known fact that one may find similar (or at least, comparable) ideas at different times. It may be argued, however, that if there is an unequivocal, one to one relationship between the theology of the dtr corpus and that of the prophetic books, or sections thereof, one could advance the claim of a redactional affliation even if it is not supported by the language of the prophetic text.

But there is no such relationship. To begin with, the basic theological ideas that are expressed in the prophetic books and that can be correlated with similar or identical positions in the dtr corpus are not unique to the latter. This is clearly the case regarding the protection of the rights of the powerless in society and the assumption that the actions of people carry consequences and that a system of retribution is in place (though not consistently implemented).[58] It is also true in regard to the unique role of Zion/Jerusalem in the divine economy, the explanation of the fall of Jerusalem in terms of wrongdoing (mainly of the monarchic elite), the explanation of the fall of Samaria in terms of its sinful behavior, along with comparisons between the northern kingdom/Samaria and Judah/Jerusalem, as well as the basic repertoire of sinful behavior (i.e. wrongful worship, disregard for the rights of the powerless, the violence of the ruling elite and the like). Whereas all of the

57. By 'particular affinity' I mean an affinity that is stronger with the works in Deuteronomy–Kings than with other biblical corpora.

58. The dtr history does not implement or communicate a consistent (and simplistic) system of reward and punishment. For instance, no wrong was assigned to Josiah, and yet not only was he killed by Necho, but Judah lost—within the world of the narrative—the independence that it achieved in the days of Hezekiah. Chronicles 'solves' this problem, but also does not communicate a consistent (and simplistic) system. (I discussed this issue in Ben Zvi, 'A Sense of Proportion: An Aspect of the Theology of the Chronicler', *SJOT* 9 [1995], pp. 37-51.) As for Proverbs, see, for instance, Prov. 16.19; 28.6; and regarding wisdom literature in general, see Fox, *Qohelet*, pp. 132-50. The simplistic and naive system of recompense that is sometime associated with Dtr 'conventional wisdom' literature or Chronicles is more of a caricature—and a 'helpful', rhetorical strawman—based on a reading of particular units within books that does not take into account that these units are integral to the larger discursive frame (/space) created within each of these books.

references to them in prophetic literature are consistent with what is usually characterized as dtr theology,[59] none of them requires the acceptance of a separate and distinctive deuteronomistic theology that could not be shared by many other literati within whom one is to locate both authorship and rereadership of prophetic books such as Micah, Zephaniah and Obadiah, and particularly (but not exclusively) so in the postmonarchic communities in which they were likely composed.[60] Albertz's position that all (official) Yhwhistic theology(ies) was (were) influenced by the deuteronomistic thought in the time that followed the fall of the monarchy reflects the same evidence, though from a different perspective.[61]

Moreover, whereas theological ideas that are commonly expressed in dtr language within the standard dtr corpus appear elsewhere, there is no single, consistent and encompassing deuteronomistic theology. In fact, to speak of '*the* deuteronomistic theology' is misleading. Thus, for instance, while the dtr corpus points to the 'choice of the people' as an important theological construct (Deut. 30.19; cf. Josh. 24.15-16, 22), Deut. 30.6 points to a glorious future in which YHWH will take away the possibility of choice, so that people will be ('biologically') conditioned to 'love' YHWH (cf. Jer. 31.31-34).[62] Von Rad, among others,

---

59. This includes, of course, passages such as Zeph. 1.8-9 (which shows no clear deuteronomic/dtr language; cf. Ben Zvi, *Zephaniah*, pp. 278-82) and Mic. 1.7 (which again as a whole is not written so as directly to evoke the style of Deuteronomy or Kings, despite the vague resemblance of a section of it with a portion of Deut. 7.25).

60. Notice that the three books refer to the exile and dispersion, and express hope for restoration. The book of Micah also contains an explicit reference to Babylon (Mic 4.10; which there is no reason to 'emend', unless one assumes beforehand that the text *must* have been composed in the eighth century BCE) and implies the 'loss of the land', the hope of a new beginning such as the one under Joshua (see Mic. 2.4-5); the perspective of the speakers in book of Obadiah is from the time after the destruction of Jerusalem; and on the book of Zephaniah I have written at length in Ben Zvi, *Zephaniah*. I also discussed some general methodological issues that have bearing on these questions in Ben Zvi, 'Studying Prophetic Texts'.

61. See Albertz, *History of Israelite Religion*, II, p. 382, and *passim*. Whether one agrees or disagrees with Albertz's reconstruction of the intellectual history of the monarchic period, it has no bearing on his observation that 'dtr theological thought' is ubiquitous at that period.

62. See M.Z. Brettler, 'Predestination in Deuteronomy 30.1-10', which appears in this volume.

observed differences in the theology (and the actual 'method of presentation') between Kings and Judges, and Albertz refers to 'the Deuteronomists of the time of the exile and the early post-exilic period' as comprised of 'very different groupings', and stresses the differences between JerD and those reworking the historical traditions.[63] Römer distinguishes between Jer Dtr1 and Jer Dtr2,[64] and two or three different groups of deuteronomists are often associated with the (so-called) Deuteronomistic History (Dtr1 and Dtr2; DtrG, DtrP and DtrN). In fact, if one accepts that the production of texts in dtr style took place for likely a few centuries, then one has to expect some significant differences.

The implications of the last considerations go beyond rejecting the claim that members of the dtr movement redacted or composed prophetic books such as Micah or Zephaniah. If (1) there was not one deuteronomistic theology; (2) much of what is usually considered to be consistent with deuteronomistic theology is in fact shared by many of the religious thinkers in postmonarchic Israel (even if they did not necessarily express or communicate it in dtr language);[65] (3) there is no reference in the Hebrew Bible to the existence of a multi-generational group of literati that kept itself separate from other groups and that can be associated with the proposed social entity called 'the deuteronomistic movement'; and (4) no particular sociopolitical objective can be associated with this proposed movement through all the centuries of its claimed existence, then it follows that (5) the only potential support for the proposal that there was a separate social group, namely, the deuteronomistic 'movement' to whom one may ascribe postmonarchic texts (such as the books of Micah, Zephaniah and Obadiah as well as Deuteronomy and Kings) is the presence of some form of shared style—notwithstanding the differences that exist within the dtr corpus—or better, the presence of some conveyed sense of textual coherence or affinity within the literary corpus usually assigned to the dtr movement. But the mentioned coherence or affinity points only to a

---

63. Albertz, *History of Israelite Religion*, II, pp. 382-83, and *passim*; *idem*, 'Le milieu des deutéronomistes', in de Pury, Römer and Macchi *et al.* (eds.), *Israël construit son histoire*, pp. 377-407.

64. See Römer, 'Y a-t-il une rédaction deutéronomiste dans le livre de Jérémie?', pp. 419-41.

65. On these and related issues, see Knauf, ' "L'historiographie deutéronomiste" (DTRG) existe-t-elle?', p. 410.

rhetorical stance taken by the implied author of these books; literary style by itself does not provide sufficient grounds to postulate the historical existence of a separate 'movement' for generations.[66]

The discussion to this point has led to 'negative' assessments such as:

(a)   the redactional models and the textual reconstructions that are necessary to claim that there was a dtr redaction of books such as Micah and Zephaniah are questionable, hypothetical and tend to fall into circular thinking by 'proving' what is assumed from the outset;

(b)   In any case, the language of the books of Micah, Zephaniah and Obadiah supports neither the idea that they were redacted (or composed) by members of the deuteronomistic movement (or that there was a dtr redaction) nor the position that these books were written so that their rereaders would associate them particularly and uniquely with those included in the proposed dtr corpus.

(c)   Considerations based on the theology(ies) communicated by these prophetic books and by that of the dtr corpus provide no convincing basis for positing that these books were redacted (or authored) by deuteronomistic groups or by 'the deuteronomistic movement'.

(d)   There is no convincing evidence that there ever was a separate social entity, 'the deuteronomistic movement' to whom one may ascribe the standard and postmonarchic dtr-corpus (i.e. Deuteronomy–Kings + Dtr Jeremiah), not to say the prophetic books discussed here.[67]

The observation regarding style in the prophetic books and its use for communicating a sense of textual coherence, however, opens the door to the development of a 'positive' approach.

66. Cf. N. Lohfink, 'Gab es eine deuteronomistiche Bewegung?', in W. Gross (ed.), *Jeremia und die 'deuteronomische Bewegung'* (BBB, 98; Weinheim: Beltz Athenäum, 1995), pp. 313-82; Knauf, ' "L'historiographie deutéronomiste" (DTRG) existe-t-elle?'; Coggins, 'What Does 'Deuteronomistic" Mean?', p. 143.

67. Whether there was a deuteronomistic movement that supported Josiah's reform in his days depends much upon one's reconstruction of the historical events during Josiah's reign. In any case, the dtr corpus cannot be assigned to that group, because both the books included in the standard dtr corpus and the books of Micah, Zephaniah and Obadiah postdate not only only the reign of Josiah but also 586 BCE. See above.

6. *The Significance of the Presence and Absence of Dtr Style or from 'Movement' to Associations and Messages Conveyed to an Intended Readership*[68]

Whereas the conspicuous presence of deuteronomistic phraseology in Joshua–Kings does not point to an independent and distinctive 'deuteronomistic movement', it clearly links together the books from Joshua to Kings—despite the different ways in which these deuteronomistic elements appear in each of these books— but also, and more importantly, it closely binds them to Deuteronomy. In fact, the entire Deuteronomistic History hypothesis is based on that sense of strong coherence.[69]

Yet to say that these books are deuteronomistic is to say that they are written so as to convey a 'Mosaic' flavor; their intended rereaders are reminded by textually inscribed markers that the texts in front of them are in the tradition of Moses who is the main character (and speaker) in Deuteronomy.

Of course, Moses is also the anchor that keeps Exodus–Deuteronomy together, and indirectly the entire Pentateuch.[70] This is the same Moses with whom the concept of the divine Torah is associated (cf. Deut. 4.4; 33.4; Josh. 7; 8.31, 32; 23.6; 1 Kgs 2.3; 2 Kgs 14.6; 23.25; Mal. 3.22; Ezra 3.2; 7.6; Neh. 8.1; 2 Chron. 23.18; 25.4; 30.16; 34.14). It is reasonable to assume that if a series of books is written so as to be read as 'Mosaic-like', then it connotes—among other things—a claim to authority and social legitimacy; that is, it attempts to spread upon itself some of the legitimacy and the authority of the Mosaic tradition. Such a claim is consistent with the ubiquitous (explicit and implicit) calls to observe and learn the Torah of Moses that characterize the dtr historical narratives as a whole, just as the Pentateuch as a whole.

If so, it is the *absence* of dtr phraseology in the prophetic books that

---

68. Some of the issues discussed here were advanced in Ben Zvi, 'Looking at the Primary (Hi)Story and the Prophetic Books as Literary/Theological Units within the Frame of the Early Second Temple: Some Considerations', *SJOT* 12 (1998), pp. 26-43.

69. Needless to say, this hypothesis is based on the mentioned textual coherence per se, but also on the implications that have been argued about actual authorship— as opposed to the authorial voice suggested by the text—on the grounds of this sense of strong, textual coherence.

70. I discussed the way in which Genesis is linked to Exodus–Deuteronomy, in my paper 'Looking'.

is most noteworthy, and the more so since it is likely that in their present form, at least, both dtr writings and the mentioned prophetic books are to be associated with (more or less) the same general period and social group (i.e. the postmonarchic, Jerusalem-centered literati).[71] It is reasonable to assume that this absence of dtr language is not accidental and that it conveys to the intended rereaders that these texts are not written in the 'Mosaic voice' but in that of other prophets (i.e. Micah, Zephaniah, and Obadiah). Each of these prophets was 'minor' to Moses,[72] but each had his own voice, and a text characterized as דבר ה' was associated with each of them. (On דבר הי and divine Torah, see Isa. 2.3; Mic. 4.2; cf. Isa. 1.10 and Zech. 7.12). This position is strongly supported by the pervading tendency to show a Zephanianic flavor in the book of Zephaniah, an Obadianic in Obadiah, and Mican in Micah, even in cases in which one can reasonably maintain that the writers of these books used some written sources.[73] This position is also consistent with the presence of textually inscribed markers that request the intended rereadership of each of the 12 prophetic books that were later included in the Twelve to understand each prophetic character and each prophetic book as clearly distinct from the others.[74]

These tendencies are all the more remarkable because it is not only that these texts (in their present form) existed within relatively similar social and cultural backgrounds, but also because they come from the very modest number of the literati who comprised both the authorship and primary rereadership of the biblical books that (in their present form) are usually assigned to the postmonarchic period. In other words, if there was no deuteronomistic (or Zephaianic, Mican, Obadianic, Isaianic and the like for the sake of the case) movement, school or socially separate group,[75] then much effort had to be extended not only to shape these books each according to its distinctive style (and language), but to avoid the use of deuteronomistic expressions in these books.[76] The fact that one finds even some degree of synchronic lin-

---

71. See Ben Zvi, 'The Urban Center'; cf. Ben Zvi, *Obadiah*, pp. 260-67.

72. See Num. 12.6-8; Deut. 34.10 and cf. Deut. 18.15.

73. See Ben Zvi, *Zephaniah*, pp. 197-205; *idem*, *Obadiah*, pp. 99-114; *idem*, *Micah*.

74. See Ben Zvi, 'Twelve Prophetic Books', esp. pp. 149-56.

75. See Ben Zvi, 'The Urban Center'.

76. Of course, one may wonder why the book of Jeremiah is so different, for surely there is dtr language there. It is worth stressing, however, that even the

guistic variation (cf. Haggai with Isaiah 40–66/56–66; see also Ezekiel) among the prophetic books associated with more or less the same general period is another testimony to that (literary and theological) effort.[77]

Yet, if this is the case, some overriding ideas (some of which are usually characterized as dtr), some basic traditions and some understandings of the past are bound to be expressed in more than one of the books written (or redacted) at that time. After all, if these texts are associated with a similar cultural space that is produced—at least in

'sermons' in Jeremiah (i.e. the often-called source 'C') contain a very substantial number of 'deuteronomic clichés' that either never or rarely occur in Deuteronomy and/or Joshua-Kings (see Weinfeld, *Deuteronomy*, pp. 352-54). So even when the book of Jeremiah is written so as to convey to its (re)readers a clear association between this book and Deuteronomy and the collection Joshua–Kings, it also communicates an individual characterization of the main personage in the book, Jeremiah. The clearly evoked association between Jeremiah and Kings, which is emphasized by the similarities between 2 Kgs 25 and Jer. 52 (cf. also 2 Kgs 25.1-12, 23-24 and Jer. 39.1-10; 40.7-9), indicates that some form of intertextual (re)reading of Jeremiah and Kings was suggested by the choice of language and text in Jeremiah. This in turn, and from a larger perspective, may be seen as suggesting a link between the collections that were later called 'Former' and 'Latter Prophets', or may be related to the characterization of Jeremiah as a prophet 'like Moses'. (Cf. C.R. Seitz, 'The Prophet Moses and the Canonical Shape of Jeremiah', *ZAW* 101 [1989], pp. 3-27; R.E. Clements, 'Jeremiah 1–25 and the Deuteronomistic History', in A.G. Auld [ed.], *Understanding Poets and Prophets: Essays in Honour of George Wishart Anderson* [JSOTSup, 152; Sheffield: Sheffield Academic Press, 1993], pp. 94-113). These issues are, of course, beyond the purview of the essay. It is worth stressing, however, that the unique (among the prophetic books) 'Jeremianic' feature of showing a significant number dtr expressions is found also in the pluses of the edition II (MT) over the edition I (the Hebrew Vorlage of LXX Jeremiah; see E. Tov, 'The Literary History of the Book of Jeremiah in the Light of its Textual History', in J.H. Tigay [ed.], *Empirical Models for Biblical Criticism* [Philadelphia: University of Pennsylvania Press, 1985], pp. 211-37 [220, 233]). From this observation it does not follow that editor II was a member of the deuteronomistic movement/school. Rather, it could be that this editor was aware that the presence of deuteronomistic expressions was one of the characteristic features of the book of Jeremiah (and of the Jeremianic voice created by the book) and, edited accordingly. Had the same editor reworked another prophetic book, it is unlikely that deuteronomistic expressions would have been used. (Compare this approach with Tov, 'Literary History', p. 220).

77. In this regard, whether this (more or less) synchronic linguistic variation was based on some diachronic linguistic variation or not is immaterial.

part—by a small number of postmonarchic literati, then some degree of intertextuality (if defined in these terms) is to be expected.[78] It is perhaps in this light that some of the textual relations between the books of Micah, Zephaniah and Obadiah and Deuteronomy–Kings, as well as those between these prophetic books and other prophetic books, Psalms and Proverbs, may be studied.[79]

78. An issue that I have addressed among others in 'Twelve Prophetic Books', 'The Urban Center' and 'Inclusion in and Exclusion from Israel as Conveyed by the Use of the Term "Israel" in Postmonarchic Biblical Texts', in S.W. Holloway and L.K. Handy (eds.), *The Pitcher Is Broken: Memorial Essays for Gosta W. Ahlström* (JSOTSup, 190; Sheffield: Sheffield Academic Press, 1995), pp. 95-149.

79. My reference to the 'tapestry' of images of the past (see above), and to multivocality among and within texts in some of the works mentioned in the preceding footnote, may suggest some of the ways in which these issues may be addressed.

My thanks are due to Professor Robert A. Kugler (Gonzaga University) for reading and commenting on a draft of this paper.

POSTSCRIPT:
THE LAWS OF PHYSICS AND PAN-DEUTERONOMISM

Steven L. McKenzie

The book of Deuteronomy is sometimes referred to as the 'Archi-medean point' of Pentateuchal criticism.[1] Archimedes (third century BCE), who studied the properties of levers, claimed to be able to move the world if given the proper vantage point. For biblical scholars since the time of de Wette, Deuteronomy has been the fulcrum upon which critical study of the Pentateuch swings.[2] This is so first because Deuteronomy is the only one of the Pentateuchal sources that can be securely dated on internal grounds; it is widely identified in its earliest form ('*Ur*-deuteronomy') with the 'book of the law' found under King Josiah in the late seventh century BCE (2 Kgs 22.8). Despite, on the one hand, efforts to derive *Ur*-deuteronomy from an earlier (e.g. Hezekian) period and, on the other hand, indications that the 'book finding' in 2 Kings 22 may be fictional, there remain good reasons for linking Deuteronomy with Josiah.[3] These are well known and need not be laid out in detail

---

1. For example, E. Otto, 'Das Deuteronomium als archimedischer Punkt der Pentateuchkritik auf dem Wege zu einer Neubegründung der de Wette'schen Hypothese', in M. Vervenne and J. Lust (eds.), *Deuteronomy and Deuteronomic Literature: Festschrift C.H.W. Brekelmans* (BETL, 133; Leuven: Leuven University Press, 1997), pp. 321-39, and M. Weinfeld, *Deuteronomy 1–11: A New Translation with Introduction and Commentary* (AB, 5; New York: Doubleday, 1991), p. 16; *idem*, 'Deuteronomy, Book of', *ABD*, II, p. 174.

2. W.M.L. de Wette, *Dissertatio critico-exegetica qua Deuteronomium a prioribus Pentateuchi libris diversum, alius cuiusdam recentioris auctoris opus esse monstratur* (Jena, 1805).

3. A good overview of the consensus positions on critical issues in Deuteronomy is T. Römer, 'The Book of Deuteronomy', in S.L. McKenzie and M.P. Graham (eds.), *The History of Israel's Traditions: The Heritage of Martin Noth* (JSOTSup, 182; Sheffield: Sheffield Academic Press, 1994), pp. 178-212. Römer points out here and in a later article ('Transformations in Deuteronomistic Biblical

here.[4] The second aspect of Deuteronomy upon which Pentateuchal criticism depends is its doctrine of cultic centralization—the proscription of local country shrines in favor of the temple in Jerusalem as the only site where worship was allowed. The documentary sources behind the Pentateuch are dated before or after Deuteronomy depending on whether they presume this rule of centralization.

If scholarship since de Wette saw Deuteronomy as the key to dating the Pentateuch, scholarship since Noth has increased both the role assigned to the book and its sphere of influence. Deuteronomy has been recognized as the key to the formation of the Hebrew Bible as a whole. In terms of physics, a better point of comparison than Archimedes is Newton: an object at rest will remain at rest until acted upon by an outside force; and conversely an object in motion will remain in motion until acted upon by an outside force. Deuteronomy was the force that got the ball of the Hebrew Bible rolling.

The immediate course of Deuteronomy's trajectory is relatively easy to chart and widely recognized by most biblical scholars. Its direct heir was the Deuteronomistic Historian, who enlarged Josiah's law book and set it at the head of his theological history (or historical theology) of Israel. Thus, I continue to subscribe to Noth's theory of a Deuteronomistic History despite recent objections as noted by Auld's article. With

Historiography: On Book-Finding and Other Literary Strategies', *ZAW* 109 [1997], pp. 1-11; see also B.J. Diebner, B.J. Nauerth and C. Nauerth, 'Die Inventio des ספר התורה in 2 Kön 22: Struktur, Intention und Function von Auffindungslegenden', *DBAT* 18 [1984], pp. 95-118) that book finding was a literary and historical motif in the ancient world for justifying social and religious change. Hence, the 'law book' may have been written to legitimate Josiah's reforms. This seems more likely than the possibility that the reformers just happened upon a book that exactly suited their needs, as R.E. Clements (*Deuteronomy* [OTG; Sheffield: JSOT Press, 1989], p. 71) observed. Nevertheless, the connection with Josiah's reign is probably not entirely fictional. It seems unlikely that Dtr would invent the story that a document as important as he makes the law out to be—the fundamental guide for Israel and the grounds upon which its kings are evaluated—existed in a single copy that disappeared for an undetermined length of time and was therefore not available for consultation until it suddenly resurfaced under Josiah. On this argument see E.W. Nicholson, *Deuteronomy and Tradition* (Philadelphia: Fortress Press, 1967), pp. 6-7.

4. For detailed discussions of the correlations between Deuteronomy and Josiah consult the standard commentaries and the works of Römer, Clements and Nicholson, already cited, as well as H.-D. Preuss (*Deuteronomium* [EF, 164; Darmstadt: Wissenschaftliche Buchgesellschaft, 1982]).

Noth, I also prefer the view that a single historian, Dtr, writing in the exile, was responsible for the History. To be sure, his History was supplemented, sometimes at length, at a number of places before it came into its 'final form'. But I am not convinced that there is sufficient evidence to indicate systematic editing by any subsequent 'Dtrs' in some kind of Deuteronomistic 'school' or 'movement'. Here I share the reservations expressed by Coggins and Lohfink.[5] Indeed, while *Ur*-deuteronomy may represent an exception in that it appears to reflect the concerns of a broad-based coalition of upper-class groups,[6] albeit one that likely dissipated quickly, literary works are not usually written by committees. That later writers responsible for additions to the Deuteronomistic History could and did copy its language is attributable to the influence of Deuteronomy and Dtr on the literary tradition behind the Hebrew Bible and does not require the postulation of a multi-generational school, circle or movement of tradents.

Most scholars would agree that the Former Prophets, either as a whole or as separate entities, passed through the hands of one or more 'Deuteronomists'. Auld tries to trace the stream of influence in the opposite direction, but I think he would admit that he is swimming against the current. Nicholson's statement is representative and offers a helpful definition:[7]

> The Deuteronomistic history represents the work of a circle who were the direct descendants of the authors of the book of Deuteronomy and who, working in Jerusalem, adopted various aspects of the Jerusalem traditions and re-interpreted them on the basis of their own specific traditions. In this they carried further what had already been done on a lesser scale by the authors of Deuteronomy itself who, as we have seen, adopted and modified certain aspects of the Jerusalem traditions. The book of Deutronomy and the Deuteronomistic history must therefore be

5.   Doubts about a 'school' of Deuteronomists have also been voiced by R.E. Freedman, 'The Deuteronomistic School', in A.B. Beck *et al.* (eds.), *Fortunate the Eyes that See: Essays in Honor of David Noel Freedman in Celebration of his Seventieth Birthday* (Grand Rapids: Eerdmans, 1995), pp. 70-80.

6.   See R. Albertz, *A History of Israelite Religion in the Old Testament Period.* I. *From the Beginnings to the End of the Monarchy* (OTL; Louisville, KY: Westminster/John Knox Press, 1994), pp. 201-206. Cf. also the discussions of this matter in Clements, *Deuteronomy*, pp. 76-79, and P. Dutcher-Walls, 'The Social Location of the Deuteronomists: A Sociological Study of Factional Politics in Late Pre-Exilic Judah', *JSOT* 52 (1991), pp. 77-94.

7.   Nicholson, *Deuteronomy*, p. 113.

seen as representing two separate phases in the history of the traditions upon which both are ultimately based.

It is not easy, of course, to distinguish the content of *Ur*-deuteronomy from later editing, as Brettler's article in this volume indicates. But at least in its Deuteronomistic form, the enormous impact of the book of Deuteronomy is clear from a brief survey of the ideological items that it either introduced or enhanced. The doctrine of centralization had far-reaching practical results for daily life, both religious and secular.[8] Deuteronomy's stress on the exclusive worship of one Yahweh went hand in hand with centralization and represented an incipient, practical monotheism that was developed further by later writers in the Hebrew Bible.[9] The 'name theology' of Deuteronomy and the Deuteronomistic History allowed Yahweh to be imminent in the temple while at the same time asserting his transcendence (cf. 1 Kgs 8.27).[10] The implications were enormous. It opened the way to thinking of God as a spiritual entity rather than a corporeal one, so that any attempt to depict God was ludicrous and demeaning (as expounded in the later addition in Deut. 4.1-40). This in turn led to an emphasis on the interior thoughts and attitudes of humans in their dealings with the divine; Yahweh perceived the musings of the 'heart' (Deut. 5.21; 7.17; 8.11-20; 9.4-5; 10.12-13; 11.13, 18; 15.7, 10; 26.16). Ironically, this concept of God and divine–human intercourse facilitated the transition from temple to synagogue in the exile and beyond when sacrifice at the temple was no longer available, but Yahweh still heard prayers from his scattered people (1 Kgs 8). Thus the theology of Deuteronomy (at least in its Deuteronomistic form) was crucial for the survival of Judaism.

Indeed, the notion of 'Israel' as an ethnic, national and religious

8.   B.M. Levinson (*Deuteronomy and the Hermeneutics of Legal Innovation* [New York: Oxford University Press, 1997]) does a good job of showing the far-reaching effects of Deuteronomy's program, although his assumption that the author(s) of Deuteronomy worked directly from older texts preserved in Exodus (specifically, Exod. 20.24 behind Deut. 12) is unproven and may be unwarranted.

9.   Cf. G. Braulik, 'Deuteronomy and the Birth of Monotheism', in *idem*, *The Theology of Deuteronomy: Collected Essays of Georg Braulik, O.S.B.* (Dallas: BIBAL, 1994), pp. 99-130.

10.   See G. von Rad, *Studies in Deuteronomy* (trans. D.M. Stalker; SBT, 9; Chicago: Henry Regnery, 1953), pp. 37-44; S.D. McBride, 'The Deuteronomic Name Theology' (PhD dissertation, Harvard University, 1969); and T.N.D. Mettinger, *The Dethronement of Sabaoth: Studies in the Shem and Kabod Theologies* (Lund: C.W.K. Gleerup, 1982), pp. 38-79.

entity may be attributed to Deuteronomy. In the wake of the events of 721 and 586, Deuteronomy and the Deuteronomistic History, respectively, reflect an ongoing struggle with self-identity, which they find in the concept of election. Yahweh, Lord of all creation, chose[11] the ancestors of Israel at the exodus[12] (7.6-8; 10.14-17; 14.2) as his 'special property' (s^{e}gûllâ, Deut. 7.6; 14.2; 26.18; cf. Exod. 19.5; Ps 135.4).[13] The relationship with Israel is expressed in terms of the covenant, which, though not original with Deuteronomy, receives its fullest development there.[14] The covenant on the plains of Moab is a renewal of the one at Horeb, consisting of the Decalogue (5.1-21; cf. 4.13), which probably originated with Deuteronomy.[15] The book's covenant

11. Deuteronomy first expressed the notion that Yahweh had chosen (*bāḥar*) Israel, although the idea that Yahweh was Israel's God was, of course, much older. Cf. G. von Rad, *Das Gottesvolk im Deuteronomium* (BWANT, 47; Stuttgart: W. Kohlhammer, 1929), p. 28; repr. in *idem*, *Gesammelte Studien zum Alten Testament*, II (TBü, 48; Munich: Chr. Kaiser Verlag, 1973), pp. 9-108; T.C. Vriezen, *Die Erwählung Israels nach dem Alten Testament* (ATANT, 24; Zürich: Zwingli-Verlag, 1953), p. 47; G.E. Mendenhall, 'Election', *IDB*, II, pp. 76-77; R.E. Clements, 'Deuteronomy and the Jerusalem Cult Tradition', *VT* 15 (1965), pp. 300-12 (305-307); L. Perlitt, *Bundestheologie im Alten Testament* (WMANT, 36; Neukirchen–Vluyn: Neukirchener Verlag, 1969), p. 57; R. Rendtorff, 'Die Erwählung Israels als Thema der deuteronomischen Theologie', in J. Jeremias and L. Perlitt (eds.), *Die Botschaft und die Boten: Festschrift für Hans Walter Wolff zum 70. Geburtstag* (Neukirchen–Vluyn: Neukirchener Verlag, 1981), pp. 75-86.

12. T. Römer (*Israels Väter: Untersuchungen zur Väterthematik im Deuteronomium und in der deuteronomistischen Tradition* [OBO, 99; Freiburg: Universitätsverlag; Göttingen: Vandenhoeck & Ruprecht, 1990]) has convincingly argued that the ancestors to whom Deut. 7.8; 10.15 and other passages in Deuteronomy refer are the exodus generation and that the identification of these ancestors as the patriarchs, Abraham, Isaac and Jacob in verses like 9.5 is the result of later editing.

13. On s^{e}gûllâ see Weinfeld, *Deuteronomy 1–11*, pp. 62, 368.

14. The two references to Yahweh's covenant with Israel in Hosea (6.7; 8.1) are questioned by Perlitt (*Bundestheologie*, pp. 139-52). But E.W. Nicholson (*God and his People: Covenant and Theology in the Old Testament* [Oxford: Clarendon Press, 1986], pp. 179-88) argues for both verses as genuinely Hoseanic.

15. The literature is too extensive to cite. See esp. F.-L. Hossfeld, *Der Decalog: Seine späten Fassungen, die originale Komposition und seine Vorstufen* (OBO, 45; Friburg: Universitätsverlag, 1982). The version of the Decalogue in Exod. 20.1-17 is widely recognized as an insertion, while Deut. 5.6-21 is perfectly suited to its context. Both versions attest Deuteronomic concerns and language. See the list in Weinfeld, *Deuteronomy 1–11*, p. 243, who refers to these as 'phrases that look

theology was a product of the time in which it was written. By means of curses partly borrowed from Assyrian vassal treaties it made Israel's tenure on the land contingent on loyalty to Yahweh and obedience to his law. Israel's fall to Assyria and later Judah's to Babylonia were the consequences of violating the covenant.

Considering the obvious importance of the foregoing set of ideas for the Bible as a whole it is apparent that Deuteronomy, especially in its Deuteronomistic elaboration, exercised a considerable influence on the formation of Hebrew Scripture. Its influence on the literati may have been enhanced by its having been composed by a coalition of upper-class groups (prophets, priests, sages, scribes, members of the royal court), as suggested earlier. One could add the notion of Scripture to the list. The idea behind Deuteronomy—namely that of a unique, holy, authoritative work containing the comprehensive divine law[16]—is the idea of Scripture.

Deuteronomy's demand for adherence to its instruction led to Judaism and subsequently Christianity (and following the same principle even later, Islam) being 'religions of the book'. It is ironic that the book that forbade adding to the divine command (Deut. 4.2; 13.1) should spark such a process. But that is apparently exactly what happened with Deuteronomy. In Newton's terms, it was the outside force that began the process of composition that eventuated in the Scripture of the Hebrew Bible.

The observation of Deuteronomy's and the Deuteronomistic History's influence on the formation of the Hebrew Bible, however, is not tantamount to pan-Deuteronomism. With the exception of Jeremiah (cf. the article by Römer but also the one by Kugler in this volume) the evidence for Deuteronomistic redaction of other biblical books is sparse and probably better explained otherwise. The difference between Deuteronomic/Deuteronomistic influence and pan-Deuteronomism is illustrated by continuing to trace the process of composition set in motion by Deuteronomy in the Tetrateuch and the book of Chronicles.

Deuteronomic' but argues unconvincingly that they indicate the northern, not Deuteronomic, provenance of the Decalogue

16. This idea is explicit in the final form of Deuteronomy (Deut. 30.10; 31.26) and in the story in 2 Kgs 22–23 and was likely implicit in *Ur*-deuteronomy. 'The term "Book of the Law" (*seper hattora*) as a sanctified authoritative work which contains all the divine law is encountered for the first time in Israel's history in the account of the reform of Josiah (2 Kgs 22–23)' (Weinfeld, 'Deuteronomy', p. 174).

Deuteronomistic influence of the sort uncovered by Blenkinsopp on the formation of the Pentateuch is widely recognized. This need not be taken as Deuteronomistic redaction, as Van Seters points out, but may simply reflect the borrowing and adaptation of Deuteronomic/Deuteronomistic language and ideas. Form-critical concerns alone suggest Deuteronomistic influence behind the composition of the Tetrateuch. A serious problem raised by Noth's theory of a Deuteronomistic History, though not generally recognized for decades, is the purpose of the Tetrateuch. With its current ending in the book of Numbers it can hardly have been an original, independent work. Everything in Genesis–Numbers points forward to Israel's occupation of the promised land so that an ending at Numbers would leave all those promises and expectations unfulfilled. Noth's contention that the account of Moses' death at the end of Deuteronomy (ch. 34) had originally belonged to Numbers and had been transferred when the Tetrateuch and the Deuteronomistic History were joined[17] only exacerbated the problem. Deuteronomy 34.9 mentions Joshua, yet the Tetrateuch does not go on to explain how Joshua led the people in taking the promised land, so the promise of the land remains unfulfilled in the Tetrateuch itself. Given the standard dating of the Pentateuchal sources, J and E, before the Deuteronomistic History, one could only assume that P or a redactor responsible for the final form of the Tetrateuch truncated them in order to prefix them to Deuteronomy.[18] But this problem eventually led to the proposal that J was later than previously imagined and had been written specifically as a prologue to Dtr's History.[19] In either case, the

17. M. Noth, *The Deuteronomistic History* (JSOTSup, 15; Sheffield: Sheffield Academic Press, 1991), p. 60.

18. So F.M. Cross, *Canaanite Myth and Hebrew Epic: Essays in the History of the Religion of Israel* (Cambridge, MA: Harvard University Press, 1973), pp. 319-21.

19. Cf. H.H. Schmid, *Der sogenannte Jahwist: Beobachtungen und Fragen zur Pentateuchforschung* (Zürich: Theologischer Verlag, 1976); M. Rose, *Deuteronomist und Jahwist: Untersuchungen zu den Berührungspunkten beider Literaturwerke* (ATANT, 67; Zürich: Theologischer Verlag, 1981); and J. Van Seters, *Abraham in History and Tradition* (New Haven: Yale University Press, 1975); *idem, In Search of History: Historiography in the Ancient World and the Origins of Biblical History* (New Haven: Yale University Press, 1983); *idem, Prologue to History: The Yahwist as Historian in Genesis* (Louisville, KY: Westminster/John Knox Press, 1992); and *idem, The Life of Moses: The Yahwist as Historian in Exodus–Numbers* (Louisville, KY: Westminster/John Knox Press, 1994). For a précis of

Tetrateuch is dependent on the Deuteronomistic History for its current existence and to that extent reflects Deuteronomistic influence.

Chronicles furnishes an even better example, as both Patton and Ben Zvi point out. There is widespread agreement that the Chronicler knew and made use of the Deuteronomistic History, especially the books of Samuel and Kings.[20] As a result, the book of Chronicles is filled with Deuteronomistic language and ideology. Yet, no one, to my knowledge, claims that the Chronicler was a Deuteronomist. There is wide recognition, to the contrary, that the Chronicler adapted and modified his sources, Deuteronomistic and otherwise, to present his own historical theology or theological history. Still, it is quite appropriate to speak of Deuteronomistic influence behind Chronicles. Not only did the Deuteronomistic History serve as the Chronicler's principal source, but one might surmise that it represented the Chronicler's inspiration or motivation for writing in the first place. Without the Deuteronomistic History it is fair to say that the Chronicler's History as we know it would not exist.

Deuteronomy and the Deuteronomistic History may have influenced the composition of other parts of the Hebrew Bible in similar ways (see the survey in Wilson's article). In the Book of the Twelve, for example, the dating formulas in the headings may draw from the book of Kings. But that hardly makes their authors Deuteronomists; other similarities in language, such as those noted by Cook in Micah, can be explained without resort to Deuteronomists, as Kugler and Ben Zvi argue. Such similarities suggest the impact of Deuteronomy and the Deuteronomistic History but not the presence of a continuing school responsible for editing virtually all of the Hebrew Bible. In the wisdom literature, especially the book of Job, I confess that I am sorely tempted to follow scholarly tradition in finding a response to the 'standard' Deuteronomistic theology of retribution, if only for the sake of being able to cite it

Van Seters's view see his article on 'The Pentateuch' in S.L. McKenzie and M.P. Graham (eds.), *The Hebrew Bible Today: An Introduction to Critical Issues* (Louisville, KY: Westminster/John Knox Press, 1998).

20. Again, Auld's suggestion that both Samuel–Kings and Chronicles are based on an older 'Story of Two Houses' is swimming upstream. See his *Kings without Privilege: David and Moses in the Story of the Bible's Kings* (Edinburgh: T. & T. Clark, 1994). My critique of this part of Auld's theory is forthcoming in an article entitled 'The Chronicler as Redactor', in M.P. Graham and S.L. McKenzie (eds.), *The Chronicles as Author* (JSOTSup, 263; Sheffield: Sheffield Academic Press).

as an analogy to Newton's 'third law': 'for every action there is an opposite and equal reaction'. But Crenshaw has shown that the alleged Deuteronomistic influences on wisdom may be accounted for otherwise. Specifically, the idea of punishment for sin was very widely held in the ancient Near East. Even if Job could be proven to be a reaction to the Deuteronomistic explanation of the exile, this would still only be a case of influence. Again no one, to my knowlege, thinks Job was written or redacted by Deuteronomists.

The articles by Coggins, Lohfink and Wilson in the first section of this book raise the question of what is meant by 'Deuteronomistic'. One might also ask what is meant by 'pan-Deuteronomism'. Coggins, in particular, notes three levels at which the first term is applied—actual authorship or redaction that imposes a viewpoint immediately derived from Deuteronomy, the use of language that is identified as distinctively Deuteronomistic, and the reflection of ideology regarded as characteristically Deuteronomistic. This is a helpful differentiation. The articles in this volume as a whole indicate that a great deal of caution is in order for the latter two categories especially. The use of the term 'Deuteronomistic' for vocabulary and ideology may be appropriate if they can be shown to be distinctive to Deuteronomy and the Deuteronomistic History. But since this is often not the case, the claims that texts outside of the Deuteronomistic History (again, with the possible exception of Jeremiah) are the products of Deuteronomistic redaction must be called into question. As Lohfink in particular has observed, the use of similar vocabulary and ideology, especially by an elite group of literati, does not constitute a social, political or theological movement. The various levels of Deuteronomistic influence in the Hebrew Bible suggest a very different picture of its development and of the social setting behind it. *Ur*-deuteronomy at the end of the seventh century seems to have been the genuine product of such a movement. It was edited into the Deuteronomistic History and in that form especially exerted an enormous influence on the composition of the Hebrew Bible and on nascent Judaism. But the label 'pan-Deuteronomism' would be inappropriate first, because there are certainly important parts of the Hebrew Bible (e.g. Esther and Song of Songs, as Crenshaw mentions) that attest no Deuteronomistic influence at all, and second, because, as amply argued in this volume, Deuteronomistic influence does not mean Deuteronomistic editing by or even the existence of a multi-generational school or movement. Deuteronomistic influence likely waned as the development of the Hebrew Bible moved in time away from Deuteronomy. The Hebrew Bible thus retains its diversity, although its composition appears to be a more circumscribed process temporally and socially than sometimes pictured in the popular and scholarly imagination.

INDEXES

INDEX OF REFERENCES

BIBLE

INDEX OF AUTHORS